By Chris Bowers

NICK CLEGG: THE BIOGRAPHY

Biteback Publishing

First published in Great Britain in 2011 by
Biteback Publishing Ltd
Westminster Tower
3 Albert Embankment
London
SE1 7SP

ISBN 978-1-84954-084-1

10 9 8 7 6 5 4 3 2 1

A CIP catalogue record for this book is available from the British Library.
Set in Adobe Garamond Pro by Namkwan Cho

Printed and bound in Great Britain by CPI Group (UK), Croydon, CR0 4YY

CONTENTS

Author's Introduction: 'A special one?'   1

1. 'A little of all these'   11
2. 'All are guilty of some atrocity'   21
3. 'Nickje'   31
4. 'Something visceral about him'   41
5. 'You scoundrels and cowards'   63
6. 'The brightest young man I've ever come across'   77
7. 'Unbundling the local loop'   101
8. 'Returning with the mark of Satan on him'   121
9. 'We have to do something about this'   149
10. 'One plus one equals more than two'   181
11. 'Might be shot in four or five years'   221
12. 'The lightning rod'   245
13. 'This is a bitter blow'   283
14. 'What is the most liberal thing to do?'   303

Bibliography   339
Index   340

'A SPECIAL ONE?'

IN SHOW business it's sometimes said that you can spend twenty years becoming an overnight star. The turn of phrase refers to someone who plays the pubs and clubs week in, week out for years; then suddenly one night a television executive happens to be in the audience, spots the talent, and within a few months the performer is a household name.

In many ways, Nick Clegg spent twenty years becoming an overnight star, but his instant stardom was somewhat different. On 15 April 2010, close to ten million people crowded round their televisions to follow the first-ever party leaders' debate in British politics. It was a phenomenal audience for a political programme, especially among a population that had taken great pride in moaning about its politicians – and with a fair bit of good reason in view of certain ridiculously audacious expenses claims that some MPs had submitted in the previous eighteen months. But with no obvious result being predicted by the opinion polls, and finally a chance to see the leaders debate with each other after years of witnessing it in America and other countries, the British people revelled in their televised political spectacle.

To some, Nick Clegg shouldn't have been part of it. As the leader of the third party in British politics, there was an argument that he represented a party that could never aspire to government, certainly not on its own, and that he was therefore cashing in on being the leader of the biggest of the non-major parties. That argument was a bit harsh – there was a big gap between the Liberal Democrats and any other party in UK terms, and the legal requirement for the broadcasters to observe 'due impartiality' meant they would have had a tough time if they had stuck to Labour and Conservatives alone. So this was Clegg's party's big opportunity in modern British politics, and he knew it.

I followed the debate from my living room, watching it with my wife, who is no political animal despite being married to me – she was one of the normally apolitical folk who swelled the audience to that astonishing figure. I didn't actually think Clegg did that well. He is a good media performer without being an outstanding one, and I felt he came over as well meaning but having difficulty hiding the fact that he was very wet behind the ears. So when I heard the newsreader on the ITN *News at Ten* say that a first opinion poll had been taken and 'there is a clear winner', I assumed it had to be David Cameron. Cameron hadn't done that well, but he'd looked like a plausible prime minister, while Gordon Brown's 'I agree with Nick' approach had clearly backfired.

I was therefore as much gobsmacked as delighted when the polls showed that Clegg had emerged as the clear winner from the debate. Was he that good? Had I missed something, locked as I was in my own Lib Dem parliamentary campaign to wrest a Tory stronghold away from the Conservatives?

Clegg did many things right that night. His trick of mentioning the questioner by name but addressing the television audience by looking straight into the camera clearly worked, and contrasted with a nervous Cameron and an uncomfortable Brown. But the biggest trump card Clegg had was that not a lot of people knew him. That was hard for those of us in the party to take, because we'd been aware of him since 1999, when he became one of the few MEPs any of us could name. To us, the idea peddled in the media that Clegg was 'Cameron-lite', because he looked too like David Cameron for his own good, was preposterous. How could anyone in their right mind mix those two up?

Well, they could, because a lot of people in Britain don't take that much interest in politics, and if they do, they generally think of it in terms of Labour and Conservative; or certainly did until the current coalition was formed. Much as we Lib Dems didn't like to admit it, we were in many cases the nicest of the protest votes, a generally cuddly way of expressing dissatisfaction with the two largest parties. As a result, quite a few people could name the leader of the Lib Dems, but not that many, and of those, not everyone would have been able to tell you what he looked like, especially as it was his first general election as leader of the party.

So after twenty years as a political animal and more than ten as an elected representative, Nick Clegg became an overnight star. In retrospect it is remarkable to think that, on the morning of 15 April 2010, he was just a name even to those who had taken an interest in the forthcoming election; and by 12 May he was the Deputy Prime Minister and one of five Liberal Cabinet ministers in the government for the first time in sixty-five years. Even in the best political fiction, people just don't rise that fast. Nor do they sink as fast as he appeared to in the months after the Conservative–Lib Dem coalition was formed, although I suspect he has not sunk as far as many in the media would have us believe.

I did some work with Clegg in the months before he became Lib Dem leader. I had met him in February 2007, when he was the guest speaker at our constituency's annual dinner, at which I was master of ceremonies. He impressed us greatly that night. In his speech, he described our local MP, Norman Baker, as 'a cross between Gandhi and a battering ram', an original formulation that will strike a chord with anyone who knows the sensitive but ebullient Baker, and the comment certainly wowed party members. Sitting next to him over dinner, I found Clegg a great conversation partner, but what struck me most was his total ease with everyone he met. Like any local party, we have a mix of personalities, from the hard-working salt-of-the-earth characters you can't do without, to those who take a fair bit of space and need a lot of maintenance. It's the politician's job to treat them all with respect and ease, but he had something special. It was almost entrancing watching him interact with someone new, male or female, seeing him look into their eyes, tilt his head slightly, and watching them go weak at the knees. Some call it charm, others call it charisma. Whatever you call it, he had it.

The line of argument I put to him in February 2007 was that Ming Campbell wouldn't last that long as Lib Dem leader, and that when he went, he, Clegg, had to take over. He was quite happy with that scenario; indeed, he had heard it enough from others. But the second half of my argument was that the next leader of the Lib Dems had to really understand the environment. The political noses of Campbell and Charles Kennedy had told them that the environment was important, but I never got the impression it was something they really felt. Faced with the onward march of the Green Party (something all Lib Dems welcome, but few dare say so because the Greens are a threat to them politically), I said that if the next Lib Dem leader didn't have a fair bit of green blood coursing through his/her veins, the party would remain vulnerable to the Greens.

Out of that began a series of meetings, at which Clegg, I and a handful of other people thrashed out an environmental policy for his forthcoming leadership campaign. This was in the middle of 2007, and none of us realised just how close the leadership campaign was. There were about five meetings; one was on the terrace at the House of Commons, another in a room in the Grand Hotel in Brighton during the party conference, which stands out in my memory for the awful sandwich (bitingly and hilariously described by Clegg) he tried to munch his way through while we chatted. Our last meeting took place – purely coincidentally – on the day Campbell resigned as leader, and while I barely saw Clegg in the three years after that, many of his early environmental pronouncements bore the hallmarks of our discussions. Whether I really got him to *feel* the environment is another matter, and this point is developed in Chapter 10, which deals with how the party worked out its first manifesto under his leadership.

When news was published that I was writing this book, a few people were quick to dismiss my Lib Dem background as detracting from the biography's credibility. It would be too much of a PR job to be truly independent, or so the argument ran. That overlooks the fact that I am a journalist first and a Lib Dem in my spare time, and that I have too much professional pride to offer up a sanitised profile of a man with a vital role in British life. In fact my professional pride was something that worried some senior Lib Dem figures, who feared I might look to be hypercritical of Clegg just to assert my journalistic independence. I hope I have been neither unnecessarily harsh nor unnecessarily lenient.

But I also think that to assume I would somehow gloss over Clegg's bad points because I'm a member of his party rather misses a stark reality of politics in a country of sixty million inhabitants.

For any political party to be viable, it has to be big enough to draw people from a wide spectrum of opinion. To that extent, all three major British parties are broad churches, and I find it journalistically fatuous when I read headlines about 'splits' in parties. If there aren't splits in parties occasionally, then the party is too small or too dormant. One person's split is another person's healthy debate, and I much prefer the healthy debate interpretation, whether in my own party or others. So the fact that I'm a Lib Dem councillor and former parliamentary candidate does not mean I feel the need to present a sanitised portrait of my party leader, just a fair one.

Moreover, there is no shortage of Lib Dems who are happy to tell you – in a quiet way that doesn't lead to headlines about 'splits' – that they're not totally enamoured of Clegg's leadership. By taking the party into a coalition with the Conservatives, he has fuelled the fires of those who always saw him as being 'on the right of the party', whatever that means. More than a year into that coalition, many feel he has not shouted loudly enough about policy successes that happened only because the Lib Dems were in government. And he won a leadership contest by the narrowest of margins against Chris Huhne, a man who, though rich enough to rub shoulders with the best of the bankers, had worked his way to the party's heart with a superb environment policy that set out a timetable for Britain to become carbon neutral by 2050.

For these and other reasons, I had no difficulty coming at this book with an open mind, expecting to find good things and not-so-good things, all of which would contribute to an overall profile of a man who still has a lot of his career to come. I have indeed found the full package, but one overriding impression has emerged over the course of several months' research: I have grown both to like and to admire the man. That realisation in itself didn't altogether surprise me. What I was slightly unprepared for was the amount of people who used the word 'special' in connection with him. The current zeitgeist in Britain is to use the word 'special' to describe a person as a bit dangerous; the media has had a lot of fun with the Portuguese football coach José Mourinho since he once said he was 'the special one'. But several people – and I mean several – who have no specific knowledge of Mourinho have said to me 'You do know you're writing a book about a very special person, don't you?' It doesn't mean one has to agree with everything Clegg says or does, but the suggestion is that here is a package of skills and attributes that is unusual, a package that, if used wisely, could have the scope to effect significant change in British society, even after the setbacks he and his party suffered in the May 2011 elections.

Yet this combination of my own findings and the observations of others presents me with my biggest problem: can I really paint a portrait of a man that is generally positive without people dismissing it as the biased analysis of a party member? At time of writing, the problem is particularly acute, given that the political media are delighting in what they see as Clegg's spectacular fall from the height of 'Cleggmania' a little over a year ago. However, as a journalist, I am well aware that the media can get very caught up in today's headlines and lose sight of the big picture, as the former sells a lot more papers than the latter. And as a sports journalist, I will just have to rely on the commentator's maxim of 'calling it as I see it', and trust the reader to see it as the honest profile I intend it to be. (And to remember that, while I have stood for the Lib Dems, the publisher of this book has stood for the Conservatives.)

Whatever one thinks of Nick Clegg, he has achieved remarkable things for himself and the Liberal Democrats. He became leader less than three years after becoming an MP. Two-and-a-half years later he was the Deputy Prime Minister, with four other Lib Dem ministers in the Cabinet and a dozen or so junior ministers further down the ministerial ranks. That is a phenomenal achievement, even if many in his party are still uncomfortable at what they see as supping with the Conservative devil.

But who is Nick Clegg? Where has he come from? What drives him? Or to use a phrase beloved of Lib Dems, what makes him get out of bed in the morning? What lies behind the boyish charm that can sometimes turn to a look of teenage grumpiness? And what makes him sacrifice the easy life that someone of his circumstances could have had, in return for life in the public eye where every syllable is scrutinised for hidden meanings, leading a party with no safe parliamentary seats, dealing with unseen abuse to himself and his family, and having to work hardest of all to ensure he doesn't miss his kids growing up? All that makes up the content of this book.

People ask me whether it's 'authorised' or not. I don't like that phrase, as it gives the impression of being somehow controlled or ordered by Clegg or his staff. It is my book, and I take responsibility for it. But I am very grateful to have had the cooperation of both Nick himself and just about everyone in the Lib Dems. I'm especially grateful to Norman Lamb, Lena Pietsch and Jonny Oates, who have been supportive of my project, even though it was clearly an irritant for them when it emerged amid the bedlam of the post-election period. The one restriction they and Nick put on me was in interviewing the Clegg family – they said that was a 'no go' area. I fully accepted this in terms of Miriam (Clegg's wife) and their three sons, Antonio, Alberto and Miguel – anyone would want their children to be protected from the kind of public intrusion Nick and Miriam are trying to shield them from. As such, the details of their private life that appear in this book are only those already in the public domain, or information close associates have been happy to tell me. But I did seek access to the family Clegg grew up in, as family background is an important part of depicting the man. I'm grateful to Clegg and his staff for the compromises they were willing to make so that I could gain an insight into the world in which he grew up.

In addition, Clegg himself gave me quality time, for which I am very grateful, and I was also able to spend time with him on the campaign trail in April 2011. But in this book I quote him from other sources than just the interviews I carried out with him. This is not simply a question of avoiding reinventing the wheel, but also to quote him as he expresses himself to others. As a result, I quote frequently from his appearance on BBC Radio 4's *Desert Island Discs* in October 2010, from an in-depth interview he gave Mick Brown for an article in *The Telegraph* magazine in March 2010, and an interview with the Ekklesia website in 2008, as well as from other articles, accounts and interviews.

And I am eternally grateful to all the people who have given me the benefit of their knowledge of Nick, and other bits of logistical help. I carried out more than fifty interviews for this book. Most of those who helped me are quoted in the text, but inevitably there were some whose help was of a more logistical than quotable nature. They include, in alphabetical order: Matthew Bishop, John Bowers, John Bridges, Joaquín Carvanna, Monica Escolar-Rojo, Richard Evans, Sebastián Fest, Anne Gorst, Sandy Harwitt, Greg Hodder, Gayle Hunnicutt, Harvey Linehan, David Mercer, Mariëtte Pakker, Chris Rennard, Alison Suttie and Steve Wasserman. And I'm also very grateful to Iain Dale of Biteback Publishing, who offered me the authorship of this book rather than taking the possibly safer option of giving it to a Westminster journalist. I agree with Iain on political matters no more these days than I did when we were students of German together in Norwich in the early 1980s, but I'm delighted to be a small part of his immense contribution to the popular understanding of British politics.

Ultimately, this book is not about being critical or uncritical of Nick Clegg, but about painting a picture of him. As such, it should be possible for those who are well disposed towards him to enjoy this book and get something out of it, as much as for those who are not. He is, after all, one of the dominant political figures of our era, so the public is entitled to know what makes him tick, whatever they may think about the man, his background, and his views.

Chris Bowers, July 2011

Chapter 1

'A LITTLE OF ALL THESE'

WATCHING NICK Clegg up close can be a daunting experience for British people. For a country not used to proficiency in foreign languages, the ease with which he switches tongues is disconcerting. 'I was staying at his house once,' recalls a close aide, 'and he was on the phone to his mother, with his wife hanging on to speak to him. He was rattling on in Dutch, and then when the call ended, he muttered a couple of words in English to me, picked up the other phone, and started rattling away in Spanish with Miriam.'

Such linguistic dexterity is nothing special in multilingual countries. In Switzerland, for example, a country with four official languages alongside the onward march of English, trilingualism is fairly common. But in Britain, even after two generations of immigration that have left many children and young adults bilingual, the ability to speak a foreign language is still held in awe. Choosing a different form of language – what the language analysts would call different 'registers' – for different people and different situations is nothing special; people use different words or modify a regional accent when speaking to children, the vicar, a solicitor and so on. So too does Nick Clegg – only in his case it's a totally different language rather than a different register.

A linguistic genius, then? Linguistically gifted, for sure, and his aptitude was always more towards the humanities subjects than the sciences, but his multilingualism stems as much from his background and upbringing as from any natural genius.

Of Clegg's four grandparents, only one was British. Two were Dutch, and one was Russian. How much anyone is influenced by their ancestry and family heritage is open to question, and it's a question that has dogged the offspring of despotic parents and grandparents as much as those from admirable stock. But there's no doubt there's a mass of drama, intrigue and entertainment in Nick Clegg's family heritage, most of it through his two grandmothers. His brother Paul, six-and-a-half years older than Nick and therefore with a more formed memory of that generation, says of their four grandparents, 'As a child, you pick out people who are defined – people who aren't defined blur into the background. All my grandparents were very defined characters, they were all interesting.'

The most colourful, even romantic, line of the Clegg family is the Russian one. His paternal grandmother was Baroness Kira von Engelhardt, the daughter of Baron Artur von Engelhardt and Alexandra Ignatievna Zakrevskaya. Baron Engelhardt was a landowner of noble German origin from Smolensk, whilst Alexandra was a Russian noble of Ukrainian descent, whose father was Ignaty Zakrevsky, a senator and one-time attorney general answering to the tsar of Russia. Kira was born in 1909, so was just eight when the Russian Revolution wiped out her family's property. The Engelhardts fled the Bolsheviks and settled in Estonia, where Kira lived with her cousins on her uncle's estate. In the 1920s she came to London and, among other things, became a lifelong supporter of the Liberal Party.

'She was a lovely woman,' recalls Paul Clegg of Kira. 'She was really gentle, and she was somebody who bore no grudges yet lived during a time in history when people could have borne an enormous amount of grudges. Her endearing quality to me was that she was endlessly interested and had no backward-looking regrets at all. She was quadrilingual [French, German, Russian and English] and we were all very fond of her.'

The most colourful member of the family was Alexandra's sister – Nick Clegg's great-great-aunt – Maria Ignatievna Zakrevskaya. For most of her life, she was known as Moura Budberg, and looked after Clegg's grandmother (her niece) as a sort of mother substitute when they were all exiled in London. She died in 1974, when Nick was seven. He does recall meeting her on a handful of occasions: 'She was a pretty imposing figure, utterly terrifying for a small boy,' he has said in interviews. 'She would visit us and look at me sternly and say in a thick Russian accent, "Speak up, boy, you mumble, you mumble." But she was an extraordinary survivor who rebuilt her life in London and became a great figure on the Bohemian, theatre and arts scene in London. She would hold soirées and salons, people would come, and she would drink everybody under the table.'

Paul Clegg, who was thirteen when Budberg died, has a somewhat more robust memory of her. 'She was quite a character, a strong older woman who people respected, and everyone in our immediate family who really knew her, mainly my parents' generation, talks about her as a key central figure, as any matriarch would be. I remember her as a really good person, and very much loved by all her family.'

Budberg was born in St Petersburg in 1892, the daughter of a wealthy imperial official. An obituary of her daughter Tania published in *The Times* in 2004 describes Budberg as 'a spoilt but exceptionally attractive and spirited girl of 18' when she married her first husband, Count Johann von Benckendorff, a tsarist diplomat. They had two children but, in the aftermath of the Russian Revolution, he was shot dead by a peasant on their estate in Estonia, which at the time was in the process of gaining independence from Russia. Kira was with her nanny, Mrs Wilson, when they found him dead on a path near the house. Many years later she and her husband Hugh Clegg went back, visited the house and located the spot where the count had died.

Nick Clegg also visited both St Petersburg and Estonia. When he was working at the European Commission on Russian and central Asian development issues in the mid-1990s, his itinerary took him to St Petersburg, and he snuck in a taxi ride past the house the Engelhardts had had there. 'I only saw the house out of the window of the taxi, but I was bowled over by the romance of St Petersburg,' he says. 'I remember being gobsmacked by the absolute beauty of the place – it was the middle of winter, you had great shards of ice coming up the river, the statue of the horseman, it was beautiful. I met a young man, he could well have been an interpreter, who took me to a library, and he became wildly excited to show me books about the Budberg family and Zakrevsky – he knew all about them.'

A more moving experience came on a separate trip, when he visited the house in Kalli Järv, Estonia, where Kira and Moura spent some time and where the Count was shot dead. 'There's a path from the big house, which is now an agricultural college, to the smaller wooden house on the banks of the lake where they lived, and there is a small wooden engraved statue where he was shot. I was in a suit, with snow up to my knees! I don't know why it hit me emotionally – it was the middle of winter and the middle of nowhere, it was where he was shot, and I'd heard all these stories about a house on a lake, and it was exactly as I'd imagined it.'

Caught up in the post-revolution chaos, Moura Budberg had an affair with Robert Bruce Lockhart, a British diplomat posted to Russia during the Russian Revolution and in reality a leading British spy. Lockhart, who legend says was the man on whom Ian Fleming based the character of James Bond, was suspected of being involved in a plot to assassinate Lenin in August 1918, may in fact have been the man behind it. Lenin was shot three times but survived the attack. Legend also has it that Budberg and Lockhart were lying in bed in his Moscow flat shortly after the attack when revolutionary soldiers burst in and arrested them both. They were imprisoned, but she was soon released and he got out a little later; much speculation surrounds what favours Budberg offered the prison commandant as part of both her own and Lockhart's release. Budberg was deeply in love with Lockhart, and felt utterly deserted when he eventually left her.

Budberg took a lot of secrets about this time to her grave, so no-one can be quite sure what really happened. As a result, and because she was a sexually liberated woman, her past gives rise to many tales and intermittent lurid headlines about Nick Clegg's 'Mata Hari aunt'. But the family is keen to make sure the good side of Budberg is also known, as she proved to be a haven of support for her friends and family over many years.

After the liaison with Lockhart, Budberg fell in love with the Russian revolutionary writer and literary giant Maxim Gorky, which helped her survive the early years of the new Soviet state. He introduced her to Lenin and Stalin, and she apparently gave Stalin the gift of an accordion. Around this time she married another member of the Baltic aristocracy, Baron Nikolai Budberg Böningshausen, but it was a marriage of convenience for her to get Estonian citizenship. Once she had it, she ditched him, but kept the title and was known for the rest of her life as Baroness Moura Budberg.

Budberg's relationship with Gorky lasted for several years, during which time he introduced her to the British science fiction writer H. G. Wells. In the early 1930s, Budberg settled in London, and began an affair with Wells, despite being thirty years his junior; she is said to have told Somerset Maugham that Wells 'smells of honey'. Her home was in Ennismore Gardens, close to one of London's two Russian Orthodox churches (although as the church in Ennismore Gardens recognised the authority of the patriarch in Moscow, it was treated with suspicion by Russian émigrés, especially during the Cold War years). Her move to Britain began a period of four decades at the core of London's international social set, in which she displayed a phenomenal ability to drink large amounts of vodka without losing her quickness of thought. Yet she could never shake off suspicions that she was a spy; in fact she may not have wanted to, such suspicions giving her a cachet in London circles that no doubt enhanced her allure. She was probably a double agent, and may even have spied on or for Germany in the First World War: the British authorities considered her 'a very dangerous woman' in the aftermath of the revolution, but they almost certainly used her knowledge of Russia during her time in London.

How much credence they gave her evidence is another matter, highlighted by an incident in 1951 that came to light when MI5 released her file in 2002. Not long after Guy Burgess, a friend of hers, had defected to Moscow as a communist spy, she told a former MI6 officer that Anthony Blunt, who was the surveyor of the Queen's pictures, was a member of the Communist Party. The officer was aghast, but passed the information on. MI5 considered adding the information to Blunt's file, but decided Budberg was too unreliable and rejected her intelligence. The decision was probably justified, since Budberg's adherence to truth wasn't always rock solid, but on this occasion she had the last laugh – or would have done if she'd lived long enough – as Blunt was exposed in 1979 as 'the fourth man' in the Burgess–McLean–Philby spy scandal that had rocked the British establishment in the 1950s.

There was a tiny frisson during Clegg's appearance on the BBC Radio 4 programme *Desert Island Discs* in October 2010 when the presenter, Kirsty Young, put it to him that, in his role as Deputy Prime Minister, he was now in a position to get to the bottom of the rumours that Budberg had been a double agent. Clegg laughed genially, and then stopped, realising that Young was probably right. He quickly added, 'Do you know, I prefer to keep it as a complete mystery.' That answer also reflects the family's wish for Budberg's good sides to be remembered and for her to not just be made into a figure of fun or betrayal.

Budberg also developed her own technique for avoiding difficult questions in one particular television interview. She was asked a question she didn't want to answer, so stared at the interviewer as if he hadn't asked it and she was simply waiting for his next question. He asked his question again, and again she stared at him as if he hadn't spoken. She was clearly keeping her dignity better than he was, and, getting somewhat flustered, the interviewer asked a different question, which she gracefully answered.

Budberg's daughter Tania was also part of the Russian aristocracy in exile, living in south-east England for many years until her death in 2004. One of her publications was a memoir of her early life called *A Little of All These*, a title taken from a statement by the philosopher and travel writer Hermann Keyserling: 'I am not a Dane, not a German, not a Swede, not a Russian nor an Estonian, so what am I? – a little of all these.' It's a title that could equally apply to Nick Clegg.

Kira, Budberg's niece, married Hugh Clegg in the summer of

1932. He was at the time a sub-editor on the *British Medical Journal*, and went on to become one of the leading figures in the British medical establishment in the twentieth century. (He is not to be confused with another Hugh Clegg, a respected professor of industrial relations, who was also prominent at the same time.)

Hugh Anthony Clegg was born in St Ives, Huntingdonshire, in 1900, to John Clegg and Gertrude Wilson. John Clegg was a clergyman and school teacher from the East Riding of Yorkshire, who had migrated to Lowestoft. The Yorkshire connection is useful for Nick Clegg, who, although he could never claim to be a Yorkshireman, makes the occasional mention of his Yorkshire roots when in Sheffield visiting the affluent constituency of Hallam, which he represents in Parliament.

Hugh was the third of seven children, and the man who raised his branch of the Clegg family from the modest surroundings of a Suffolk parsonage to a source of leading figures in British society – both through professional aggrandisement and in marrying an aristocrat, albeit an émigré one. He gained a scholarship to Westminster School and an exhibition to Trinity College, Cambridge, where he went on to become a senior scholar in natural sciences. He missed service in the First World War by a few months – he was entered as an ensign in the Irish Guards, but the war finished too early for him to see active service.

He worked his way up the medical ranks, becoming an eminent doctor, and was contemplating a career as a general physician specialising in chests when he joined the staff of the *British Medical Journal* as a sub-editor. Although he continued to practise, and did a lot of valuable work in London treating patients during the Second World War, his career was established on the ladder that would see him become one of the most significant mouthpieces of the British medical community. He was the editor of the *BMJ* from 1947 to his retirement at the end of 1965, but was effectively in charge for nearly thirty years; he became deputy editor in 1934 and, from the late 1930s, frequently had to stand in for his ailing boss, N. G. Horner.

With the foundation of the National Health Service in 1948, it was a momentous time to be the editor of a world-respected medical journal, and Hugh's editorials were widely read. As such, any history of British medicine in the twentieth century must feature some mention of Hugh Clegg, but he had a rough character trait that, if not his undoing, perhaps prevented him from going as far as he might have done. Those who knew him said he was often tactless, if not downright rude, and his attacks on medics he disagreed with often became unnecessarily personal. A good friend from the medical world, Bradford Hill, said Hugh always regretted not making a career in clinical medicine, a step he felt unable to take because of a lack of finance resulting from his relatively poor background as one of a country parson's seven children. Hill also believed the personal nature of Hugh Clegg's attacks was largely responsible for him getting 'only' a CBE when he retired, as opposed to the knighthood given to his opposite number at the *Lancet*, Theodore Fox. Fox, Hill maintained, was better able to separate the subject matter from the personal when he disagreed with someone. In its obituary of Hugh Clegg in 1983, the *BMJ* pointedly said, 'He was not one to let current events pass without coming to his own conclusions about them.'

But if that is a veiled reference to his forthright views, there's no doubt that those in the medical profession couldn't afford to avoid Hugh Clegg's publication. He had taken the *BMJ* from a somewhat boring voice of the British Medical Association – more preoccupied with the BMA's annual general meeting than with advances in medical research – to a highly respected journal, publishing a raft of statistics-based papers which were unfashionable at the time. He widened its accessibility by introducing summaries or abstracts at the start of all the leading articles, so people didn't need to read everything, and when contributors asked him how long their article should be, he was known to reply, 'As long as it has interest; stop when it has not.' As a result, the magazine's appeal widened to take in most British doctors and a readership well beyond the BMA.

Nick Clegg invoked his grandfather in a speech in early 2010 in which he railed against Britain's libel laws. With the *BMJ* having recently declined to publish an article on child abuse for fear of it being defamatory, and a journalist, Simon Singh, being sued for libel after questioning the efficacy of chiropractic methods, the Liberal Democrat leader quoted Dr Hugh Clegg's belief that 'scientific debate is at its most robust, most fruitful, when it is conducted in public'.

Hugh and Kira made their home in the Buckinghamshire village of Little Kingshill, and had two children: Nicholas (Nick's dad) and Jane. They eventually moved back to London, and were living in the capital when Nick and his brothers and sister were growing up in Buckinghamshire in the 1970s.

Slightly less colourful but arguably more dramatic is the maternal, Dutch side of Clegg's family.

His Dutch grandfather was Herman Willem Alexander van den Wall Bake, known as 'Hemmy'. A tall man, he studied at the Technical University in Delft, during which time he fell in love with a fellow student, Louise Hillegonde van Dorp, who he had met on a student boat trip (the Dutch *van* means 'of' but doesn't denote the same degree of upper-crust breeding as the German *von*). She was studying English, but was also a very gifted musician, playing the piano to a high standard and doing very well at the violin. After graduating, Hemmy went to the Dutch East Indies, now Indonesia, to work for the Batavian Oil Company and later Shell. Much later, he became president of the Dutch banking giant ABN, and was reported to be a friend of the Dutch royal family.

Hemmy and Louise married in early 1932, and she followed him to the Dutch East Indies. For the first ten years of their marriage they were very happy, and had three children, all girls. The middle daughter, Eulalie Hermance, is Nick Clegg's mother, born in November 1936 in Palembang.

The family was living on the island of Java when war broke out in early 1942. The Japanese, who were fighting on the side of the 'Axis' powers led by Germany and Italy, attacked the Dutch East Indies,

hoping to capture the country's rubber and oil supplies to aid the
Axis war effort. With the independence movement gaining strength
in its campaign to rid the area of its Dutch colonial masters, it was
the start of a turbulent time in the history of the territory that was
to become Indonesia.

When war broke out, Hermance was five. She remembers the
air raid sirens beginning, which meant the family had to go into
a bunker that heavy rain had turned into a huge puddle of mud.
Louise used to give her girls a piece of rubber to put between their
teeth, a saucepan for their heads, and cotton wool for their ears.
After Japan had attacked Pearl Harbor in December 1941, Hemmy
was made a first reserve lieutenant in the Dutch cavalry, and was
moved to a garrison in West Java called Batujajar. To be close to
him, Louise and the three girls moved to a friend's house nearby.
But he was soon called up for action, and when the friend's house
was commandeered by the independence leader Sukarno, later
Indonesian president, they were sent to a Japanese internment
camp, Kramat. During the takeover of the house, Louise was kicked
so hard by a Japanese soldier that she developed a tropical ulcer on
her shin which never healed during the years of the war.

At first Kramat was an open camp, which meant Louise and her
three girls were fairly free to come and go and life was just about
bearable. But things got gradually worse, and fights frequently
erupted over the dwindling supplies of food. Then on 23 August
1943, 2,500 women and children were forced to leave Kramat for
Tjideng. Tjideng was another internment camp, just for women and
children, set up by the Japanese in Batavia (now Jakarta). Over the
two-and-a-half years Nick Clegg's mother, aunts and grandmother
were interned there, Tjideng developed a reputation for being one
of the worst places in Asia. A survivors' website describes it as 'Hell
on Earth'. Louise later told Hermance, 'If we had been there one
more month, you wouldn't be here.'

Chapter 2

'ALL ARE GUILTY OF SOME ATROCITY'

WHEN NICK Clegg talks about why he is 'a liberal to his fingertips', the influence of his mother, Hermance van den Wall Bake, is never far from his reasons. He talks about 'her no-nonsense Dutch egalitarianism', and in an interview with *The Telegraph* magazine he said, 'My mum also retains a slight bemusement at the idiosyncrasies of the British class system, and I think that's rubbed off on me too.' But it is what Hermance, and his grandmother Louise, went through during the war – and the approach the family took to looking back on it – that has the biggest influence over his outlook on life.

Astonishingly, or perhaps not, Hermance hardly ever spoke about her war-time experiences with her four children. She finds it difficult talking about the war and says she doesn't want to 'pass on the fear'. Inevitably the subject would crop up from time to time, and she would occasionally mention her time in the 'camp', but the word meant so little to her children when they were young that they would sometimes say 'Mum, when you were in those tents...'! As a result, stories of her war experiences seldom featured in discussions at home. 'It would never have occurred to us to have asked her about it,' says her eldest son, Paul.

Nick himself said on *Desert Island Discs* in 2010, 'I've realised now, aged forty-three, how much she didn't tell us – she sheltered us from a lot of those harrowing, harrowing memories. I think it strengthened my mum's resolve to try and create the most happy, protected childhood for myself, my two brothers and my sister, and I think she succeeded, I mean we had an extraordinarily happy childhood. If you're a young girl and you see people being beaten to a pulp in front of you, and being dragged off and shot, I can only imagine what that must be like for a child of the age of my oldest boy.'

In 2010, Hermance finally broke her silence, agreeing to give an interview about how she survived Tjideng to a Dutch magazine, *De Aanspraak*, a publication specifically for Dutch survivors of the Holocaust and the war in the East Indies. Paul Clegg says the four-page article that resulted from the interview contained more than twice as much as she had ever told her children about what she went through in the war. Of Tjideng she said, 'There were seventeen of us in one house. My mother and sisters and I all had to sleep in one bed, with nine people to a room. We were constantly plagued by bedbugs, impossible to get rid of. Every day our ball rolled into the open sewer at the side of the road. My mother kept repeating that we had to wash our hands. It's a wonder we managed to get out of it alive. At first there were 2,500 people in Tjideng, but we had to keep making room for a steady stream of new prisoners. By the end of the war there were 14,350 women and children in the camp. Although there was a lot of petty theft, there was also a feeling of solidarity. If one of the mothers got ill, someone would step in and take care of the children.

'There were lots of times when the women panicked and some of them started to beat their children. The camp commandant, Sonei, was a cruel lunatic who made us stand on parade for hours on end, day and night, so we could be counted. We had to make a very deep bow, in the direction of Japan, with our little fingers on the side seams of our skirt. If we didn't do it properly, we were beaten. The Japanese would lose count and were forever having to start again, but my mother always stayed very calm.'

Like other camps, Tjideng was initially under civilian administration, with a certain amount of freedom. It was when the military took over – in Tjideng's case under the command of the despotic Lieutenant (later Captain) Kenichi Sonei – that things became desperate. Accounts from survivors talk not only of a massive growth in the camp's population, but at the same time a gradual reduction in the amount of land on which the camp stood, which made the overcrowding much worse. Savage beatings and kicking were commonplace for the slightest misdemeanour; heads were shaved; doors and windows were burned for firewood, leaving no protection from the elements; and all boys over twelve – later reduced to ten – were sent to the men's camps. All caged inside a fence of matted bamboo called *gedèk*.

'Our worst fear was that we would lose each other,' said Hermance in her *Aanspraak* interview, 'so my sister and I were very worried about my mother's tropical ulcers. She was covered with them because of a vitamin C deficiency. For her sake, we would go out early in the mornings and gather cherries that had fallen from the trees in the night. When the war ended she only weighed 36 kilos. Later, she would often say to me "If it had lasted one more month, you wouldn't be here". I was listless by that time and unable to eat anything at all.'

Perhaps more remarkable than the suffering was the attitude towards it. Hermance said her mother was keen not to get involved with any confrontation, often offering food to squabbling mothers to end a conflict, even if it meant she and her daughters became even hungrier. During the long days in the camp, Louise would say to her girls, 'You have to learn to read and write – if you go to school in Holland in the future, you'll want to be in the right age group.' She read *Alice in Wonderland* in English with her eldest daughter, she made Hermance a dictionary for her birthday, and when she found her maths knowledge insufficient to teach the numerical skills she thought were necessary, she bought some lessons by bartering with baked sago starch, even if that meant less food for her and the girls.

Hermance says of her mother, 'She was an exceptionally strong person with an enormously positive character. She never wanted to dwell on people's weaknesses. She preferred to ignore the bad side, which is what she did in the camp.' She recalls similar positivity from her father. 'He taught me not to harbour prejudice against any race whatsoever, because all are guilty of having committed some atrocity in the past. He did not want to pass anti-German or anti-Japanese feelings on to his children, and neither did I, as nothing would be gained by it.'

Both Nick Clegg and his elder brother Paul say that their mother has come through her war-time experiences without bitterness and recriminations. 'If you can do that after all she had been through,' says Paul, 'you have to have a very strong character.'

Just before giving the *Aanspraak* interview, Hermance spoke with her youngest son Alexander, Nick's younger brother, with whom she had visited Tjideng on a pilgrimage two years earlier. She told him, 'They want to know how my time in the camp affected your upbringing.' Alexander replied, 'We learned never to make a fuss about food.'

The end of the nightmare began on 6 August 1945, when the USA dropped the first atomic bomb on Hiroshima. Hermance's father was the first Dutch man back in the camp, telling the guards at the camp entrance, 'Either you open the gate or I'll drive straight through it!' He didn't recognise Hermance at first, as he had been away for more than three years and his five-year-old was now eight.

Attempts to live in a house owned by the Batavian Oil Company came to nothing, as the end of the war was the trigger for Indonesian freedom fighters to start attacking the Dutch. So the five of them were put in another camp, this one for families, and the girls sent to a temporary school. One day, Hermance and her elder sister witnessed a murder in the square in front of the school, watching the victim collapse in a pool of blood. As the situation became more tense, Hemmy took to sitting in front of his house brandishing an axe, just to send the signal that he was defending his family.

During a train journey from Batavia to Bandung, Dutch citizens were attacked by freedom fighters when the train went into a tunnel. Shots were fired, and women and children began screaming. People crammed into one end of the train, making it very difficult to breathe. Louise calmly told her daughters, 'Stay very still and you won't need so much air.' They survived the ordeal, but knew then that they had to get out of the country.

They left on one of the first flights to the Netherlands via Cairo. While in Cairo, the Red Cross provided them with their first real food for several years. By the time they arrived back home, Hermance and Louise were in a terrible state, and spent about nine months convalescing. For several years, Hermance suffered from anaemia and inexplicable fevers, and despite her mother's best efforts to keep her daughters at the same level as their contemporaries, there were times when Hermance just couldn't keep up with children her own age.

As Louise recovered her strength, there was another addition to the family – she gave birth to a fourth girl in the early 1950s. Hermance meanwhile gradually caught up with her education, going on to train as a special needs teacher. At the age of nineteen, she wanted to brush up her English, so she went to Cambridge to do a language course, and while there fell in love at first sight with an Englishman called Nick Clegg.

The idea that no anti-German or anti-Japanese feeling should result from the appalling treatment Hermance had suffered at the hands of the occupying Japanese forces found expression in her marriage and her children. While all her children proved proficient in German (it was Clegg's best learned language, certainly until he met his wife Miriam and became fluent in Spanish), her husband spent many years working with Japan, and was eventually awarded a CBE for services to Anglo-Japanese relations.

Nicholas Peter Clegg, Nick Clegg's father, was born in London in May 1936, six months before the woman he was to marry. In 1940 he was sent with his mother (Kira) and his sister Jane on one of the last refugee boat convoys to America, spending time in New York, Long Island and Connecticut, before being allowed to fly back to Britain as early as 1942. He went to school in the West Country, first at a prep school in Port Regis and then at Bryanston.

Nick Clegg Sr did his national service in the intelligence division of the Royal Navy, during which time he learned Russian, and he was stationed in Germany and Cyprus. He then went to study international law and economics at Trinity College, Cambridge, where he met his bride-to-be. After graduating from Cambridge, he married Hermance, and worked for a while in London. Shortly after their first child was born, he took a job in the Netherlands with the Dutch steel works. Two years later he got a job with Procter and Gamble in Belgium, so the family, by then with two children, moved again. A further two years passed, before they moved back to England, setting up home in the Buckinghamshire village of Fulmer, where their third and fourth children were born.

From then, Clegg Sr pursued a career in banking. He was a director of the merchant bankers Hill Samuel (who were eventually taken over by Lloyds TSB), and later joined Japan's second-largest securities firm, Daiwa Securities, first as managing director of their London operation, Daiwa Europe Ltd, then becoming co-chairman of the securities operation as well as chairman of their new bank, Daiwa Europe Bank. It was the start of a long relationship with Japan that continued until after his retirement. He helped conceive and establish the Daiwa Anglo-Japanese Foundation, a UK charity funded entirely by Daiwa to promote better understanding between the people of Japan and Britain by educational 'cross-fertilisation' initiatives, whereby Japanese students going to Britain would be given financial help, as would British students going to Japan. It is now arguably the leading organisation in its field, and it was doing this role, over more than twenty years, that earned him a CBE in 2009.

He also had various other roles in the banking world. He was a director of the International Primary Markets Association, he sat on the supervisory board of the Dutch bank Insinger de Beaufort, he was a senior adviser to the Bank of England on banking supervision, he joined the board of a Hungarian bank, and was an adviser to a bank in Brazil. On retirement, he became non-executive chairman of the United Trust Bank, a relatively small bank which describes itself as one of Britain's leading suppliers of funding for UK-based property developers. He remains in that role today.

With the performance of the banks a major issue in the two years leading up to the general election of 2010, the media enjoyed speculating on whether the Liberal Democrat leader's paternity was likely to make him tackle the banks with the same vigour that went into his speeches on banking. On a couple of occasions, he invoked the name of his father as an example of 'good old-fashioned banking principles', and said his dad was furious at the behaviour of today's banking community. It's hard to know whether Clegg is likely to be more understanding of the banks because of his father's background, or more contemptuous about the absence of noblesse oblige in the way modern banks have behaved. Ultimately, it probably doesn't matter, as the pragmatics of getting big money to stay in Britain (and thus to pay significant amounts of tax) are always likely to win out over the kind of pre-election statements that will appeal to voters, or even the best of intentions.

Certainly, some of Clegg's political foes have made a little mischief over his dad's banking background. Speaking to Channel 4 in the run-up to the 2010 election, the Conservatives' then business spokesman, Kenneth Clarke, said Clegg should have followed his father's 'political wisdom'. Clarke worked with Clegg Sr for a year at Daiwa Securities, and describes him as 'a very nice, very wise man'. The dig at Clegg Jr was that his dad was a Conservative, but even in that, Clarke didn't seem entirely sure. 'He was a very successful City man,' Clarke told Channel 4, 'but he wasn't a flash City man in any way. He was a Tory, I think, quite definitely.' How definite Clarke can be is a little uncertain. He clearly *assumed* the banker was a Conservative, but the Clegg children never knew how their parents voted. 'We knew it wasn't Labour,' says Paul, 'but we never knew if it was Conservative, Liberal or anything else.' And Nick says his folks were 'small-L liberals', though that also says nothing about which way they voted. The only certainty was that Kira was a long-time supporter of the Liberal Party.

Like their respective parents, Nick Clegg Sr and Hermance van den Wall Bake (she uses the name 'Clegg' in Britain but largely goes by her maiden name in the Netherlands) are clearly 'defined' people. David Brown, who became housemaster to Clegg at Westminster School, recalls being invited back to the Clegg house as part of getting to know the parents of the boys he was in charge of. 'What I remember most about the Cleggs', he says, 'was the very nice mum – very bright, broad minded, intelligent, supportive, so that is probably one of the many reasons why we didn't have any trouble with him. Nothing against the father, who was also very nice – in fact I have kept a letter Nick's father sent me – but the mother stands out more. Nick came from a very strong home life.'

While Clegg Sr pursued his banking career, Hermance mixed raising a family with her career as a special needs teacher. She taught dyslexic children, starting in Montessori schools. Having witnessed her mother's fear that the window for learning can sometimes be quite small, she was keen to find the right approach to releasing what she has always felt is the huge amount of potential that lies in all young people. 'She believes passionately in children,' says Paul, 'and if you look at Dutch society, it's very family oriented, not just now but going back hundreds of years. She exemplifies that in many ways. She's a very natural teacher.'

Shortly after Nick Clegg Sr retired at the age of sixty-two, he and Hermance bought a badly run-down French farmhouse, the idea being to renovate it as a labour of love. Set amid rural farmland in Charente-Maritime, south of the Cognac region, it is a rambling building with a fair bit of space both within the house and also in the form of outlying sheds and barns. 'We really wondered if they would have enough energy to do it,' says Paul Clegg.

They did have enough energy, plus enough money to buy in specialist help when needed. The house is now in much better shape, and acts as a venue for occasional gatherings of the Clegg clan. It also acts as a stick with which the less Lib Dem-friendly sections of the British press can beat Nick Clegg – in an article published two weeks before the 2010 general election, the *Daily Mail* described the French farmhouse as 'a chateau'. Few, it must be said, are lucky enough to own a second home, and the house does have enough space to put down a fair few camp beds, but some elegant Louis XIV chateau in the Loire it is most assuredly not.

The Cleggs have access to another house, a chalet in Switzerland that came through the Dutch side of the family. Clegg's grandfather, Hemmy, built it in 1962, and it provided the venue for a number of family holidays. When Hemmy and Louise died, it passed to Hermance and her three sisters and remains their joint property. Again, it didn't stop the *Mail* saying Clegg comes from a family with 'a chateau and a chalet' – at least the alliteration is attractive, even if factually it's stretching a point.

Chapter 3

'NICKJE'

NICK CLEGG's description of his nearest and dearest as 'a bit of a mongrel family' is not just a reflection of his Russian, Dutch and Spanish relations. It also applies to himself, his brothers and his sister, who were each born in a different place across a period of ten years in which the family lived in three countries.

His elder brother Paul was born in May 1960 in London, just before their parents moved to the Netherlands. His sister, Elisabeth, who is known in the family as Ibe (pronounced 'ibby') from Paul's early inability to say 'Elisabeth', was born in the Netherlands, but spent the first couple of years of her life in Belgium. The family moved back to the UK in 1964, and Nick was born in a maternity home in Chalfont St Giles on 7 January 1967. The fourth child, Alexander (who Nick sometimes calls 'Ax-an'), was born in 1970 at the family home. All have given names from the family's history.

Nicholas Peter William Clegg was named Nicholas and Peter after his dad, and William as an anglicised version of his Dutch grandfather's Willem. At home he was never Nicholas. Because Paul and Ibe spent their early years in the Netherlands and Belgium, their first language was Dutch, and they adopted the Dutch habit of forming a diminutive by adding the syllable *je* (pronounced like a sudden 'yer') to the end of words and names. So their younger brother became 'Nickje', and is still largely known as that in the family today, albeit most family members refer to him as 'Nick' when talking to people outside the family. There were various short-term nicknames, but nothing stuck. All four children were nicknamed 'Clog' by various people outside the family, but that is hardly original; indeed, many of Clegg's nephews and nieces get called Clog at school a generation later.

All four children enjoy a sinister dexterity when it comes to languages. Paul, a father of four who works for an environmental technology firm specialising in wood products and sits on the board of a Hampshire-based biotech company, has four languages (English, Dutch, German and French). Elisabeth, who Nick describes as the funniest person he has ever met because of her razor-sharp humour and ability to see the funny side of situations, mixes being the mother of two children with working part-time in a small design company in Berkshire; she speaks the same four languages as Paul. Nick has added Spanish since his marriage to Miriam González Durántez, so he has five. But the award for linguist of the family goes to the youngest of the quartet, Alexander – he is based in Saigon working in advertising as part of the WPP Ogilvy & Mather consultancy, and speaks English, Dutch, German, French, Mandarin and Vietnamese, and even has a few words of Korean left over from a stint in Seoul. (He once protested that his Mandarin wasn't very good – a relative comment given how many British people speak the language.)

There was no default language at home. With both parents fluent in English and Dutch, the language changed constantly. Paul didn't speak much English until he was five, while Nick and Alexander spoke English from the start. 'It was very fluid, and still is,' says Paul, 'but the Dutch we spoke was very much around the kitchen table at meal times, and that kind of language probably doesn't really develop until you take it outside. I think Nick in his teens spoke worse Dutch than I did, but now speaks better because he used it in Bruges and Brussels. At a family level when he was growing up, it was more English with flitting in and out of Dutch, but we all understood Dutch. Nick would speak 60 per cent English and 40 per cent Dutch. We all grew up in a multilingual environment, and it was always encouraged.'

These days Clegg still uses Dutch with his mother, and often with his brothers and sisters, especially when phoning them in public situations where he doesn't want his conversation to be overheard. More importantly, he has massively impressed the Dutch political classes with his command of their language, and allowed a Dutch television team to follow him during the 2010 general election campaign.

Nick Clegg clearly had a happy and largely unremarkable childhood. There were, of course, deaths of grandparents, and one house move in the early 1980s: from Fulmer to a delightful house on the Oxfordshire–Buckinghamshire border a little further out of London (so picturesque that one Lib Dem friend refers to the family at this time as the 'Swiss Family Clegg'). But there were no massively pivotal moments, no upheavals that shaped the development of the future Deputy Prime Minister.

To some, this lack of drama is a sign of blandness, but that would be a harsh judgement. True, history is littered with figures who dragged themselves up by their bootstraps from extreme poverty and suffering to become national and world leaders – whether admirable icons like Gandhi and Mandela, or despotic dictators like Stalin and Hitler. But there are an equal number of world figures who are presented with the knowledge of what poverty and tyranny can do but who never experience it themselves, and who therefore become equally – or more – effective leaders, perhaps because they don't have the chips on their shoulders that those with the personal scars carry. All the drama in Clegg's life happened one and two generations back, and it is the way he has absorbed it, rather than any powerful personal experiences of his own, that has shaped the political figure he is today.

Part of the exposure to the family's horrors came in discussions around the kitchen table. 'I grew up in a household where ideas, if not party politics, were discussed,' Clegg told *The Telegraph* magazine, and his brother Paul recalls it similarly. 'We discussed world affairs, but discussions around the news rather than politically skewed stuff. I have no recollection of any polarisation over a political discourse. Many of our discussions were defined by the events of the 1970s, in particular the miners' strike, the three-day week and inflation going well over 20 per cent. I remember having candles for light, and at one stage we had baths full of water to store it when there were shortages.'

It was clearly an affluent household, but not ostentatiously so. Even at the worst of the 1970s recession when British inflation went above 25 per cent, there was never any doubt that the four children would continue to go to independent schools, but the family did not feel that their wealth shielded them completely from the impact of what was a very low period in British economic fortunes.

Paul makes another point that characterises the family's underlying philosophy. 'The politics of ideological extremes never featured. I don't remember any member of my family ever coming up with an extreme view, and it was a big family and we'd meet regularly. We had people from histories that were blighted by extreme ideological politics, catastrophically so. Everybody in Holland remembers the war very clearly, or did in the 1970s as it had only been a couple of generations before. And when I look with the benefit of hindsight, it was always felt that it was terribly important to be objective and free-thinking. My mother drummed into us the concept of standing up for the rights of an individual, and the responsibility of an individual to their surroundings – we were strongly reminded about our responsibilities if there was a cousin or friend in need. She had a very strong sense of right and wrong, and therefore I think we're all a bit too stubborn or headstrong. We've been encouraged to speak openly and bluntly, so we all have strong opinions. But she was very keen to make sure that things were done in the right way, and Nick has inherited that.' (Both Paul and Alexander have made financial contributions to Clegg's election campaigns, notably his first one in the East Midlands European region.)

Nick Clegg also talks about his mother's Dutch attributes as a driving force behind the morality and mentality of his childhood household. 'The irritating side of the Dutch', he told *The Telegraph* magazine, 'is that they can be slightly finger-pointing and moralising. The really good side is that there's a very strong Low Church Calvinist tradition of fairness and that people have to hang together.'

His mother herself says such ethics and internationalism were very much part of how she and Nick Sr tried to bring up their children. 'We are proud of all our children, and that includes Nick,' she said in her interview with *De Anspraak*. 'We did our best to give them an international upbringing and encouraged them to go on exchanges to other countries as part of their studies. We wanted them to see that there are many different ways of approaching a problem.'

The wider family met at every reasonable occasion, whether in their Home Counties home, grandparents' houses in London or Holland, or in various holiday venues. Birthdays and Christmases were very family oriented, with lots of people gathered round a table. Christmas presents were opened the continental way on Christmas Eve, following communal singing of carols and listening to a recording of *Stille Nacht* (Silent Night) sung in German. As the four Clegg children started their own families, the continental format allowed them to visit English in-laws on Christmas Day, though certain English customs like playing charades and hunting for coins in the Christmas pudding were regularly observed.

Although Hermance was reluctant to say too much about her war-time experiences, there were plenty of tales from the Dutch East Indies. Paul remembers his grandfather Hemmy, 'an imposing man of about six foot four, with a cluster of grandchildren who would sit on his lap, and he'd tell us stories about tiger-hunting in Indonesia – I have no idea whether they were true or not, they probably weren't, but we would sit there wide-eyed; it was very exciting.'

It was a very normal middle-class childhood. Children were allowed to behave like children, they got into scrapes and bumps, they fell out with each other, and then made up. There was always a dog around, or several, mostly spaniels. And also a succession of guinea pigs, plus the odd rabbit or two. Hermance says Nick 'grew up amazingly quickly and was always an oasis of calm in the family', an attribute that has come in very useful since.

When Clegg went on *Desert Island Discs*, he chose the Johnny Cash number 'Sunday Morning Coming Down' as his second record, because, he said, 'we used to go on road trips across Europe, often driving through the night, and my parents often used to play Johnny Cash'. On such trips, the entire family was loaded into a Peugeot 504 estate car, with an extra row of seats at the back that meant it could seat everyone plus the dog, and they would drive to wherever they were going. Often it was to the Dutch grandparents and cousins half an hour east of Amsterdam, with all the border crossings that transnational motoring entailed in those days. Other times it was Italy, France or Switzerland. And there were plenty of trips within the British Isles, to destinations in Wales, Yorkshire and Scotland. The luggage would be strapped on to the roof with an old Second World War canvas groundsheet held in place by a couple of bungees; every couple of hours a corner would come loose and cause a serious flapping, prompting a stop for re-strapping.

Sports were very important to the four children, in particular skiing, tennis, squash and rugby. As well as doing well at tennis and hockey, Nick was a particularly good rugby player (see page 39), but the family sport was tennis, something that had come largely through Nick Sr. The problem was that no-one appears to have told the Cleggs that the knock-up doesn't actually count for anything. 'We were very good in the knock-up but crap at the games,' Clegg says, 'so we'd whack the ball in the knock-up and think we were terribly good, but then hit the ball in the net in the first competitive point. My sister used to get really annoyed and veto actually play-ing games. There were plenty of teenage tantrums, and I guess my younger brother was the best of us. We were very enthusiastically amateur, but we were all in our school top teams so I suppose we weren't too bad.'

Music was also ever-present in the Clegg household, largely clas-sical. Nick proved the least musical of the four; he played the piano from eight to thirteen, and reached grade four, but never seriously got into it. His mother says he was the most insufferable child to practise with, because if he set out to play a whole piece but then made a mistake, he'd insist on going back to the beginning, so he'd get up to the same mistake, make it again, and head back to the beginning. 'I really regret that I didn't stick with it,' he says, 'but then I dabbled with playing the drums, and dabbled with playing the guitar.' He has since made up for his own lack of musical talent by marrying a very gifted pianist in Miriam González Durántez.

As the four children began to have their own families, the Clegg clan spread out but remained very tight. These days Clegg has three boys of his own, plus four nephews and two nieces. They still have their kitchen table discussions, these days fuelled by a little more alcohol than in his formative years. Paul recalls one holiday discussion when he was twenty-three and Nick seventeen, when his brother's debating skills really struck him. 'We were staying in a farm building near Lucca in Italy,' he says, 'in a place that barely had hot and cold running water. We had some great fun with very lively debates over Chianti and whatever else. Again, it wasn't neces-sarily political – we were sparring with our ideas – but it struck me how very eloquent Nick is, lucid in the way he describes complex issues. He was never somebody who went to conferences at sixteen – that wasn't him, politics emerged post-university rather than in his formative and teenage years – but he had the ability at that time to sum up complicated ideas very simply and efficiently.'

At seven, Clegg was packed off to a local prep school, Caldicott, about ten minutes' drive away, largely as a day boy but with occa-sional boarding. He describes it as 'stiflingly conventional', which it no doubt was, though he admits that this description stems from his adult days looking back, rather than what he felt at the time. 'Like any child I just got on with things as I found them,' he says, 'so it's how I remember it.'

There's a theme running through Clegg's life of a mild insecu-rity about the privileged upbringing he had, almost as if he isn't comfortable, as a liberal, having had such good fortune through his birth. To that extent, calling Caldicott 'stiflingly conventional' could be seen as belonging to the handful of reactions he's shown to his affluence that betray this slight nervousness. Yet that is too simple in this instance. In fact his experience at Caldicott says as much about how his mother encouraged an affable disobedience as about the conventionality or otherwise of the school. 'Both my parents were small-L liberal,' he says, 'and my mum in particular was slightly horrified by the very phenomenon of British country prep schools, so I think even then I was aware that it was quite strict. My mum would mischievously urge us not exactly to disregard the rules, but not to take them too seriously. We were constantly challenging authority: there were teachers that I and my mother would completely send round the bend, if not through insolence at least by constantly asking "Why?".'

One victim of the Clegg personality was Malcolm Boyden, who at one stage got so exasperated by it that he took the empty plastic cup he happened to have in his hand and threw it down in frustration. The reason this event stands out in Clegg's memory is that the cup bounced in a great arc and hit another boy on the head, which drove the hapless teacher even further round the bend. He also got terribly frustrated with Alexander Clegg a couple of years later – the most junior Clegg was a very good swimmer but could never be bothered to participate in the swimming races with enough gusto for poor Mr Boyden, who once bellowed at him in a swimming gala, 'You're swimming as if you're swimming in the Mediterranean.'

And yet there was always an awareness of how far not to go. People who knew the Cleggs at that time speak of 'the right kind of cheekiness', and while it wouldn't have made the teachers sleep any easier at night, there was a certain morality to the constant questioning. Clegg adds, 'My mother's philosophy was that it's good to question authority if it's arbitrary and doesn't explain itself, but if it's fair, then it's OK. It wasn't insolence for the hell of it, it was insolence for a purpose – at least that's the way I romanticise it.' His brother Paul says, 'Nick has always had the energy to challenge authority; he challenged most teachers at his prep school, and he challenged his teachers at Westminster – almost at every turn he has challenged the status quo if he feels it needs to be challenged.'

One teacher who left his impression on the youngster was Peter Smith, who could claim to have begun the politicisation of Nick Clegg, or at least built on the general morality instilled by his mother. 'I was about ten,' Clegg recalls, 'and was very alarmed by the Cold War and the threat of the Soviet invasion, I got quite anxious about that. So I got our history teacher, Mr Smith, to give us a special lesson on what the Soviet threat was. In retrospect, I realise he was a bit potty. He literally told us, a bunch of nine- or ten-year-olds, "You're all going to be dead by Christmas." He got this great map and said, "Look, the Soviet Union needs warm-water ports, so it will sweep through central Europe, and that will elicit a nuclear reaction." There was a boy in our class from Hawaii – I even remember his name, Roberto los Baños – who was driven to tears because he'd been sent to school here from Hawaii, and hearing this he said he would never see his parents again because there was a big naval base in Hawaii. But even without Mr Smith's experience, I was very much a child of the looming threat of nuclear disaster; at least that weighed very heavily on my mind from a young age.'

However challenging he was of his teachers, he at least had academic rigour to fall back on and create some goodwill when those in authority felt their blood pressure rising. He impressed staff with his essays, showing an ability to put things straight onto paper with very little need for correction. He also impressed with his general conduct, to the point that he was made head prefect. His mother recalls that, in one of his prep school reports, 'they said he took on too much for his age, but it was his own choice'. Plus he had that quality beloved of all private schools: the ability to contribute to the school's prestige through sporting prowess. Clegg loved rugby, and played a lot of it at Caldicott, mostly as flanker. The headmaster at Caldicott, Peter Wright, had an abiding, all-consuming obsession with rugby, and consequently the school excelled at it, winning various national competitions. As a member of the school's top team, Clegg found himself twice on the hallowed turf of Twickenham in the late 1970s, when the school was invited to a fill a pre-kickoff slot demonstrating passing, tackling and other manoeuvres before the Oxford–Cambridge varsity match. 'For an eleven- or twelve-year-old, to run onto this ground was amazing,' he recalls. 'The thing that stands out for me was how long the grass was, it was so much longer than I'd expected. We had these little cones, we'd run around them and pass the ball. There was endless practising to do.'

But at thirteen, disaster struck – he went to a school that didn't play rugby! 'That was where my career went all wrong,' he jokes, but adds seriously, 'I loved rugby, absolutely loved it, and I missed it immensely when I went to school in London.'

Chapter 4

'SOMETHING VISCERAL ABOUT HIM'

THOSE WHO like to lump David Cameron and Nick Clegg together as two of a kind because of their similar upbringings cite their schools and universities as evidence. It couldn't possibly be denied that two traditional English public schools (now sensibly termed independent schools) followed by Oxbridge higher education represents a truly privileged start in life. But to assume that Eton and Westminster were the same, or that Brasenose College, Oxford and Robinson College, Cambridge were two of a kind, would be to miss some important nuances of both the independent schools sector and Oxbridge.

For a start, Eton and Westminster are significantly different in size. Eton, where Cameron went, has vast playing fields and buildings, and a much bigger staff, while Westminster makes its home in a number of historic and characterful if at times dingy and dark central London premises. While Eton nestles by the Thames looking over to Windsor Castle, Westminster is a metropolitan institution just behind Westminster Abbey, which means that moving from one classroom to another frequently involves crossing some of the picturesque back streets a stone's throw from the Houses of Parliament. It also means some exercises of almost military precision in bussing kids to sports lessons at various fields around London. At the time Clegg was at Westminster, the school had around 600 pupils, around half the number Eton had when Cameron was there.

If Eton has always been a traditional school for the offspring of affluent English families, Westminster has prided itself on its liberal arts and internationalist background. A look at former Westminster pupils who have gone on to big things shows a large number of top-level arts performers, as well as a lot of children of mixed-nationality parentage. It is, if you like, a Liberal Democrat school, while Eton is very much a Conservative school, and the mock election at Westminster in May 2010 produced a landslide victory for the Liberal Democrats (some of that may have been out of loyalty to a former pupil who had starred in the television debates, but even without him, the Lib Dems would probably have walked the Westminster School poll).

By attending Westminster, Nick Clegg can today be classified as an 'old Wet', the term for the school's alumni. And the Westminster he attended from 1980 to 1985 was arguably in its heyday. It was run by one of the most prominent and reforming independent sector head teachers of the twentieth century, Dr John Rae. A forthright figure who, despite his doctorate, was never a high-flying academic, Rae had established himself as a free thinker, partly with his thesis on conscientious objectors in the First World War, but also with his views on modernising private education. One of his innovations was to allow girls into the Westminster sixth form, and even to have a head girl one year as opposed to a head boy, though he never made Westminster co-educational for the under-sixteens. Some of his staff recall him as very present for the boys, frequently appearing in the school yard at break times to ask for shirts to be tucked in or top buttons to be done up, but Clegg remembers him differently: 'He was this almost comic figure, so distant and so grand; he had a sort of baritone presence.'

Rae was also very present in the media. By the standards of the time, he was a skilled publicist, more for his school than for himself, but not backward in pushing forward his own educational ideas; in particular, he incurred the ire of the independent school sector by opposing the government's Assisted Places Scheme, which funded a few places for poorer kids to attend top-notch private schools. His appearances in the media, which included letting the television cameras into the school in 1979, irritated some of his governors and parents, and when once asked what he would do if a group of rebellious students approached him asking for some of the school's rules to be changed, he replied he would 'invite them in for a glass of sherry'. By today's standards it's all rather tame: he was probably doing no more than any independent school head looking to steal a march on his rivals would do, but in the 1970s it was really quite racy. As his time at Westminster drew to a close in the mid-1980s, Rae joined the Social Democrats, but is believed never to have stood for election. For all his public progressiveness, he was still seen by the boys as 'establishment'.

The liberal arts influence is reflected in the fact that a number of Clegg's contemporaries have gone on to make their name on the global stage. Many are in the arts, such as Marcel and Louis Theroux, Helena Bonham Carter (the Bonham Carters are a family steeped in English liberalism), and the pop star Gavin Rossdale. Many of these have mixed-nationality parentage, like the Theroux brothers (sons of the American travel writer Paul Theroux) and Mika, though Mika's website denies any English parentage, nor does it even acknowledge his schooling in England.

So the idea that a product of Westminster would be a natural for the Conservative Party just doesn't hold water. There have been numerous Westminster graduates who have joined the Tories, like Margaret Thatcher's chancellor of the Exchequer Nigel Lawson, but if anything, it was more normal for those at Westminster to go the Liberal Democrat or Labour (or even anarchist) route. Among the healthy crop of politicians to have been educated at Westminster are Tony Benn and Clegg's rival for the Liberal Democrat leadership Chris Huhne (as Huhne is twelve years older than Clegg, the two didn't overlap at school).

For all its liberal arts attributes, Westminster had its fair share of weird and not always wonderful traditions. The Associated Press journalist Christopher Torchia, who was a contemporary and friend of Clegg, says it was 'quite a humane place with some eccentric traditions and punishments', and others speak of 'a lot of pushy egos' which led to a lot of putting people down, though those who remember Clegg say he generally kept his ego in check and was normally eager to please.

One of Westminster's more eccentric traditions was a bizarre, medieval spectacle called 'the Greaze', in which participating students would show up in fancy dress, gather in the presence of staff and parents, and then scramble for scraps of a pancake that had been tossed over a high bar. The winner would be the person who got most of the pancake, measured by weight, and prizes awarded by the Dean included Maundy money and 'begging a play' (Westminster terminology for the Dean asking the headmaster if the boys could have a half-day's holiday). 'It was a form of institutionalised thuggery,' says Torchia, an American citizen whose schooling at Westminster provided a bit of stability in a nomadic existence coat-tailing his father's journalistic career around the globe, 'and the scrum would sometimes spill over into the audience. I think it has been toned down over the years for safety reasons.'

The traditional English 'public school' practice of fagging, whereby a junior student acted as a personal servant to a senior one for various domestic tasks, had also existed at Westminster, but was being phased out in the 1980s. On the BBC programme *The One Show* in the run-up to the 2010 general election, the television presenter Louis Theroux offered the throwaway line that he had been Clegg's fag, to the extent that he claimed he was obliged to bring Clegg a newspaper as the night owl struggled to get out of bed in the morning. Clegg denies any memory of it, though that could be because he was too deep a sleeper. Theroux's elder brother Marcel says it was common practice for the younger boys to take on a number of chores for the older ones: 'At 7.30 and 7.50 they had to switch the lights on and wake people up. Louis also used to make toast, so he would have made toast for a lot of people and woken a lot of people up, including the Deputy Prime Minister. But the idea that he was a fag in the sense of *Tom Brown's Schooldays* is ridiculous.'

The decision to send Nick to Westminster was not an automatic one. His elder brother Paul had gone to their father's school, Bryanston, but his parents had found the trips to Dorset from a village just north of Slough somewhat tedious, and with Elisabeth having gone to Queen Anne's in Caversham, near Reading, a school closer to home was a more attractive proposition for their third child. It didn't need to be Westminster, but Clegg's grandfather Hugh had been a scholar there, and as Nick had by then shown that he had an excellent brain and a willingness to work hard to achieve what he wanted to, his parents took the plunge and sent him to Westminster (despite its lack of rugby). Alexander was to follow three years later.

The Nick Clegg who went to Westminster in 1980 was something of a country boy amid a largely urbanite school population. 'It was a big change for me,' he said, 'because I grew up in a rural area outside London, and I remember going to Westminster School, and I'd never spent even a night in London, so it was like the scales falling from my eyes. It was an extraordinary experience being in this very precocious, intense atmosphere, and I found it all very new.'

One could reasonably argue that a Home Counties boy was hardly the country bumpkin that Clegg likes to portray himself as, but again there are degrees of nuance. The son of a banker and a special needs teacher growing up the London side of Oxford was never going to be as rustic as a child growing up on a farm in mid-Wales, but many of Westminster's intake came from schools like The Hall in Hampstead, Arnold House in St John's Wood, Dulwich College Prep School and Westminster's own Under School, so coming from Caldicott in Buckinghamshire did make him one of the less streetwise kids.

Clegg's friend Marcel Theroux, now an accomplished writer, recalls him as being 'very spotty and quite neurotic' at thirteen, but already carrying a strong degree of innate confidence. 'When I first met him,' the elder Theroux says, 'I was quite intimidated by him. He had a kind of Steerforthian confidence [Steerforth is a character from *David Copperfield*, a confident if unprincipled and despotic senior schoolboy], almost bumptious, but very likeable, much nicer than Steerforth. He was very unfashionable, but quite proud of the fact that he wasn't a follower of fashion, which took some doing because it was a very trendy, fashionable, knowing school – being

in central London, there was a trend that you bought your shoes
from various fashionable places in the King's Road. He wore cord
trousers and Kickers, but he was blessed with the confidence to not
mind. All the hard lads liked Nick and they didn't care that he wore
all these silly shoes. You couldn't not know who he was, he was a
famous person around the school because he'd been in plays and
was known. But people never seemed to resent him because he's a
nice guy. And he was quite cheeky to the teachers, he seemed to me
preternaturally mature because he related to the teachers as though
they were people rather than authority figures, and that was a trick
I never figured out. He would just look them in the eye, make jokes
to them, and teachers love that because they don't want to be treated
as authority figures but as the human beings they are.'

Like most Westminster pupils whose parents didn't live in
London, Clegg was a weekly boarder, accommodated during the
week in Liddell's, a Dickensian building named after Henry Liddell,
a former Dean of Westminster and classical scholar whose greatest
claim to fame is arguably that his daughter, Alice Liddell, was the
inspiration for Lewis Carroll's *Alice's Adventures in Wonderland*. The
housemaster was David Brown, a teacher of French and Spanish.
He was effectively in loco parentis for the boys, looking after both
pastoral and academic interests. Brown made it his duty to invite the
parents of all his charges to dinner in his Westminster flat, and was
frequently rewarded with return invitations, including to the Clegg
family home in Oxfordshire. 'With Nick Clegg there was never a
problem,' he recalls, 'largely I guess because of the supportive family
he came from, but you can imagine that with so many talented
and intelligent kids in the middle of London, there were problems
we had to deal with. People sent their children to Westminster
for differing reasons, and one of them was that if you're running
the World Bank or some similar high-flying institution, you don't
have time to check that they're doing their homework. So I could
tell you horrible stories about lots of people, but there aren't any
about Nick.'

Brown picked Clegg to be head of house, a job that entailed

running Liddell's in the housemaster's absence. He had a team of prefects or monitors, and had to get the other boys up on time, make sure they were on time for 'Abbey' (what most kids know as 'assembly' but in this case it actually took place in Westminster Abbey), and various extraneous tasks like dealing with smokers and even pub checks, the practice of sending prefects into local hostelries just to keep the lid on drinking as far as was possible. One could argue that the need to manage one's contemporaries is good training for becoming the leader of a political party. 'I don't think we spotted that,' says Brown today, 'but I picked him because I knew he could be reliable, thoughtful and helpful, which he was. The word that most comes to mind about him is "conscientious".'

Clegg developed a broad circle of friends, including some people who were hardly safe figures. Christopher Torchia remembers him as 'smart, articulate, extrovert, engaged in school activities, and able to resist getting dragged too deeply into dark-side stuff'. Torchia remembers a close friendship Clegg had with a boy who had a 'self-destruct button' – 'they shared a study for a couple of years, and I always found it an interesting relationship, because Nick was able to engage with him without getting dragged too near the edge.' This particular relationship has proved more than just a schoolboy friendship – the boy's name is Andrew Foord, and Clegg says he is arguably his closest friend these days. 'We're like brothers,' he says, 'we couldn't be closer, even though in a sense we couldn't be more different. He thinks I'm completely mad to be in politics; I suspect he's barely aware what party I'm in. He's probably the most authentic and gentle person I know.' Brown describes the schoolboy Foord, with some genuine sadness, as 'not a happy bunny for quite a lot of the time', constantly running the risk of being 'rusticated' (suspended). 'Andrew was not what you'd call a successful member of the school, he was very different from Nick,' adds Brown.

Westminster prides itself on its somewhat deprecating sense of humour, and Clegg clearly picked up on a lot of it. 'Thank you for your miserable notelet,' he wrote to Torchia in 1991, which old Wets will understand as expressing delight at having heard from his old friend, and Clegg christened Torchia 'the fried crisp' after Torchia had returned with a deep tan from a trip home to Kenya during the holidays. 'The sense of humour was right on the border of being gentle and being abusive,' says Torchia, 'and Nick was able to go along with it without it becoming too nasty. Maybe in this respect he was a bit ahead of his years.'

Torchia also remembers there being plenty of cigarettes and alcohol available, and, being a central London school, the range of extra-curricular distractions for the boys would have been vast compared with more rural schools. But he says the amount of hard drugs was relatively limited. 'When I went to university in the US,' he said, 'I compared notes with students who had come from other schools, and it became clear that, relatively speaking, there weren't a lot of hard drugs doing the rounds at Westminster.'

There were also plenty of trips, and on one of them, Clegg displayed what was to become something of a reckless streak while out in the wilds. It was a lower school expedition to Dartmoor, a practice-run for the Duke of Edinburgh award, so the boys went camping near Widecombe-in-the-Moor, going potholing and kayaking by day. Marcel Theroux, who describes Clegg at fourteen as 'outgoing and bold, while I was bespectacled and wimpy', recalls him jumping off a high bridge into the water. 'That was all part of the very confident air he had about him,' Theroux says.

Perhaps because of his Dutch–English bilingualism, Clegg excelled at languages, counting French and German among his best subjects. And he was lucky to have some very respected teachers. Under John Rae's leadership, Westminster School's teaching staff included some of the leading figures in their fields, which, almost inevitably, brought in some off-beat teaching methods. One of the more off-beat was Richard Stokes, who taught Clegg German for four years. 'Richard was unusually good at his job and got amazing results,' recalls David Brown. 'I always struggled in Spanish because I was up against such strong German teachers. There was Chris Wightwick, who went on to be head of KCS [King's College School] in Wimbledon; there was Chris Martin, who went on to be head of Bristol Cathedral School and Millfield – these were very good teachers. And then there was Stokes, who was the best of them all, and a bit on the boys' side with his unironed shirts and no tie – rather groovy. Stokes's pupils used to get 'A1's effortlessly because of Stokes's methods; we saw it because our son was one of them. There were also teachers like John Field and Jim Cogan, who had had jobs outside education, which is a great advantage.'

Stokes remembers Clegg as 'a very lively student, bright eyed, cheeky in the best sense, great sense of fun, with a mind of his own. You get a lot of students who take notes and do what you say, but not Nick – he was more individual. You do get students who say things for show, but he simply wasn't like that. There was something visceral about him.

'He was not only good at languages, he relished them – some people learn languages like maths, but he didn't, he clearly loved the sound, though he wasn't a sharp grammarian. I taught largely through music. What kills languages is studying a textbook about the "Familie Schmidt" which takes you 240 pages to get through the present tense. I taught them grammar very quickly, and then chose poems, operatic excerpts, *Lieder* [a form of German song for solo voice and piano], oratorio, pop songs, cabaret etc., so they would learn more about rhythm. Nick was genuinely interested, he came along with us to a couple of recitals by Dietrich Fischer-Dieskau [arguably the greatest exponent of *Lieder* of his generation]. He had an independent mind; when studying literature for example, a lot of students regurgitate things they read in books, but Nick always had a very personal take on the text. He was a pleasure to teach, I clearly remember that. He even learned some Kafka off by heart.'

Stokes's teaching clearly rubbed off on Clegg. When appearing on Michael Berkeley's *Private Passions* programme on BBC Radio 3, he listed Schubert's song *Erlkönig* sung by Fischer-Dieskau as one of his six choices, alongside two other vocal works and three piano pieces.

Given that Clegg has often put education at the top of his political priority list, it's worth noting just who was teaching him, or

more importantly, how he was being taught. Stokes's 'enthusiastic'
teaching methods clearly got results, but didn't always find approval
with state authority. At the age of about fifty, long after Clegg had
left Westminster and having taught some of the nation's brightest
youngsters for the best part of three decades, he was confronted by
an Ofsted inspector who had asked if she could observe him giving
a refresher lesson on Goethe's poetry in the run-up to A-level exams.
Stokes recounts the tale with such venom that he pronounces the
common name for the Office of Standards in Education as if it were
a soulless East German industrial town (Off-shtett).

After Stokes had explained to his students, in English, some of
the finer points of Goethe's meaning – and also how Schubert had
set Goethe's poetry to music – the Ofsted inspector got up, took
him very sensitively by the elbow, turned him confidentially away
from the class, and told him, 'This has to be done in the target
language.' Stokes was so angry he feigned ignorance of the term
'target language', whereupon he was told he should be explaining
the finer points of Goethe's poetry in German, not English. He
thanked the inspector for her enlightening information, and carried
on with his lesson. In English. Two minutes later she was out of her
seat again, took him this time outside the classroom, and told him
it had been 'prescribed' that he had to do this part of the course 'in
the target language'. Stokes suggested that she do one of two things:
either stick to her role as an observer and actually observe what he
was trying to do, or 'run along and do something else'.

Because Stokes is somewhat unreconstructed, and male, the
good lady would probably not have been the only person to have
taken offence, and indeed she went straight to the headmaster to
express her considerable indignation. Her problem was that the
headmaster had been enjoying Stokes's results for many years,
and, short of hearing of downright abuse, was not about to tell his
teacher how to teach. 'Westminster not only tolerated or condoned
but actually encouraged the sort of teaching that stemmed from a
teacher's soul rather than from a book that tells you how to teach,'
says Stokes proudly, adding, 'Languages are easy if they're taught

enthusiastically, and teaching is good if a teacher does what he does enthusiastically, instead of doing what he's told to by the state.' Whether Westminster would stand by its teachers against Ofsted today is a matter that some of the longer-standing members of its teaching staff doubt.

Education is arguably the single biggest driving force behind Clegg's own political activity, so how does he square the privileged education he enjoyed with the kind of education he's trying to establish in today's state schools? 'The freedom to teach is exactly what we're trying to do now,' he says. 'It's become a bit obscured by people getting overexcited by what "academy status" really means, but if you strip away the headlines and the language, what you're actually talking about is giving teachers and headteachers more autonomy to get on with it, so they can do the kind of things I benefited from. Look, I was acutely aware then, and even more now, of what an extraordinary privileged education I had, and one of the reasons I was very lucky was that it didn't feel like a school – to be honest, it felt like some sort of overprivileged educational commune. We had these teachers who were a genuine inspiration, the teaching there was unbelievable, and when I think back, particularly to my English literature classes, it instilled in me an absolute love of reading, which has been with me ever since – I still read constantly.'

Clegg's English literature teacher was Jim Cogan, an inspirational figure in more ways than just his ability to enthuse about English literature. Struck by the massive gap in wealth between the developed world and Africa, Cogan established Students Partnership Worldwide, one of the earliest gap year schemes, encouraging pre-university students to spend time in Africa, India or Nepal. He set up the scheme while still at Westminster (in Clegg's last year, 1985), and was recognised with an OBE in 2005, two years before he died. 'He was extraordinary,' says Clegg, 'one of those people straight out of a film, probably a little bit vain – I suspect if I met him as an adult I'd view him as a bit self-regarding because the greatest teachers are also showmen and showwomen, but he was very good to me, very generous. And he just had these teenagers completely rapt, so much so that we didn't really do the curriculum we needed for the A-level until a few months before the end of the last year. We just roamed over all this literature, then did the curriculum with breathtaking arrogance, and everyone got As. It was an astonishing example of how, if you can inspire pupils, then the teaching comes next, and that's how it felt – it felt like an inspiration first and an education second, and boy am I lucky, I really am unbelievably lucky.'

Clegg left Westminster with A-levels in English, German and History (the first two with As, the third with a B). It was a package that he himself feels was too limited for his own good. 'One of the reasons I personally am very relieved that A-levels have become broader based', he says, 'is that people are doing more subjects, plus there's a move to the International Baccalaureate. When I look back on it, I basically did no maths or science at all, nothing of any numerate or scientific value, from the age of fifteen or sixteen – despite going to a fantastic, very expensive school – which I think is rubbish. When I look at my nephews and nieces, they tend to now do four or five, rather than three, and they have the AS-level, so we've now got a bit more breadth in the system, which is a good thing.'

Another member of the teaching staff, albeit in a somewhat unorthodox role, was Michael Fields, who taught Clegg the guitar. Born and raised in California, he is a leading authority on, and player of, medieval musical instruments, and joined the Westminster staff in the mid-1970s. As a one-to-one teacher responsible for a non-standard subject, he had a slightly different status to other staff, and his guitar lessons in a basement of the College boarding house (one of the school's oldest buildings) alongside the pottery studio were sometimes something of a confessional, although Clegg did less confessing than some. 'I got a strong sense of the personalities of the students,' says Fields. 'I remember Imogen Stubbs [now a world-renowned actor] would stare sultrily up from under her long fringe and give me the impression that it was all going to be on her terms – I got a sense then that she was going to be big. With Nick, I remember a bright "Let's make things happen" personality. He had charisma, a keenness for life; he was affable, confident, friendly. He would always do what he wanted and needed to do and somehow encourage others – in a very nice way – to fit in with that.'

If Fields remembers Clegg's personality, that's probably because there isn't a lot to remember about his guitar-playing. Clegg came to the instrument late, and left it early, working with Fields during his lower-sixth year (age 16–17). 'Nick would sometimes have to miss a guitar lesson,' adds Fields, 'but he was always very polite and apologised for having to do so. And it was always because something urgent or more important – like a play rehearsal – would take him away. But it was always great when he came. He had a lot of natural competence, so that even if he hadn't practised between lessons, there was still enough to work with because he took to it so easily. And we talked about life, the universe and everything as much as we played guitar.'

Fields says he never took it too personally when his students missed their guitar lessons. 'Kids at Westminster are very busy,' he says. 'It's an academic hothouse, so the ability to make choices and prioritise is something students have to learn early. We're dealing with young people approaching adulthood who often have to learn to juggle a lot of conflicting desires and commitments, so it's a smart kid who knows when to cut their losses and set priorities. I never pushed Nick about why he missed a guitar lesson – if he'd made the decision that learning lines for a play he was in was more important than his guitar lesson, I respected that.'

Clegg's take on his guitar lessons is somewhat more perfunctory. 'I was crap,' he says.

It was while at Westminster that Clegg committed the peccadillo that has come to be the one black mark on his childhood. Not that he claims it to be the only black mark, but the 'cacti escapade', as he calls it, has taken on a life of its own as a good enough story that it can act as a shield for any other deviations that may have arisen as part of the process of developing a lively intellect.

Westminster's German teacher, Richard Stokes, had organised an exchange visit with a school in Munich for the summer holidays of 1983, housing his students with families who had children at the school. Clegg was housed with the family of a judge, a man whose hobby was collecting rare cacti.

Stokes takes up the story. 'I was staying with my own host family, enjoying a fine bottle of Mosel, when the telephone went. It was the host father, and it was about eleven o'clock at night. Nick in his unwisdom had, after drinking a fair bit, gone into the greenhouse, got out his lighter and singed the "beards" of around five of the cacti, obviously not realising that these were priceless samples. It's a bit like him coming into my study and singeing all my first editions. The judge was incandescent, and we had to decide what to do. I said we should sleep on it. Nick comes out of it quite well, if that's not too much of a contradiction. He was anguished and very ashamed, gutted by what he had done – he hadn't realised what he was doing. It wasn't a wish to inflict clandestine damage – I imagine there was a party going on and then this happened. He was appalled.'

Stokes and the judge decided the best thing to do was not to send him home but to get him to atone for his actions while still in Munich by doing some community service. So he was banished to a courtyard in a community centre in scorching summer heat and asked to dig over a number of flower-beds. 'The judge was very much OK with that,' says Stokes, 'he didn't want him punished. His parents were extremely good too – they tried with Nick to find examples of all the cacti that had been burned, and find replacements, but it wasn't easy because this was a collection of rare cacti. Nick, without any grumbling, just got on and did his community work cheerfully. He didn't come on any of the outings – he may have come on cultural events like operas and *Lieder* recitals, but he didn't go on cycle rides through mountains, didn't go to Oberammergau, didn't go to Nuremberg – so he was punished that way and did his penance in the community.'

Clegg was not the sole guilty party in the cacti escapade. Another student, Tom Browne, was also involved to an equal degree, and shared the flower bed digging with Clegg. A letter sent by a boy who went on the trip to one who didn't talks of a week of drunken escapades, and ends with: 'After we left the party Nick Clegg and Tom Browne proceeded to destroy 15 ... cactuses. Lots of trouble for them. So Germany was a good grin.' The '15' appears to be something of an exaggeration, but alcohol as the driving force behind the prank appears to be beyond doubt. 'We were very drunk, we behaved very badly, and we did a lot of flower bed digging,' says Clegg. He is still in touch with a number of his school friends, but Browne is not one of them.

The cacti escapade appears to be one of those stories that Clegg feels he cannot possibly laugh about, but he finds it hard to resist the comic side. Indeed a Dutch author, a friend of his mother's, found the tale so funny she wrote a short story about it that was published. Clegg also says he doesn't like to boast about his teenage misdemeanours – some sections of the media have suggested he has played up his laddish past to detract from his affluent background – but acknowledges that he had a lot of fun at that time, and that inevitably meant the odd step out of line.

Stokes also had responsibility for the Westminster school tennis team, in which Clegg was a regular. He wasn't the best – Christopher Torchia was clearly a couple of rating categories better – and in tennis terms the name 'Westminster' wasn't a brand to put fear into the hearts of opposing teams, but he was always enthusiastic. 'Nick was a stormer,' recalls Stokes, 'he loved going to the net. He was a natural player rather than a coached player, very energetic, very competitive, very enthusiastic.' Clegg still plays today, albeit much less often than in his teens.

A much bigger feature of his school days was drama, and he acted in a number of plays with some rising stars. His acting career had begun at Caldicott, where he had the leading role in *The Government Inspector*, Nikolai Gogol's send-up of the pomposity and corruption of local government. His acting really took off at Westminster, where he was a regular both in school plays directed by a teacher (normally John Field, another of Westminster's original characters) and in house plays directed by one or other of his contemporaries. 'He was quite nervous as a little boy,' says David Brown, 'and I think they got him onto the acting to help with that. The dividend came in the TV debates when he wiped the floor with Gordon Brown and David Cameron. Nick's timing was in a different league, and I think that comes from the acting.'

His brother Paul has a slightly different take on the role acting played in dealing with nerves: 'Nick does have a lot of nervous energy and always has had, so it could well be that acting has helped him channel his energy. But it's definitely a channelling – I don't think he's ever been nervous in the sense of being intimidated. His energy is to challenge, and if you can channel that energy into an adrenaline rush on a stage, I can imagine that would be pretty good.'

While at Westminster he played another lead role, this time in a Jacobean play called *The Changeling*. The changeling was the pivotal character, albeit without many lines, and acting opposite him was a sixth-former from the year above, Helena Bonham Carter. At one stage in the play, Bonham Carter had to kick Clegg between the legs, causing him to collapse in melodramatic agony in a crumpled heap. It was a bit of business Clegg remembers all too well: 'We got it down to a fairly fine art of her missing the crown jewels, so to speak. But once she got it spot on, and no acting was required.' Bonham Carter recalls working with Clegg in the play but says, 'I wish I remembered more about kicking him in the balls. My memory of that time is all rather fuzzy, but I do remember Nick being very nice.'

Another role he played was the suave Charles Condomine in Noël Coward's *Blithe Spirit*, a man who boasts about all his sexual conquests which he claims to have listed in his diary. When a photo of the seventeen-year-old Clegg, costumed in purple velvet jacket, was unearthed, the *Daily Mail* enjoyed poking fun at his expense, especially in the light of his remark to Piers Morgan in 2008 about the number of sexual relationships he had had. But he went on to more challenging acting roles while studying for his first two degrees at Cambridge and Minnesota (see page 70).

A feature of Clegg's relationship with Westminster School was that he made some friendships that have lasted to this day; indeed, many of his Westminster friendships are his release from the breathless world of politics, given that most of them have kept a safe distance from anything political. The quartet of Andrew Foord, Tom Buehler, Paul Thomson and Clegg were very close and have remained so to this day – they still meet up about once a year. Foord now lives outside Britain, Buehler works in publishing and Thomson nearly had a breakthrough with an indie rock band. Clegg is also close to the Theroux brothers, particularly Marcel. 'I made friendships from school that are often the most intense friendships, because you go through some intense experiences as teenagers, and these relationships have remained with me, which is lovely. The others are all so utterly removed from my world.'

Gap years were not quite as popular in the mid-1980s as they are now, but Clegg did one in 1985-86. Yet he ended up spending it doing rather more involuntary research into the health services of Austria and Finland than he would have wanted.

Having done his A-levels in the summer of 1985, Clegg did what was known as 'seventh-term Oxbridge' at Westminster – staying on at school for the following term to concentrate on the Oxford or Cambridge University entrance exam. That was the time his friendship with Marcel Theroux really deepened, as they were both taking English literature. But their paths diverged, Marcel going to Clare College, Cambridge, while Clegg got fed up with English literature so opted for archaeology and anthropology at Robinson College, Cambridge. 'We were doing practical criticism,' says Theroux, 'and he got frustrated because he said you can say anything you like about poems, good or bad, and he found that too woolly.'

Having secured his university place for the autumn of 1986, Clegg opted to spend the main winter months of 1985–6 in the Austrian ski resort of Hochfügen in the Tyrolean Zillertal, where he got a job as a paid ski instructor, a profession that goes down on his CV as his first job. He went for the season but ended up spending just four weeks on the slopes, and the following three months on crutches.

On arrival in Hochfügen, he was given the most junior classes to teach, an experience that made him feel more like 'a glorified Kindergarten childminder' than a ski instructor. 'I was in these pens at the bottom of the ski slopes, decorated with Mickey Mouse figures. It was the hardest work I've ever had to do in my life, because if one of the kids suddenly had to go to the loo, you had to take the whole class, walk them across a snow field, which was exhausting because they kept falling over, go down some steps, supervise the kid getting undressed and doing their business, and then bring them back – it was just a nightmare.'

After three weeks of serving his apprenticeship, he was allowed to take a slightly better class up to the top of the mountain. At the end of every day, all the ski instructors would assemble at the top lift and then show off by skiing in a great snake formation all the way down to the bottom. Clegg was always the last, because although he was a pretty good skier, he wasn't in the same league as the other instructors, most of whom were locals who had grown up on the slopes.

Clegg takes up the story. 'There was one bit towards the bottom of the slope where you fly over this lip into a long jump, and then you'd land, and then had to slow down quite quickly because it became a sharp gully with moguls [bumps] down to a wooded path. So I flew over the edge, and suddenly saw this line of kids straight in front of me, who I obviously had to avoid. Before I knew it, I was going straight down this very steep gully at absolute breakneck speed. I hit something with a thud and I remember flying up in the air, and literally very slowly and calmly saying to myself, "Oh dear, I'm going to hit that tree." I flipped over, hit the ground, blacked out, and I then woke up and felt a pain I had never felt in my life and never felt since. I looked down and my right leg was stretched out next to me – it had come out of its hip socket. It was so painful I couldn't even locate the pain. Apparently it's very, very difficult to dislocate your hip, it only happens in high-impact accidents or Formula 1 racing, so I must have landed in a particularly bad way.'

It was an obvious case for a helicopter rescue, only the slope's rescue personnel couldn't get a helicopter, so they had to make do with a snow plough. 'I remember saying "You cannot move me",' Clegg says, 'it was so painful. But they had to move me, so they put me on a horizontal platform on the snow plough, and bumped me all the way down – the pain was just indescribable. I was driven to Innsbruck in an ambulance, and I remember lying in the corridor of the hospital, and this doctor finally came and said, "*O, das ist sehr schlimm, das ist sehr schlimm* [Oh, that's very bad, very bad]," and I shouted back, "How dare you just say that!" Then they knocked me out, obviously put my leg back in, and I woke up in a room next to a farmer who had been kicked hard by his cow, and a lift attendant; I don't know what the lift attendant was in hospital for, but I quickly established that he had a seething dislike of ski instructors.

'I had to lie there with my leg up for several days. When I was finally able to get up after about a week, I was desperate to just wander around, so with nothing more than my hospital night shirt on, I took my crutches, walked to the end of the corridor, and I found a lift which had the symbol of a television room. So I pressed the button, but instead of going up, the lift went down, and opened up in the underground car park, with snow swirling in. I was there in my night shirt, being buffeted by snow, and I thought, "I've just survived this accident and now this!" It was obviously the service lift, so I put one of the crutches against the emergency switch and waited an eternity – well it was probably only ten minutes, but it felt like an eternity – until I was rescued again. Afterwards, I painted one of my crutches with a metal laminate paint in quite psychedelic colours.'

The recovery has been largely successful, especially given that the hip was out of its socket for about six hours, which can cause serious blood and structural problems; Clegg has been warned he may need a hip replacement in his fifties. 'Sometimes I get some gyp in the winter, and I do a lot of stretching in the mornings,' he says. He also had some back problems, which he's convinced stemmed from his skiing accident. About four years after the accident, he slipped two discs quite badly, one playing tennis, the other playing squash, so he had several years of very bad back trouble, which landed him in a Brussels hospital a few times. 'It's never really gone,' he says, 'but I've become much better at handling it. I did a lot of physio to strengthen the back, and my stretching helps.'

Step two of the gap year was supposed to be a spell on the India–Nepal border as part of Jim Cogan's embryonic Students Partnership Worldwide scheme, but the skiing accident put paid to that. In fact the winter and spring months were spent vegetating out at home. For a young man with boundless energy and a lively mind, this was about the worst thing that could happen, and he admits to tearing his hair out, but relief came in the form of an idea from his Westminster friend, Andrew Foord. He suggested Clegg take up Transcendental Meditation.

'It was one of those junctures in life,' Clegg says. 'I was a classic eighteen-, nineteen-year-old: I was trying to discover myself, I was at home, I had a bad time after the accident, my childhood sweet-heart and I had just split up, so when I heard about this through Andrew, I did it. I don't think of it as a great route to spiritual enlightenment, but it's a brilliant and precise technique to help people deal with stress.'

TM became an integral part of his life, even to the point of doing it in the passenger seat of the car he and the Theroux brothers used to drive across America a couple of years later (see page 68). He did his twenty minutes in the morning and twenty minutes in the evening, sitting cross legged and thinking of his mantra. Given that he now struggles to get six hours' sleep a night, it would probably be a very good technique to use to cope with the stress of being Deputy Prime Minister, but Clegg abandoned TM four or five years after he learned it. 'The reason I stopped was very precise, even if it sounds a bit pretentious,' he says. 'After a while, I felt it was becoming a bit of an anaesthetic, and I didn't like that. I did it non-stop for four or five years, but when you do it for too long, it develops a slight "I'm all right, Jack – as long as I do this, then everything else is OK" mentality. I felt I was losing a bit of compassion – you become a bit enclosed, you think "As long as I have my TM shell around me, then everything is OK", and I didn't like that because you have to be affected, angry, upset, moved, overjoyed etc., otherwise you're not a proper human being.' There are those in the Transcendental Meditation world who would disagree that it has to be like this, but maybe by twenty-four, Clegg had got what he needed out of it and was simply ready to move on.

There was one other activity he undertook during his conva-lescent period. He wrote a novel, one that has never seen the light of day, and which the author insists never will. 'It's a truly awful novel, which will never ever surface,' he says. 'If I ever find it, I'll destroy it.' Legend has it that only one of his friends, a chap called Nick Mayhew, has ever read it, and his verdict was pretty damning. Visitors to his flat in Brussels in the late 1990s say it was present on his shelves, but no-one was allowed to look at it.

Once he was fit enough to travel again, Clegg took on an unpaid internship with a Finnish bank in Helsinki, an assignment that would have been a tiny footnote in his career were it not for the British press seizing on it in the spring of 2011. He came to the internship through his father's contacts in the banking world, so when he announced that he wanted to encourage work experience opportunities that didn't depend on who you knew rather than what you could do, he was pilloried in the media for having taken the Finnish job.

Clegg recalls that summer of 1986 with a big smile: 'It was the now infamous internship that, according to the Great British press, launched my career – it launched it precisely nowhere, and it wasn't even the Posti bank, which they said it was. But it was a lovely time, I was there for about eight weeks, making tea and coffee in various departments. I found a room in a university campus just outside Helsinki, and went on plenty of outings which left me with an absolutely indelible love for that kind of archetypal Nordic land-scape: the huge forests, the lakes, the light nights. I remember going with some friends and we found a classic log cabin in the middle of nowhere, by a lakeside, with a wood-burning sauna, it was beautiful. If the weather is good in the long Scandinavian summers, there are very few places on earth which are quite as lovely. It's a huge country, even though there aren't many people, there's an immense sense of space And they love jazz. We went to a couple of jazz festivals in the west.'

Yet such memories obscure one other ineradicable impression – a big scar on his left knee. On one of the trips exploring this beautiful country, he went for a late-night swim in a lake having had too much to drink, bumped into a submerged rock and smashed his knee open, an injury that needed several stitches. After experiencing hospital care in Austria and Finland, and with a sense of balance emanating from injuries to both his right and left legs, it was time for the somewhat more sedate environment of Cambridge University.

Chapter 5

'YOU SCOUNDRELS AND COWARDS'

IF WESTMINSTER and Eton were very different types of school, Robinson College in Cambridge, where Clegg studied anthropology, is light years in cultural terms from Brasenose College in Oxford, where David Cameron studied politics, philosophy and economics. While Brasenose (originally Brazen Nose) dates from 1509 and is rich in Oxford traditions, Robinson is the newest of the Cambridge colleges. It was founded in 1981 with money from the industrialist and philanthropist Sir David Robinson, who had made his fortune through a radio and television rentals business, and people often felt that going into it was like boarding an ocean liner. Clegg says what he liked about Robinson was that 'it had none of the stuffiness of the established colleges. There was a very human, unpretentious attitude about it.'

But Cameron and Clegg did have something in common in their undergraduate days – neither was involved in student politics. For many politicians, their student days are an apprenticeship for the council chambers and Houses of Parliament they aspire to. Rules about interrupting and chairing, when to build alliances with people of slightly different persuasions, when and how to attack opponents, and how not to get yourself caught up in the laws of defamation – these are often learned in the hothouse of student politics. Witnessing a student union debate is often akin to watching a litter of puppies scrapping with each other – good harmless fun taken terribly earnestly by the participants, but with a serious edge to it in terms of what lessons can be learned for the big bad world to come.

The man Clegg succeeded as Lib Dem leader, Menzies Campbell, cut his teeth in student politics. He rubbed shoulders with Robin

Cook, Donald Dewar, John Smith and Derry Irvine, all of whom became ministers in Labour governments. But Clegg himself says he only once looked at formal politics in his university years, and instantly turned tail. 'I remember going to the Student Union and thinking about whether or not I wanted to dip my toe into student politics,' he told Robinson College's *Bin Brook* magazine in 2010. 'I remember seeing all these young men and women braying at each other, much like MPs do across the floor of the House of Commons, with all these rigid party certainties, and I found it completely off-putting. In many respects, I was like any student, I had a number of ideals, but at that age I didn't know exactly what my subtle view was on a whole range of things. I had more questions than answers, so I certainly wasn't attracted – if anything I was repelled – by the idea of shrill tribal student politics.' That is a toned-down version of an earlier interview he gave *The Telegraph* magazine, in which he said, 'It was very Tory at the time, all these girls in pearls braying at each other and seeming to think they knew the answer to everything.' But the picture is the same, and he is not alone in being an interested citizen of the world turned off by the bickering of student debating.

Clegg remembers being interested in politics, and used to scream 'You scoundrels and cowards!' at the television. His three years at Cambridge (1986–9) coincided with the later Thatcher years, and he has talked about being affected by Thatcher's ethos. 'I remember being galvanised by Margaret Thatcher,' he says, 'and being infuriated by all this stuff about there being no such thing as society. I remember being immensely angry at this dog-eat-dog sort of social view that she took – it was a very ungenerous, harsh political environment at the time. That, combined with the complete obsession with Europe and the constant insularity there was at that stage in the Conservative government, had quite an effect on me.'

He has also recalled a moment towards the end of his university days when he first equated his social and internationalist conscience with the Liberal Democrats. It was 1989, he was twenty-two, and the party was just a year old in its new incarnation as a merger of the old Liberal Party and the seven-year-old Social Democrats. In the run-up to the return of the British colony of Hong Kong to Chinese rule, the new Liberal Democrat leader, Paddy Ashdown, went out on a limb by arguing that the 3.2 million British passport holders in Hong Kong should be allowed to live in Britain after the colony reverted to Chinese rule. With the party doing so badly in the polls, it was a highly risky strategy, but Ashdown says he felt it was important for a party whose existence was in doubt that it should remind itself what it was there for. 'It really caught my imagination,' says Clegg, 'because he was saying something that was deeply unpopular. But it was very clear: Britain had a duty to these people.' Twenty years later, Clegg would go out on a similar limb to say that the Gurkhas should be allowed to stay in Britain, arguing that if you ask people to fight and die for your country, surely you should give them the right to live in it (see page 199).

Yet it genuinely seems to have escaped his imagination that he might get involved in politics. He talks now of his view from that time that politicians were 'a different species', that he could observe them and criticise them, but never join them. 'There were several years that elapsed between university and me finally entering politics. There was no great "Eureka!" moment. But those influences certainly acted as a catalyst to push me in a slightly different direction, into a more liberal, internationalist, socially liberal direction.'

This perhaps part-explains one confusion from his university days, one that revolves around whether he joined the Cambridge University Conservative Association, as some people have suggested. The Tory MP Greg Hands, who was in the year above Clegg at Robinson, says the Lib Dem leader was a paid-up member of the association, and has produced evidence showing an 'N. Clegg' as a member. He has also provided documentary evidence showing there was no other Clegg at Cambridge during that period. Clegg himself says he has no recollection of joining the association, and certainly didn't join the Conservative *Party*. Much has been made of this by some sections of the tabloid press, but it seems hard to think of it as a big deal. Many a student, daunted by the freshers' fair (a parade of university societies all looking for recruits among new students at the start of the academic year), has signed up to associations that look welcoming, only to show no subsequent interest, and Hands admits Clegg is listed as being a member of the Conservative Association only for his first year. Even if Clegg did sign up, was that really a summary of his political views? And if it was, is a student not entitled to modify his/her political views on the basis of a burgeoning knowledge of the real world? Plenty of students have – and moved in various directions. The only notable aspect of this business is the minor discomfort Clegg (or possibly his staff) appears to feel about the fact that he might have signed up – almost as if he senses it will undermine his credentials as a real liberal. As Hands himself says, 'If I were Nick, I would come clean about it – it is long ago – and move on.'

If Clegg found politics at university offputting, he found his studies inspiring. He went to Cambridge to do social anthropology and archeology, but dropped the archeology in his first year. 'Social anthropology is not the most practical discipline to learn,' he says, 'but it does hardwire you with this idea that in applying your own judgements you have to do so with care, because people inhabit different cultural universes.'

Two lecturers clearly impressed Clegg. One was Keith Hart, a very radical Marxist anthropologist who had done a lot of work on the informal economy in west Africa. 'He had quite a radicalising effect on a lot of students, including myself,' Clegg told *Bin Brook* magazine. 'Not in an indulgent cardboard cut-out way, but he was very provocative and keen to challenge people's ideas and certainties.' The other was Ernest Gellner, who was one of the leading figures in anthropology at the time. During Clegg's three years at Cambridge, Gellner published a book, *Plough, Sword and Book*, that explored evolutionist ideas about how society has evolved from agricultural communities. 'All of that had a thought-provoking effect on me, but it didn't at that stage make me think I wanted to become an MP.'

Clegg lived in university halls in his first year, in a block opposite the porter's lodge, inhabited by a notorious head porter called Fred Boyne. Revered and feared in equal measure, Boyne was responsible for keeping everyone in line, and Clegg boasts about having avoided 'the Boyne treatment' by keeping a sensible distance from him. In his second year he shared a house in Mill Road, and then in his final year shared a different house not far from Magdalene College. Like most Cambridge students, his principal means of transport over his three years there was a bicycle.

His two main hobbies of tennis and acting (rugby had been left behind at thirteen, and his skiing accident had dented any serious hopes of a reprise) both prospered. He captained the Robinson tennis team, and worked with some serious talent on stage. He was directed by Sam Mendes in a production of *Cyrano de Bergerac*, though his part was little more than a spear bearer. Of greater significance was his role in the play *The Normal Heart*, about the rise of the HIV/AIDS crisis in New York in the early 1980s. Clegg played the part of Felix Turner, the secret lover of the lead character Ned Weeks, the founder of a prominent HIV advocacy group. The play, in which Clegg had to die on stage, reached the final of the National Student Drama Festival.

Most students have tales to tell of the adventurous trips they undertook in their university holidays, and Clegg is no exception. His major trip covered three weeks of the 1987 summer vacation, when he and Marcel Theroux, and later Louis Theroux, trekked across America.

Clegg had never been to the USA, and as the Theroux brothers are half American it seemed an obvious way to do it. So on Sunday 2 August, they left the Massachusetts town of East Sandwich on Cape Cod Bay in Paul Theroux's Ford Tempo, and set off for New Orleans, where Clegg has some distant relatives. There they were joined by Louis, who had travelled by train, and the three of them drove to Los Angeles. Marcel kept a diary, so he can report that on 3 August they drove through the Blue Ridge Mountains, where they had a puncture that required sitting for hours staring into green wooded scenery while waiting for the breakdown operator. They also went into Mexico on 15 August. Among other highlights of the trip, Clegg cites seeing the blues guitarist Stevie Ray Vaughan play in Phoenix, running over a roadrunner, and getting into alligator-infested waters in Louisiana.

One of Marcel Theroux's strongest memories from that time was of Clegg doing his Transcendental Meditation in the passenger seat while he drove their car, a practice that was obviously much more relaxing for Clegg than for Theroux. 'He was a bit neurotic and could get wound up about things,' says Theroux, 'so the TM was a way of relaxing and centring himself and calming down. He smoked a lot at school, even though it was against the rules, and he would always work too hard and get very pale and tired – he'd be in a play and having some sort of disastrous love affair and trying to write a thesis about something. Interestingly, I don't remember him smoking on that trip, he certainly didn't smoke in the car, so maybe the TM was helping. But I remember thinking it was very weird having him doing his meditation in the passenger seat while I drove.'

The Theroux brothers nicknamed Clegg 'Grizzly Fish' on that trip. 'Louis and I found Nick a bit annoying,' says Marcel, 'because he had this persona of being someone who could tell what the weather would be by looking at a flock of geese overhead. We felt he was a cross between Grizzly Adams and Michael Fish, so we referred to him behind his back as Grizzly Fish.'

Clegg's memories are more of the landscape and particularly the lakes. 'I got an intimidating sense of space,' he says. 'It was my first time in America, and as a European I was struck by the vast expanses of space, especially in Texas. Marcel had brought a great camping guide, a phone directory of campsites, so we went from campsite to campsite, and we'd specifically pick the ones with a symbol for 'other swimming', which meant there was some sort of lake or creek. After a whole day in the car, there's literally nothing nicer on a warm evening than jumping in a lake. And we really did find some spectacular campsites with lakes. We often went swimming in these beautiful lakes with barely anyone else around.'

There was no psychological after-effect of his knee accident in Finland; in fact Clegg still loves swimming in lakes. He once delighted in swimming in a lake filled with icy cold water – literally melted snow – while walking in the Alps, and has transferred his pastime to Chevening, the grace-and-favour mansion on the south-eastern edge of London that he is allowed to share with the Foreign Secretary, William Hague, and which has its own lake. 'I love swimming in lakes and the sea, but then doesn't everyone?' Clegg says. 'In fact I've taught William Hague to go for swims in the lake at Chevening.'

Clegg graduated from Robinson in the summer of 1989 with a 2:1 bachelor's degree. These days he can boast it's an MA, because of a custom at Cambridge whereby graduates with bachelor's degrees can attend a ceremony a couple of years later and get their bachelor's degree turned into a master's degree. It is generally thought of as an outrageous custom by anyone outside Oxbridge, and to his credit Clegg considers it outrageous too (though he still went to his ceremony).

Just a few weeks before, Margaret Thatcher had celebrated her tenth anniversary as Prime Minister, but there was a strong sense that her grip on office was becoming increasingly precarious. She had lost her feisty and previously trusted political ally, Michael Heseltine, over the sale of the Westland helicopter company, and her desire to show that she had not run out of steam and was still pursuing a dynamic agenda was leading her into controversial territory. She made her comment that 'there is no such thing as society; there are individual men and women, and there are families', which alienated a lot of people across the political spectrum, and she had embarked on her controversial 'community charge' project that became known as the poll tax, a blunt instrument to raise money for local government that treated poor people the same as rich and therefore was much harder on the poor.

'I was quite angry about what I saw Thatcher doing to Britain at the time,' Clegg told *Bin Brook*, 'so I left Cambridge open to further political influences. I didn't come out of university fully formed in my political views, far from it; it took several years and working elsewhere for that really to happen. In hindsight I'm immensely grateful for it because I actually started active politics quite late, and all those things that happened in the decade after university were incredibly important in giving me a perspective before I finally took the plunge.'

If there was no 'Eureka!' moment in Nick Clegg's decision to become involved in politics, it began to take shape in the five years between his graduating in 1989 and going to work at the European Commission in 1994. And if there was a starting point in his political career, it was probably the scholarship year he spent at the University of Minnesota in Minneapolis (1989–90), studying political philosophy, in particular the politics of environmental campaigners. This year is interesting in the context of his environmental background, something that worries a large section of the Lib Dems because he clearly doesn't eat, sleep and breathe environmental issues the way many of them do. When he talks about his year in Minnesota, he gives the impression that he viewed the environmental campaigners he observed as overdogmatic. He has told friends that he felt the Minnesota green movement tended to 'elevate the means over the ends' and that this 'produces a deeply illiberal philosophy' that can be excessively dogmatic, narrow-minded and unable to see the wood for the trees. At least that is what he got out of his year – whether he phrased it quite so bluntly in his master's thesis is not known.

He appears to have revelled in life in America. He continued his amateur drama, including acting in a student production of Samuel Beckett's *Krapp's Last Tape*. At least that's how he explained it to *The Guardian* in 2010 – the paper seems to have missed the point that the work is a one-hander, so when Clegg says he 'acted in it', it means he was the whole cast (or to put it less kindly, he was Krapp). He was directed by a friend from Westminster and Cambridge, Kate Bassett, with whom he shared a flat in Minneapolis, and who is now theatre critic for the *Independent on Sunday*. 'Sharing a flat with Nick in Minneapolis was terrifically enjoyable,' Bassett says today, 'a year of very interesting conversations, affectionate mutual mockery, and risibly bad cooking. When we worked together on *Krapp's Last Tape*, as part of a theatre-directing module I was doing at the university, Nick happily buckled down to the task. Being talented and confident, he brought a lot to the table instantly, but also listened and was responsive: it was an easy collaborative process. As Krapp – a decrepit oldster who's in part a tragicomic clown – he was impishly funny, having a ball, scuttling out from behind his desk and gobbing bits of banana. Standing in at Prime Minister's Questions surely isn't such a lark. Nick also quickly got the lyrical rhythms of Krapp's more regretful reminiscences – rhythms more delicate than those of political rhetoric – though this wasn't the most emotionally probing rendition of Beckett the world has ever seen. Maybe we had few regrets to plumb at age twenty-three.'

It was Clegg's first encounter with Beckett, the man he described to *The Guardian* as his hero. 'It's that willingness to question the things the rest of us take for granted that I admire most about Beckett,' he wrote; 'the courage to ask questions that are dangerous because, if the traditions and meanings we hold so dear turn out to be false, what do we do then? Every time I go back to Beckett, he seems more subversive, not less. The unsettling idea, most explicit in *Waiting for Godot*, that life is habit – that it's all just a series of motions devoid of meaning – never gets any easier.'

He also discovered a passion for the artist then known as Prince, following him to several gigs. 'I saw him there a couple of times,' he said on *Desert Island Discs*. 'It's such clever, quirky music. I just think he's brilliant.'

After his time in Minnesota, Clegg stayed in America for a few months, basing himself in New York, where he took a flat in Manhattan and got an internship as a fact checker on a newspaper called *The Nation*. Its editor at the time was Christopher Hitchens, the abrasive atheistic British journalist, and some reports say Clegg worked directly with Hitchens. All Hitchens will say is that Clegg 'briefly worked as my intern in the NY office while I was in Washington; we barely met.'

There's one photo of Clegg and Marcel Theroux from this New York period, in which the two of them had dressed up for a Halloween party thrown by one of Clegg's fashionista friends. Theroux went as Marge Simpson, Clegg just went in drag, with a glitzy red wig and over-the-top multicoloured make-up. The photo is so garish as to make Clegg unrecognisable, but the sting in the tale is that Theroux and Clegg were mistaken in thinking it was a fancy-dress party, so found themselves the only guests not in civilian clothing.

Theroux saw a lot of Clegg at this time, and admits to feeling very sad when Clegg returned to Europe at the end of 1990; in pre-email and Skype days, the two kept in touch via spoken letters on micro-cassette. Does Theroux recall any signs of Nick Clegg the politician emerging? 'I seem to recall that he did express an interest in government and politics,' he says, 'so I think there was something bubbling away there. I thought when he was nineteen that he might become an actor. He was good enough, but at the time he was too arrogant to realise how tough it is – acting's not a profession like others, there's so much luck involved. It's not the biggest turn-up that he has become a public figure. He was interested in issues of fairness and justice, but not as a policy maker would be.'

Clegg returned to Europe, where he got an internship at the European Commission in Brussels, working in the G24 Coordination Unit, set up by the then president, Jacques Delors, to coordinate aid for the group of twenty-four newly liberated countries of central and eastern Europe and the former USSR. It was to prove useful experience for his more formal work in the Commission later in the decade.

In the summer of 1991, Clegg embarked on a second postgraduate degree, this time at the Collège d'Europe in Bruges. The college is a mini-university, set up by the founding fathers of the European Economic Community, that offers year-long courses to people wanting to attain a Master's degree in politics, law, economics or history. It has around 300 students a year, and all the courses are shaped towards giving its students a thorough grounding in EU affairs. The college's master's degrees in law are particularly useful, as the EU has a legal system that is very strongly based on case law, while many of the national legal systems around Europe are based on statute law, some of them very heavily prescribed.

At Bruges, Clegg studied European affairs, which fell under the 'politics' heading. The word in the Brussels cafés about Collège d'Europe graduates is that if they came from law or economics courses, they would have worked very hard for their degrees, but if they came from politics or history courses, there would have been ample time for partying – no doubt received wisdom for law and economics graduates but a vicious rumour for those who have done history and politics. Comments Clegg made to a friend after a few weeks in Bruges expressed pleasant surprise that the course was useful, something he didn't always feel about his studies at Cambridge and Minnesota.

Another piece of received wisdom from Brussels circles is that the Collège d'Europe is sometimes nicknamed the College of Love, because so many long-term relationships begin in Bruges. And while Clegg didn't study law, he fell in love with someone who did.

Miriam González Durántez came from Olmedo in north-central Spain. Her father was the mayor of Olmedo and had gone on to become a senator in the Spanish Parliament. When Clegg first met her, he had not long split from his Cambridge-years girlfriend, Corisande Guest-Albert, whose brother Justin had been at school with him at Westminster. And a good thing he had ended that relationship, because he fell head over heels in love with Miriam at first sight. But there was a problem – they didn't have a common language. 'I barely understood a word she said for the first weeks of our courtship,' he says. 'We certainly had a linguistic tussle in a sense that I spoke no Spanish and her English was almost entirely incomprehensible, so the first few weeks was in halting French. Frankly, I didn't understand much of her French, but it didn't matter – I stared at her bewitched for the first few weeks. I thought she was magnificent. It was a real thunderbolt.'

Miriam's introduction to the Clegg clan added a new national-ity to the multinational family. 'Spanish was for us quite exotic,' says his brother Paul. 'We had no connection with Spain or South America, so when I think about when Miriam was introduced, there was something exotic about it. She has a very powerful character. She is also the most beautiful piano player – once you hear Miriam play the piano, we all need to give up.'

Clegg today says Miriam is 'very, very beautiful, and so authen-tic and so true, and so direct. I've never met anyone before or since who's anything like her. She's very unspun, but I'm not even sure if she's aware of that gift.' Friends of the pair confirm that they were indeed besotted with each other, but it was by no means plain sailing, and theirs was very much an on–off relationship for the six years until Clegg popped the question in 1998 while out campaign-ing for the European elections.

Despite being able to claim three Masters degrees, Clegg appears to have drifted somewhat in the two years between his graduation from Bruges and his return to Belgium to work for the European Commission. He spent nine months working in London for a lobbying firm called GJW, an interesting company for someone who was to go on to become a Liberal Democrat. GJW had been set up in 1980 by Andrew Gifford, Jenny Jeger and Wilf Weeks. All were researchers in the House of Commons; Gifford had worked with the Liberal Party leader David Steel in the 1970s, and when he and Weeks wanted a third person, they approached Peter Mandelson, who Weeks says recommended Jeger. The aim was to set up a lobbying company to help people who were sympathetic to Labour and the Liberals to work better with Parliament and the government.

Clegg describes his duties at GJW as those of a backroom researcher. One report in the *Daily Mail* questioned whether his role had really been so backroom, quoting 'a well-placed source who worked alongside him at the firm' as saying he was trusted enough to work with clients on a face-to-face basis. At the time, GJW had the government of Libya as one of its clients (Muammar Gaddafi was looking to restore Libya's image in Britain after the shooting of a woman police officer by Libyan embassy staff in London in 1984), and the firm was later named in the 'cash for access' scandal in the late 1990s. Clegg denies any wish to play down his time with GJW – he says he had 'no knowledge' that it had an account with Libya, and has only found this out afterwards. (That same *Mail* article quoted a 'former colleague' from GJW as saying Clegg had specifically said he would go to the European Commission, then become an MEP and then an MP. Clegg describes this as 'utter nonsense', adding: 'If anything I've been very lucky because I never had a fixed plan – it really didn't occur to me that I could become a politician until Leon Brittan put it to me.' Others who spoke with him at that time, and later, confirm the absence of any expressed political ambitions.)

Clegg's time at GJW took him to the spring of 1993, when he went to Budapest to work as a journalist as the recipient of a *Financial Times* writing prize. 'That was Nick!' laughs Marcel Theroux. 'He writes an essay and wins a prize with a trip to Budapest attached to it. He always landed on his feet somehow.' But there was still a lack of focus in those years. After spending the summer in Budapest he returned home without knowing really where to go next. 'It's probably quite good for him to have had those drifting years,' says Theroux, 'because he had this underlying belief that someone with his good fortune had to do something with his life, something that's worth doing, but it sometimes takes a long time to find what exactly that is.'

After several months at home, Clegg hit on the idea of returning to the home of one of his internships, the European Commission in Brussels. It was to be the move that set in train his entire political career.

Chapter 6

'THE BRIGHTEST YOUNG MAN I'VE EVER COME ACROSS'

IN THE autumn of 1998, former Conservative Home Secretary Leon Brittan – by then Sir Leon Brittan, now Lord Brittan of Spennithorne – was standing on the Eurostar platform at Waterloo station, reading some literature he had in his briefcase. A member of the Liberal Democrats not only spotted him, but spotted that what he was reading was the Lib Dem pre-manifesto for the 1999 elections to the European Parliament. 'Oh, are you coming over to our party?' the Lib Dem asked optimistically.

'No,' replied Brittan, 'my assistant is standing for the Liberal Democrats, and I want to find out what his platform is going to be.'

Legend has it that the former Defence and Foreign Secretary, Lord Carrington, had recommended Nick Clegg to Brittan. It wasn't quite like that. One of the Cleggs' neighbours in Oxfordshire heard that young Nick was keen to work for the European Commission, so they contacted their friend Carrington, asking if he could smooth the way for their neighbours' son. Carrington wrote to Brittan, who was just starting his second five-year term in Brussels, saying the son of a friend and neighbour was looking for work in the Commission, and asking whether Brittan could meet the young man and, if he liked what he saw, help him. Brittan agreed to meet Clegg and was instantly impressed with him. 'I thought he was quite exceptional,' he recalls, 'and entertaining and interesting, and we got on very well together.'

The rules about Commission jobs are that you have to pass an entrance exam first, the Concours, and then apply for a job in one of the directorates (the Commission word for department). It was a very competitive exam, and Clegg took his in Wembley Arena. 'I remember this Orwellian experience', he says, 'of being in the arena with literally hundreds of people in rows, scribbling away at these written exams in English and French. It was ludicrously competitive, a couple of hundred thousand people applying for about 100 jobs.' But Clegg passed, and Brittan got him a job in the directorate he was responsible for, external trade. It was April 1994, and Clegg was twenty-seven.

There Clegg stayed for two years, working largely on aid programmes for countries formerly part of the Soviet Union (all the '-stans', as many in that department describe them). They were called 'aid programmes' – in reality they were more advice programmes, as the EU had insufficient money to hand out to nations emerging from seven decades of Soviet rule. The Commission had two programmes: Phare, to help the emerging states in central and eastern Europe, many of which joined the EU in 2004, and Tacis, to help the states south of Russia that had been ruled from Moscow since 1917, and in some cases even before.

Clegg's work on Tacis involved some pretty eventful journeys in central and southern Asia. He met an eclectic mix of people who were keen for western help, some of whom saw him as an expert in some unlikely fields. 'I remember the slight comedy of going round the bus depots in Tashkent and the locals expecting me to provide expertise on how they should reorganise their local transport network. I remember being appalled by some really aggressive lobbying by some French companies on an air traffic control project we were funding at the time. I was bowled over by the Muslim seminaries in Samarkand with their amazing frescoes. And once when I was staying in Tashkent I had a knock at my hotel room door and heard this male voice shouting something incomprehensible. I opened the door to find a man with a grizzly beard brandishing a Kalashnikov machine gun – I stared at him, he stared at me, and then I closed the door and he went away. I never found out what that was about.' One of his biggest projects was as the EU's representative at a summit involving all the central Asian and Caucasian republics in Almaty, the then capital of Kazakhstan, for a project called Traseca, aimed at establishing a new transport corridor from the Caucasus to central Asia, a kind of rediscovery of the Silk Road from colonial times (it has never got off the ground).

In 1996, when Brittan was forced into a minor reshuffle of his *cabinet* (a team of half-a-dozen or so personal assistants working to a European Commissioner, pronounced the French way), he seized the opportunity to bring Clegg into his inner circle. He was aware he was taking a bit of a flyer on a relatively inexperienced recruit. 'I'd been in the Commission for about seven years,' Brittan recalls, 'and my *cabinet* was very close. It was made up of people with different backgrounds, though most of them were British, and then I said I'd be appointing this guy Nick Clegg who'd been working at the Commission. There was a considerable degree of scepticism. There was nothing against him personally, but this did seem a somewhat arbitrary decision on the face of it. He wasn't well qualified, he'd been in the Commission for just two years, so it was thought of in some quarters as favouritism. Everyone was perfectly polite, but they looked as if to say "Who is this creature that Leon has dreamed up and inserted in our number?" I think it took about two weeks, three weeks max, for them to be completely won over, for them to realise that he was serious and competent and agreeable, and that he wasn't just some personal favourite of mine.'

As a member of Brittan's *cabinet*, Clegg assisted in the negotiations over China's application to join the World Trade Organization. The negotiations were centred on reform in China, specifically an assessment of how far the Chinese had gone in meeting the criteria the WTO sets down for aspiring members to meet. The experience gave him a first-hand insight into dealing with China and what he calls China's 'immense sensitivity about its image in the world, its appearance, its face. There's an extraordinary complexity of decision-making within the Chinese government: nothing would happen for months and months, and then suddenly there was an alignment of some of the top officials, and you'd get an acute feeling that you'd spent hours talking to people who'd had no ability to negotiate at all because they had no mandate.'

As with his earlier job on the Tacis project, Clegg found that working for Brittan paved the way for some weird and wonderful experiences. On one of his many visits to China, he was in a restaurant when the staff brought out large platters of bees fried in batter. 'They were completely tasteless, and slightly chewy,' he recalls with more bemusement than disgust. And on one trip to Australia, he landed the prize guest bedroom right by the swimming pool in the Sydney home of one of Rupert Murdoch's nephews, who was married (at the time) to a family friend of the Brittans.

Brittan also tells the tale of one trip with Clegg where he (Brittan) felt Clegg was most uncomfortable because of his Dutch roots. The two men were on a trip to Madrid, and once the business part was over, Brittan's host, knowing the Commissioner was keen on art, said he'd take him to the ancestral home of the Duke of Alva, who had an impressive art collection. 'When we got there, I sensed that Nick was becoming a little uneasy,' says Brittan, 'and I wondered if it was because the duke was the direct descendant of the Duke of Alva who laid waste to much of the Netherlands a couple of hundred years back.' Clegg finds this story highly amusing. 'I don't think it was quite like that,' he says. 'The Alva name is not exactly popular among the Dutch, and that duke razed whole Dutch towns to the ground – my aunt lives in a town which still has the military defences against attack from the Duke of Alva – but I don't blame the current duke for the sins of his forebears. I think Leon is slightly overegging it.'

Whatever past conflicts there may have been between Spain and Holland, the relationship between Clegg and Miriam González Durántez had been given the chance to wax as well as wane. She had become Middle East desk officer in the *cabinet* of Britain's other Commissioner, Chris Patten, and established herself as an emerging expert on Palestinian issues. It meant they were back in the same city, and by now had more in common linguistically.

But one day Clegg showed up for work and Brittan instantly noticed something was wrong. 'Nick, who was normally calm and unflappable, came in and looked absolutely white,' he says. 'I asked him what had happened. He told me Miriam's father had been killed in a car crash. I said, "You'd better go and look after her."'

It would be wrong to say José Antonio González Caviedes was one of the leading politicians in Spain, but he was massive in his own locality. He became mayor of Olmedo in 1975 as a member of the centre-right party founded by Spain's first post-Franco president, Adolfo Suárez, and in 1989 he became a senator at national level for the Partido Popular party. After twenty-one years as mayor, he had become a legend in Olmedo.

At around eight o'clock on the evening of 4 December 1996, the Mercedes he was driving home from Madrid was involved in a head-on collision with a lorry in Montuenga, near Segovia. He was on his way from the Senate to meet six councillors at Olmedo town hall. His death was fully covered by the regional media and was also a national story. A few days after the crash, a rumour began circulating that he had had a heart attack at the wheel, but this was never officially confirmed. These days a statue of him adorns the entrance to the town hall, and the local industrial estate carries his name.

The role González Caviedes has played in Nick Clegg's career is difficult to assess. Given that Clegg was little more than the senator's daughter's on–off boyfriend at the time González died, there are limits to how much one can attribute to him. But he has clearly played a big role in allowing Miriam to accept her husband's political career. She is a highly successful woman in her own right, earning considerably more money than he does, but having grown up in a household where public service through politics was part of the reality, she is much more accepting of Clegg's career (even if she does occasionally mutter to friends that her husband 'has a hobby called politics'). In 2007, she told the Spanish newspaper *El Norte de Castilla*, 'There are many similarities between my father and my husband. They are both vocational politicians amid so many professionals. My husband, just like my father, loves politics, and he couldn't do anything else. They have a vocation for public service.'

Since marrying Miriam, Clegg has taken annual holidays in Olmedo, and since he became Lib Dem leader, the local media there have taken a considerable interest in him. These days, many media outlets refer to him as '*el caballero de Olmedo*' (the gentleman or knight of Olmedo).

Lord Brittan claims 'one success and one failure' with Clegg. The success was to persuade him to stand for election; the failure was in not getting him to stand for his own party, the Conservatives.

'I remember him saying to me, "You've got a very strong set of views"', Clegg says, '"so why don't you think about going into politics?" I don't want to be melodramatic about this, but it hit me with a sense of "Oh, right". Until then, I would look at politicians on the television and think they were a different species of people. It never occurred to me that I might go into politics – it was a world I wasn't familiar with, I had no family connection in it. Leon made me make that leap from just having my own views to making me think I could have a role to play.'

The implicit assumption on Brittan's side was that Clegg would be a Conservative, albeit on the liberal wing of the party. He was not alone in that assumption. When Brittan held a press conference, Clegg would generally be there, and so the press got to meet him. One of the press regulars was *The Guardian*'s Europe editor, John Palmer. 'He was very personable,' recalls Palmer, 'and could glad-hand a room full of different nationalities, and move effortlessly from one language to another. He was at ease working with people of different nationalities, which wasn't surprising for someone working at the EU but sometimes less obvious for someone from Britain. That attracted him to various people of non-British nationality. I assumed on first impression that he was a Conservative, primarily because he was working with Leon and it would have been normal for personal appointments – as opposed to senior officials transferred from another civil service – to come from the same party as the Commissioner. I remember asking about it and somebody who knew him from the Collège d'Europe told me he probably wasn't a Conservative, because he was very pro-Europe.'

Brittan is reluctant to take any credit for initiating Clegg's political career, saying it was always in the back of Clegg's mind, but there's no doubt he encouraged his young protégé, and as the two men had become friends very early in their acquaintance, it was a voice Clegg respected that was urging him to go into elected representation. 'I said, "You are a natural for this and you should do it,"' says Brittan. 'He had the unusual combination of interest, principle, intelligence and charm – two of the four is pretty good, three out of four is very good, and four out of four is extremely unusual. There's one other quality that's needed, perhaps the most important quality of all, and that is resilience: the ability to pick yourself up when you've been knocked down. I couldn't really judge then whether he had that – he hasn't had to show it until now.'

This is a crucial time in the Clegg political story for those who wonder whether he really is a Liberal Democrat, as opposed to a displaced Conservative. When he went to Brussels, he was politically aware, but had not taken the decision to make a career in party politics. As such, he wasn't a member of any party. There was no lack of salesmanship for the Conservatives, as Brittan was doing his best to recruit a man he clearly believed was top notch. If Clegg had been ambitious for power alone, as distinct from power as a means to enact idealistic beliefs, he would have recognised the practical advantages of joining the Conservatives (or Labour, although he has said that was never really an option for him). After all, in the mid-1990s the Liberal Democrats were a party of just eighteen MPs at Westminster and two MEPs, and still something of a joke in the eyes of many in Britain.

But there was one big obstacle to the Tories, certainly the way Brittan recalls it. 'He was very unhappy with the Conservatives' European policy. I told him I didn't really agree with it very much myself, "but a handful of youngsters like you who are keen, active and able could change things quite dramatically, so why don't you do that?" But he didn't buy that.' (The issue of whether Clegg is a 'real liberal' is discussed at length in Chapter 7.)

Having failed on the ideological line, Brittan also tried the pragmatic line. 'I said that if he wasn't happy with the Conservatives and wasn't happy with Labour, all that left was the Liberal Democrats, "so you've really got to make up your mind: do you want to join a party of power or a party of influence? There's nothing wrong with influence, it's very important, and you can direct policies in useful directions, but it's very different from being in power. And if you join the Liberal Democrats, you'll only have influence, whereas if you join the Conservatives or Labour, you'll at some stage be in power."' The irony is not lost on Lord Brittan that his protégé ignored the warnings and has gone on to have both.

'He was very scathing,' says Clegg of Brittan's attitude towards his political allegiance, 'extremely scathing, in fact – I remember him once saying, "Oh for heaven's sake, joining the Liberal Democrats is like joining an NGO." It made no impression on me at all. I was very clear I always have been a liberal and I always will be a Liberal Democrat.'

Scathing or not, Brittan was ultimately impressed with Clegg's response to this choice between pragmatism and idealism. 'His attitude was he'd take his chance,' Brittan recalls. 'What was the alternative? To join the Labour Party, which was New Labour at that time, and a lot of people of his age were indeed joining it, but he didn't like Labour at all and didn't like the Conservatives enough. So for him, it was joining the Liberal Democrats or giving up on the idea of a political career.' Brittan also recognises that this was a major statement of principle on Clegg's part, and says his respect for Clegg's beliefs have allowed the two to remain good friends, despite being members of different parties. In 2009, when Brittan celebrated his seventieth birthday and his Commission officials decided to throw a dinner for him in Brussels, Nick and Miriam both took time out of their busy schedules to attend.

Having given up trying to win over Clegg for the Conservatives, Brittan did the decent thing and recommended him to the Liberal

Democrat leader, Paddy Ashdown. In late May 1997, Ashdown was in Brussels with a Lib Dem delegation for a meeting with Brittan about EU trade issues, and despite it overrunning, Brittan used the opportunity to tell Ashdown about his colleague.

'Leon took me aside, shooed his officials out of the room', says Ashdown, 'and said, "Look, I've got this really bright young man working for me – by the way, he's the brightest young man I've ever come across. I've tried to persuade him with all sorts of blandishments to join the Conservative Party, but none of them work, and for some mad reason he wants to be a Liberal Democrat. Can you help him?" I said, "Look, Leon, Liberal Democrats aren't like Tories. The assistance of party leaders is rarely an advantage and often a disadvantage, but obviously I'll do anything I can by way of advice." So I met him afterwards, and I concluded very quickly that this was one of those rather rare politicians whose scope for growth is the thing that attracts most. There's a lot that attracts about Nick, but I like to see politicians who have room to grow. Blair always gave me the impression that he had more in reserve – I don't say Nick's like Blair, he's absolutely not, but you always felt there was something else there.'

Ashdown's ebullient, high-octane manner means that some of his stories take on a phrasing that serves multiple purposes. His idea that the assistance of party leaders is rarely an advantage has a strong element of truth in it, especially in a party that prides itself on independence of thought. But to give the impression that the Lib Dems don't go in for talent development or nurturing potential future leaders would be misleading. In fact, that meeting in the summer of 1997 was in effect the start of Ashdown's post-leadership role. He is clearly Clegg's unofficial godfather in the party, and as the founder of the Liberal Democrats, he has always taken a paternalistic interest in Clegg's career.

One of the people who was 'shooed out' was Andrew Duff, a twelve-gold-star federalist pro-European who was chair of the English Liberal Democrats and at the time had his eye on a Lib Dem seat in the European Parliament. He was also involved with

Ashdown through his work in a body called the Federal Trust, so had joined the Lib Dem leader's mission to Brussels. And the reason Brittan shooed out his officials was that Clegg was one of them, which left him with an impromptu encounter with Ashdown's delegation.

'It was my first time meeting Nick in a professional capacity,' says Duff, 'and I think we knew what Leon was going to tell Paddy. We knew they wanted to talk about Tory/Lib Dem European connections, and I was pleased they were going to talk privately. When Paddy came out, he briefed me about it on the trot, and that led to a meeting a few weeks later involving Nick, me, and two other liberals: Alison Suttie and Simon Nuttall [Suttie was a British Euro civil servant working for the Liberal group of MEPs; Nuttall was director of the Commission's External Affairs Directorate]. The four of us had a discussion over early evening drinks about the direction of the party and whether Nick should throw his hat into the ring as a candidate for the 1999 European elections, even though he was very new in the party at that time.' By the time Clegg met Lib Dem representatives for dinner two weeks later, he had had further chats with the Lib Dems' Director of Campaigns and Elections, Chris Rennard, in London. 'He wasn't immediately sold on becoming an MEP rather than an MP,' Rennard says, 'but I tried to make it clear that it was more appropriate and achievable in the short run.'

Clegg's first port of call at Lib Dem HQ was Kishwer Falkner, who in the mid-1990s was the party's European and international officer. 'He phoned me', she recalls, 'and came straight to the point, saying he wanted to join the party and then wanted to become an MP. I laughed at the directness of the approach, and he laughed too. I asked him about himself, and he told me about his background and that he was working for Leon Brittan. My first reaction was that he might be a disgruntled Tory, irritated at the Conservatives' stance on Europe. I also wondered, with his exotic background, whether he might run up against the parochialism that even the most internationally minded of Britain's three parties is not immune from, so I was quite candid about that, saying that if he wanted to stand for election, he had to find a home and work bloody hard there. He got it instantly. A couple of days later he came back, asked for more information, and by then I was quite excited about him. It's easy to forget that people of Nick's calibre, and that of David Laws and Chris Huhne, were not regularly attracted to the Lib Dems at that time, so once it was clear he was serious, it was exciting.'

There's no doubt that the meeting between Brittan and Ashdown was the start of Clegg's formal induction into the party, but it's not totally clear whether it was the first that Lib Dem HQ had heard about Clegg. For, around the same time, Graham Watson, one of the two British Lib Dem MEPs in the 1994–9 Parliament (and now Sir Graham Watson), tipped off Rennard about him.

Watson had formed a supper club in Brussels – called the Bagehot Club after the British political historian Walter Bagehot – involving MEPs, Commission officials, party workers and other Brussels-based professionals who were either members of a liberal party or proven liberals in their thinking. In 1996, he invited Clegg to join the group, and became sufficiently impressed with the young man that he told Lib Dem HQ about him. When exactly that was is something Watson is not certain of; Rennard says it was Suttie who first drew his attention to Clegg after the meeting with Duff and Nuttall, so Watson's tip-off may well have been a few months later. What is remarkable about this period is the speed with which things moved. Word got around the party that there was this bright young thing in Brussels willing to stand in the European elections, so he suddenly met a lot of leading Lib Dems, many of whom might, in a moment of weakness, claim to have discovered him.

Suttie's recommendation to Rennard was not the kind of testimony a senior figure in the Lib Dems was likely to overlook. 'He struck me as a special kind of guy,' she says. 'I remember thinking at that drinks evening that this is somebody who's really going to go places. I immediately thought we have to help him because this is the sort of person we should want to get involved with the Lib Dems but we wouldn't have automatically attracted previously. '

Word spread quickly. Ashdown told a number of people he'd spotted a great talent. One of them was Ian Wright, a businessman and former speech writer for SDP leader David Owen, who had co-founded Lib Dems in Public Relations, an informal network of Lib Dem sympathisers in PR who sometimes did pro bono work for the party and had helped Paddy Ashdown with some of his conference speeches. Wright met Clegg at a drinks evening and was so impressed that he phoned another of Lib Dems in Public Relations' co-founders, Neil Sherlock, while driving home, saying, 'I've just had a drink with someone who'll be a future leader of the Lib Dems!'

Sherlock replied, 'What? You've just met someone who Paddy recommended, he's barely thirty, not yet elected, and you say he's a future leader of the party?' Wright affirmed that that was exactly what had happened and exactly what he meant. Sherlock resolved to meet this young man, and when he finally did so in 1999, he realised 'Ian was absolutely right – this was a future leader of the Liberal Democrats'.

Having joined the party at the end of 1996, Clegg decided to do a bit of homework with a view to his post-Brittan career, and sought the advice of someone who had trodden a similar path a couple of decades earlier, Simon Hughes.

Hughes was one of the highest-profile Liberal Democrat MPs, having won an ill-tempered by-election in 1983, turning a hitherto safe Labour seat on the south bank of the Thames in central London into a Liberal one, thanks in no small measure to his cashing in on Labour's choice of Peter Tatchell as candidate. From today's vantage point, Tatchell's platform seems fairly harmless, but it was based on a strong core of gay rights, which at the time was still something of a taboo subject, and Tatchell himself was a prominent homosexual. Hughes fought the by-election with the slogan 'It's a straight choice', which some people chose to interpret as him playing an anti-gay card. Hughes has always denied it, and it was – and remains – a classic Lib Dem election message to squeeze the third-placed party's vote in a seat the Lib Dems could win. Whatever his underlying motivation, Hughes cashed in on lots of protest votes, and built the seat into his own fiefdom thanks to years of hard work, so hard that he gained a reputation for being the worst timekeeper in the Liberal Democrats. Tatchell must have smiled wryly when Hughes admitted in 2006 that he had had 'both heterosexual and homo-sexual relationships', though he has apparently never borne Hughes a notable grudge.

Before entering Parliament, Hughes had done a year at the Collège d'Europe in Bruges, and also worked in Brussels and at the Council of Europe in Strasbourg. So Clegg visited him at Westminster for an informal pep talk. What does Hughes remember about the young man who sought his advice? 'He was engaging, warm, charismatic, relaxed, interesting, and there was a lot of kindred spirit, so my first impression was good. He was a class act, even at that time, and I'd been in the party long enough to see all levels of player – there are a small number you're instinctively impressed with, both in terms of their intelligence and intellect, and their personality, and he was one of them.'

The two had a general conversation about careers in the party and politics – the upsides and the downsides – and then had a more specific conversation about the mechanisms, selections, processes, and logical routes to take. 'It was a workmanlike, businesslike and time-efficient encounter,' recalls Hughes, 'without being a Paddy Ashdown-type machine gun encounter in which he came in with seventeen questions and you had twelve minutes to answer them. It was much more relaxed talking to Nick than talking to Paddy normally was, but it was still businesslike. I told him it was a good thing, given his European experience and broad European herit-age, for him to stand for the European Parliament as a first step. It seemed the right landing place for him.'

Another person Clegg had a good heart-to-heart with was a young Scotsman he had met in Brussels, who had joined the Lib Dems a few years earlier. Danny Alexander was, like Clegg, a convinced pro-European, who went on to work for the Britain in Europe pressure group, which was campaigning for Britain to join what was then commonly referred to as the single European currency (now the euro). Alexander felt the prospect of the Lib Dems one day getting into government was a real one, if only the party would get its act together.

During the party's conference in Eastbourne in 1997, the two escaped from the official proceedings and took themselves onto the South Downs for a philosophical walk. 'We have a shared outlook about the party, and about liberalism,' Alexander says. 'As a party, we felt we had a huge opportunity, because liberalism is the basic philosophy of an awful lot of people in this country, but the party had never quite managed to capitalise on that. We both felt there were possibilities in front of us, including getting into government, but that we needed to be very disciplined and organised in order to take them. We also discussed our personal ambitions – Nick was thinking about the European Parliament, and I chose to stay with campaigning for European integration rather than standing for election at that time.'

From that early acquaintanceship has developed Clegg's closest political friendship, and the two are friends outside politics, too. They represent the Liberal Democrats in the government's 'quad', the four-man committee that resolves policy differences within the coalition. Alexander is never far away when Clegg is politically active; in fact, so close are the two that some senior Lib Dems feel they can't really influence party policy without breaking into the Clegg–Alexander nexus.

In order to put himself forward for selection as a Lib Dem candidate in the 1999 European parliamentary elections, Clegg had to go through an approval process to assess him for the skills needed to be a candidate, including an interview on policy issues. As part of his preparation, he went to Lib Dem HQ in Cowley Street, just behind his old school in Westminster, to collect some policy briefing material. The party official who briefed him was Christian Moon, who remembers, 'He was clearly very bright and a good person, and I thought, "This is great, we're getting some excellent people in to stand for these elections." I didn't think, "Wow, this man will be the party leader within ten years," but I do remember being very impressed by him.'

If Clegg was going to stand for the European Parliament, he had got his timing spot on. Since the first direct elections to the Parliament in 1979, Britain had adopted a variant of its Westminster first-past-the-post system, by which the country had been divided up into eighty-one largish constituencies (the number of seats given to Britain in the 1999 parliament), with only those from Northern Ireland being elected by a proportional system. As with Westminster elections, the result was a paltry and disproportionately low number of Liberal MEPs elected from Britain – in fact it was worse than that, because until 1994 the Lib Dems didn't have any, and in 1994 achieved just two (other parties suffered too, notably the Greens, who polled 15 per cent of the British votes in 1989 but got no seats at all).

But the system to elect MEPs in the 1999 European elections was going to be proportional for the first time. In the run-up to the 1997 general election, much was made of the good political relationship between Tony Blair and Paddy Ashdown, and there were high hopes on the centre-left of British politics that some sort of significant constitutional reform could take place. Labour's 179-seat majority meant it didn't happen, but one concession that did emerge from the Ashdown–Blair project was that the European elections would henceforth be fought under a proportional electoral system. And it was a major concession by Blair, as first-past-the-post had served Labour well at European level (Labour won sixty-two of the eighty-one British seats in the 1994 elections).

The voting method to be used was known as the regional list system. The good news for the Lib Dems was that they were likely to get a reasonable number of MEPs; indeed, they went from having just two to being the biggest national representation in the grouping of liberal MEPs known as the ELDR (European Liberal Democrat and Reform group). The bad news was that if a candidate didn't come top or second in the party's regional list, they had no chance of being elected. This is because, unless the party's vote were to collapse to well below 10 per cent, the first person on the list of Lib Dem candidates was always likely to get elected. And in certain regions the second one might get in too, but unless the Lib Dem vote rocketed never a third. Therefore, the challenge for an unknown figure like Nick Clegg was to find a region where he could get to be top of the list – and to do that, he needed to impress his fellow party members who vote for the order of the list.

There was a further complication in the Lib Dem system. In order to promote gender equality – something that's at the heart of the party's ethos but has not been well reflected in the gender balance of Lib Dems at Westminster – the European list was 'zipped', which meant it went man-woman-man-woman (or woman-man-woman-man) and so on, depending on whether a region was designated male led or female led. So if someone came a close second to a candidate of the same sex in the vote to get onto the party's list for the Euro elections, he or she ended up at best third on the list, with virtually no chance of getting elected. In many ways, it's a bigger battle within the party than among the electorate.

Discussions about where Clegg should stand had begun in Brussels shortly after the Brittan–Ashdown meeting in May 1997. All the regions with which he had any connection – notably London, the South East, and East of England – had prominent Lib Dems as declared candidates, so the question of the East Midlands came up as it was to be a male-led list and there was no obvious front-runner. Many claim to have suggested it was the place for Clegg to run, but the person whose recommendation carried most weight was Chris Rennard, who had been a party organiser there ten years earlier so knew the area. But there were two problems: Clegg had no connection with the region (an associate from Brussels days says he even had to look up where it was), and another ambitious Lib Dem had also made a beeline for the East Midlands nomination with the endorsement of a past party leader.

His name was Atul Vadher, a successful businessman who had

based himself in Skegness (which is in the East Midlands region), and he had the backing both of a leading East Midlands parliamentary candidate, Paul Holmes – later an MP – and of the former Liberal leader David Steel. Campaigning under the name Ash Vadher, he had promised to use his wealth to support various Lib Dem candidates in the East Midlands, in particular Holmes's bid to win the Westminster seat of Chesterfield, where about 10 per cent of the East Midlands' 3,500-or-so Lib Dem members were to be found. The Vadher camp was therefore less than amused when a bright-eyed, golden boy, who clearly carried the seal of approval from the party's HQ, was suddenly thrust into their midst.

Yet Clegg was a political virgin. 'He didn't know much about campaigning,' says Russell Eagling, a Lib Dem activist who met Clegg for the first time in 1998 and went on to be his regional organiser earning the princely sum of £60 a week. 'We met on the roof terrace of the Houses of Parliament, and he was very impressed that I should have a camera with me. To me it was basic politics – he was standing for us in a region where we hadn't been very successful, we knew we had to do some good campaigning, and I had a chance to take a picture of him with Big Ben in the background. So it was obvious to me but new to him. He hadn't done any canvassing either.'

Perhaps this inexperience explains the mild outbreak of panic when news reached Clegg that Steel was phoning round various prominent East Midlands Lib Dems asking them to back Vadher. One of them was Tony Rogers, a veteran councillor on Chesterfield Borough Council who had stood three times for the Chesterfield parliamentary seat. 'I got this call one Friday night,' says Rogers, 'and it was David Steel. He said, "This is a voice from the past – I want you to support Ash Vadher. He works for me in the House of Lords, he's a good bloke and will make a very good MEP." So I said yes, and that was it. The very next day, I got a knock at the door from a young man who introduced himself as Nick Clegg and asked if I'd support him. I said I was very sorry, but that if he'd arrived the day before I could have done so, but that I'd given my word to

David Steel and I wasn't in the habit of going back on my word. He didn't even get to say goodbye, he just walked out, slamming the door as he went.'

Such outbursts of pique – if indeed it was that – are very rare in the Clegg story. Many people who worked with him say they never saw him lose his temper, and Rogers speaks very highly of Clegg to this day. But there's no doubt Clegg was worried about the competition he was facing, and the Clegg–Vadher battle did threaten to get nasty. There were even suggestions of whispering campaigns denigrating Clegg's international family, though the Vadher camp denies it was involved in them. 'Nick didn't seem to know how to counter it,' says another East Midlands activist and later parliamentary candidate, Ed Fordham. 'He wasn't used to using his contacts. If the immediate past party leader had phoned the chair of Skegness Lib Dems to endorse Nick's opponent, Nick had to get the current party leader to phone the chair of Skegness to endorse *him*. He didn't think of that – he thought he'd have to go to Skegness, but that would have been a terrible use of his time. He also had a curious shyness. I'd say to him "Mention that you were in China" or something when he was in conversation with people, but he didn't really want to use his anecdotes. Maybe it's modesty, or a desire not to show off?'

Although not a massive region in relative terms, the East Midlands is very spread out, embracing six counties and lots of flat land between villages – it goes south to Corby and north to High Peak, and there are active Lib Dem groups in all parts of the region. Having had very little political success, the Lib Dem organisation there was sparse; although there was a regional committee, the closest they had to a regional organiser was a long-serving activist, Jane French, doing desk-based administration with one book and a biro in the quaintly named village of Dogdyke. Clegg drove through much of the region at weekends, trying to drum up support for his battle to top the Lib Dem list. 'The party in the East Midlands was so weak,' he recalls. 'We hadn't had an MP in the East Midlands since the 1930s, so it literally was a question of going from place to place. I spent hours and hours in service stations off the M1, driving round, meeting activists, joining in little local campaigns, but there was no coordinated East Midlands campaign at that time.' It was the complete antidote to the urban sophistication of Brussels, where he spent his weekdays. Fordham recalls him phoning in, saying 'Where am I?' when stuck in a tiny village. 'Rural campaigning is a totally different world,' he says: 'you go out of mobile phone reception, you drive for miles through nowhere. But he adjusted well. He was impressive because he got down to work, but not in the way that made you think a suit had swanned in; in fact, we had a constant joke about his dreadful cardigans. He gave the impression of being a good bloke.'

The new boy learned very quickly, and Vadher's problem was that the Clegg magic, allied to his capacity for hard work, instantly seemed to win over Lib Dem members. If at first there had been a sense that an outsider had invaded the ranks of East Midlands Lib Dems, it was soon replaced by a realisation of 'Ah, now I see why', as one activist put it. The man from Brussels who had no connection with the area won over the locals, even those who were somewhat sceptical.

'Learning that he was working for Leon Brittan increased my suspicion of Nick,' recalls Peter Harris, an East Midlands activist who later became Clegg's constituency chair. 'I had got a very good impression of him on first meeting, but the second meeting was a bit more circumspect because I'd found out in the meantime that he was working for Brittan and was therefore uncertain what his motivation was – I was not hugely supportive of Leon Brittan. At the hustings I raised the question that he came from a conservative political background, so what assurance did I have that he was a Liberal Democrat in terms of the party's philosophy and the implications of putting him No 1 on the list? I got a direct answer, and it was a very positive response to the question. He left me with the impression that he was sympathetic to the core principles of the party and aligned with where I stand.'

In short, Clegg charmed the East Midlands party, but still the vote was close. Although he topped the poll from the start (it was

run under the alternative vote system), it took five rounds of counting before he gained the necessary 50 per cent, finishing ahead of
Vadher by a tiny margin. But it was enough to top the list.

In most circumstances, this would have been enough to get him
into the European Parliament, but in the region he had chosen,
it wasn't quite that simple. The East Midlands had never had any
elected Lib Dem higher than councillor level, so the working
presumption that at least the No 1 on the list would become an
MEP wasn't totally watertight. Indeed, the East Midlands Lib Dems
were so unsure that they could get their No 1 in that they had a
lengthy debate on whether to resource the 1999 European campaign
or not. The fact that the lion's share of the funding for it came from
party HQ, with the region merely topping it up, meant the eventual
decision to fight a proper campaign was an easy one. Once it was
taken, a website was set up and a campaign office sought. Clegg also
got himself a cottage in the Nottinghamshire village of Ruddington,
which was not only near East Midlands airport (of practical use for
getting to and from Brussels) but was slap bang in the middle of the
East Midlands region.

The website was an interesting one in that Clegg asked for it
to carry the Lib Dems' audited accounts. This was very unusual at
the time, and his local activists felt the need to point out that the
website should have been about how to contact the leading candidates and what they stood for, but Clegg was insistent he wanted
the accounts on the website. It not only laid down a marker that
he wanted the funding of his political activity to be totally above
board, it also came in useful when journalists suddenly wanted
details about expenses when Cleggmania struck in April 2010.

Finding an office in a region that had seen little or no campaigning for the Lib Dems was somewhat harder. Several places were
looked at, including one in the village of Gotham – it's pronounced
'goat-um', but that would have been no impediment to some nice
Batman-related headlines and cartoons. Interestingly, none of
the potential offices were in Chesterfield, which was Vadher and
Holmes's patch; Clegg has never hit it off with Holmes, even during

the five years they were both MPs. In the end, Clegg's political career started in an auspicious little room just off Trent Bridge in the centre of Nottingham. The room, next to a hairdresser's in a row of shops, had been discovered by a local larger-than-life supporter called Kevin Mulloy, who Clegg describes as 'a marvellous fixer who always had the latest business wheeze that was going to make him into a millionaire'. When Clegg arrived, there was Mulloy already in situ with a suitcase full of cheap jewellery that he was trying to sell. Despite various reservations about what a cheap jewellery salesman would do for the image of a hopeful politician, that room did indeed become the East Midlands Lib Dems' European campaign HQ.

Clegg went about campaigning for his European seat very assiduously. He sent out press releases, and for some local papers this was news in itself – they weren't used to a candidate for the European Parliament sending them anything, as all the local MEPs were thought to be in safe seats. It certainly helped his profile, and he was featured on the front page of the Mansfield *Chad* newspaper four weeks running, such was his novelty value.

The process of adjusting to rural politics in an unfashionable part of England had its moments. At one stage he visited the chief executive of Lincolnshire County Council and took the opportunity to ask about ethnic diversity. The chief executive replied, 'Well, we have a Chinese takeaway in every village.' Lib Dem staff teased the metro-wise Clegg about his welcome to rural politics. For his part, Clegg invited his East Midlands friends over to Brussels. On one occasion he introduced them to his boss, Leon Brittan, who told them, 'This guy is on the up, do what you can to help him. At the very least, get him elected.'

With the elections due in June 1999, a campaign launch was planned for October 1998 at a garden party to be held in the utilitarianly named Electric Station Road in Sleaford, at which a number of balloons were to be released. On this occasion, Clegg was to appear with his Spanish girlfriend, with the two of them arriving by train to great acclaim, to highlight the need for improved rail links in Lincolnshire. On the way, the two found themselves alone at Rauceby, a tiny station in the middle of the Lincolnshire countryside on the Boston–Nottingham line. 'Literally as the train came into sight,' Clegg says, 'I turned to Miriam and said, "Will you marry me?" and she said, "Yes." We were both so stunned by this very brisk transaction that we got on the train and were very silent for a while as we digested this massive step that we'd suddenly taken. I've never been back to Rauceby station since, but I love Lincolnshire, I still love the openness of the countryside and the skies.'

As well as galvanising the local press into talking about MEPs and potential MEPs, Clegg brought some big names into the region. His biggest triumph was his adoption meeting at Nottingham University's Senate in May 1999, just a fortnight before the elections, where he brought in Paddy Ashdown and Shirley Williams (Baroness Williams of Crosby). One activist described the event as 'probably the best attended Liberal Democrat event in the East Midlands in twenty years – it added a previously missing piece of glitz to the campaign, and raised the spirits significantly'. It was upping the ante on the kind of electioneering the East Midlands had seen for a Euro election before, and helped raise both the Lib Dems' profile and Clegg's. A poster for the campaign featured a cartoon of Clegg, drawn by a Lincolnshire street artist who disappeared without trace, little knowing that he had drawn the first cartoon of the future Deputy Prime Minister.

Having said that, bringing in Action Man Ashdown is fraught with dangers. He returned to help the Clegg campaign, happily initiating and taking part in a white water rafting stunt with Clegg and the rest of the East Midlands European election team at Holme Pierrepont, Nottinghamshire's international-standard rowing and watersports facility. Ed Fordham, who observed the invasion of Ashdown's infectious enthusiasm, said, 'Paddy was at the helm, obviously – he loved it and Nick achieved the impossible of keeping up the same level of enthusiasm for such outdoor sport!'

* * *

Elections to the European Parliament are strange affairs in Britain. The British have Thursdays as their traditional polling day, while most of mainland Europe has Sundays. So the British are allowed their Thursday voting, as long as no votes are counted until the polls have closed across the whole of the EU, thus necessitating a three-day wait once the British polling stations have ushered out their last voter. But that doesn't mean there was no activity between Thursday night and Sunday evening in June 1999. Because the boxes could be opened ahead of the count, a number of Lib Dems had been doing calculations based on 'box counts', and the initial indications made them unsure whether the party would even get its No 1 elected in the East Midlands.

When the results came in on the evening of Sunday 13 June 1999 showing that Clegg had been elected, there was euphoria among the East Midlands Lib Dems. In South Derbyshire, he was the first liberal parliamentarian elected since 1916, and the first Liberal Democrat parliamentarian anywhere in the six counties since the Lib Dems emerged out of the Liberals and Social Democrats in 1988. Only one person couldn't share the joy – Clegg himself. 'On the night of the election after the results had been declared, he was very downbeat and disappointed,' says Russell Eagling, 'because the turnout was so low. He was saying "I don't see what the point is if you're not engaging with anyone", he felt his mandate was not legitimised. It was a shock to him to see how little the EU mattered to the British people after his time in Brussels, where it means so much. We had to explain to him that in local terms this was a great result, that I'd spent a lot of the campaign evangelising in the local parties about how good it would be to have someone like an MEP who we could all draw on, and that we'd succeeded.'

Clegg remembers his disappointment well. 'I do remember the unalloyed joy of being elected was mixed with this feeling of "What kind of mandate is this when there are so few people voting?". The turnout was lamentable, and the question of how you get people engaged in politics is something I remain very preoccupied about to this day.'

The turnout was indeed low. Britain came bottom of the then fifteen-member EU for voter turnout, and it was Britain's lowest-ever turnout in its European Parliament elections. The overall turn-out in Britain was 23.3 per cent, and the East Midlands was below that on 22.8 per cent. There may have been 92,398 people who voted for the Lib Dems in the East Midlands, but they represented less than 3.5 per cent of those able to vote in Clegg's Euro-constituency.

Yet Clegg soon saw that it was indeed a success, and the spring was back in his step when he returned to the EU's centre of power. Barely two years after first being introduced to the top brass of the Liberal Democrats, Nick Clegg was a member of the European Parliament. At the age of thirty-two, his career as an elected repre-sentative had begun.

Chapter 7

'UNBUNDLING THE LOCAL LOOP'

ANYONE WHO was frustrated at the monopoly British Telecom had over fixed telephone lines in Britain in the 1980s and 1990s will have rejoiced in 2001, when the company was ordered to make its fixed infrastructure available to other telecom service providers. Until then, if you didn't live in a street with cable television facilities and you wanted a landline, you had to go to BT, the private commercial giant that had been established in the early 1980s when Margaret Thatcher's government privatised the telecoms part of the state-owned post and telecommunications industry. But that all changed – and Nick Clegg was one of the principal architects.

One of the most significant pieces of legislation passed by the 1999–2004 European Parliament was a package of telecommunications liberalisation measures, freeing up formerly nationalised infrastructure and opening it up to competition. The part Clegg was responsible for was called 'Unbundling the local loop', which meant his challenge was to open up to free competition the last few miles of telecommunications wires from the local exchange to private houses. He was the Parliament's 'rapporteur' on the issue, a name that implies the role of a spokesperson or chair of a piece of legislation, but in reality, the rapporteur is more a fiercely proactive shepherd, steering it through various legislative obstacles.

'It was his greatest single legislative achievement, and perhaps the biggest achievement of that Parliament,' says Chris Davies, a fellow Lib Dem MEP who is still in the European Parliament today. 'It was a classic case of rapporteur negotiations, where the rapporteur plays a lead role in securing the deals necessary to advance legislation. Some of the deals are done through the formal structures, deals with ministers and the [European] Commission, but some need a lot of behind-the-scenes negotiation. He lobbied for the right to be rapporteur, which is no small achievement in itself, he steered the dossier through Parliament, and he sorted out various problems associated with it. He made his mark as an MEP with real influence.'

Marcel Theroux has a more tongue-in-cheek way of recognising Clegg's achievement. 'In the world of local loop unbundling,' he said, 'he's a demi-god.'

Clegg was clearly keen to set out his stall as an MEP early. Any disappointment about the turnout in Britain was wiped away when he arrived for his first plenary session in Strasbourg and resumed friendships with a number of people he had worked with during the previous five years. 'He bounced down from the plane at Strasbourg airport', recalls Davies, 'and met up with Lousewies van der Laan.' Van der Laan had pursued a similar path to Clegg – they were only a year apart in age, had both studied in America, and both ended up in the *cabinets* of European Commissioners, in van der Laan's case as press spokesperson for the Dutch Commissioner Hans van den Broek (she had earlier worked for another Dutch Commissioner, Frans Andriessen). She became an MEP in the same elections as Clegg, as head of the list of the Dutch social-liberal party D66. 'They were both very bouncy,' adds Davies, 'and Lousewies told us we should all campaign to get rid of Strasbourg!'

Ah yes, Strasbourg. The EU's institutions are spread across three cities – Brussels, Luxembourg and Strasbourg – but effectively based in Brussels. The European Commission sits there, as do the European Parliament's committees. But the monthly full sessions of the Parliament take place in Strasbourg, a symbolic location as it's the capital of Alsace, a region that has been disputed by differ-ent countries over the centuries and is therefore supposed to be a symbol for the peace dividend of European unity. The problem is that it costs the EU about €200 million a year (and allegedly 20,000 tons of extra CO_2) just transporting all the papers from Brussels to Strasbourg – both expensive and heartily inconvenient, especially for the poor souls who spend much of their time packing boxes for the monthly temporary relocation.

So Clegg, van der Laan and a Swedish liberal called Cecilia Malmström (now a Commissioner) got together to campaign for the Parliament to meet in Brussels. They never succeeded in their explicit aim – they were up against the French government, which earns a fair bit of money from the Parliament being on French territory – but they did succeed in getting rid of Fridays in Strasbourg, which effectively reduced the Strasbourg week to Tuesday, Wednesday and Thursday mornings. Strasbourg may be fairly central in western Europe, but in transport terms it isn't easy to reach, and for those coming from eastern Europe, Ireland or the Canary Islands, the original four-day week (from Monday lunchtime to Friday lunchtime) often involved a full week away from home. So it was a meaningful concession for the three to have gained.

Among many of the liberals, Clegg and his associates were known as the 'young dogs' or 'young hounds' (the name comes from the Dutch *jonge honden* as the term originated among the Dutch liberals), denoting a younger generation of politicians. Arne Richters, a Dutchman who worked as an assistant to liberal MEPs, says, 'In the past the fossils went to the European Parliament, the old politicians that one wanted to park somewhere strategically and not have back. That went for the majority of the institution, so these guys stood out because they were generally young and dynamic. The name was used for more than just liberals – it denoted the new, ambitious group of MEPs.'

Clegg also showed he meant business among his own colleagues. In July 1999, he came to one of the meetings of the British Liberal Democrat MEPs, armed with a paper about MEPs' expenses. The topic of expenses had been alive and kicking in broader EU circles, as the 1994–9 Commission had had to resign early because of expenses scandals involving several high-ranking officials, most notably one of the Commission vice-presidents, Manuel Marin, and his colleague, the former French Prime Minister Édith Cresson. But the scandal had not reached MEPs, and Clegg was convinced it shouldn't. 'It was a very principled paper,' recalls the leading British Lib Dem MEP Graham Watson, 'basically saying that we should not abuse the gravy train of EU largesse. It was in many ways ahead of its time.'

One man who observed Clegg at close quarters, both as a Commission official and as an MEP, is John Palmer, who was *The Guardian*'s Europe editor from the mid-1990s to the mid-2000s. 'It was clear that he was very ambitious,' Palmer says. 'I knew a lot of the Lib Dem MEPs, and listening to them talk it became clear that Nick was emerging as a player. He had his conflicts within the Liberal group, but then there were several personality conflicts within the Lib Dem group. He took part in a number of activities organised by the European Policy Centre, and people were saying he was ambitious. My first impression was that I didn't quite believe it, because he was a bit self-effacing, a very well-mannered young man, clearly at ease with different people of different international social backgrounds. But it soon became clear he was ambitious in an economic liberal sense.'

As a Lib Dem MEP, Clegg found himself a member of various groupings. He was obviously a member of the LDEPP, the Liberal Democrat European Parliamentary Party. But more importantly he was a member of the ELDR (the European Liberal Democrat and Reform group), an eclectic grouping of centre ground members who called themselves liberals: everyone from the German FDP (Freie Demokratische Partei or Free Democratic Party) to the British Lib Dems, and including two Dutch parties (D66, which is more to the left of the British Lib Dems, and the VVD (Volkspartij voor Vrijheid en Democratie or People's Party for Freedom and Democracy), which is more right wing but without the Christian element found in many European Conservative parties). The ELDR had fifty-five members, of which the British Lib Dems had suddenly become the largest single bloc.

All MEPs have an office in Brussels, and Clegg struck lucky with his. All the offices in the European Parliament's building in Rue Belliard in Brussels are identical, but not all have a view. He got a room with a view on the tenth floor; it looked out to the east, which meant the sun streamed in most mornings. But no sunshine could hide the constant chaos that comes when masses of documents are packed into coffin-like trunks once every four weeks for the trek to Strasbourg. And yet it was an environment that did nothing to dent Clegg's eternal optimism. 'He really enjoyed it,' says Charlotte Harris, the daughter of his constituency chair, who did a two-week internship in 2001 at the age of sixteen. 'He was really happy all the time, he used to bounce in – it was chaotic, but he seemed to thrive in it.'

Not that being an MEP was always a bag of laughs, but in some of the more boring moments Clegg established a good friendship with Chris Davies, who had become an MP in 1995 in a by-election in Oldham, but had lost his seat at the 1997 general election and decided to pursue his political career in Europe. Davies says, 'Nick and I saw a lot of each other, because in a group of fifty-five, Clegg and Davies are alphabetically next to each other, so classically we spent five years sitting next to each other in Strasbourg during voting sessions, bored out of our minds, voting on amendment after amendment, and chatting about the world, other MEPs, and everything. Voting in Parliament is, with a few exceptions, the most tedious time of the week because you're voting on matters about which you've had no involvement, so you're just pressing the green button.

'He was struck by the self-confidence of members,' Davies adds. 'One of his first comments to me in the European Parliament came as we were walking across the bridge between the hemicycle and the office block. He said, "Tell me, in the Commons, are they all as pompous as this?" I said, "They're much more pompous in the Commons than they are here." Well, now he knows from his own experience!'

There are arguably three key relationships in Clegg's rise to become leader of the Liberal Democrats and Deputy Prime Minister. The first was the relationship with Paddy Ashdown, who steered him through the early waters and still plays a paternalistic role today. There is also the relationship with Danny Alexander, who he has known as long as he's known Ashdown, and with whom he is closer than with any other politician. And then there's the relationship with Chris Huhne, which has echoes of the Tony Blair–Gordon Brown relationship in the Labour Party of the 1990s but seems to be enjoying a harmonious third chapter which the Blair–Brown psychodrama never really achieved.

Clegg and Huhne were among the new boys in the 1999 Lib Dem European parliamentary intake, and soon struck up a very close political relationship. 'We were definitely kindred spirits, and we had similar interests,' says Huhne. 'When we were elected in 1999, there was an assumption that we would have a referendum fairly soon on Britain joining the euro, so there was a lot of interest in the related matters: the economic interests, the creation of the European Central Bank etc. Nick was involved in the Britain in Europe campaign, so we had a lot of agenda in common.'

Huhne and Clegg both had a journalistic background, though Huhne's was much more thorough. He had been Brussels editor of *The Economist* in the late 1970s and then joined the staff of *The Guardian*. He had been a member of the Labour Party, thinking of himself very much on the Roy Jenkins wing, so he was one of the Labour members who joined the new Social Democrats in 1981. He went on to stand for Parliament twice for the SDP in the 1980s: in Reading East in 1983 and in Oxford West & Abingdon in 1987. He fought good campaigns and got reasonable results, but ended up somewhat dispirited with the electoral system, and decided he wouldn't stand again until there was a decent chance of getting elected. With a proportionally representative system being used for the 1999 European elections, he put himself forward for the South-East England regional list, was the top male performer in a female-led list, and got in thanks to a good Lib Dem showing in that part of the country.

One of the first people Huhne ran into when he arrived in Brussels was John Palmer, *The Guardian*'s Europe editor. Palmer greeted his former colleague warmly and asked him what he was doing there, to which Huhne replied that he'd just been elected an MEP. Palmer says, 'I knew he'd gone into the City, and he explained he'd made some good money in commodities broking. He then said, "Look, I've been in business and I've done rather well, and I think the time has come for me to put something back in."'

Palmer makes another observation about Huhne that was to prove significant eight years later. 'He seemed to have some of his radical youth left. The way he spoke about the Tory Party was more adversarial and resonated more with people on the left.' With his detailed knowledge of finance and banking, Huhne gave the impression of being very much a Europe-minded economic liberal, but his roots in the Labour Party had not been totally severed, and in the 2007 Lib Dem leadership election he was to woo the left-of-centre vote with such success that he very nearly won.

Given that the question of Britain adopting the euro is way off the agenda at the moment, one struggles to recall that Clegg and Huhne's political relationship was established largely on the basis of mutual support for the single currency. 'We struck up a good, strong friendship,' says Clegg; 'he was one of only two Lib Dem MEPs invited to my wedding, and the only one who could come. We thought fairly alike on a lot of issues. He's obviously a formidably intelligent guy, had a very strong background on the economics of European integration, and he was passionate about the single currency, as I was. What drew us together was that Chris and I shared an absolutely passionate conviction to make the case [for Britain to join the single currency], but not to make it in endlessly fluffy terms, which is always the danger of the pro-European movement. If you're constantly talking about intergovernmental conferences, you'll never get the British people on your side.'

Throughout their first four years in the European Parliament, Clegg and Huhne were very close. They clearly developed a strong friendship, and as the two had both been at Westminster School, there was a certain amount of solidarity. 'I got the impression that Chris was something of an elder brother to Nick,' says the most senior British Lib Dem MEP, Graham Watson. 'There was twelve years between them, and Nick was so much less experienced in politics than Chris was, that I felt it was a very healthy relationship.' Clegg feels the elder-brother interpretation is somewhat 'overegging it – it didn't feel like that,' he says now.

More importantly, word was seeping through from London that the two were highly regarded, and were being tipped as possible future leaders of the party. Huhne today plays down the idea that he was a potential leader at the turn of the millennium, but Clegg must have felt Huhne was a rival. For in 2003, when Watson was promoted to leader of the ELDR, it created a vacancy in the LDEPP. Huhne stood for it and asked for Clegg's backing. It came, but very late. 'I was surprised,' says Huhne, 'because we'd been quite close, so it introduced a slight edge, and I wondered if Nick saw me as something of a rival.'

It's easy to think of an MEP as flitting seamlessly between Brussels and Strasbourg, paying just the occasional royal visit to his constituency. But that was never the deal once Clegg became the top-listed candidate on the East Midlands Lib Dems' list. Part of his dismissal of Atul Vadher's challenge was that he said he would match Vadher's promise to use his membership of the European Parliament as a lever to get more Lib Dems elected to Westminster.

He visited his constituency most weeks. His strategy was to work the whole region, but selected six councils and parliamentary target constituencies – one in each East Midlands county – to focus on, with Chesterfield as his top target. 'It wasn't a case of "Right, I'm the MEP, I'm off",' says the East Midlands Lib Dem activist Ed Fordham; 'he really did want to help. He was very conscious that he was the first elected Lib Dem to represent the region and wanted to use that role as a platform for other campaigners across the patch. Most counties had target constituencies and target councils that were supported from the regional Lib Dem office, places like Northampton, Leicester, Derby, Broxtowe, East and West Lindsey, and Chesterfield. By coming in to support these places, he energised – or re-energised – campaigns and campaigners, and over time the work drew significant rewards. Since that time, the Liberal Democrats have had control of all those councils, and most would accept it was down to that early seedcorn at the start of Nick's time as MEP for the East Midlands.'

At parliamentary level, the targeting of Chesterfield paid off. After three elections in which Tony Rogers had narrowed Labour's majority (the original MP had been Tony Benn), Paul Holmes won it in 2001, and held the seat until narrowly defeated in 2010. Despite the fact that Holmes had backed Vadher, and had clearly not seen eye to eye with Clegg, Clegg put a considerable effort into Chesterfield.

The MEP also spent a fair bit of time cultivating links with the region's universities. He had a regular series of meetings with vice-chancellors, which not only kept him connected with the intellectual environment of higher education, but also allowed him to connect politics with the student generation, given that he was only thirty-two when he became an MEP and only seven years removed from his last master's degree.

One other minor development at that time was the decision by Ian Wright to return to his job working for Boots in Nottingham. Political parties tend to be known for their high-profile politicians, but no party could function without a few talented supporters strategically placed in industry and other walks of life. Sometimes they are referred to by the media as donors, other times as advisers or friends – very seldom as Liberal Democrats, Conservatives or Labour people, because their day job is outside the political world. The Lib Dems are no exception, and people such as Wright, Neil Sherlock, Chris Fox and others are crucial to the Clegg story for their help behind the scenes. Wright had worked for Paddy Ashdown, but then went back into the private sector as a public relations executive when Charles Kennedy became the party's leader. Working in Clegg's patch brought him back into a more hands-on involvement with the Lib Dems and helped smooth Clegg's rise to greater prominence.

* * *

Away from work, Clegg was a very gregarious member of the Brussels social set. He was into the close-knit British, Dutch and Spanish expat communities, and people around him at that time say he was very popular and very well liked, and many talk about having 'enjoyed themselves', a euphemism for getting drunk. Evenings involved the customary Clegg cigarettes – he has never been a heavy smoker, only ever smoking in the evenings, but as an evening wore on, a couple of Marlboro Lights would generally emerge and get lit.

Even then – and despite the relatively low profile of most British MEPs – Clegg had perfected his now distinctive mixture of engaging sociability and keeping his private life very private. For much of his time there, he had a flat of his own; once he and Miriam were engaged, she was very much a fixture in it, yet when he threw parties, they were generally in private clubs rather than his flat. Arne Richters said, 'He wasn't the type of MEP who was in Les Aviateurs every night [a bar in Strasbourg near the cathedral where one would find MEPs most nights, often on the dance floor]. He preferred more a dinner and a chat.'

In September 2000, he and Miriam got married in a colourful celebration in Spain. A few nights before, Clegg had had a get-together in Brussels with most of his Euro friends, though it wasn't a typical stag night. Even though the wedding had several hundred guests, relatively few of Clegg's Brussels acquaintances had been invited to Segovia, which was to be the base for the wedding, largely because he has such a wide circle of friends. Among the Brussels brigade were his political adviser Katie Hall, the ELDR's press officer Alison Suttie, the recently ennobled Lord Brittan, and his East Midlands organiser Russell Eagling (accompanied by his partner, Ed Fordham). Chris Huhne and Andrew Duff were the only British MEPs invited, and Duff couldn't make it – Huhne sat with Brittan at the reception. That was not the sum total of his British guests; in fact, his guest list served to emphasise that his political friends made up only a small part of his overall circle of friends, and to this day he keeps up a number of long-standing friendships with people outside politics.

Most of the guests were accommodated in the Parador de Segovia Castilla y León (a parador is a very Spanish concept: a state-owned luxury hotel, often in a castle or monastery), which is just north of Madrid, between the capital and Valladolid. It's an impressive red-brick building, fairly modern, with spectacular views towards a rolling valley and Segovia's perfectly preserved Roman aqueduct. For those who had arrived the day before the wedding, the Clegg family hosted a meal. Some Britons made the mistake of turning up at around 7 p.m., totally misreading the local custom of going for a walk around that time, and sitting down to dinner around 10 p.m. The following day, the guests were bussed out to the small country church in Olmedo for full Roman Catholic mass in mid-afternoon, during which the marriage ceremony took place. The whole of Olmedo turned out to welcome the wedding guests, a tribute to the standing in which Miriam's father José Antonio González Caviedes had been held. Then after the customary photographs, they were bussed back to the parador for the main reception.

Paul Clegg, Nick's elder brother, is one of many people glowing in their recollections of that Spanish summer's day. 'It was a very strong Spanish wedding, and a lot of our family turned up. Their family had been in that region forever, you could feel that – everyone had known the family, you could feel that everyone was there. The service was great, it was hot, it was alien, new, exotic, and I remember I wished it had gone on for longer. It was a really nice occasion, as stereotypical as you would hope it to be.'

It was also a real United Nations wedding. At least five languages were spoken: English, Spanish, Dutch, French and even some pre-revolutionary Russian, thanks to some of Clegg's Russian émigré relations having made it. Clegg made the traditional groom's speech, switching from English to Dutch to Spanish to keep everyone happy. Then when he had finished, Miriam grabbed the microphone and gave her own speech in response, which alternated between Spanish and English. Both speeches went down superbly, and one of the British Lib Dem contingent remarked 'She should stand for election, not him!'

Another guest described the wedding as 'big and fun, vibrant, boisterous – and unbelievably late'. The celebratory meal began around 10 p.m., dancing began sometime after 1 a.m., and at about 5 a.m. – by which time many of the British had conked out and gone to bed – out came one of Miriam's gastronomic specialities: *chocolate con churros*, a Spanish tradition that's almost an alternative to breakfast when you've had a heavy night and are about to go to bed. It's chocolate sauce with deep-fried breadsticks that you dip in and eat – fattening but tasty.

Miriam made it clear from the outset that she would keep her maiden names as is generally the custom in Spain (Durántez is her maternal grandfather's surname), and while she is sometimes referred to as 'Miriam Clegg' in sections of the British media, such nomenclature never comes from her or her husband. Another deal the couple worked out was that if their marriage were to be 'blessed with children', they would have the surname Clegg but be given Spanish first names. By the spring of 2001, Miriam was pregnant, and on 21 January 2002, their first child, a boy, was born. He was named Antonio, in memory of Miriam's father, the one grandparent the boy was not to know. And if he one day grows up to have a love of Chopin's piano music, it could be because Miriam frequently played Chopin's Waltz in A minor during her pregnancy with Antonio, a piece of music Clegg chose as one of his eight desert island discs in 2010.

Clegg has been keen to emphasise that he took a lot more time off work than his wife did after Antonio was born, but he also makes no attempt to hide the fact that it happened to fit with his professional circumstances to do so. 'Miriam was in a very busy time in her career, so she went back to work pretty quickly after Antonio was born,' he says. 'I'm full of admiration that she was able to do that. At that stage I'd pretty much decided I wasn't going to carry on in the European Parliament, so I was my own boss, and therefore I had this lovely luxury of being able to spend time at home, pretty much for that whole year. Obviously I did my work, but I was able to spend a huge amount of time with Antonio in his first year, because I wasn't running to be re-elected and Miriam was working very hard for Chris Patten at the time. It was something I wanted to do, and to be able to spend that much time with your first child was one of the most lovely things – I wouldn't trade that in for the world.'

The thing that is easy to forget about Clegg's time as an MEP was that he had very little knowledge of Britain politically. He had grown up in an international household, gone to a very international-minded school, and had then spent most of the intervening decade outside his homeland. Simon Hughes says, 'I don't think he'd ever really been exposed to the political agenda in Britain until he came back [in 2004]. He'd not been political at home, he'd not been political over the road [at Westminster School], he'd not been political in Cambridge in a partisan way, he'd gone to the States, he'd become more wedded to liberalism as a counter to what was going on in the States, his internationalism was strengthened in Brussels, and he did all the trade stuff which is pro-free trade.'

Trade was indeed Clegg's big thing, and he was clearly very good at it. Perhaps because he was so at home with the trade brief, he gave the impression to many Britons of being very much on the right wing of the Lib Dems, if not in that overlap of the Venn diagram that could have seen him in the Conservative Party. There was even a British Lib Dem MEP who said at the time 'I sometimes wonder whether Nick's not a Conservative sleeper'. Yet most people who knew Clegg then – and now – say the argument that he's a displaced Tory just doesn't hold water.

For a start there is the fact that he could have joined the Conservatives from the outset; indeed, with Leon Brittan's help it would almost have been easier to do so than to join the Lib Dems, where he had no real contacts. That is a powerful argument in itself. Chris Huhne, Clegg's rival in the 2007 Lib Dem leadership election, believes there were two obstacles between Clegg and the Conservatives. 'You have to ask what makes people tick politically,' Huhne says, 'and there's no doubt there are two things that make

Nick tick. One is that he is a passionate believer in the whole civil-liberties, human-rights agenda, and that goes back deep into his personal life and the experience of his family – he feels that very strongly, and it is not something you would traditionally associate with a Conservative. Nick is, in very classical terms, a liberal on the civil-liberties agenda. The other thing is that he is a passionate pro-European. He believes very strongly, as I do, that Europe is a positive force for good, that it's really crucial to develop arrangements that can stop what happened in Europe in the two world wars ever happening again. Europe is a patchwork quilt of different ethnicities and language groups – which the English tend to forget, even though it's true of the United Kingdom – and you can't solve all your problems through borders as you have so many speakers of the language of one country living in another country; so you need a framework that provides an overarching guarantee of fundamental civil liberties and freedoms, and that's essentially what we have with the European Union. For someone like Nick or me, it would be very uncomfortable to be in a modern Conservative Party where the *lingua franca* is hostility and scepticism about Europe.'

Some talk about 'his instinctiveness on equality and gay rights' as being a long way from the Tory agenda, certainly the Conservative Party of the early 2000s. And the left-of-centre (on most issues) MEP Chris Davies says, 'There is certainly no evidence in the way he voted or the way he spoke in the Parliament that he was right wing.' Davies adds, 'Some of my colleagues would say Nick's a Tory, but that's complete snobbish nonsense. I've never thought Nick was instinctively a Tory in any sense. I think of him more as a continental liberal than perhaps a mainstream British liberal. He doesn't carry the baggage with him that some of us do. I campaigned against all sorts of privatisations carried out by Margaret Thatcher – Nick didn't go through the baggage-carrying experience of campaigning against these things.'

The Lib Dem activist and environmental thinker David Boyle takes a slightly different slant. 'I regarded him as a liberal radical,' Boyle says, 'emphatically not part of the Social Democratic wing of the party, but not right wing. Nick reached initially for market solutions for want of any other alternative, and simply because he was asking the right questions: how could you get more capacity into the public system, how could you make the public sector more human and less bureaucratic? That doesn't mean he was committed to market solutions – it was more a measure of how much he was searching for new ways forward, and the search continues.'

Friends of Clegg's say there was another reason for him being a Liberal Democrat: he just didn't like the Conservatives. This was not a personal judgement, in the sense of disliking what he saw as a typical Conservative personality (if such a thing exists), but more a leaning towards the quirkiness of the Liberal Democrats in preference to the more mainstream parties. It was almost a logical conclusion to his mother's encouragement to look at problems from various different angles, a philosophy that tends to rule out tribalist approaches. To that extent, the fact that the Lib Dems were a slightly offbeat minor party would have been an attraction rather than a turn-off.

The MEP who wondered if Clegg was 'a Conservative sleeper' is Andrew Duff. His suspicion came not from a position on the left of the party, but because Clegg wasn't federalist enough. 'I certainly don't think he's a fifth columnist,' Duff explains, 'but I do think that if the Conservative Party had been how it used to be under Edward Heath, Nick would be a Tory, albeit a natural liberal, pro-European Tory like Chris Patten and Ken Clarke. I have always had a great regard for these people, they're the sort of British pro-European who want the union to prosper and would like full British engagement with the EU, but they will the ends without willing the means. So they are decidedly not federalists, and they do not subscribe to the constitutional evolution of the EU. They're frankly a bit bored by institutions, procedures, rules and treaties. Nick, when he was an MEP, found it hard to disguise his contempt for people like me who were engaged with these dossiers in the Parliament.'

Leaving aside whether one might perhaps forgive someone for not getting excited about dossiers to do with institutions, procedures, rules and treaties, Duff's argument loses traction on two fronts. Firstly, parties change as times change, and therefore people who would belong in a party in one era don't necessary belong in it in the next. If the Labour Party had remained the party of Harold Wilson and James Callaghan, an awful lot of today's prominent Lib Dems – from the former Labour Cabinet minister Shirley Williams to the 'SDP intellectual' Chris Huhne – might still be Labour members. Secondly, Duff may have a logical argument on Britain playing a more engaged role in Europe, but trying to sell that in the British political climate is akin to trying to sell Indian flags in Pakistan. Vince Cable describes Duff as 'way out, a bit of a Euro-fanatic – a very nice guy, but in a different league', while Duff's colleague Chris Davies goes further. 'Andrew is the extreme federalist, he doesn't take account of British political realities. Nick is acutely conscious of British political realities: what you can sell and what you can't, what, to use a classic Nick word, is "bonkers" and what is not. What is bonkers is what you can't sell in the pub, and there are things Andrew thinks you could sell in a pub when there's a cat in hell's chance – you wouldn't come out alive!'

Someone who supports Duff's notion that Clegg would have been a Conservative in a different era is Ed Vaizey, the Conservative minister who struck up a good relationship with Clegg when the two went with three other MPs to the Arctic Circle in 2007 (see page 176). Vaizey feels Clegg is one of a type of people who is 'essentially Tory but divided by one issue, in his case Europe'. Vaizey admitted to trying to tempt Clegg over to the Conservatives in their five days in -30°C temperatures, but conceded defeat. 'He wasn't having any of it,' says Vaizey. 'We have different views on different issues, but I do think Nick is a very, very impressive politician. I just think he's in the wrong party. He thinks he's in the right party, so unfortunately we have to leave it at that.'

All this raises several questions, most notably: what is a liberal? Does it change meaning through the years? Does it mean different things in different countries? (In America, 'liberal' is used synonymously with supporters of the Democratic party, frequently as an insult.) Are the British Liberal Democrats traditional liberals, modern liberals, or any other brand of liberals? And if Clegg is a 'continental liberal' as Chris Davies suggests, what is that? And is it understood in Britain?

The liberal tradition in Britain has been through several incarnations, but it had to rethink itself most in the post-war years. Having been totally eclipsed by Labour as the left-of-centre party in an essentially two-party system, the Liberal Party needed to invent a role for a third party – and fill it – or die (a brief history of the Liberals in British politics is given in Chapter 9 – see page 152). The fact that the Liberal Party survived the barren years of the 1940s and 1950s is largely down to a patrician figure called Jo Grimond.

Grimond, a Scottish lawyer who went to Eton and Oxford, was Liberal leader from 1956 to 1967, and the man who saved the Liberals from extinction. At the 1955 general election, there were only fifteen constituencies (out of 630) in which Labour and Conservative did not occupy the top two positions, and only eight the two main parties didn't win (six Liberal, two Sinn Fein); the Liberals contested barely 100 seats, such was the strength of the two-party system. The niche Grimond created for the Liberals was as the party that rejected the class-based allegiance of the two major parties. With the beneficiaries of the 1944 Butler Education Act becoming young adults, Grimond created a party that people could support and join without feeling they were letting down their working-class (Labour) or privileged (Conservative) roots.

Liberal historians say Grimond reasserted the traditional liberal insistence that ideas and principles were more important than interests. In terms of policies, he was a convinced opponent of the idea that socially progressive policies could only happen through a strong role for the state (what has become known as 'statism'), believing that relying on the state primarily created self-serving bureaucracies and a generation of handout-dependent citizens. Grimond's defenders on the left of today's Liberal Democrats emphasise that he was more anti-bureaucracy and anti-centralisation than explicitly anti-state, and that the difference was important for his ability to attract so many liberal radicals into the Liberal Party. This may be a fair distinction, but Grimond was sufficiently anti-state that he joined a liberal faction called the Unservile State Group. Yet he also believed that you could have central planning without having to sign up to the socialist idea that the state should own the means of production.

This is essentially what most of the continental liberal parties stand for – best summed up as a 'free trade, low state intervention' philosophy. It is also essentially what the Liberals in Britain stood for until the 1980s, and perhaps it was no coincidence that they did better when fighting the Conservatives than fighting Labour – suggesting that disaffected Conservative voters felt better exercising a protest vote for the Liberals than disaffected Labour voters did. But once the breakaway Labour group founded the Social Democrats in 1981, the centre ground shifted in emphasis, and when the Liberal Democrats were formed out of a merger between the Liberals and Social Democrats in the late 1980s, more Lib Dem members saw themselves as being closer to Labour than the Tories. This culminated in the 2005 Lib Dem general election manifesto, which had twenty-five pledges to increase public spending and was described by one senior Lib Dem as 'us trying to out-left the Labour Party'.

So, in many ways, Nick Clegg the MEP represented an old-fashioned British liberal in the Grimond mould: deeply concerned about social injustices, passionately pro-European, but highly sceptical about any greater role for the state than absolutely necessary. The journalist John Palmer recalls, 'When he first entered the Parliament, I became aware that he was an economic liberal as well as a political liberal. His work with Leon in and around the single market and competition policy probably had quite a strong influence on him. He was quite markedly to the right of some of his colleagues. There were some in the British Lib Dem group in the European Parliament who were more clearly socially centre-left.' Although that view was shared by a number of people, a note of caution is necessary. Palmer is known in some circles as having pronounced left-wing views, and Chris Huhne says, 'I'm not sure John, coming out of the Labour Party, is totally reliable when it comes to calibrating the nuances.'

Richard Allan, who Clegg succeeded as MP for Sheffield Hallam in 2005, has a more colourful way of explaining why Clegg is, in his words, 'a proper liberal'. Allan says, 'My crude characterisation is this: Labour people essentially believe people are bad, so you need a strong regulated society to force them to be good; Conservatives believe people are bad but say "Hey, let's just get over it"; Liberals believe people are essentially good, and if you enable them, they'll be even better, but it doesn't mean you have to have a whole bunch of rules and regulations. Nick is a liberal in that camp, because of his background. He's an old patrician liberal, for whom education and internationalism are core beliefs. His philosophy has come from various places, like the adversity in his family history, and a lot from having done very well. He is a proper liberal, and that was difficult to grasp early on, because the party between the mid-90s and through into the early 2000s had acquired a lot of people who were frustrated left-wing folks, and the party activist base was already oriented that way. He's a liberal to his core, he's not a conservative, and what he has done is to re-establish the Liberal Democrats as a liberal party.'

That may be true, but with a generation of Lib Dem members having learned to think of themselves as competition to Labour for the progressive voters – with the Conservatives the traditional opposition – Clegg's economic liberalism has been hard for some in the Liberal Democrats to swallow. It was a dilemma reflected in the publication of *The Orange Book* in 2004 (see page 130).

As it happened, the Duff–Vaizey argument that Clegg would have been at home in a 1970s-style pro-Europe Conservative Party remained largely academic, as the British Tories showed no inclination to grant Europe any favours. In 2000, the Conservative MEP Bill Newton-Dunn defected to the Lib Dems, bemoaning the Conservatives' negative attitude towards Europe. He was the second Conservative MEP to do so in less than two years, following a similar move by James Moorhouse in 1998 over William Hague's attitude to the euro. Newton-Dunn was one of the Conservative MEPs representing the East Midlands, which meant that the Lib Dems had gone from no MEPs there to two in barely a year.

That, however, created a potential problem with a view to the 2004 European elections. As sitting MEPs, Clegg and Newton-Dunn could have been first and second on the Lib Dems' regional list in the East Midlands (the male-female 'zip' rule was altered after 1999), but realistically, only one of them was likely to get in. As the one elected under the Lib Dem label, Clegg was always likely to be top of the list, which would have meant no chance of Newton-Dunn getting re-elected for the Lib Dems. It was a problem Clegg resolved by announcing that he was not going to stand for a second term in the European Parliament. He had decided his future lay at Westminster.

Chapter 8

'RETURNING WITH THE MARK OF SATAN ON HIM'

NEVER IN the history of mainstream British politics had an MEP been tipped as the next leader of a party. Getting oneself elected to the European Parliament has, for many, been a stepping stone to becoming an MP, as well as a career in its own right for politicians never likely to make it to Westminster (people such as Andrew Duff, whose stammer would be mercilessly exploited by the media, even in a post-*King's Speech* era). But the British gave too little value to the European Parliament for anyone to use Brussels/ Strasbourg as a springboard to prominence in their own party. That is until Nick Clegg and Chris Huhne came along.

Even the Liberal Democrats, the most open to the EU of the three main British parties, had difficulty seeing their next leader as being in Brussels, as this piece of phrasing from Mark Oaten, the former chair of the Lib Dem parliamentary party, shows: 'There were two figures that everyone kept talking about as being really, really bright who were not known around Westminster. They were Nick Clegg and Chris Huhne, but they were both stuck in Brussels.' Although one could defend that approach for its pragmatism, there is a bit of British arrogance inherent in it. There is the suggestion that one can't achieve much in Brussels, when the more influential and bright MEPs clearly can. There's even a school of thought that says the calibre of MEPs is better than the calibre of national politicians (in all countries, not just Britain), because the immersion in policy is greater than is typical in national parliaments, and MEPs have to deal with bigger issues, so they have to get a handle on what's happening at the macro level. Indeed some member states admit MEPs to national select committees as non-voting members, because they know more about the issues than national parliamentarians. Yet even if this argument holds water, it is well-nigh impossible to imagine a British MEP having a senior position in his or her party, and certainly not as the party's leader.

Clegg was well aware of this, as Oaten testifies. 'It certainly was very clear that he was interested in what was happening in Westminster – he was engaged with people in London, he wasn't isolated, he hadn't gone native in Brussels. He's too charming, too nice, too mature, too sophisticated to show crude outward ambition, but it was clear that he wanted to be networked into the party in Westminster, and he certainly shared the frustrations about how to make the party move. He felt we should have been doing better than we were, given that at the time we had Hague as Conservative leader and the unpopularity of the Labour government.'

Paddy Ashdown announced his resignation as leader of the Lib Dems in January 1999, but agreed to stay on until the summer. Having taken the decision to go, it seemed sensible to announce it so it didn't leak out, and also to avoid any suggestion that it was prompted by the Lib Dems' showing in the European elections in June. For a man who took such pride in being the founder of the Lib Dems, Ashdown appears to have done remarkably little grooming of a successor. Once it became clear that Charles Kennedy was the front-runner, he did try to give the party a choice by gently pushing Nick Harvey, the MP for North Devon, who was a very entertaining public speaker but had a much lower profile than Kennedy. There were, in fact, around nine Lib Dem MPs who expressed some interest in standing for the leadership, but it eventually came down to Kennedy or Simon Hughes, and Kennedy emerged the clear winner.

The assumption was that Kennedy would fight at least two general elections, but inevitably the pundits began looking for the emerging next generation. There were obviously a lot of new MPs in the 1997 intake as the Lib Dems' number had gone up from eighteen to forty-six, but the two names from the 1999 intake of MEPs kept on cropping up. 'There was absolutely no doubt that we were starting to think about these two characters,' says Oaten, who became chairman of the parliamentary party under Kennedy's leadership. 'One of my jobs was to go out to Brussels and talk to the MEPs to keep them on board, keep them happy, so I spoke to both Chris and Nick and had fairly candid conversations with both of them. I said, "Look, I think you should be coming to Westminster." It didn't come as a surprise to them, it was clearly something they had both been thinking about, it was no magical revelation. I remember being amused that I'd had two separate conversations with them where they both gave outline thought processes that were heading in exactly the same direction. It would be wrong to say they were wasted in Brussels, but the potential for them to do much more was enormous. The difficulty was: how do you make it happen? I tried to make myself as supportive for them as I could, but still said, "Get yourselves over here as soon as you can."'

Both Clegg and Huhne had meetings at this time with Chris Rennard, the Lib Dems' campaigning linchpin in London. They discussed switching from Brussels to Westminster, which meant that Rennard's antennae were henceforth alert for any winnable Lib Dem seats that might become available.

Ashdown tells the story of a conversation he had with Kennedy shortly after the latter had taken over as party leader. He says he told Kennedy that the next leader of the Liberal Democrats was someone who wasn't yet elected to Westminster. Kennedy verifies that part of the story. Ashdown maintains he had Clegg in mind, whereas Kennedy recalls Ashdown saying, 'Whenever the next change of leadership comes, I'd risk a prediction that the next leader is not yet a member of the parliamentary party – I think it'll very easily be Chris Huhne or Nick Clegg.' The discrepancy is both minor and immaterial. It's quite possible Ashdown meant only Clegg, and Kennedy heard Clegg *and* Huhne (Kennedy aptly describes both Clegg and Huhne as 'self-firing'), but the anecdote serves to emphasise that, at the turn of the century, the Lib Dems were clearly wondering whether their next leader was serving an apprenticeship in Brussels and Strasbourg.

While both MEPs were being touted in the party, Ashdown was clearly championing Clegg. Shortly after he stood down as leader, Ashdown and his wife Jane held a dinner party at their home in Kennington, south London. They invited six bright young things: the MPs Richard Allan, Ed Davey, Michael Moore, Mark Oaten and Lembit Öpik, and one MEP, Nick Clegg. His main message was to tell them 'The future of the party is in your hands'. At one stage the discussion got onto the subject of the pressures on MPs of life in prominent public positions, yet a lot of the guests were treading carefully as it was only eight years since Ashdown had admitted to having an affair with his secretary. Although he had been given the nickname 'Paddy Pantsdown' by a few sections of the media, the speed and cleanness of the admission allowed him to survive with his reputation undamaged; indeed, it's possible to make the case that Ashdown's affair marked a watershed, in that it set the trend for clean, low-key, no-fuss admissions of extra-marital affairs that subsequent politicians have been able to follow – and emerge largely unscathed from. But it was still a slightly touchy subject that night. After a while, the Ashdowns recognised this, so they put it out in the open. They said it had been a ghastly business that had led to them having to access their home via the back fence for a few days because the press were camped out at the front, but that it served to emphasise what a goldfish bowl high-level representation is. Once the subject was out in the open, the participants relaxed, and they speak warmly of both the dinner and the Ashdowns' hospitality.

That group, augmented by David Laws and Steve Webb, began referring to themselves as 'the young guns'. Rennard says, 'They all wanted to see what they could do to help the party advance, and how they could work together. We had one dinner at my London house over a Chinese takeaway in which we explored fund-raising possibilities. What was interesting was that they all recognised that they might be rivals for the leadership at some point in the future.'

One person who pours a fair bit of cold water on the idea that Huhne was thought of as a future leader is Huhne himself, and it's interesting in retrospect that the 'young guns' group included

Clegg but not Huhne. 'I think that might be a bit of ex-post-facto rationalisation,' Huhne says today. 'Nick clearly was thought of as a leader of the future; the rumour mill had it that Paddy had been pushing him, but I had never been in that position. I wasn't aware that anyone thought I was the great white hope of the party. The more normal view of me would have been, not that I'd be a potential leadership figure, but that I was a specialist economist, helpful on technical matters on the euro and other monetary affairs. And I'm twelve or thirteen years older than Nick so was too old to be a young hopeful.' The laid-back, affable Huhne makes a reasonably convincing case, but it does need to be taken with a pinch of salt, as he was only forty-six in 2000 and has no shortage of self-confidence. As Richard Allan puts it, 'It was obvious that their [Clegg and Huhne's] long-term aim was to be significant in the party, and you can't do that in Europe – in British politics, Europe doesn't count for enough.'

Not that everyone wanted Clegg back in Britain. The MEP Graham Watson says he felt Clegg had worked out how to be effective as a European parliamentarian, and having done a very impressive apprenticeship over his first five years, he was throwing in the towel just at the point where he was likely to be at his most influential. And another MEP, Clegg's friend Chris Davies, with a glint in his eye that mocks his own reading of the situation, says, 'I spent some time trying to persuade Nick not to go to Westminster. If you're going to be out of power forever, why trade in the chance of influence? I'd had my two years as an MP, we all try to get to Westminster, I'd spent thirteen years or more trying to get into Parliament, and I'd had two years on the back benches – you make all your speeches, but what is there to show for it? Whereas here [in Brussels], you know you have influence, you know the relationships are different, the separation of powers means there aren't the same barriers, you can go and talk to a Commissioner, you can talk to Commission officials, they listen to you, they take on board what you say and they make changes without feeling that to do so is to give in to the hordes of barbarians. You do deals all the time, deals across parties. It's more grown-up. I told Nick, "You don't want to go to the House of Commons."'

But he did, and the process started as early as the summer of 2001, just after the British general election of that year. Some believe it was always on his agenda, and the only reason he stood for the European Parliament was that he had missed the general election of 1997 (that argument is a bit thin, as standing for Europe meant missing the 2001 election too, not that there were that many winnable seats for a Lib Dem in that election). Others say he realised very quickly that the European Parliament just doesn't cut any ice in Britain. Clegg himself says of his work as an MEP, 'It was not the type of politics that interests me. You have no meaningful relationship with your constituents. It's very bloodless.' For a man who is at his best relating one to one with people and who had done a lot of acting, the lack of a meaningful relationship with constituents was a big deal, and regardless of any long-term motivation he had when he stood for the European Parliament (and he insists there was no long-term career plan), it seems entirely logical that Brussels should lose its attraction after one five-year term.

Watson has another theory: that Clegg needed to stand for his national Parliament to get a sense of being British. 'If you think about the time he had spent outside Britain,' Watson says, 'I got a sense that it was very important to him to connect with his own country.' Perhaps the most likely explanation is that he had a young family, so needed a place where his child (later children) could grow up, where his wife could further her career, and where he didn't have masses of commuting – London fitted the bill better than the itinerant Brussels–Strasbourg–East Midlands package, even if he were to end up with a seat outside London. Chris Rennard says Clegg talked a lot at that time about the lifestyle factors that played a role in his choice of career path, so no-one should be too surprised that he was aiming for Westminster. Whatever the motivation, by the start of 2002 it was clear he was looking to make the switch to his national Parliament.

John Palmer says he perceived Clegg's gradual preparation for immersing himself in British politics. 'As time passed and he got closer to moving back to national politics, I got the impression he was refining his political stance within the Liberal family in two ways. One was that he became less enthusiastic about the free market and welfarism; the other was that it became clear he was taking a more reserved position on Britain's continuing integration into the EU. I went to some dinner parties where he and Miriam were present, and I began to form the impression Nick was becoming a British pragmatist on European issues. You might say "Big deal", but quite a lot of his colleagues had remained committed to a longer-term strategic process of integration. He knew that in returning to British politics from European politics, he came with the mark of Satan on him.'

Yet if he was to make the transition to British politics, he needed a constituency to fight, and one that a Lib Dem could win. There were a few winnable ones, but precious few safe ones. Lord Brittan, who had been MP for Richmond in North Yorkshire (now William Hague's seat), advised Clegg to get a seat a reasonable distance from London, as such seats give members 'a different view of things, allowing them to see that people are passionate about matters that those at Westminster don't know a thing about and aren't interested in'.

One seat that many in the party pushed him towards was Oldham East & Saddleworth, the Pennines constituency Chris Davies had won in a by-election in 1995 but lost at the 1997 general election, albeit under somewhat revised boundaries. The Saddleworth end is moorland country, while Oldham is greyer and more urban. Davies encouraged Clegg to stand there, as the Lib Dems believed the sitting MP, Phil Woolas, was eminently attackable (by 2002, the Lib Dems had almost all the councillors in the constituency). But the weather gods obviously didn't want Clegg as the Oldham & Saddleworth MP. On the day he visited Oldham, there was torrential rain, and even the prettier parts of the constituency – in particular the moorland that should have appealed to Clegg's fondness for walking in unspoilt countryside – looked grim. Clegg couldn't see how he could sell it to Miriam, and wasn't sure he even wanted to. Davies admits it was 'vile', and he wasn't even there. He had been detained in Brussels, so instead of having Davies's sense of humour to guide him, Clegg was driven around the constituency by Davies's wife, whom Clegg didn't know. 'I think he might well have been the candidate for Oldham East & Saddleworth if I'd been able to take him around and if the sun had been shining,' Davies says today. 'He'd certainly have given it a second look.'

Other seats that came into consideration were two in the West Country, traditionally fertile ground for the Lib Dems. He went with Graham Watson to look at Wells in Somerset, as that was mathematically a winnable seat for the Lib Dems, but they had done less well there in 2001 than in 1997 and there were issues of local personnel which meant it wasn't one of the party's top targets. And there were discussions about Cheltenham, where the sitting Lib Dem MP, Nigel Jones, was still coming to terms with the trauma of having had one of his constituency surgeries in 2000 invaded by a sword-wielding intruder; Jones survived, but only because a close friend of his, a local councillor and member of his staff, was killed fighting off the assailant, an act that allowed Jones to escape. Clegg never visited Cheltenham, as it was a while before it became clear that there would be a vacancy, but it was certainly on his list of possibles.

At this time, Clegg had regular meetings with Chris Rennard (by now Lord Rennard). Rennard had been actively trying to persuade Richard Allan, the bright young MP for Sheffield Hallam, to stand for a third term as Allan was having doubts about his long-term future. The moment Rennard realised he couldn't persuade Allan to stay on, he suggested to Clegg that Allan's seat would be a good one for him to target. He also introduced the two men to each other, as he was sure they would get on. They are good friends to this day, and Allan played a prominent role in Clegg's campaign for the Lib Dem leadership in 2007.

In 2002, the two men found themselves at an East Midlands conference. 'A couple of people came up to Nick and me', Allan explains, 'and said, "We've joined the Lib Dems – we used to be

Labour, but Labour's gone all right wing, and now we're joining the true left-wing alternative." Nick replied, "Look, if that's what you think the party is, you're wrong, and maybe you ought to be joining the Socialist Workers Party if that's what you want. You can join this party, but you need to understand that we're not the left-wing social-ist alternative to Labour, we're a liberal and democratic party." I was quite taken aback that someone could be so frank. The tradition of the party at the time tended to be "We'll be whatever you want us to be; if you want to come from Labour or the Greens, we'll take you". But Nick said "No, this is where we are". I was seriously impressed.'

On its own, that little incident doesn't mean a great deal, but in terms of helping cement the Clegg–Allan friendship, it was important. And having established his links with the MP for Sheffield Hallam, Clegg had a foot in the door of his future political base camp.

That little incident also shows how Clegg was keen to play a part in the ideological development of the Liberal Democrats. He may have been adjusting to the pragmatism of British politics after nearly a decade in the European theatre, but he had ideas about what liberalism should mean in a modern society.

In 2000, the Lib Dem activist David Boyle had written a pamphlet for one of the party fringe's magazines, *Liberator*, entitled 'After Community Politics', about what a political party might look like in the future. 'It was motivated by a bout of canvassing in a housing estate', Boyle said, 'where everybody was in and not one person was voting at all. It was clear to me this was not apathy – they had actively decided not to vote for positive reasons, for moral reasons, so the days when there was mass membership of politi-cal parties was over.' On reading the pamphlet, Clegg sought out Boyle and said he really liked it. He was still smarting from the low turnout at the previous year's European elections, and was keen to explore ways of getting people more interested in politics.

There are constantly essays and pamphlets written about politi-cal philosophy in all parties, but in 2004, one freelance publication sent the Liberal Democrats into some public convulsions. The publication concerned created a lot of hot air, but in retrospect was a natural stepping stone in the party's semi-reinvention following the Ashdown era. In fact, with the benefit of 20:20 hindsight, these convulsions helped to pave the way for the Conservative–Lib Dem coalition of 2010.

The convulsions were caused by *The Orange Book*, a collection of essays by rising Lib Dem figures, edited and coordinated by two who saw themselves as modernisers of the party. One was an MP, David Laws, the man who had taken over Paddy Ashdown's seat in Yeovil; the other was Paul Marshall, an investor and philanthropist who stood for Parliament in 1987 and now chairs the liberal think-tank Centre Forum. The other leading figure behind the book was Vince Cable, the Lib Dems' treasury spokesman (or Shadow Chancellor, to give him the grand title the party enjoyed using), as Laws was Cable's deputy.

'A few of us felt a sense of frustration about party policy,' says Laws. 'We felt that, quite often, policy had got disconnected from the liberal roots of the party, and that we suffered too much from a lazy "oppositionitis" where we would oppose anything the government of the day was doing. It led to a frustration that we were being defined, not by our own values and liberal policies, but by being opposed to whatever was being done by the government. We also had a tendency to go for rather statist solutions to many of the problems that society faced.'

The result was a book that brought together the young Lib Dems – MPs elected in 1997 and 2001, plus Clegg and Chris Huhne from the 1999 MEP intake – in presenting a set of essays covering all the main policy areas. They were separate essays written by different people, but in a way that produced a common narrative that set out some views about where Lib Dem policy could be developed and how it could be reconnected with liberal roots, particularly in relation to the economic liberal history of the party. Clegg wrote on how Europe should be shaped in the future, Steve Webb wrote a chapter on the family and the impact of family breakdown on society, Huhne's chapter was on global governance, while Cable wrote about building a liberal economy.

In principle it all sounds very positive and admirable, and the party leader, Charles Kennedy, even wrote a foreword to it. But there were two problems. One was that the call for a revival of economic liberalism led to the media tagging it a 'lurch to the right' for the Lib Dems, which in turn prompted many Lib Dems who felt they were on the left of British politics but just not in the Labour camp to wonder whether they were in the wrong party. The second was that at least one author claims not to have seen the chapter Laws himself wrote about reforming the National Health Service until it was published, and that was the chapter that was quoted most often by those saying *The Orange Book* was a right-wing publication.

There's an irony here. The authors were worried *The Orange Book* might sink without trace as just a worthy piece of liberal philosophising, so they tried to pick out something that would interest the press. There were two possibilities: one was Cable's chapter, which had some pretty provocative things, such as privatising Royal Mail; the other was Laws's views on health service reform and social insurance. They plumped for Laws's NHS chapter. The tactic worked, as the press picked it up, but it had a dramatic effect on the party. 'The members were absolutely scandalised,' says Cable, 'it was almost a star chamber. David Laws was hung out to dry. It was a seminal moment.'

Huhne, who like Webb sees himself more on the left of the Lib Dems, was the leading contributor who felt compromised by *The Orange Book*. '*The Orange Book* was meant to be a platform for the parliamentary talent in the Liberal Democrats,' Huhne says, 'that was the way it was sold. I agreed to contribute to it on the strict understanding with David Laws that we would all see each other's contributions before they were printed. And they were all circulated, except for David's contribution on the NHS, which I didn't see. He went back on that agreement – he said it was a mistake and I accept that, but it was *the* chapter that was spun as being the market-oriented Lib Dem manifesto. If there was an agenda there for driving that more market-oriented approach, then that wasn't something I was happy with.'

Laws says he doesn't recall failing to show Huhne his chapter, but believes Huhne is sufficiently assiduous that he would have read a chapter if it had been sent to him. That, though, is a small detail. What is more important was the incendiary nature of *The Orange Book*, as it threatened to undermine the ability of left-leaning voters to support the Lib Dems. A couple of authors subsequently distanced themselves from the project, a launch at the party conference was cancelled to try and dampen down the ire, and Laws himself says he was almost lynched by Lib Dem members in the immediate aftermath of its publication. Yet Laws says the whole idea was to make the party more liberal and less conservative (with a small c), both of which should have been beneficial to the party's electoral prospects.

'It was perceived as right-wing,' he says, 'but that was really a misunderstanding of what *The Orange Book* was seeking to achieve. We wanted to breathe life into all aspects of the liberalism of the party. The party had certainly become associated with its social-liberal heritage in terms of social justice, which is very important, but we felt it had lost track of the economic-liberal heritage. We had lost our way, even at times on the social-liberal agenda – for example, on personal liberal issues we were becoming somewhat illiberal, there was a lot of "nanny state" liberalism creeping in, telling people they couldn't buy goldfish at funfairs, and such like, which was out of kilter with the idea of people living their lives as they wanted. But we also wanted to show that economic liberalism is not only important for wealth creation but for creating responsive public services that are good for everybody in society. We challenged whether the social-liberal agenda that the party had been pursuing was likely to lead to social justice being promoted; indeed, some of us said that many of the supposedly social justice policies the party was promoting probably wouldn't do much to advance social mobility.'

Cable tells a similar story. '*The Orange Book* had quite a spread of opinion on topical issues, but in general we were the market end of the party, as we brought together the ambitious people who wanted the party to be credible as opposed to just feeling good about what we stood for. It was a return to Grimond (see page 117). I read Grimond's stuff at the time and I hadn't realised how radical he was. He was arguing for education vouchers, and other ideas which even today would be considered quite fundamentalist and right wing in Lib Dem circles.'

About his chapter on the NHS, Laws says, 'That was the chapter that most challenged people's assumptions, so was most newsworthy and was most distorted. People wilfully went out of their way to portray it as an attempt to bring private insurance into running the NHS, and it wasn't that at all. If people had actually read it, it would be clear this was still a publicly funded NHS, where the money was raised on the basis of progressive taxation. The vision of my health chapter was that, with healthcare free at the point of need, with money raised through progressive taxation, with everybody being able to access healthcare on the basis of need rather than ability to pay – all of which are fundamental tenets of the NHS – there would be more freedom of choice about the way health services are delivered. And like in some continental countries, people would be able to join different providers of NHS services who would then make different offers on diagnostic tests, treatment times etc. My experience of the NHS was that it was a monopoly service with all the flaws that monopoly services have, like failing customers on unacceptable waiting times and standard of service. Under the NHS there's nothing you can do about that.'

Listening to Laws today gives some explanation about how and why the Lib Dems got themselves into such a mess over the Conservatives' plans to reform the NHS in 2010–11. As the reforms were not in the coalition agreement, the Lib Dems could easily have opposed them, but looking at what Laws was trying to promote through *The Orange Book*, it is at least partly clear why Clegg believed it was inherently liberal to support the abolition of primary care trusts and put commissioning of services into the hands of family doctors. One might equally argue that the barrage of criticism that *The Orange Book* ran into, and the resulting fears that it could seriously damage the party, should perhaps have been a warning about what the Lib Dems in government could expect if they went along too keenly with reforms of the NHS which were too easy to equate with privatisation.

In some ways, *The Orange Book* was a product of the Blair years, when the centre ground of British politics became very crowded. If the Lib Dems were to be different to a very free-market social-democratic Labour Party, they had to show it. In some areas, that meant promising to outspend Labour. In others, it meant challenging the role of the state.

It would be wrong to say *The Orange Book* approach appealed only to those on the right of the Lib Dems. Norman Lamb, an ambitious but softly spoken and less shrill member of the 2001 Lib Dem parliamentary intake, describes himself as 'centre-left' but found himself attracted to some of the *Orange Book* ideas. 'I have very little faith in the central state for directing and effecting change,' he says. 'As a result, I often feel I share similar objectives to many people in the Labour Party but have a very different vision of how you get there. I believe in having more faith in people, empowering communities, having much more decentralised power, and yes, a belief in the power of the market on occasions – I don't have an ideological view that the state should run services, preferring instead to empower the citizen as much as possible. I believe firmly in public services, but I don't mind if some services are provided by the voluntary sector or the private sector, as there's an awful lot of evidence to suggest that if you have a bit of competition between service providers you might drive up standards. I'm very opposed to monopolies of power, whether they're public or private.'

Another reason for the screams that *The Orange Book* was right wing came from some of the headline measures it advocated. These included the privatisation of Royal Mail (though not the Post Office), and an end to the Lib Dems' policy of opposing tuition fees in university education, a policy that was to ignite before and after the 2010 general election. On this issue, Laws says, 'In 2004 we still had this policy of scrapping tuition fees when it's quite clear that the problem in our education system is not with able people who don't go to university because they're afraid of debt; it's because people with poor backgrounds don't get good qualifications at sixteen and eighteen so can't get to university whether there's a debt problem or not. All our education policy priorities were being defined by us wanting to oppose tuition fees, rather than by us looking at the education system as a whole and asking where we should be spending scarce resources if we really want to make Britain a fairer place to live in, and if we want to make sure that people from any background can get ahead in life.'

The reaction to *The Orange Book* was certainly excessive. It has to count as entirely reasonable for someone who calls himself a liberal with a good understanding of economics to ask whether there are better ways of guaranteeing quality public services without such recourse to state intervention, which is always likely to lead to higher taxation. But maybe it was a little naive of Laws to expect his party's members to react with cool academic detachment to the idea that aspects of the National Health Service might prosper in private hands. After all, it was less than twenty years since the Thatcher doctrine of 'private good, public bad' had raised the hackles of the progressives in British society, so any attempt at bringing in private help to health – and indeed education – was always going to be a red rag to a bull in a party featuring many of Thatcher's opponents.

In some ways *The Orange Book* was overhyped, and it made relatively little difference to the Lib Dems' manifesto for the 2005 general election. By then, the Lib Dems' trump card was their opposition to the Iraq War, along with opposition to university tuition fees. Detractors of the 2005 manifesto feel Iraq provided rather useful camouflage for a platform that was somewhat unfocused, but the Lib Dem electoral results in 2005 were good. It also needs stressing that Nick Clegg played only a peripheral role in *The Orange Book*, but the book was important in setting out the new generation's stall, as Clegg was to become leader of the new generation of Lib Dems less than four years later.

Moreover, the principles underlying *The Orange Book* were not only to have an impact on the Lib Dem manifesto for 2010, but also served to narrow the gap between the Conservatives and the Lib Dems, a narrowing that made the current coalition a possibility it might not have been in 2005. Chris Davies says both *The Orange Book* and Clegg's own leadership have 'rewritten what being a liberal in Britain means', with the new liberalism being unhampered by the baggage of having fought the Conservatives. 'People like Ming Campbell, Charles Kennedy and Paddy Ashdown defined themselves by fighting the Tories,' says Davies, 'squeezing the Labour vote to edge out the Tories, whereas Nick doesn't come from that.'

An interesting postscript to *The Orange Book* came at the end of 2004, with the publication of 'Neither Left nor Right: the Liberal Democrats and the Electorate'. It was a study by two Manchester University academics, Andrew Russell and Edward Fieldhouse, into the Lib Dems' 'struggle for identity, distinctiveness and votes'. The study found that Lib Dem voters were closer to the Conservatives in their economic profile, but closer to Labour in their ideology. It also found that, by being an essentially classless party, or at least one that couldn't mobilise support on the basis of social divisions, the Lib Dems had to rely on 'issue-based' campaigning. That made sense of the outcry against *The Orange Book* – it may have been good liberal theory, but it had the potential to frighten off Lib Dem voters who were ideologically closer to Labour than to market-friendly solutions.

Nonetheless, Laws is unapologetic about the need for *The Orange Book* in 2004. 'The party had become incredibly conservative in its thinking,' he says, 'and the fact that the kneejerk reaction was so strong tells me it was worth having that debate. Whether you agree with them or not, both the Conservatives and Labour had become innovative in their policies to get elected, while we were becoming a very stodgy, safe, small-C conservative party, always wanting to default to the easy position. That's OK when you're not expecting to be in government, but it doesn't test you by the standards of what you need to do if you do want to be in government. The party needed a bit of a shake-up.' Not everyone in the Lib Dems would agree that the party had become small-C conservative, but they would agree that *The Orange Book* provided a very definite shake-up.

With the benefit of hindsight, it's easy to see the Liberal Democrats as at least a fixture on the British political landscape, if not a rising force, in the first half-decade of the new century. But concerns about the party's vulnerability were never far from the surface, especially with a Labour government in power that seemed to have taken up some of the Lib Dems' political floorspace.

Just a few weeks before the 2001 election, an opinion poll was published that showed the Lib Dems heading for a dismal result, and Charles Kennedy's morale was hardly boosted when he heard Bob Worcester of Mori on BBC Radio 4's *The World at One* saying the party's forty-six seats from the 1997 election had been an aberration and the Lib Dems would lose half their MPs. This goes down as one of the many false alarms from those who predict the Lib Dems' demise, and the party ended up with six more MPs than it had done in the 'aberration' four years earlier. But the first half of 2003 proved a troubling time for the Liberal Democrats – both on specific policy and in narrowly avoiding a potentially damaging leadership contest. And if things had worked out otherwise, it would have been a very different party that Nick Clegg inherited a few years later.

Two things threatened Kennedy's leadership. The first was the issue of Iraq, a topic that ultimately helped establish the Lib Dems as a serious force for the 2005 general election. Given how much the Lib Dems reaped the rewards of their opposition to Britain's decision to join America's war against the Iraqi dictator Saddam Hussein, it seems strange to think that it was a risky strategy. Indeed some Lib Dem insiders take the view that the party was never going to support the war. It's not a line Kennedy himself gives much credence to.

'In my private moments I was staring resignation and bringing the party to its knees in the face,' he says now. 'When we took the decisions on Iraq, 70–80 per cent of people in the opinion polls thought Blair was right and thought Iraq did have weapons of mass destruction, despite the million out demonstrating on the roads.' Although Ming Campbell, then the Lib Dems' foreign affairs spokesperson, was to make a lot of political capital out of his party's opposition to the war, he was initially in favour of it, and made Kennedy aware that opposing the war was a high-risk strategy, especially with the invasion being started in March and local elections due for the first week in May. Kennedy adds, 'Ming pointed out that there was every possibility that by the end of April – quite convenient for polling in the first week of May – you would have George Bush and Tony Blair in downtown Baghdad with a grateful populace, and where would that have left the one party that decided to stand out and say "We're against all this"? It sounds fanciful to say it now, but that was how it felt at the time.'

If the dragged-out nature of the military campaign in Iraq spared Kennedy the humiliation that could have led him to question his position, another problem closer to home was taking its toll. By mid-2003 his drink problems were well advanced, and a press briefing was scheduled one Saturday in July at which he would admit that he had 'personal health issues' and that these were already being dealt with. But Kennedy cancelled the briefing at short notice because he felt the admission would make him a hostage to fortune.

The existence of that cancelled briefing was first revealed in Greg Hurst's biography of Charles Kennedy, a book which Kennedy studiously maintains he refuses to read. Yet if he was right about being a hostage to fortune, it implies that the admission of a drink problem might well have brought him down then, rather than two-and-a-half years – and a general election – later. If one bears in mind the fact that his resignation in January 2006 began with a pledge to fight on as leader while seeking help for his drink problem but two days later he was forced to resign, there is a good chance that would have happened had he made his admission in July 2003. The two situations are not similar in every detail – in 2003, there was a strong feeling in the party that Kennedy was a good leader, so the parliamentary party wanted him but not the alcohol; by January 2006, he had had so many 'last chances' that he had little support left. But an admission of a drink problem in July 2003 might have unleashed such a chorus of disapproval through the media that he could have been doomed irrespective of the level of internal support.

Had there been an election in mid-2003, Campbell would probably have won (against Simon Hughes); in fact, the only doubt surrounds the cancer that was detected in his hip, which was fresh at the time. Had Campbell become Lib Dem leader then, he would have had two years to ride high on his popularity stemming from opposition to the Iraq War, and he would have had the oxygen of publicity from fighting a general election as leader, something all party leaders need but especially those leading the 'third party'. There might then not have been a leadership election at all until after the 2010 general election. It's all speculation, or, to paraphrase the historian A. J. P. Taylor, a turning point at which Lib Dem history failed to turn.

If 2003–4 was a convulsive period in Lib Dem thinking, 2004 was a convulsive year in the Clegg family.

A feature of the 2010 general election was that all three party leaders had sustained brushes with hospital services over the welfare of a child. Of the three, Clegg's was the happiest experience, as his son Antonio came through his life-threatening illness, while Gordon Brown lost his daughter Jennifer-Jane ten days after birth and has a son, Fraser, with cystic fibrosis; and David Cameron's son Ivan died at age six. But the Cleggs' experience in 2004 was the kind of nerve-wracking situation no parent ever wants to go through.

It started when Antonio, by then two years old, was diagnosed with pneumonia. Or more accurately, it was misdiagnosed, and before they knew it, the boy had pleurisy. 'We ended up taking him to three different hospitals,' Clegg says, 'and they misdiagnosed it, and they kept pumping him full of antibiotics and he just got iller and iller. There was a moment when we thought we were going to lose him, which was just horrific. And then finally we got him to a specialist hospital, and they drained his left lung, which was full of pus. He had pleurisy that got out of hand.' As the Cleggs were still in Brussels, it meant a lot of travelling for the broader family. Clegg's parents were constantly on the phone, and made several trips to Belgium to offer support. 'It was just a shocking time,' says Paul Clegg. 'I remember it very clearly because we were all on the phone. If you see a baby of that age really struggling, it's very, very worrying – this is as personal as it gets. It was a shocking reminder about how tenuous life can be. Thank goodness it has left no lasting scars.'

One thing Clegg is insistent on is that his experience is not in the same league as Brown's and Cameron's. 'It was traumatic for us as young parents, but I would never seek to compare that with something like losing a child. It was awful, but what Gordon Brown and David Cameron went through was a lot worse. Ours was nowhere near that.' Well, no, but really only because Antonio survived.

There was a second part of the drama. While Antonio was in intensive care, Miriam was pregnant with the Cleggs' second child. He, Alberto, was born a few months later, but the birth went horribly wrong, Miriam ended up in intensive care, and at one stage her condition was so perilous the doctors were seriously worried about her. No wonder Clegg describes it as 'a horrible year'.

At the time all this happened, he had been selected to fight a Westminster seat and was gearing up for the campaign. He has been asked if he ever thought this just wasn't the right time to enter the big bad world of national politics. 'Yes, a lot,' he says. 'I'm sure it's the same as everybody. I sometimes think "Gosh, wouldn't it be better to do this when the children are grown up?" because you always want to spend more time with the children. I think a lot of people think the same in their own working lives. I just took a whole lot of time off. I remember sleeping night after night in the hospital with Antonio, taking the time off to make sure he and Miriam were healthy and strong. I would hope I'd do exactly the same now. I really am a father before I'm a politician, I'm completely besotted with my little boys, they mean everything to me.'

The *Daily Telegraph* journalist Mick Brown, who followed Clegg for a couple of days in the run-up to the 2010 general election campaign, reported him suddenly going absent for a few hours after his third child, Miguel, was rushed to hospital with breathing problems. 'Breathing and babies just makes us go cold,' was Clegg's pithy but understandable explanation.

By the time these twin health scares hit the family, Clegg was as good as guaranteed he would become an MP. He had taken the decision not to stand for the European Parliament in the 2004 elections well before he was selected for a Westminster seat. That timing has led some to say he showed immense courage, and to compare him favourably with Chris Huhne, who remained an MEP until elected to Parliament for the Hampshire seat of Eastleigh in 2005. Both observations are a little simplistic. Clegg had decided as early as 2001 that he didn't want to stand for another term in Europe, having realised that life in the European Parliament was too limiting in an MEP's relationship with constituents and too intrusive on his wish for a stable family life. So to have hung on until he was selected for a winnable Westminster seat would have been tantamount to keeping a safety net he could never see himself using. On Huhne's part, one of the reasons he stayed on in Brussels until the summer of 2005 was that he was working on European legislation that he wanted to see through.

Having decided not to stand in 2004, Clegg needed to set about the serious business of finding a winnable Westminster constituency. He had visited Sheffield in 2002 in his capacity as an MEP – it was the nearest major city in a neighbouring constituency – and impressed the constituency chair of the Lib Dem-held seat of Hallam, Allan Wisbey. 'I found him a fresh-faced young fellow, very able, totally in command of his world,' Wisbey recalls.

It wasn't initially clear that there would be a vacancy in Sheffield Hallam. The seat was held by a man just a year older than Clegg, Richard Allan, who had won it in 1997 with an 18 per cent swing from the Conservatives, the second-biggest swing to the Lib Dems in that election. Allan was thought of as one of the rising stars of the Lib Dems. He had a degree in archaeology but had become an IT expert working in the National Health Service. At thirty-one, he was one of the bright stars of the forty-six Lib Dems elected in 1997, and with his IT background, he became the Lib Dems' parliamentary whizzkid for all things to do with computers.

But Allan is a character for whom variety and new challenges are crucial to enjoying life. His constituency officials always sensed he would not be an MP for ever, and Allan himself tells a story from his time in Parliament that affirms this. 'I did this thing called the Industry and Parliament Trust, which basically finds work placements for MPs so they can understand how the world of industry works. I'd done twenty days with Centrica, and I was spending a lot of time working with the IT sector in Parliament, and I felt less and less legitimate in my parliamentary work. The more I learned, the more conscious I became of my own ignorance around how business works, which is the thing we were supposed to be regulating.' When a Conservative councillor came up to Allan on Remembrance Sunday in 2001 and said, 'You've got a job for life here, we'll never be able to win against you and nor will Labour,' it tugged at a doubt that had been crystallising in Allan's mind: did he really want to be an MP from thirty-one until his mid-sixties or whenever he chose to retire? 'When I looked into the future, that wasn't the future I wanted,' he says.

In early 2003, Allan formally announced that he would not be standing for re-election at the next general election, expected to take place in 2005 or 2006. That prompted the Hallam Lib Dems to draw up a 'spec' for the kind of parliamentary candidate they were looking for. The selection committee decided to go for a candidate who had the capacity or promise to operate successfully on the national stage. Wisbey explains: 'In so far as any Lib Dem seat can be regarded as "safe", we reckoned Hallam was a safe one, and we should therefore use it to best advantage for the party. And in our view, that meant finding a candidate who could be more than just a good local rep. That was not to denigrate in any way the concept of the backbencher, but to recognise that the party as a whole did – indeed does – need a good supply of what we might call above-average performers in the House, and so we should aim to send one such there. We were, after all, losing Richard Allan, a man of many talents who is above average and had made a name for himself in the House, and we wanted someone of that calibre to replace him. The candidate spec therefore included the requirement to show "potential to exercise a leadership role at national and parliamentary level".'

It's one thing saying you are happy to provide a safe base for a national figure, but having made their gesture to the party, the Sheffield Hallam Liberal Democrats had to ensure that their selection procedure actually attracted some top-quality candidates. They knew there were some good-quality people in the market, but would they be enticed to one of the six Sheffield constituencies, an oasis of liberalism amid five safe Labour seats?

Hallam is an unusual seat for northern England – in many ways, it has more characteristics of a southern seat. When Clegg came to see it in 2003, it was in the top three constituencies in the country in terms of percentage of graduates, and in the top 10 in terms of disposable income. It had a lot of doctors, a lot of university academics, public sector professionals, businesspeople – the kind of constituency in which letters to the local MP frequently have numbered footnotes. With London just two hours away by train, it was a perfect constituency for an ambitious Liberal Democrat.

'We've got a membership that has always been interested in national and international affairs,' says the long-standing Sheffield Lib Dem councillor Andrew Sangar, 'so most of the members weren't looking for a candidate who would talk dog dirt and potholes. We wanted someone to talk CO_2 emissions, trading with the developing world, having a critical-friend relationship with Europe – the membership wanted someone who would reach out. Nick was the right kind of candidate for this kind of seat.'

Yet despite all it had going for it in demographics and Richard Allan's majority, Hallam attracted only twelve applications. From that, a shortlist of four was compiled, with none of them local (Allan is a Sheffield boy). Three were men: Clegg and two councillors from Tyneside, and there was one woman, a feisty 23-year-old from Dunbartonshire, Jo Swinson, who had taken a flat in the constituency and had lived in Yorkshire for some years.

The four candidates set out their stalls in the summer of 2003 to around 100 Lib Dem members of the constituency gathered in King Edward's Lower School. Swinson fought a strident campaign, making a powerful case for having a woman MP in a party that had not done too well on its gender balance at Westminster. But she was no match for Clegg's personality and general worldliness. At one stage, someone asked a question about the World Trade Organization and world affairs, which Clegg took in his stride while the other three struggled to look credible. 'He's always had that leadership air about him,' says Wisbey, 'and he charms people. He doesn't set out to do that, but that's just the effect he has. He bowled a lot of the party members over. He became very popular.'

It wasn't quite a landslide, but Clegg won the nomination comfortably, and while he didn't take anything for granted, he knew he was into Westminster. He even attracted the interest of *Politico* magazine, a short-lived publication emanating from the then popular political bookshop near the Houses of Parliament, Politico's. It listed Clegg as one of its politicians to watch in 2003. It even predicted he would be a future party leader, but the source of that prediction, which the editor of *Politico* took on trust, would never have predicted it would have happened as quickly as it did.

One of the first things Clegg did was to rent a semi-detached house in Sheffield that he could buy if he were elected to Parliament. The domestic plan was to get a house in London, which would be the family's permanent base given that Antonio would start formal school sometime after the ensuing general election, but that they should have a place to live when Clegg wanted to spend time in Sheffield. And he did spend a lot of time in his constituency, certainly up to the end of 2007 and even in the two-and-a-half years up to the 2010 election. He worked out a great fondness for a piece of unspoiled countryside only about ten minutes from the city called Stanedge Edge, where he loved to go walking and process the myriad thoughts emanating from the mad world of politics.

In the eleven months between the end of his time as an MEP and getting elected as an MP, he did a bit of freelance lecturing as an associate professor at the University of Sheffield. He also took on two days' work a week with a lobbying firm, G-Plus, though those who knew him then said his heart wasn't really in it, and he was more keen on campaigning for the forthcoming general election.

With Richard Allan retiring as a very popular local MP – he had taken a principled stand against the Iraq War, which had angered the other five Sheffield MPs but gone down well among the public – he and Clegg worked as a team to get Clegg elected as Hallam's next MP. After Clegg ceased to be an MEP in 2004, he and Allan did a form of synchronised diagonal campaigning, Clegg in Sheffield during the week before retiring to his family in Brussels at weekends, Allan spending the week in London on parliamentary business before retiring to Sheffield for the weekend. Their strategy was that Clegg was 'the natural successor', as Allan describes it: 'I wanted us to be elided one into the other, on the basis that if people liked one guy, they'd like the other; that Nick was just as good as me if not better.' Given that Allan was thirty-eight and Clegg thirty-seven, the strategy had a certain logic to it, but it came to grief when the two men met an elderly constituent.

'Hello,' said Allan, 'this is my successor, Nick Clegg. He's just like me if not better.'

The lady said, 'Oh, he looks a little young for a job like this.'

Allan replied, 'Well he's pretty much the same age as me.'

'Well, one of you has clearly aged a lot better then.'

Clegg proved an enthusiastic campaigner. 'He wasn't taking it for granted,' says the Sheffield councillor and Lib Dem activist Andrew Sangar, 'he was very keen to go out canvassing, and we had a lot of fun. We'd frequently go out in groups of six, with one person designated "the fat controller" who filled in the canvass returns while the other five knocked on doors. At that election we were promising to introduce a 50p rate of income tax for people earning over £100,000. On one occasion we went down this street where every house was worth more than a million pounds, and everyone on the doorstep was saying how dare we introduce a high tax rate. But we were all really going for it, and seeing how much we could wind these Conservative voters up. We had nothing to lose, because you never know where you might get a voter, and if you get one rich supporter, you can do very well.' That particular sortie proved fruitless, but Clegg did attract some moneyed backers, including John Stevens, a defector from the Conservatives who had made his money in the City.

They were also able to dovetail the job of improving Clegg's profile with campaigning in council elections. With Sheffield City Council electing its councillors a third at a time, there were elections most years, and the Lib Dems had lost overall control in 2002. But in 2004 there were new boundaries, so the whole council was up for election. Clegg campaigned with the Lib Dem council candidates, but couldn't help them retake control of the city.

In the run-up to the 2005 election, Ming Campbell came to the Sheffield Hallam constituency dinner. In his speech, he said Clegg would be a future leader of the party. The build-up of people tipping him for the top was impressive, yet none of them realised how soon it would come.

There was one other local obligation that Clegg was happy to observe. The Sheffield Lib Dems have a tradition of staging a pantomime every Christmas as a fund-raising event for the party, and the tradition requires the sitting MP to have some part in it. In 2004, the pantomime was *Jack and the Beanstalk*, with Allan and Clegg cast as the giant's two evil henchmen, Rumsfeld and Wolfowitz (Donald Rumsfeld was at the time President George W. Bush's Defence Secretary; Paul Wolfowitz was Rumsfeld's deputy). Allan played the evil henchman, Clegg the dumb one, who at one stage had to be programmed into life in a scene which looks strangely reminiscent of John Cleese's legendary 'Ministry of Silly Walks' sketch for *Monty Python's Flying Circus*; somehow this made it into a video profile of Clegg compiled by *The Observer* in 2007 which is still available on the internet. The pantomime ended with Clegg and Allan engaged in a swordfight up and down the central aisle of the hall, culminating in Clegg, with his foot on Allan's neck, declaiming 'I'm in charge now'. It was a symbolic handing over of the constituency, which Clegg won comfortably six months later, increasing Allan's majority. Allan now works as director of policy in the London office of Facebook.

At a fringe meeting during the Lib Dems' Blackpool conference that took place three months after the 2005 general election, Clegg found himself debating with his old mate from MEP days, Chris Davies. Davies, by then the leader of the British MEPs, was once again making his point that you have more influence as an MEP than an MP. Eventually, Clegg threw up his hands and said in mock resignation, 'OK, Chris, I admit it, I've swapped the chance to have real legislative influence for the chance to be on *Newsnight*.'

Chapter 9

'WE HAVE TO DO SOMETHING ABOUT THIS'

THE LIBERAL Democrats could be forgiven for feeling quite pleased with themselves after the 2005 general election. With sixty-two seats, the party had more MPs than at any time since the 1923 general election, when the Liberals gained 158 seats. But all was not well within the ranks, and at an internal meeting shortly after the election, one of the twenty new MPs had the gall to describe the party's election platform as 'technocratic mush'. That MP was Nick Clegg.

Political strategists would say he was already setting out his stall for a push for prominence, but that would be to make it sound more calculated than it was. The general feeling within the party at the time was that, in terms of ideas, the Lib Dems had offered a very poor selection of policies at the 2005 election. Some would say it doesn't matter, that getting too hung up on policies is unnecessary in a political world dominated by twelve-second sound bites on the news and feel-good factors that owe more to the image makers than to political, economic and philosophical thought. Certainly the Lib Dems got their broad tactics right at the 2005 election, as Charles Kennedy and his respected foreign affairs spokesman, Sir Menzies Campbell, cashed in on their opposition to the 2003 war in Iraq, to say nothing of their opposition to tuition fees.

But the Liberal position has always been a very cerebral one, standing as it must between the policies of the two major parties who have traditionally represented the haves (Conservative) and have-nots (Labour), and who thus have a stronger gut instinct to rely on among their core voters. There were a number of people in the Lib Dems distinctly uneasy at the lack of thought that went into the 2005 election policies. Indeed it's generally only the candidates, who had to know the party's manifesto by heart, that can remember many of the ten headline policies the party campaigned on.

Clegg says, 'We had this list, with posters to highlight the ten things, and I remember thinking and saying at the time "There's no point having a list, people don't vote for shopping lists – you have to have a story", and I still believe that now. The story is more important than the list. You can do all the focus groups you like and find the most popular policies, but it doesn't mean people will vote for you if there isn't a narrative. I was saying that, as a party, we needed to get beyond popular lists and start telling a story. This is why I think the manifesto of 2010 was a very good one because it summed up where we thought we were and what we felt we needed to do.'

Clegg's comments about the Lib Dem manifesto of 2005 are partly backed up by the party's chief executive, Chris Rennard. He said in a submission to a post-election meeting in January 2006 that the party had 'lacked an effective message', because its message was too spread out and not focused enough. He told the story about the beaten 1956 US presidential candidate Adlai Stevenson, who made a brilliant speech on the campaign trail, so brilliant that someone from the audience shouted out, 'Mr Stevenson, with arguments like that, I can guarantee you the votes of every thinking American.' Stevenson replied, 'That's not enough, I need a majority!'

It's possible to view the 2005 manifesto as the last of the 'opposition' Liberal Democrat manifestos. Much as the party had to talk publicly about what it would do if it were in government, any dose of realism would indicate that its best bet was to hope for a hung parliament and then use what influence it had as a kingmaker or junior party in a coalition. Even that scenario was fairly optimistic, such was the inability of the still-fractured Conservative Party to dent Tony Blair's stranglehold on power, a stranglehold that should have been eminently attackable, given that Blair's justification for Britain's involvement in the Iraq War had been to rid Iraq of its weapons of mass destruction, weapons that were never found. As a result, the Lib Dems were able to make a lot of capital out of their Iraq opposition without too much close attention being visited on their manifesto.

The 2005 manifesto had twenty-five pledges to spend more money; in fact, the Lib Dems were promising to spend more on public services than any other party. It was all costed, and most of the spending commitments would have been funded from the revenue of the 50p tax rate that the party had as one of its policies. The approach wasn't ideologically driven in the sense of trying to be more left-wing than the more social-democratic Labour Party of the day, it was just thought to be good politics. But it alarmed the man responsible for the Lib Dems' finance plans, Vince Cable. 'There were a lot of people in the party who liked the idea of spending a lot of money,' Cable says, 'some of them close to Kennedy. But it wasn't philosophical – if you want to dignify it, it was a Swedish approach with lots of public spending and taxation, but it had nothing to do with public ownership or trade unionism. It wasn't a deliberate attempt to outdo Labour, it just sort of happened. It was the way a lot of the party tried to think at that time, and was the source of many of the problems later, like tuition fees.'

Clegg, who had been appointed Lib Dem spokesperson on Europe by Kennedy, made his 'technocratic mush' comment at the first meeting of an initiative called Meeting the Challenge. This was an internal think-tank chaired by the party leader aimed at working out a narrative for the party for the subsequent ten years. One person who attended that same meeting says Clegg's comment was like a breath of fresh air: 'I was hugely excited about that, it was a very important moment. The manifesto had contained the sort of stuff I'd never have voted for if I hadn't been a member of the party – it was a patronising idea of human nature. I had already identified him as a thinker and I felt we desperately needed to regain some of the intellectual high ground, we needed someone who was prepared to think in public, and he did that. He was prepared to question sacred cows, both in terms of a lack of ideas, and the way we were running our campaigns, so I identified him as a future leader.'

Clegg himself was totally unapologetic about wanting to change things. 'Any new MP will be conscious of being branded a young man or woman in a hurry,' he told *The Guardian* in an interview in October 2005, 'but I can't understand the point of being in politics unless you want to advocate change. British politics has been in a holding pattern for some time.'

It is no exaggeration to say Clegg could easily have become the Lib Dem leader at the age of thirty-nine, just seven months after becoming an MP. That would normally be far fetched, but in January 2006, the Liberal Democrats found themselves in a leadership election with something of a missing generation of leaders. To get the full measure of how a man who had been in Parliament such a short time came so close to becoming the leader of the third-biggest party, it's important to understand the broad state of the Liberal Democrats after the 2005 general election.

The party in its modern form was only eighteen years old, though if you count the old Liberal Party, it goes back much further. The Liberal tendency in British politics has a glorious tradition, with paintings of prime ministers such as Pitt, Gladstone, Asquith and Lloyd George adorning the walls of Liberal Democrat buildings. The Liberals (known until 1877 as the Whigs) were the 'left-wing' party in a two-party system that dominated British politics throughout the nineteenth century and into the twentieth. Over the first three decades of the twentieth century, the Labour Party, representing the swelling ranks of the industrial working classes, gradually took over from the Liberals, the Liberals having suffered a disastrous split during the First World War which lasted through most of the 1920s. By the end of the Second World War, they had virtually no members of Parliament.

There was a revival of sorts in the 1960s and 1970s under Jo Grimond (see page 117) and Jeremy Thorpe, which established a new centre ground in British politics, but it was not big enough to dent the two-party system dominated by Labour and the Conservatives. Indeed, in the only general election between 1945 and 2010 not to produce an overall majority (February 1974), the Liberals, with fourteen seats, were too small to help either of the main parties form a coalition government with a majority. There were around a thousand Liberal councillors up and down the country, many of whom had strong followings for their local hard work, but at national level, the Liberals were little more than an affable bunch of political intellectuals: a sort of refuge for the free-thinking middle classes, rather as the Quakers have often been the refuge of religious believers who have no truck with mainstream churches.

Then, in 1981, the centre ground received a massive boost. A group of Labour MPs, led by four highly prominent former government ministers, broke ranks from Labour and set up their own party, the Social Democratic Party (SDP). Forming an electoral alliance with the Liberals, the two parties had a phenomenal result in the 1983 general election, gaining 26 per cent of the vote, and did almost as well at the 1987 election. But they couldn't translate this into parliamentary seats. It seemed obvious for the two to merge, which they did in 1987–8, forming the Social and Liberal Democrats, initially known for short as the 'Democrats', but shortly after that as the 'Liberal Democrats'. (There are plenty of people, even two decades later, who still delight in calling the party 'the Liberals'. A few Lib Dems who are happy to use the term 'Liberals' about themselves nonetheless feel it is deeply insulting for anyone else to eschew the term 'Liberal Democrat'. Hence Peter Mandelson's exhortation to Gordon Brown on the eve of coalition talks with the Lib Dems in 2010: 'If you're serious, perhaps you should stop calling them "the Liberals" and get their name right.')

The first Lib Dem leader was Paddy Ashdown, a former Special Boat Service officer with the Royal Marines and later intelligence officer for MI6, who had turned to politics moderately late but had risen quickly, having built a powerful following as MP for the Somerset town of Yeovil, largely from scratch. Ashdown was crucial to the new party's survival, because the merger was frankly something of a disaster. The leader of the now defunct SDP, David Owen, refused to accept the merger and maintained the SDP – or arguably formed his own new SDP – as a breakaway party, fighting several parliamentary by-elections. The breakaway SDP was never going to be more than a spoiler, but it did its fair share of spoiling, including splitting the Lib Dem vote at a crucial by-election in Richmond, North Yorkshire, in 1989, allowing a bright young Conservative called William Hague to win an election he looked for all the world like losing.

The Lib Dems almost came to grief when barely a year old. In the elections to the European Parliament of 1989, the party polled just 6 per cent of the votes, while the Greens had their breakthrough moment, polling 15 per cent. With Margaret Thatcher having announced an unexpected commitment to the environment in a speech to the Royal Society in September 1988, the environment was the talking point of the moment, and the Greens' spectacular election result seemed to confirm that the Liberal Democrats were the final flame of a dying centre movement, with the Greens likely to become the new third party of British politics.

The fact that it didn't happen, and the Lib Dems recovered to be stronger than any of their predecessor parties had been since the last Liberal-led government in the early 1920s, is largely down to Ashdown, along with a lot of help from his chief election strategist, Chris Rennard. Ashdown was nicknamed 'Action Man' and 'Tigger' by friends and enemies alike, because of his boundless energy – his successor-but-one as Lib Dem leader, Ming Campbell, describes him as 'living off scorched earth'. But he also had political judgement.

Ashdown's buccaneering style had first saved the newly merged centre party from oblivion, and then built it up into a plausible political force. The third stage of the Ashdown plan was quite blunt: 'I deliberately went round building up my popularity,' he says of his early years as party leader, 'both by delivering results and by being very consensual, conscious of the fact that when I began to play on the field [in the final phase of his leadership] I was really going to have to use up this political capital and ... make myself unpopular with the party.' Ashdown saw the future of the Lib Dems as part of a broad progressive coalition with Labour, and built up a fairly close relationship with Tony Blair in the run-up to the 1997 general election. This might well have led to some form of post-election deal, leading in turn to meaningful electoral reform, but when Labour gained a massive majority at the 1997 election to end eighteen years of Conservative rule, it had no need of Lib Dem support. Ashdown, who still speaks constantly of the 'realignment of the left' in British politics, continued to hope for a while that Blair would deliver an elected House of Lords and proportional representation for general elections, but it soon became clear that those hopes would remain unfulfilled, and by the time he resigned as Lib Dem leader in January 1999, many in his party felt he was beyond his sell-by date.

Ashdown was succeeded by Charles Kennedy, a genial Scotsman whose media appearances had given him a high profile, which counted for something at a time when the number of people who could name more than three Lib Dem MPs was painfully small. He was even nicknamed 'Chatshow Charlie' by the media due to his willingness to appear on jocular television programmes.

Kennedy admits that, in leadership terms, 'there is an inevitable human reaction to go for something different from what you've just had. So a Major follows a Thatcher, a Brown follows a Blair, a Smith follows a Kinnock, and so it goes on to a laid-back Kennedy following Action Man Tigger Ashdown. They're caricatures, but there's an element of truth as well.' The biggest contrast in Kennedy's leadership was that he was less antagonistic towards the party than Ashdown was – he lost his temper much less often, and was perceived as a breath of fresh air. He was a very consensual leader, always consulting people within the party; he was also likeable, self-deprecating, and very amenable.

Kennedy proved a great success electorally; indeed, in mathematical terms, one could argue he was the most successful Liberal leader for 100 years for enhancing the party's positions at the 2001 and 2005 general elections. But there are two polarised views of his leadership, and in some circles of the party he is judged almost brutally.

In an essay in the *Political Quarterly* in early 2007, the long-standing Liberal Democrat activist Duncan Brack contrasted the Ashdown and Kennedy leaderships, concluding that Kennedy's period in office was a 'wasted opportunity'. In one of the more damning passages, Brack says, 'Kennedy disliked and actively avoided confrontation. This meant there were none of the leader-ship defeats at the party conference that Ashdown had suffered on a number of occasions; since Kennedy never actually adopted a posi-tion on a key conference vote, he could never be defeated.' Brack says Kennedy never had an agenda for his leadership, he did not manage his party, his communications skills largely deserted him, and he did not appear to believe in his own capacity to lead.

There are a number of people in the party who share at least elements of Brack's view that Kennedy squandered Ashdown's legacy. Even those who supported him felt he wasn't making the most of the situation. His former speech writer Richard Grayson said Kennedy's leadership style was 'more chairman than leader', and he said in an interview with the BBC that the party 'wants to be led rather than necessarily being chaired'.

But there is a counter-argument. This is not just rooted in the fact that the Lib Dems did better in 2005 than they had done since 1923 in terms of seats won, but in two other factors. One is that Kennedy was generally thought of as a good operator, typified by his winning the Politician of the Year award run by *The Spectator* magazine in 2004, with a good nose that could sniff out what would go down well with the British voting public. The other is that the party membership liked him, to the point where his resignation in January 2006 unleashed fears in the rank and file that the Lib Dems had no-one of Kennedy's standing to replace him with. Clegg describes Kennedy as 'on his day one of the most supremely gifted figures in British politics of any party'.

Kennedy also rejects Brack's argument that the party was always going to oppose the Iraq War, and believes the dividend the party earned at the 2005 election for doing so was ample reward for taking a bold stance against it at the time when it wasn't an easy option. And while Kennedy won't say so in as many words, he clearly feels there's an irony in Ming Campbell having gained a lot of the credit for opposing the Iraq war when Campbell had had to be persuaded that opposing it was the right thing to do.

Much debate still surrounds the effectiveness of the Lib Dems' 2005 election campaign, and whether it could – or should – have been better than it was. That can be left to the liberal historians to thrash out. What was clear is that the party gained its highest share of the vote (22.7 per cent) since the second election fought by the SDP–Liberal Alliance in 1987, to give it its sixty-two seats. The significant detail is that it did better against Labour than it had done since Labour had come into existence more than 100 years before, taking twelve seats with no losses. And yet the impressive result masked two crucial behind-the-scenes developments.

The first was that the calibre and ambition of Lib Dem MPs had gone up dramatically since 1997. The 1997 intake included a generation of people who were not content to sit by and let the Lib Dems be a nice, centre-ground alternative point of view without any realistic hope of ever being in government. Ashdown's hope that the Lib Dems could be a party of government was perhaps ahead of its time, but was also thwarted in part by a relative lack of ambition among many senior Lib Dems. Among the 'Young Turks' he invited to dinner shortly after he handed over the reins to Kennedy was Mark Oaten, who says, 'If you look at the Young Turks at the time, of whom Ed Davey and I were perhaps the most prominent, what brought us together was not a desire to become leader but to make the party ambitious. We felt the 1997 intake was a different intake, we hadn't come to hang around on the back benches, we'd come into politics to do things, and there was a frustration and irritation at how slow that was. So there was a hunger to look around and find fellow-travellers who wanted to get there quickly, and it was very clear to all of us that Clegg and Huhne were part of the crowd who wanted to get into power and make the party grow.'

Campbell makes this identical point about the 2005 election. 'By 2005, people were being elected as MPs for whom being elected wasn't enough,' he says. 'Their ambition was more than just being an MP, their ambition was government, and it was possible because of the rising tide of the party's fortunes. What had seemed inconceivable to us in the 1980s had suddenly become conceivable in the 1990s and early 2000s.'

So, far from seeing the 2005 election as a high-water mark in the party's history, the sixty-two Lib Dem MPs elected in that year were ambitious and ready for action. Clegg denies that his quest for the party manifesto to 'tell a story' was an attack on Kennedy, of whom he says, 'When Charles is on form, there's no-one who can touch him; he was and remains an extraordinarily intuitive politician who has an emotional intelligence that I think very few people have.' But it did reflect a feeling that the party needed to become more hard nosed in the way it presented itself to the public and fought elections, whoever its leader happened to be.

For the eight months between the general election of 2005 and Kennedy's resignation in January 2006, the Lib Dems operated in two very discrete universes. While the membership exalted in the good election result and didn't consider that the leadership was up for discussion, Kennedy was becoming increasingly vulnerable at Westminster.

There was a by-election in July in the Greater Manchester seat of Cheadle, where Patsy Calton had died from cancer (she had been too ill to campaign in the election, but still increased her majority, and was sworn in to the House of Commons five days before she died). Had the Lib Dems lost that, which seemed a distinct possibility, Kennedy's position would have become very precarious, and even at the party's conference in Blackpool in September 2005, the BBC's newly installed political editor, Nick Robinson, said 'The only thing keeping Charles Kennedy going is that many senior figures in the party don't want Simon Hughes as leader.' That comment, indeed the idea of a leadership crisis, was thought of by many as a bit of journalistic hyperbole, and even Campbell, who was to emerge victorious from Kennedy's demise, says he had 'little sense of its potential at the time'. But it was much closer to the truth than most Lib Dem members knew.

The second factor that did for Kennedy was his long-suspected alcoholism, which finally came out in January 2006. It could, perhaps should, have come out much earlier. There had been a story before he even became leader about him being carried legless out of a party at the Irish embassy, but this had been largely laughed away. When it was put to Paddy Ashdown at the time he was resigning that Kennedy was his most likely successor but had this drunken episode on his CV, Ashdown reportedly dismissed it with 'Oh, Highlanders like a drink'. Kennedy's decision to cancel his press briefing in July 2003 (see page 138) had bought him two-and-a-half more years – and a general election – before the demon drink caught up with him. In theory, he was only going to stand down as Lib Dem leader temporarily in the summer of 2003, but it's hard to see how that would have washed – it would have been a temporary standing down for about two days, before he'd have had to resign. That's what happened in January 2006: he announced on the Thursday night that he had a drink problem and was seeking help, and was therefore calling a leadership election in which he himself would stand. By Saturday lunchtime, he was gone.

It's a either a testament to the loyalty Kennedy inspired or a sign of how weak the Lib Dem mind was in being politically ruthless that so few people were willing to speak out against Kennedy's leadership until the drink problem finally nailed him. That in itself has led to an urban myth that Kennedy's leadership was undone by alcohol, whereas the common theme amongst many Lib Dems who were in positions of influence during the Kennedy leadership years was that he was a mediocre leader, and the drink problem got worse as he realised he was providing little or no leadership. The Lib Dem MP Nick Harvey was one of the few people to say publicly in 2005–6 that they wanted Kennedy to go because he

was a poor leader, not because he was an alcoholic. Whatever the
merits or demerits of Kennedy's leadership, the loyalty shown to
him by his MPs and staff is both touching and daft, admirable and
lacking in Realpolitik.

Kennedy's drink problems have also fuelled the feeling in some
party circles that the Lib Dems could have achieved an awful lot
more in 2005, had so many efforts not been directed towards keeping the Kennedy show off the bottle and on the road. As Oaten, by
then a leading light as the party's home affairs spokesman, put it,
'It was a great opportunity, foiled by a lack of ambition.' Whether
that is true is another matter – as already mentioned, there's a plausible theory that, drink problem or not, the Lib Dems got as much
in 2005 as the most perfect campaign would have delivered – but
there's no doubt a lot of effort was spent on avoiding distractions.

Kennedy was in several cases very lucky. He botched the launch
of the party's manifesto, totally failing to explain the details of the
Lib Dems' policy on a local income tax, but he was able to pass off
his inability to get his words out as a sign of sleep deprivation as
he'd become a father for the first time in the small hours. The nation
found it very sweet, little suspecting that it was more drink fuelled
than caused by his time in the maternity ward.

To those who knew about the drink problem and therefore saw
themselves caught between loyalty to the party leader and loyalty to
the party, the assurance that kept them moderately calm was that
Kennedy was having treatment, and that the treatment was working.
But in the autumn of 2005 there was a major relapse. He attended
a series of events in a state which caused concern to members and
sympathisers, a series that culminated in him setting out on a trip
to the north-east and never making it, an accompanying assistant
having phoned Lib Dem HQ from King's Cross station asking for
advice as the party leader was in no fit state to travel.

Much of this was kept within Kennedy's core group of advisers,
but word gradually began to seep out to the parliamentary party.
Clegg was also becoming aware of these growing problems. One
day, walking past Norman Lamb in the impressive atrium of the

Westminster administrative building, Portcullis House, he said quietly, 'We have to do something about this.' He was not alone, and it would be wrong to read into this a bid for power – in fact he stayed right out of the plotting that eventually toppled Kennedy. He had already discussed his own leadership ambitions with Lamb and another prominent Lib Dem MP, Michael Moore, who went on to be Secretary of State for Scotland. But it was a discussion based on there not being a leadership election for a while, and when Kennedy's problems became harder and harder to hide – 'by the end of 2005 we were having to lie through our teeth,' says one Lib Dem MP; 'whenever a journalist asked us whether our leader was an alcoholic, we just had to lie' – the question of whether Clegg was ready to be the leader of his generation took on a different hue, given that he had only been in Parliament a few months.

Among activists at the time, Clegg was clearly thought of as the great hope of the party. If his 'technocratic mush' comment had inspired many of the handful who heard it, a wider audience was impressed when, at the Lib Dems' Blackpool conference in September 2005, he spoke about 'liberalism as an optimistic creed'. He was saying things that resonated with the party membership, and word was spreading that this was a guy heading for the top, so people were keen to court him. One of the more audacious examples of this came from a young woman called Polly Mackenzie, who had joined the Lib Dems after working for the party on housing issues. She heard the 'optimistic creed' speech, and was determined to meet Clegg when she attended the Liberal Democrat Ball in November 2005. 'I saw we were seated fairly close to each other,' she says, 'but not next to each other, so I quietly moved the place names so I could sit next to him. I remember we had a fight about whether elected mayors were a good thing – he was pro, I was anti. When I told him that I had switched name tags, he was appalled.' But obviously impressed too – a few months later Mackenzie applied for the job of policy officer on the home affairs brief and got the job, becoming one of Clegg's most trusted policy officers; she now works for him in government. (She is one of many Lib Dems who wanted to work on home affairs in 2006–7 solely because it was a chance to get to know the rising star.)

But it was more than just a few admirers. Three prominent behind-the-scenes Lib Dem supporters put their money where their mouths were, and funded a second member of Clegg's research staff. The three were Neil Sherlock and Ian Wright – two of the original founders of Lib Dems in Public Relations, who are often cited in the same breath – and Michael Young, a former head of Edward Heath's private office and the man who, as head of corporate affairs for the gold-mining company Consolidated Goldfields, had secretly brokered talks between the African National Congress and the South African government that led to the release from prison of Nelson Mandela and the unbanning of the ANC. The money was used to hire Matthew Hanney, an enthusiastic young political activist whose job it was to work on matters that would prepare for Clegg to become Lib Dem leader at some stage in the future. Clegg himself contributed to the fund, although the way he did it provided the basis for the *Daily Telegraph*'s attempted smear at the height of Cleggmania in 2010.

In the months after the 2005 general election, an informal supper cabal had evolved. It was put together by Paul Marshall, the Lib Dem activist who had compiled *The Orange Book* with David Laws, and featured many of *The Orange Book*'s authors. Marshall had got together a group of six MPs (Clegg, Chris Huhne, David Laws, Ed Davey, Vince Cable and Norman Lamb – Sarah Teather also attended one or two suppers) who saw themselves as ambitious for the party, so they met regularly to discuss policy options. When the group met in late 2005, they found themselves chatting about who would be the best leadership candidate if Kennedy were forced to stand down. The general consensus was that it should be Ming Campbell, even though he wasn't a member of the group. There was only one dissenter, Cable. He says there were three reasons for his reluctance to back Campbell: he wasn't aware of much evidence that Kennedy had a problem (though he has since admitted that this was because the information was kept secret, and Cable now accepts that Kennedy probably did have to go by late 2005), he felt that while Campbell had strengths he also had limitations that would be exposed, and he felt he himself was a member of the leadership team, so was mulling over a challenge of his own.

Ultimately, though, the group agreed to back Campbell, and it was the outcome of this discussion that has been used to feed the idea that Clegg and Huhne made a pact not to stand when Kennedy resigned. There appears never to have been a bilateral agreement between the two ex-MEPs, but they were part of the group that felt the party needed a fairly amicable leadership election without leaving any blood on the carpet, and that Campbell was the best candidate. Huhne says he missed some of the discussions, but he was certainly consulted on the issue of the leadership and had left others with the impression that he would support Campbell.

The act that signalled the end for Kennedy was effectively carried out by four MPs: Lamb, Laws, Teather and Davey. Because Teather and Davey did most of the media work, reports at the time suggested that they had pulled the trigger, but it was as much down to Lamb having broken ranks, given that he had been Kennedy's parliamentary private secretary prior to the 2005 general election and so became the first of Kennedy's inner circle to say the situation was untenable and was only going to do the party harm.

Just before all hell broke loose, Teather and Davey phoned Paddy Ashdown (now Lord Ashdown of Norton-sub-Hamdon) to tell him what they were planning. Ashdown, who was in Bosnia, wanted to know who was going to stand for the leadership, and asked specifically if Clegg would be a candidate. It was put to the former leader that he wouldn't be, because the supper group had felt it was too early for Clegg to become the leader of the new generation of Lib Dem MPs, so they were going to support Campbell.

Ashdown says he wasn't happy with this, and says he was blunt when Campbell phoned him to ask if he would support the Scotsman in his bid for the leadership. 'I said I needed to know whether Nick was standing first,' says Ashdown today, adding that he tried to persuade Campbell not to stand. 'I said to him, "Ming, I

wouldn't do this, I don't think it'll do you, or the party, any good."
And I tried to persuade Nick to stand. I told him this was the only
election in his political career he could afford to lose, as he'd mark
his card as an ambitious young man with places to go. In my view
Nick would have won. I didn't think so at the time, but I do now.
But he took the decision, and it was a highly mature decision that
has proved over time to be right, that he wasn't ready for that, and
decided not to do it. For Nick it was probably the right decision.
Whether it was right for the party I'm not so sure.'

Clegg talked to a lot of people at that time about whether he
should stand for the leadership, mostly from within the party but
also outside. The day after Kennedy admitted to his drink problem,
several Lib Dem MPs were talking about Clegg standing, and it
would be wrong to assume it was only Ashdown's ebullient recommendation that forced Clegg to think seriously about running.
Among the people whose views he sought was his old friend from
Brussels days, Leon Brittan. Brittan says, 'The line I took was: can
you win? If you can win, go for it; if it's a long shot, don't. Politics is
a very chancy business – you could think you're well placed for the
future so you bide your time, but then someone else comes along.
You can never be sure, so I just said, "If you can win, go for it."'

In retrospect, the idea of Clegg standing was never really a starter,
and he seemed to realise it. It also wasn't on his agenda. 'I was a
new MP, I wanted to settle in, get my family moved across from
Brussels to settle here, I was really keen to get my feet under the
table at Westminster and do my constituency work, given that I'd
inherited this wonderful constituency from a very popular outgoing
MP – that was my mental frame. Standing for the party leadership
was literally the last thing I thought of doing.'

So he decided to throw his weight behind the Campbell
campaign. Just after Kennedy gave up the fight, Clegg was lunch-
ing with Campbell and another Lib Dem MP, Jeremy Browne, and
pledged his support for Campbell. He also agreed to help him with
communications, writing many of the articles that would carry
Campbell's name (Paddy Ashdown says Clegg is a seriously under-

estimated writer, and that he should do more writing as his ability to clearly encapsulate complex ideas in words is so good). Clegg also agreed to stand in for Campbell at certain hustings, and become an unofficial spokesperson for him. Ian Wright, the PR activist who ended up in charge of media relations for the Campbell campaign after sussing out Clegg's own leadership ambitions, says, 'Nick was a key player in Ming's campaign. His support for Ming was pretty crucial because Nick was already identified as the star of the next generation so his backing carried some weight.'

With Ming Campbell the clear front-runner, two other candidates said they would also stand. Simon Hughes had been a darling of the Lib Dems' progressive wing since being elected in the very nasty Bermondsey by-election in 1983 that had been dominated by the issue of sexuality (see page 88), and as the losing candidate to Kennedy in the 1999 leadership election, he put his name forward. And Mark Oaten also said he would stand. Oaten had built up a good majority in Winchester after originally winning the supposedly safe Conservative seat by just two votes in 1997, an election that was rerun after his beaten Conservative opponent, Gerry Malone, had claimed there had been election irregularities; Malone's strategy backfired as it made him look a bad loser, which in turn played into Oaten's hands, allowing the Lib Dem to bolster his support and increase his majority.

To the general public, Oaten's candidacy looked reasonably good, and Campbell believes he was Kennedy's preferred candidate. He had been the Lib Dem home affairs spokesman since the general election and had evolved the concept of 'tough liberalism'. It was an attempt to reverse what had come to be seen as the Lib Dems' soft stance on crime in the sense of not being enough on the side of the victim, and he talked about forcing prisoners into the classroom to make them employable when they came out. The policy seemed to be going down well in public but had confirmed Oaten as a figure of the party's right wing, and therefore narrowed his support among fellow Lib Dems.

But Oaten never made it to the starting line. There's a belief that the scandal that engulfed him did for his leadership chances, but it wasn't quite like that. The media had evidence that he had paid for the services of a male prostitute for about a year in 2004–5, but they had never used the story, probably because Oaten wasn't a big enough fish for it to make waves. Oaten announced he would stand for the leadership, but found only one MP (Lembit Öpik) and one MEP (Sarah Ludford) publicly supporting him, so he withdrew. A couple of days later, the *News of the World* published the rent boy story, probably sensing that Oaten would never be as prominent again as he was in that particular week. It is a salutary lesson in how the fortunes of politicians form a betting game for media outlets looking to use their destructive information at the most financially lucrative time; the *NOTW* was clearly waiting to see if Oaten would become party leader before unleashing its story.

So then there were two: Ming Campbell, by now knighted and known as Sir Menzies (pronounced 'Mingus') Campbell, and Simon Hughes. Hughes was still thought of as something of a maverick within the party – the party's social conscience, certainly, but not everyone felt he was a safe pair of hands. Campbell cut a more patrician figure. He had been a former Olympic athlete, the holder of the British 100 metres record from 1967 to 1974, and an accomplished rugby player (the 'Ming' came because his speed meant he played on the wing so became known as 'Ming on the wing') who had just come through treatment for a malignant tumour on his hip that was probably a legacy of his running days. He had done very well for the Lib Dems in representing the party's opposition to British involvement in the Iraq War, but were his best days behind him? He was three months younger than the ever-youthful Paddy Ashdown, but he seemed older, and concern about his health was hard to fully suppress.

Campbell thought he could beat Hughes, but wanted to be the unity candidate of the party. He is a proud man who did not want to stand if he was unlikely to win. To this end, he held a meeting on a Sunday afternoon with all those who had said they would support him. But one person didn't show: Chris Huhne. At first it was reported he had been delayed on a trip back to London, but by the end of the meeting, those present felt Huhne's absence might well indicate that he was considering a challenge of his own. Clegg walked back from that meeting with Kishwer Falkner, by now Baroness Falkner of Margravine, who had been his first port of call at Lib Dem HQ when he decided to join the party. Falkner asked Clegg why he didn't throw his own hat into the ring if, as seemed likely, Huhne would be doing so. Clegg explained that he had given his word to Campbell, and wished to honour that commitment. 'It struck me how honourable and loyal he was,' Falkner says.

Matters came to a head when Campbell invited Huhne in for a discussion about the latter's intentions. Campbell made it clear he wanted a clear run against Hughes, and by the end of the discussion, Huhne had apparently agreed not to stand. The two men shook hands as Huhne left Campbell's office. Campbell says in his autobiography that Huhne had assured him he wouldn't stand; Huhne says he felt at the end of the chat that he 'probably wouldn't', but that he wanted to mull it over with his wife. Three-quarters of an hour later, Huhne was back in Campbell's office to say that his assurance that he wouldn't stand had been part of a group pact agreed at a meeting he didn't attend, and he therefore asked Campbell to release him from his promise. Campbell is not the sort of man who would ever say no to such a request, but when the two men parted for the second time in an hour, it was without shaking hands.

When Clegg heard Huhne was standing for the leadership, he was horrified. He sent Chris Davies a text: 'My worst fear realised, Chris Huhne has just announced he's going for it. I've given Ming a commitment that I'm not going to go for it, and now Chris is.' When news that Huhne would stand became public, the whispering telegram around the party suggested Huhne had broken a gentlemen's agreement with Clegg that neither would stand. Both men deny that such a bilateral agreement ever existed, although the supper club agreement clearly did (even if Huhne missed some of the discussions), and some friends of Clegg's maintain Clegg said at the time that he and Huhne had both agreed in a phone conversation that neither would run. In an interesting twist to this story, Huhne says he had encouraged Clegg to at least think about running, though he can't remember the conversation clearly. Huhne also says he probably wouldn't have stood if Clegg had. But Clegg had promised Campbell he would support him, in return for a promise that Campbell would support Clegg at the end of his time as leader.

Clegg certainly gave his friends the impression that he felt he might have missed the boat by declaring his loyalty to Campbell and therefore feeling morally bound not to enter the contest. He may have secured Campbell's support for the next leadership election, but Clegg's fear was that, by then, Huhne might have been the obvious leader-in-waiting. In retrospect, Huhne's candidacy in early 2006 did give him a head-start in the 2007 election, in the sense that he had a campaign structure ready and waiting to be activated.

So why did Huhne run in 2006? He says there were two reasons. The first was that something about his tête-à-tête with Campbell caused him to wonder whether the 64-year-old really had the energy for the leader's job, a concern he only processed after the meeting. 'One thing you do require as a political leader is energy,' says Huhne, 'particularly for the third party because you have to grab the agenda.' The second was that he felt there had to be a candidate from the ambitious wing of the party. Both stand up to some analysis, but Huhne burned some bridges with Clegg with his decision to stand, and to close observers of the two bright lights in the Lib Dems, relations between them became much more strained during Campbell's leadership, after eight years in which the two ex-MEPs were fairly close politically. At the very least, it pitted the two against each other in a few hustings when Campbell asked Clegg to stand in for him, which meant it was Clegg arguing against Huhne (and Hughes). That in itself prompted some concern within the senior ranks of the party that the election was proving something of a proxy contest; indeed, one senior official even floated the idea of asking Campbell to stand down so the Clegg v. Huhne contest could happen then, rather than a couple of years later.

To the public at large, and indeed to large swathes of the party, Huhne's decision to stand made him look like the leader of the new generation of Lib Dems. He was distinctly younger than Campbell and seemed a lot younger than Hughes, but despite his good showing, it didn't improve his standing in the parliamentary party very much. Although he is immensely popular and claims never to have seen the party leadership as a goal he was aspiring to, he has such a profound streak of self-confidence that he sometimes ploughs too much of his own furrow. It is impossible to say this with any certainty, but the circumstances surrounding Huhne's decision to stand in 2006 may have done some of Clegg's spadework for him in 2007, simply because Clegg seemed so much more of a team player by the time the 2007 leadership election came round. It may also have helped secure Clegg's position in 2011 when the going got tough and Huhne was, for a short while, seen as a possible alternative Lib Dem leader.

In the end, Huhne fought a very good campaign, but could only poll 75 per cent of the votes Campbell polled. Some people think Huhne was undone by being an MP of just seven months' standing, which, if true, would mean Clegg would have struggled too. For the party, the clarity of the result was encouraging, Campbell emerging a clear winner, with Hughes a distant third. By then he had been acting leader for two months, so the transition to full leader seemed fairly seamless. But that two-month period did have one other side-effect nineteen months later. Because Campbell had been both acting leader and a candidate, he was somewhat stretched, and indeed got off to a bad start in his first Prime Minister's Questions, when he asked a question centring on how many caretaker headteachers there were in Britain's schools – he appears to have totally overlooked the fact that he was a caretaker leader himself, which allowed Tony Blair to dismiss him with a fair bit of easy mockery. When Campbell stood down in October 2007, Vince Cable slipped into the role of acting leader, and decided that he couldn't be both caretaker and a candidate. He may well not have been elected, but that realisation about the difficulty of playing both roles played a significant part in his decision not to stand for the Lib Dem leadership.

Campbell's election as leader came in only the tenth month of a new parliament, yet the Prime Minister, Tony Blair, was increasingly embattled over his pre-election statement that he would not remain in office for the full five-year term. With the possibility that he might soon depart, and that his successor might call a snap general election, it was clear that the new Lib Dem leader would not have long to get his feet firmly under the table.

With hindsight, it is clear that the battle to succeed Ming Campbell began the moment he was installed as Lib Dem leader. That may look like unseemly haste on behalf of Nick Clegg and Chris Huhne, the two candidates who eventually fought out the leadership contest at the end of 2007, but there was reason for it.

Those in charge of Lib Dem strategy figured that Tony Blair would resign in the summer of 2007, a date Blair himself announced in mid-2006, and that he would probably be succeeded by Gordon Brown, but that whoever succeeded him would see the honeymoon period as the only chance Labour would have of winning the next general election. There would therefore be an election in the autumn of 2007, and unless Campbell led the Lib Dems into a coalition government with Labour or the Conservatives, he would resign as leader shortly afterwards. Subsequent events show that reading of the runes to have been remarkably accurate, certainly more accurate than Brown's strategists proved to be.

There's a weekly tabloid newspaper that goes to many Liberal Democrat members, called *Lib Dem News*. It has eight pages, and page six is the gazette page, listing vacancies for candidates, election results and constituency engagements. A trawl through the page sixes in the period of Campbell's leadership reveals both Clegg and Huhne regularly speaking at dinners. They were on the campaign trail, though decorum prevented them from describing it quite

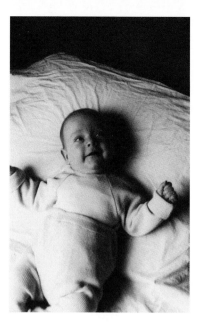

LEFT: Despite being the third-born in his family, Clegg was born to Nick Sr and Hermance in Buckinghamshire after the family returned to Britain after spells in the Netherlands and Belgium.

BELOW: Clegg (second from left) was a member of the Westminster School tennis team, known as a net rusher. His teammate Chris Torchia (third from right) remains friends with him to this day.

ABOVE: The Clegg clan pictured in 1990 at their grandparents' house east of Amsterdam. From left: Nick Jr, Nick Sr, Louise (maternal grandmother), Elisabeth, Hermance, Alexander and Paul.

LEFT: Paddy Ashdown, pictured here with Clegg at the 1998 Lib Dem conference, has played almost a godfatherly role to his successor-but-two since the moment Leon Brittan told him Clegg was 'the brightest young man I've ever come across'.

LEFT: The adoption meeting for the European elections of 1999 galvanised the East Midlands Liberal Democrats into action, thanks to Clegg's ability to bring in big names such as Shirley Williams and Paddy Ashdown.

BELOW: An unknown street artist drew the first cartoon of Nick Clegg as part of this recording of the East Midlands adoption meeting. The 'mystery chair' from the poster was the then Lib Dem president, Diana Maddock.

ABOVE: The first twenty-nine months of Clegg's leadership of the Lib Dems was characterised by his having to accept Vince Cable's very high profile and immense public respect following his warnings about the impending economic downturn that struck in 2007–8, but the two got on well.

BELOW: A major fillip to Clegg and his party came from the support they received from the former Democrat US presidential candidate Howard Dean in 2009.

ABOVE: Perhaps a little too keen to escape from the economic shadow of Vince Cable, Clegg boldly denounced the Tories' 20 per cent 'VAT bombshell' early in the 2010 general election campaign, but the Lib Dems conceded the 20 per cent rate as part of the coalition agreement.

BELOW: The Clegg team preparing for Britain's first-ever televised leaders' election debate. To Clegg's immediate left is the former Sky News anchorman Scott Chisholm, to Chisholm's left is Neil Sherlock, and to his left Polly Mackenzie. Two to Vince Cable's right is Lena Pietsch, Clegg's press officer.

Clegg appears to be at his best when relating face to face with groups of people, and has therefore developed a series of 'town hall meetings'. Above right, he signals to a questioner at a public meeting in Liverpool; top of this page, addressing a meeting of party members in Cornwall.

LEFT: An MP's and party leader's life involves trips to all sorts of different places, including a food factory in Camborne, Cornwall.

RIGHT: Children are central to Clegg's political thinking and, as the father of three under-tens, he relates easily to youngsters, like these two girls at a school in Cardiff.

Clegg's performance in the first TV debate on 15 April 2010 unleashed massive support for him and the Lib Dems, dubbed 'Cleggmania', but they were unable to turn it into an increase in parliamentary seats.

The bedrock of Clegg's affability and ability to get through masses of work is his marriage to Miriam González Durántez, pictured here in his Sheffield Hallam constituency.

so crassly. Clegg did a lot of writing at this point, mostly under Campbell's name, but some under his own.

Campbell's initial appointments were very shrewd. He gave Huhne the environment brief, knowing how much 'green' issues mattered to his defeated opponent, and he promoted Clegg to home affairs. The home affairs brief can be a poisoned chalice. Some get bogged down in its widespread issues and become invisible, as if blending in with the civil servants whose job it is to remain largely faceless, while others make something of it. The best example of someone who made it work for him was Blair, whose pithy 'tough on crime, tough on the causes of crime' slogan was coined in his time as Labour's shadow Home Secretary and was arguably the single most powerful factor in establishing him as a plausible prime minister.

Clegg never made the impact that Blair did, but he did go at the job with great excitement, and impressed those willing to listen to him. He had sought a meeting with the Metropolitan Police Commissioner, Ian Blair (no relation to Tony), during which he asked whether Britain's top policeman felt Britain was a police state. No, came the answer, it wasn't, but it would be if the police used all the powers available to it. Both the question and the answer provided powerful material with which Clegg was able to push the civil liberties agenda, in particular in fighting the Labour government's plans for personal identity cards.

He had taken over home affairs from Mark Oaten, and in many ways, Clegg continued Oaten's attempt to show that Lib Dems were on the side of the victim, but he marketed the policy differently, both to the public and to the party. 'He showed his ability to quickly analyse a difficult portfolio,' says Oaten. 'He quickly grasped where the party needed to be on ID cards, holding terror suspects, control orders, the whole liberal freedom agenda. Whereas I was quite happy to risk incurring the party's wrath in terms of what I described as "tough liberalism", he was politically astute enough to not confront the party on some of those things. He understood exactly what I was trying to say, he recognised that he had to ditch language and change the party quickly, and he rebranded some of the party's thinking in that area without fundamentally disagreeing with what we were doing on prison reform and other things.'

In many ways, the job of Liberal Democrat home affairs spokesperson was a massive challenge to Clegg's ability to explain complex concepts in simple terms. He knew that the average voter was somewhat illiberal in terms of wanting criminals locked up for life, but he also knew they wanted less crime, so he set out to explain that you get less crime when you don't lock people up for longer, even if that came across as counter-intuitive. He was effectively trying to explain that a more liberal policy in terms of rehabilitation of offenders and restorative justice would make people safer, however much it might seem like being soft on criminals.

His stance certainly did him no harm, and he became a go-to politician whenever the media wanted someone to counter the 'hang 'em and flog 'em' and 'send 'em home' lobbies. One such instance happened in early 2007. A story broke in February involving a build-up of potential immigrants at Sangatte, near the French entrance to the Channel Tunnel. The French government announced it was building a second refugee centre for those seeking entry to Britain who did not have the appropriate permission; although the centre was not going to include sleeping facilities, the British press whipped itself into a frenzy. It even coined the name 'Sangatte 2', and portrayed the camp as bursting with people wanting to enter Britain who the British authorities were struggling desperately to deny entry to. In an interview on BBC News 24, Clegg came as close as he has ever come to being genuinely angry. 'It is a soup kitchen,' he said, 'so what do you want to do? Start denying people soup?'

Within the party, he contributed a chapter on terrorism to a book, *Reinventing the State: Social Liberalism in the 21st Century*. It was compiled by three leading Lib Dem figures, Duncan Brack, Richard Grayson and David Howarth, and was intended as a response to *The Orange Book*, but some of the *Orange Book* authors were invited to write chapters, so it wouldn't be seen as a challenge to the party leadership. The title of the book is interesting, in that it hints at the ongoing debate within the party about how much the state should be expected to play a role in bringing Lib Dem ideas to fruition. It's also interesting that the chapter Clegg opted to write was not a topic on which there would be a split between the social liberals and economic liberals, so it was fairly safe.

Perhaps Clegg's biggest job at this time was in keeping his own leadership ambitions under wraps while Ming Campbell struggled to make an impression. Campbell's nineteen-month stint as Lib Dem leader is generally dismissed as an aberration, almost as if the party picked the wrong man and gradually realised its mistake. History can be a little kinder to the Scotsman, who despite his patrician exterior is someone who has fought his way up from an upbringing in modest Glasgow surroundings to become a highly respected figure of his era. He gained a command of party policy in a way that Charles Kennedy had not, and he also restarted a long-overdue process in the Liberal Democrats of professionalising the leader's office and its interface with the party, a process that had begun in the early days under Paddy Ashdown but had rather broken down under Kennedy. Part of that professionalisation process involved putting proper recruitment procedures in place for taking on staff, rather than hiring someone known to the leader or one of the leader's senior lieutenants. Yet the time involved in putting such processes into place, and then following the new procedures before making appointments, meant Campbell's office was frequently understaffed in the early months, a factor which contributed to the poor public perception of his leadership.

Campbell was also a very cautious man, as was his principal political ally, Archy Kirkwood, which meant many in the party felt not a lot was happening. Campbell's followers boasted that meetings ran to time, which was a welcome relief after the somewhat haphazard timekeeping of the Kennedy era, but not a lot came out of them. And Campbell was not always the fastest off the mark in responding to events.

Perhaps the most damning example of this came in the summer of 2007. The new Prime Minister, Gordon Brown, promising 'a government of all the talents', offered a handful of positions in his government to Liberal Democrats, among them Ashdown and Shirley Williams. Brown contacted Campbell on a Monday, to make the offers. Campbell said he would think about it and come back. But he was torn, and the matter dragged into the next day. On the Tuesday evening, Campbell's phone rang – it was *The Guardian*'s political correspondent Michael White asking if there was any truth in the story that Lib Dems had been offered posts in the government. Kirkwood responded that the Lib Dem leader 'did not comment on tittle-tattle', an unfortunate phrase to use in relation to an offer of government posts. The paper ran the story on the Wednesday, by which time Ashdown had turned down the offer of Northern Ireland Secretary (Williams and Julia Neuberger accepted low-key roles as government advisers). The story, which named Clegg as a possible minister, ran only in later editions of *The Guardian*, which meant Clegg hadn't seen it when he appeared at an event at ten o'clock that morning. When asked whether he was about to take up a position in Brown's government, he was quite honestly able to say that he hadn't a clue what the questioner was talking about.

The interesting feature of this episode is that Ashdown had said for years that he would never join a government led by another party unless there was a policy platform. He was aware that he could easily be used to glorify a set of policies he was unhappy with, and rumour had it that during his time as leader he always travelled with 'heads of agreement' in his briefcase, a list of minimum Lib Dem demands in the event of some form of cooperation in government. Without an offer on policy, it was hard to see why Campbell should not have turned Brown down instantly, as Ashdown did. This incident helped sow the seeds of doubt in many leading Lib Dems' minds that Campbell might not be the man for the leader's job.

Ultimately, Campbell was probably undone, not so much by

indecision, as by the timing with which he became leader, as he came across as old. Some had urged him to stand against Kennedy in 1999, and despite his cancer he would probably have won in 2003 if Kennedy had stood down then. His biggest contribution to the party was perhaps in giving the next generation of leadership a little extra time to get used to Westminster life. He also unwittingly created the conditions for Vince Cable to flourish as the Lib Dems' popular hero, as Cable is unlikely to have had the public profile for his wisdom about dealing with an unfolding economic crisis had he not been stand-in leader for the two months after Campbell resigned. Cable's comment about Gordon Brown, that he 'had moved from Stalin to Mr Bean', really hit home, and helped make him something of an anti-political hero from among the political classes.

Although he was making a good fist of the home affairs job, Clegg was shining almost more brightly beyond British shores. Many Europeans from his MEP days had recognised that he was a rising star in British politics, and therefore invited him to speak at events. In fact he turned up at the September 2007 Lib Dem confer-ence in Brighton somewhat short of sleep after attending various events on the mainland of Europe, among them a convention staged by François Bayrou, the founder of the European Democratic Party which was set up to counter the growing influence of Eurosceptic parties throughout Europe.

Mark Oaten recalls having tea with Clegg in the early stages of Campbell's leadership, saying he needed to make his mind up on his long-term plans, specifically whether he was going to run for leader or not. 'He was aware he needed to make some decisions and he had to speak out about where he thought the party was going,' says Oaten. 'He clearly sensed he was more than just the home affairs spokesman, he was one of the people who could decide on the future direction of the party, and he was giving a lot of thought to that. He was ambitious for the party.'

And yet it was not an ambition accompanied by great scheming – in fact in some ways there was a remarkable absence of street savvy-ness about him. He had hopelessly few photos for campaigning purposes, and his assistant, Tim Snowball, frequently ended up asking people if they could email him a photo of an event Clegg had attended. And it wasn't until the summer of 2007 that he had his first suit made for him. Up to then he bought them off the peg, one of his favourite places being the mainstream Spanish department store El Corte Ingles ('the English court'). His close political colleague Norman Lamb says, 'Nick and I used to joke that I bought my suits off the peg at Marks for £150 or whatever, but he would top that by saying he got his from a Spanish supermarket for €130 – he may have immense self-confidence, but he's not self-obsessed.'

Clegg met regularly with leading Lib Dems, sometimes just socially but always keeping tabs on the current thinking. On one occasion he was eating with David Laws, Ed Davey and Norman Lamb in a restaurant in Marsham Street, just behind his old school, when discussion was interrupted by the appearance of a large cockroach on Laws's plate. After the waiter had removed it, the four were given a free meal.

There was one striking event he took part in, which enhanced his leadership credentials, albeit with a different group of people. In 2006, he was asked to take part in the Westminster Challenge, a six-day trip planned for February 2007 in which five MPs and a handful of journalists would travel to the Arctic Circle and live in vicious weather with only a light wooden sledge and four huskies. The event was the brainchild of Richard Stephenson, a Conservative who went on to run Royal Mail's communications, and it gained a lot of media coverage, which in turn raised considerable sums for the charities Crimestoppers, The Children's Society and Cancer Research UK. The five MPs were Tobias Ellwood and Ed Vaizey (both Conservative), Emily Thornberry (Labour), and Jenny Willott and Nick Clegg (both Liberal Democrat), and at times they were in temperatures of minus 30 Celsius. Willott said the clothing involved 'two layers of thermals, a fleece layer, all-in-one Arctic suit, a huge jacket on top, plus massive mitts, balaclava, snood and furry hat.'

'I absolutely loved it,' says Clegg. 'What I learned is that I feel completely at peace in a place that's stunningly beautiful and miles away from anywhere. I had this unbelievable sense of space, literally placing footprints in the undisturbed snow. It's a thrilling and very peaceful feeling, disturbed only by Ed Vaizey saying something – he says so much. He's a very nice guy, very funny, but I often don't know what he's saying from one moment to the next.'

Much of the talk after the event was about the relationship that Clegg and Vaizey had struck up on the Swedish–Finnish border. They clearly got on very well, so well that the political commentator Iain Dale wrote in his blog on 21 February 2007, 'I'm told that the two MPs became quite close during the trip – perhaps a sign of easing relations paving the way for a possible coalition after the next election?' (Dale then wrecks his chances of being hailed as a prophet by adding 'Probably not'.) Vaizey, now a minister of state, says, 'Nick was always in a good mood. He showed a natural leadership air, very naturally charismatic.' Vaizey told the political commentator Steve Richards on GMTV's *Sunday Programme* that he kept falling off the sledge while Clegg tended to stay on it. In conversation it emerged that Clegg had been a ski instructor in his gap year, though Clegg appears to have kept the lid on his ghastly skiing accident.

Another thing that unites Clegg and Vaizey is that they're both among the best-looking MPs, and both know it. Towards the end of their trip that took them from northern Sweden into Finland, they suddenly came back into mobile phone range and all their PDAs started ringing and beeping. And one of the messages Clegg and Vaizey received was the result of the Sky News Valentine's Day 'Most Fanciable MP' award. Vaizey had come a very creditable ninth, but had been totally eclipsed by Clegg who finished third overall (behind Caroline Flint and the winner, Julie Kirkbride), thus making him the most fanciable male MP. This became the talking point of their last Nordic evening, though both men have since made the top 10 in subsequent years, Vaizey sometimes finishing above Clegg in BSkyB's somewhat less than scientific poll.

Throughout the summer of 2007, the Lib Dems languished in the opinion polls. Gordon Brown was still basking in the novelty

value of being a new prime minister, and his move to preside over
'a government of all the talents' was going down well. With Brown's
popularity high, the Lib Dems were being squeezed.

As a break from this, Ming Campbell visited the Edinburgh
Festival. One of the things he went to see was the première of a
film called *Hallam Foe*. It was to prove a symbolic title for him, as
at that very time, the dilemma for the MP for Sheffield Hallam was
how loud to speak out, and how not to become the leader's foe.

One of Clegg's appealing features is his ability to engage with
the person talking to him, but when that person happens to be a
media figure trying to beef up a story they are working on, then
engaging becomes a more precarious business. 'He hates faking it,'
says his then policy officer, Polly Mackenzie, 'and he's terrible at
faking. When we have something we have to get him to say but we
don't have time to explain it, he's totally unconvincing if he's not
convinced. He has to be persuaded – then he'll be great because
he'll develop his own way of explaining it.'

Clegg's inability to fake came to a head at the Lib Dems' 2007
conference in Brighton. Having agreed to speak at a fringe meeting,
all his advisers warned him that Andrew Rawnsley of *The Observer*
would ask him whether he harboured ambitions to be leader of the
party. Mackenzie recalls, 'We said to him, "It doesn't matter what
you say, if you say anything about some time in the future, it'll be
news." So he tried line after line after line, and kept saying "But
it sounds so disingenuous", and he hates being disingenuous, he
hates sounding slippery. So when Rawnsley asked the question, all
the things he'd practised just disappeared.'

Clegg's reply was, 'If you're asking me "Would I stand against
Ming?" the answer is no. If you're asking me "Would I throw my
hat in the ring if there was a vacancy in the future?" I probably
would – but my crystal ball is no clearer than yours.' The answer
was entirely reasonable, as Campbell himself has admitted, and he
said something that everyone knew at the time. But the media were
trying to stir up a leadership crisis, and the fact that Clegg had
engaged in talk about the leadership – even if only in terms of

a future leadership election that everyone knew would take place sometime – had fuelled the media's fire. The irony is that the public always says it wants real politicians rather than media cut-outs, so criticism of him needs to be tempered; indeed, some applauded his genuineness. Huhne's response was much more media-savvy: he said, 'There is no vacancy and it would be premature to even talk about the position of there being a vacancy.' That's what the manuals on dealing with the media tell you to say.

A couple of days later, Clegg was out for a stroll along Brighton sea front, when he bumped into Campbell and his formidable wife Elspeth. 'I don't know if you're being helpful or not,' she said to Clegg. 'I'm trying to be,' he replied. The problem with party conferences is that there are masses of television crews, many of them roving, so the chances of a camera being close by are pretty high. And indeed there was a camera that caught this exchange. Campbell noticed it, and interjected quickly, 'He's being very helpful.' It was a good way of calming the waters, but Elspeth's parting shot to Clegg was 'It's so tough'. Needless to say, the footage was aired extensively for the next few hours.

Irrespective of whether Clegg should have been tighter on his media technique, just being himself was in some ways undermining Campbell. Celia Thomas, who was head of the Lib Dem whips' office in the House of Lords for many years, says, 'He can't help being charismatic in fringe meetings. Even when trying not to attract attention to himself, which was the case when Ming Campbell was leader, he can't help it. He couldn't help it, not just because he connected with people; he was asking interesting questions, asking "What if" things, and that was very exciting.'

'The election that never was' is a journalistic term that is probably overused. But the British general election of autumn 2007 really was an event that everyone was prepared for but at the last minute didn't happen. The former Labour general secretary Peter Watt has written about the preparations Labour had made, including spending £1 million on direct mailshots – in the end, the letters were withdrawn from their mailbags and pulped.

The Liberal Democrats also had their manifesto ready. All it was missing was the cover photograph, and the presses would have rolled. That was how close Britain was to going to the polls in 2007. But Gordon Brown pulled out, perhaps unnerved by George Osborne's gamble of pledging to raise the inheritance tax threshold to £1 million per person, and decided to take a chance on at least three years of a term as Prime Minister. And with it, he killed off the chances of his friend Ming Campbell ever leading his party into a general election.

It took a couple of weeks for the message to filter through. In fact on the Saturday before Campbell resigned, he had given a speech to a Lib Dem conference in Suffolk which he felt had gone well, and which many in his party felt was a signal that his fortunes were on the up. But he was pilloried in the press, and on the Monday – 15 October – he gave up the fight. Earlier that day, Clegg had been talking liberally – albeit in private – about 'the forthcoming leadership election', yet even he was taken by surprise. One of his friends received a text from him at about 4 p.m., which read, 'Oh fuck, Ming's just resigned.' Even with all the writing on the wall, Campbell's resignation still seemed to come more quickly than many had expected. Some people who were very close to the Scotsman believed he engineered the timing of his resignation to maximise Clegg's chances of succeeding him, though he never said this in his autobiography. Then again, he never told anyone except his wife that he was resigning, largely because he had made up his mind to go, and knew his close associates would try and persuade him to stay on.

Unlike the chaos when Kennedy stepped down, the party was ready this time. At 6.10 p.m. a press conference was called for 6.30 on 'the leadership of the party', and by that time Vince Cable was acting leader, with a timetable set out for an election campaign which was expected to feature just two candidates: Nick Clegg and Chris Huhne.

Chapter 10

'ONE PLUS ONE EQUALS MORE THAN TWO'

WHAT DID the Liberal Democrats have in 2007 that Labour didn't? They both got new leaders, but the difference was that the Lib Dems actually had an election. While Gordon Brown found no-one willing to stand against him and thus became Labour leader – and Prime Minister – via a 'coronation', the Lib Dems had a contest. And it was a genuine contest that came down to the wire and was decided by a margin of 1 per cent of the votes cast.

Yet how different were the two candidates? That was the question exercising the minds of party members, who had to vote by the middle of December 2007 on who should succeed Ming Campbell. Despite the fact that Chris Huhne was twelve years older than Nick Clegg – fifty-three to Clegg's almost forty-one – both were young enough to offer a more go-getting style of leadership, candidates who, in Charles Kennedy's words, 'just had more of a sense of zing about them, fairly or unfairly'. The party, indeed British politics, was guaranteed its first leader to have been an MEP, they were both passionately pro-European, and they were still reasonably close personally. But there were differences in both personality and politics.

Of the two, Huhne seems to have the more laid-back manner in a suave sense, yet Clegg comes across as more personable. They have contrasting voices, and voices can be important in media terms – while Huhne has a deep lyrical voice, Clegg can sound a little like a shrill schoolboy who's getting a sore throat; yet Huhne's baritone can sound slightly nerdy at times, while Clegg's higher-pitched voice has surprising depth to it (perhaps mildly tar assisted).

Both men have great self-belief. As one leading member of the Lib Dems, who asked not to be named, put it, 'Chris and Nick are absolutely convinced they're right all the time, but they have different ways of handling people who disagree with them. Nick generally likes to debate, though he gets tetchy from time to time, while Chris is too intellectually arrogant to think that he's wrong, so it doesn't worry him – he'll happily argue the case but remain convinced the other person is wrong.'

Chat to Lib Dems in a bar, and they're convinced they would always choose a leader on substance over style. Yet given how Ming Campbell had bombed because too few people could relate to him through the media, factors of appearance played a very important role. At the time of the leadership election, it was by no means clear that there would be televised debates at the next general election, yet the Lib Dem members knew they needed to have a media-friendly leader. That perhaps explains why Clegg started the campaign as a clear though by no means overwhelming favourite.

Mark Oaten, who by then had decided not to defend his Winchester seat at the next general election, campaigned for Clegg largely because of the figure he cut. 'It was a no-brainer as far as I was concerned, because I didn't feel Chris could have done what Nick did in those television debates. It was a question of reaching out more, and Nick could reach out more than Chris could. I felt he would be a star in the election campaign. As it turns out Chris is very popular in the country, but it was definitely the right choice. Having worked closely with Charles in two general election campaigns, I knew how absolutely critical the leader's charisma was to this party at elections.'

Clegg started as a slight favourite, but Huhne had a massive administrative advantage – he had the same team in place from his leadership campaign in early 2006, a team that included the best campaigning strategists in the party (at least among those who didn't have to stay neutral), and he had a lot of supporters on a database. In a party election, that is a significant head-start. But Huhne knew he had to do something to make use of his advantage, and he seized his chance. Having originally joined the Labour Party and then defected when the SDP was founded in 1981, he decided to play up his centre-left and environmental credentials. 'Candidates in leadership elections try to gravitate to the position they think will gain them the maximum support,' says Huhne, 'so I made a lot of the fact that there was quite difference between our agendas on public service reform. And although I share with Nick his enthusiasm for Europe and civil liberties, what gets me out of bed in the morning is the green agenda, which Nick wouldn't claim. So if you were a party member concerned about the green agenda, you'd gravitate towards me rather than Nick; and if you were more concerned about the social-liberal element of public service reform and equalities, you'd gravitate more towards me than Nick. To that extent I was the centre-left candidate, but I'd like to think I was economically hard headed.'

It didn't persuade everyone on the left of the party. Simon Hughes says, 'Chris moved to the left of Nick during the campaign, and picked up the activists and left-wingers, but with some exceptions, like me. Nick doesn't come from the liberal tradition, he doesn't come from a politically Liberal family, but he was clearly traditionally liberal on all the civil liberties things. He was more of a pro-competition and economic liberal in the free market, which is explicable partly by the Brussels culture and partly by his Dutch parentage. Liberals on the mainland of Europe are generally to the right of Liberals here. Oversimplistically, Nick was to the right of me by quite a long way, but not in any way that worried me that he was off the Liberal Democrat linear radar. I could still count him as a kindred spirit because of his very positive internationalism and commitment to civil liberty and individual freedom.'

Another MP from the left wing of the party proved an enthusiastic supporter of Clegg. 'There's a kind of person who makes a leader,' says Norman Baker, 'and it's a very rarefied group, because there are plenty of people who are very good parliamentarians but couldn't be leaders. Take the Tories – there was a succession of leaders before Cameron came along who clearly weren't up to the mark, although they had their own qualities. And it's the same with Labour, who are finding that out now with Ed Miliband, and they'll go through

several incarnations before they find the right leader. There's something about a leader – he or she either cuts it or doesn't cut it. It was
clear to me that Nick was going to cut it, he'd be able to make that
extra step up that others couldn't make. While Chris Huhne would
have hit the ground running more quickly and would have made
the party feel better, at least initially, and would probably have had a
better scorecard six months on, I felt that, two years on, Nick would
have a better scorecard than Chris and be a better leader. Especially
following Ming, who was out of his time, Nick was a leader of the
future rather than the past. He had a very refreshing way of being
prepared to look at issues from a new lateral perspective, and say "Is
this the right policy?", which I felt was right.'

While good natured – if a little dull – in the first couple of
weeks, the campaign got nasty on national television, when the
two men were interviewed on the BBC's *Politics Show*. Prior to
the programme, the BBC had been sent a briefing document from
Huhne's office entitled 'Calamity Clegg', which featured a list of
quotations implying that Clegg had changed his position on various issues. Facing Clegg on the programme, Huhne apologised for
the document and dissociated himself from it. His office later said
the title had come from 'an overzealous young researcher' and it
should never have gone out until approved by Huhne himself. The
title may have been written by an overzealous young researcher, but
the contents are widely believed to have been written by Huhne's
media adviser Carina Trimingham, a woman who is now his partner following the break-up of his marriage to the economist Vicky
Pryce in 2010.

Despite his apology, Huhne stuck by the thrust of the dossier's
contents, insisting Clegg had 'flip-flopped' on various policy issues,
notably nuclear weapons, schools and the NHS. 'I don't support
describing anyone else in the party as a calamity,' Huhne said, 'but
I do think we've seen a series of flip-flops from Nick,' and went on
to accuse him of 'attempting to face both ways'.

Clegg replied, 'I have said to you until I'm blue in the face that
my position is very clear on all the issues. What you're seeking to

do is believe the worst that is said about me. As a colleague, I will do you the respect of listening to what you've said.' It was an ill-tempered discussion, with both men interrupting each other, and the moderator, Jon Sopel, left with the role largely of lighting the blue touchpaper and retiring to a safe distance.

In terms of political experience, Huhne was considerably ahead of Clegg, and it was starting to show in their tactics. While Huhne had been fighting elections for the SDP in the early 1980s, Clegg was still making the transition from a political world where throwing around unformed ideas for debate and discussion was a central feature to one in which every utterance was likely to be recorded and scrutinised, and could be used in evidence against him. And Clegg had left enough material in his wake for Huhne to work with. One example was a pamphlet Clegg had written not long after becoming an MP, in which he aired ideas about how to improve provision of medical care; in it he had talked about 'breaking up the NHS'. Among those who had confronted Clegg about his pamphlet was the then MP Evan Harris, himself a medical doctor. 'He said he meant it more in the sense of organising the NHS more regionally,' Harris says, 'but more importantly, it seemed not to have occurred to him that using words such as "breaking up the NHS" could be construed as an attack on the nation's venerated health service. I didn't quite know what to make of that.' Harris ended up voting for Huhne in the leadership election.

Clegg's irritability may well have been down to the fact that his lead over Huhne was narrowing. As the campaign progressed, Huhne seemed to be gaining ground, and many people close to Clegg were distinctly worried. Huhne's experience of having fought a leadership election in early 2006 was becoming a major advantage. But there was another factor, one that goes to the heart of a Lib Dem dilemma. As a party that prides itself on free thinking and an absence of interest-based tribalism, the Lib Dems would like to think all issues are resolved by means of respectful, reasoned debate. Many are, but one of the reasons the Lib Dems have become a more powerful force than the old Liberal Party is that they have embraced many of the techniques of modern political warfare. Huhne in his campaign did just this – some of the techniques he adopted were non-malicious, like building up databases and sending out direct mail, but some, like the 'Calamity Clegg' dossier, had an edge to them, and senior figures in the party had to urge Huhne to apologise for overstepping the mark.

'Chris crossed a line at that point,' says Clegg's campaign manager, Richard Allan, of the dossier, 'but that was almost symbolic of the whole campaign; Chris was fighting it like a Lib Dem will fight a by-election, while Nick was quite hesitant. Chris had more of a killer instinct than Nick: Chris was gloves off, Nick was gloves on. If you knew Nick, you knew he was great, but if you didn't know him, he just wasn't coming across, and not a lot of people did know him.'

Allan's comments are part of a general admission that Clegg's campaign was strangely disorganised. To some, that is an understatement – one Clegg insider described his leadership campaign as 'absolutely rubbish'.

The policy platform of modernising the party but emphasising its liberalism was an appealing package that was consistent with Clegg's own outlook. Among its specific features were the importance of flexible working and family-oriented policies, reforming public services, and having an open economy. But in the words of one activist, 'there were too many chiefs and not enough Indians'. Ed Davey and Danny Alexander were supposedly in overall charge, but Anders Hansen fronted the Sheffield end of the operation, while Richard Allan ran the campaign in London. There were lots of press officers, but very few people to stuff envelopes and get the message out. 'Lots of people volunteered but there wasn't a strong ability to coordinate them,' adds Allan. 'The people we really needed, the classic Lib Dem by-election organisers, we didn't get, so the bit that was missing left us with the wrong mix. Chris was better at attracting some of those folks, so things like stuffing envelopes just didn't get done.'

The back-room Lib Dem activist Ian Wright says the campaign

was not only disorganised, it was misguided in its basic assumptions. 'It started from the incorrect premise that we could assume that all those who had voted for Ming would transfer straight across to Nick,' he says, 'and then you'd add on a number of people based on Nick's pizzazz or star quality. That simply wasn't the case. Ming may have endorsed Nick, but he had been chairman of the party in Scotland in the 1980s, so he was bound to have a personal connection with lots of people who would vote for him but who wouldn't necessarily vote for Nick.'

'I thought this was Nick's worst campaign,' says Paddy Ashdown. 'I didn't think he did all those things we now know him for – making choices, staking out a clear agenda, being prepared to argue that, and I have to say that those of us who admired him very much and saw him as potentially a considerable leader of the party were very depressed and even had our confidence shaken by the fact that he did not do what we expected him to do. Chris ran the better campaign, there's no question about that. Nick ran a bad campaign.'

There were also some strange moments. At one stage, Miriam phoned the Clegg campaign office, asking what she could do. Everyone, even people who had worked with Clegg since 2005, froze slightly, wondering how they should handle this person they were slightly scared of. In the end, Ed Fordham, who had been at Nick and Miriam's wedding, went off to have coffee with her. 'I think we all needed to calm down because she's phenomenally normal,' he said. 'There's this assumption that she's amazing, which is true, but slightly scary, which is also true, but because of the scariness, people don't see how normal she is.' In the end, she turned up to selected leadership functions.

Not everyone is quite so hard on the Clegg campaign. One of his confidants, Neil Sherlock, says it was much better for uniting the party after the election. 'If Nick had put out "Hopeless Huhne" material to counter "Calamity Clegg", it would have been much harder for him and Chris to work together after the election. Nick realised that Chris needed to be in the leading group of Lib Dem figures after the leadership election, which is why he was less antagonistic.'

With two weeks to go, Huhne was thought to be running neck and neck with Clegg, but then the Clegg campaign received a boost in the form of some organisational help it badly needed. Willie Rennie, the Scottish MP who had won the by-election in Dunfermline & West Fife, the seat next door to Gordon Brown's, was brought in. He had been an organiser for the party, and he provided some discipline and direction in the last two weeks. It all helped to just about take Clegg over the line.

Ultimately, the fates were with him. He scraped home by 20,988 votes to 20,477, or 50.6 per cent to 49.4 per cent. How much a Royal Mail strike in the last week of voting affected the result will never be known. It held up 1,300 votes, but with Clegg winning by 511, Huhne would have had to take 70 per cent of those missing votes to win, an unlikely percentage in such a close race, though with Huhne finishing fast, one can never be sure. A decision had to be taken as to whether the closing date for votes of 14 December should be moved; the rules of the Electoral Reform Society, which ran the election, made it clear that the closing date should stand, the party abided by those rules, and on 17 December 2007, Clegg was declared the winner.

From the moment Clegg became leader, the atmosphere in the party leader's office changed. 'He had a whole list of things he wanted done,' says a senior aide, 'he was absolutely clear what he wanted to achieve – he was ambitious for the party, and wanted us to move from being peripheral to being a mainstream party of government. He increased the leader's office staff, bringing in a bunch of very bright, clever, dynamic, driven people, and engendered a "busy-busy" culture. It created a really positive office, a really great atmosphere.'

Another feature of the new leader's office was that the number of women in senior positions increased. Despite a commitment to gender equality, the Liberal Democrats have never managed to get that many elected to Parliament (probably because liberals are as averse to discrimination as they are to inequality, and without positive discrimination it's hard to get as many women as men into winnable seats), but Clegg's office has always had a number of women high up. The most senior figure was Alison Suttie, who was one of the first Lib Dem officials to have met Clegg before he was even a candidate. Polly Mackenzie had become a trusted policy adviser and speech writer, while towards the end of his first year as leader, Clegg took on Lena Pietsch as his media spokeswoman, a role that requires her to accompany him to most of his engagements. When *The Guardian* ran a feature at the start of the 2010 election campaign, highlighting ten key people in each of the three major parties, the Lib Dems had four women, while Labour and the Conservatives had just one apiece.

Going from Lib Dem home affairs spokesperson to party leader was arguably the biggest step up for Clegg logistically. 'I don't think I fully appreciated until I'd become leader quite what demands are made of you,' he said in an interview with *The Telegraph* magazine. From working with a couple of policy researchers and a constituency organiser, he suddenly became a man whose every move (well, nearly) was managed, so that he could manage the party. 'The demands are not just as a manager, but also the extraordinary amount of flak you get. There isn't a relationship between the Lib Dem Party and established parts of the press, for instance, which creates a protective barrier that other parties and leaders enjoy. I needed to toughen up pretty damn quickly to create space and not just get buffeted around.'

When a new man (or woman) takes over at the helm of a political party, a lot of attention is normally focused on him (or her). Everyone wants to interview the new leader, and it provides oxygen for some publicity. Whether it's good or bad publicity depends on how the subject deals with the questions, many of which might be unexpected.

The morning after he was elected, Clegg was invited onto BBC Radio 5 Live's *Breakfast* programme, and the presenters had a series of quick-fire questions to which they wanted one-word answers. It's a trap many a politician has fallen into – with the public clamouring for 'straight answers' there is a strong desire to give them, but it means bowing to the interviewer's agenda, which can sometimes drive the politician into a corner. And so it was when Clegg was asked for a 'yes or no' answer on whether he believed in God. Choosing to give a one-word answer, he said 'No'. That led to various headlines about him being an atheist, which he says were totally unfair. 'I thought for a few seconds and concluded, "Well, I don't know whether God exists, so I can't say yes, so the only logical answer is no,"' he told Simon Barrow in an interview for the Ekklesia website in March 2008. 'But I'm not some rabid atheist by any stretch of the imagination, more of an agnostic. If anything, I feel almost inadequate that I don't have a faith.' And to Shelagh Fogarty, who interviewed him for *Total Politics* magazine, he said, 'I thought that, as I didn't know whether God exists, it would be totally dishonest of me to say yes. It wasn't meant to offend anybody, I just think politics and religion are completely separate.'

A few weeks later, something of greater gravity happened when he was interviewed by Piers Morgan for an article in *GQ* magazine. The two men clearly established some easy banter, which Morgan used to get very personal. He asked Clegg whether he was 'good in bed'. Clegg responded, 'I don't think I'm particularly brilliant or particularly bad. Since the only judge of that is my wife...' Morgan sensed he was close to some juicy information, and suggested there had been other women in Clegg's life. 'Yes, OK,' Clegg replied, 'but not for a very long time.' Morgan then tried to ask how many, which Clegg tried to dismiss with 'Not a list as long as yours, I'm sure'. The rest of the interview, as printed in *GQ*, has Morgan asking: 'How many are we talking: ten, twenty, thirty?' and Clegg replying 'No more than thirty, it's a lot less than that.' But Clegg disputes the final bit – he says he was continuing his previous answer, but Morgan barged in with his 'Ten, twenty, thirty?' which Clegg never responded to.

Once again, the detail is less important than the wider issues. Was it wise for Clegg to be doing an interview as a new leader with a journalist who specialised in trying to trip up politicians, and who wasn't well disposed towards the Lib Dems? Was it wise for Clegg to let Morgan get so far on a subject Clegg should have limited the access to, whether or not he'd responded to the number 'thirty'? Clegg was certainly upset about it, feeling that he had been not so much backed into a corner as barged into one, but was it entirely of Morgan's making? Clegg was riding out on his natural, easy-going charm, but some media people see it as utterly fair game to exploit that for their own aims, and maybe Clegg was a little naive in allowing Morgan down that route (or maybe his advisers were naive in setting up such an interview).

The broader media had a field day, even before that edition of *GQ* was published. Some of them dubbed him 'Cleggover', and others sought out his past girlfriends to check whether there was any truth in the number. As Clegg did 'toughen up', his total number of sexual conquests remains a matter of speculation and is probably well below thirty, though having been a tall, handsome, young and affable ski instructor, one has to assume there were a fair few opportunities.

A more serious error came in November 2008, when his relaxed manner of conversation strayed into the realms of indiscretion. He and Danny Alexander were sitting next to each other on a packed plane en route to a meeting in Inverness when they began discussing senior Lib Dem personnel. They were perhaps unlucky to have a *Sunday Mirror* journalist in the row in front, but it has to count as seriously injudicious to have been discussing public figures in any non-confidential environment. According to the story that resulted from it, several senior Lib Dems felt Clegg's tongue in the journalist's recounting of that conversation, notably Steve Webb, who may be one of the party's less charismatic figures but whose understanding of the minutiae of social welfare rules, regulations and legislation is probably well ahead of anyone else at Westminster, from any party. 'He's a problem, I can't stand the man,' Clegg is reported to have said of the hapless Webb. Chris Huhne was also attacked for his apparent 'lack of emotional intelligence'.

The journalist concerned, Adam Lee-Potter, rather let Clegg off the hook. His story was somewhat rambling, which suggested he hadn't heard that much, and it also betrayed a stark inability to understand the pecking order of government and opposition jobs. That dovetailed nicely with Clegg's damage limitation strategy, which was, the moment he knew the story was being published, to phone the people he had allegedly maligned, tell them he had been overheard discussing personnel in a noisy plane, that the journalist couldn't possibly have heard everything that was being said, so anything that was published could only amount to fragments of the truth. Webb survived to become a junior minister in the coalition, and Huhne briefed lobby journalists that it was another of his shadow Cabinet colleagues Clegg had been referring to over the emotional intelligence remark, not him (after the 'Calamity Clegg' dossier, Huhne may not have been in a good position to argue back, so shifting the accusation to someone else was good tactics from his perspective). It was a sharp reminder to both Clegg and Alexander that their lack of stuffiness should not stray into the realms of talking about confidential matters in a place where they were likely to be overheard.

Such tales suggest that Clegg was establishing himself as a leading public figure, but there was actually concern in Lib Dem circles that he wasn't striking enough. He was dubbed 'Cameron-lite' by various sections of the media, amid suggestions that people couldn't tell the difference between the new leaders of the Conservatives and the Liberal Democrats. Even the compliments tended to be half hearted, such as Shelagh Fogarty's in *Total Politics*: 'Your mum would like him; he's handsome in a head boy kind of way, and wears good threads. His problem seems to have been that people think he's David Cameron with less troublesome hair.'

In retrospect, the twenty-nine months between becoming Lib Dem leader and Deputy Prime Minister were Clegg's chance to get himself known to the nation at large. It did his profile no harm when, in February 2009, he became a dad for the third time – his son Miguel became his first child born in Britain, delivered at Kingston Hospital just a few miles from the family home. Nine months earlier, in May 2008, Clegg had undertaken another high-profile trip, travelling to Helmand province in Afghanistan to visit British troops serving there. Many of the photos of him chatting with the military were used in the Lib Dems' 2010 election material, but there was another picture on his mind while in Helmand. On learning that his dad was about to visit British soldiers in Afghanistan, Clegg's eldest son Antonio, by then six, did his own drawing to illustrate the optimum British strategy for winning the war, and asked Clegg to give it to the head of British forces stationed in Helmand. Clegg did his paternal duty and duly handed over Antonio's strategy document.

Yet this period was a tricky time for the new leader. He may have been the new kid on the political block, but he had inherited a situation in which he was in something of the shadow of another, highly popular, Lib Dem, who had risen to prominence during the party's leadership campaign.

'Leaderships inevitably become seen through the prism of what characterised them at the time,' says Charles Kennedy. 'Some of them can be in your own control, but 80 to 90 per cent is frankly forces outwith your control, and it's how you respond to things that defines you. If you think of Blair in the early days, the response to the death of the Princess of Wales probably gave more people at that point a focus on what they thought about Prime Minister Blair than all the other things he was going on about.' If that is true, then Clegg had to define himself according to the two dominant political themes of the 2008–10 British political period: the collapse and bailout of the banks, and the scandal over MPs' expenses.

The collapse of the banking system began in the summer of 2007, in Ming Campbell's last weeks as leader. There was a run on Northern Rock, a former building society that had demutualised to become a bank, which raised the question of whether the bank needed bailing out by the state. The Royal Bank of Scotland soon looked to be on the brink of similar turmoil. A number of people had been warning about the timebomb in British finances, and one of them was suddenly acting leader of one of the three main political parties.

Vince Cable, a former economist with Shell who had entered Parliament at fifty-four after a political career that had seen him serve as a Labour councillor, had been warning for three or four years that a crash was coming. For much of that time he was dismissed as a voice from the political wilderness, but when Northern Rock and RBS hit major difficulties, many of Cable's prognostications were dug out and dusted off, and his softly spoken manner with remnants of a Yorkshire accent made him seem something of a political sage.

The upshot was that, when Clegg was elected Lib Dem leader in December 2007, many people wondered why the party had elected a new man when the acting leader (Cable) was doing as good a job as any Lib Dem had done for years. It was certainly a challenge for Clegg, one that lasted for well over two years: he had to make his mark but not be seen to be trying to usurp his deputy and principal finance spokesman. By and large it worked – there were clearly a few fraught moments behind the scenes, but he and Cable built up a relationship of trust that survived some of the mischief-making that the media tried on in search of a story.

'It was quite tricky,' says Cable, 'and it continued pretty much up to the televised debates. Nick's very intelligent and quite a sensitive individual, so he knew the relationship had to be managed properly. I was loyal and constructive, not trying to undermine him, but we had newspapers making invidious comparisons between us the whole time, partly to wind him up – it was their way of getting at the Lib Dems. Every week there was some article about how I'd done something brilliantly and he'd failed to do it, but neither of us were trying to create problems for each other. We had a good relationship, he knew I wasn't after his job or trying to undermine him. It was awkward sometimes, but he understood that I was important to him and we had to work together, and that tended to dominate over the niggles.'

In some ways, Clegg could use Cable as cover, allowing the

older man to take much of the limelight while he himself got the hang of the leader's job. But Paddy Ashdown thinks the situation was potentially very dangerous for Clegg. 'To have been elected leader of the Liberal Democrats after less than one parliament,' he says, 'and to have somebody who has won the nation's hearts and respect – that wasn't an advantage to Nick, it was a great disadvantage to him. That is no criticism of Vince; Vince was a huge asset and played his role impeccably. The temptation for him to play on his popularity with a young leader must have been very great, but he never put a foot wrong, and he acted with great dignity and integrity. I think Nick showed real maturity in dealing with that. The easy thing would have been to take steps to somehow diminish Vince, but he didn't fall into that trap, he showed personal grandeur to incorporate Vince, to have him stand alongside him. Nick knew that the patient approach to this would be the one that drew the right conclusion. We talked about it on several occasions, and he said "This must not develop into a competition between me and Vince, it has to be 'One plus one equals more than two'". Lesser people would not have seen that, and it shows extraordinary understanding about the true values of leadership.'

The expenses scandal had two implications for Clegg – for himself as an MP, and for the party's campaigning at the 2010 general election.

He had to defend himself against allegations that he had claimed parliamentary expenses on his second home and that he'd claimed for private phone calls. He did indeed claim £84,000 for renovations to his Sheffield home, but they were legitimate (on one occasion his monthly expenses exceeded the maximum allowable amount, but this was because of a sudden concentration of outgoings and was explained at the time to the House of Commons authorities). More importantly, he had made it clear at the time that he had bought a house in serious need of renovation, and when it was sold, public coffers would claim their share of the enhanced value of the house. The house, which Clegg had bought for £280,000, was indeed sold in the spring of 2011 for £325,000, making a profit of £45,000. After deduction of fees and other costs, his profit was £38,750, so he wrote a cheque to the House of Commons authorities for that amount. He told the Sheffield *Star* newspaper, 'It's not something that is required of me and I expect not all other MPs will do the same, but it's my personal choice to lead by example. I don't want to be holier than thou about it, but the old expenses system made people very angry, and I pushed for MPs to get out of the property game.' In retrospect, it seems astonishing that the Lib Dem publicity machine didn't make more of this at a time (April 2011) when Clegg needed all the positive PR he could get his hands on.

He did have to apologise for a few phone calls on his private number that should not have been claimed, and he subsequently paid back £80.20. These were indeed embarrassments, but seriously small beer compared with some of the claims being made, such as for a 'duck house' in one MP's second residence, and cleaning out a moat in another MP's constituency abode.

In a broader context, the whole expenses saga gave the Liberal Democrats some opportunities that became a cornerstone of the Lib Dem manifesto for the 2010 general election. Clegg made it a characteristic of the Lib Dem image that the party was for 'cleaning up' politics. Cleverly, he linked the campaign for a fairer voting system with the expenses scandal, though he couldn't sustain the momentum into the spring of 2011, when the referendum on the alternative vote was heavily defeated.

Yet such campaigning was not without its pitfalls. The call for a 'new politics' resonated strongly, not just because of the expenses scandal but also because politics had already fallen into serious disrepute. Scandals in the previous ten years, such as those nick-named 'cash for questions', 'cash for access' and 'cash for honours', had seriously undermined the public's confidence in its politicians, so Clegg had struck a chord. His problem was that the party was reaping the rewards of certain political techniques that don't sit easily with a claim to the moral high ground.

A generation of keen young activists had been trained by Lib Dem HQ in exploiting popular concerns to the full. Some of their techniques were largely uncontroversial, such as direct mailing, and keeping messages short, sweet and visual, but many were outright negative. The upshot was that some campaigning fired cheap shots at opponents and relied more on slogans than arguments. Many intellectual members of the party became unhappy with some of the literature put out in their name, and had to hold their nose while putting it through letterboxes. The party was particularly lucky that a potentially damaging article by Andrew Gilligan in the *Daily Telegraph* during the election campaign, which highlighted some of the Lib Dems' less honourable electoral tactics, was buried deep inside, as the paper published it on the same day as its 'Clegg Accused' front-page story (see page 217). The Gilligan story was at times a little cheap, relying in part on material going back to the mid-1980s (there was one Lib Dem leaflet in a 1985 by-election in Brecon & Radnor that was seriously below the belt), but the article did have some substance, and arguably had a greater potential to damage the party than the hysterical and weakly founded front-page story, which looked like a hatchet job after Clegg's success in the first TV debate.

One of Clegg's first policy decisions as leader concerned the troublesome issue of Europe. Several years earlier, the most pro-Europe of Britain's three parties had had to recognise the political reality that Europe was not a vote winner in Britain, and increasingly a vote loser. Indeed many Lib Dems, while comfortably pro-European in a cultural sense, were becoming distinctly sceptical about aspects of the EU. Hence the Lib Dems' platform to go into the 2005 general election promising a referendum on the planned 'constitution for Europe' before it was ratified by Parliament.

In the reshuffle of the Lib Dem frontbench team after the leadership election, Clegg had promoted Ed Davey, who had chaired his campaign, to foreign affairs spokesperson, replacing Ming Campbell's choice, Michael Moore. When it became clear that the planned constitution wouldn't win approval elsewhere in Europe, there was much debate in the Lib Dems over whether or not the party's commitment to a referendum on the constitution should apply to the Lisbon Treaty. The Lisbon Treaty was clearly a modification of the EU Treaty (originally the Treaty of Rome, but updated several times), which acts as the union's guiding document, but was it a constitution that justified a referendum? You could argue it both ways, and both arguments were heard within the party.

Davey suggested a compromise position that would change the Lib Dems' Europe policy to say 'If there is any referendum on Europe, we want it to be on whether Britain stays in or gets out'. Clegg adopted the position, and wrote in *The Guardian*, 'We've all gone crazy. Pro and anti, Europhile and Eurosceptic, trading blows about the Lisbon Treaty in grand rhetoric that obscures the facts. If you're pro-European, like I am, you're accused of being a sell-out. If you're anti-European, like most of the Conservative Party, you're accused of being a headbanger.' He said that no-one under the age of fifty-one had had the chance to say whether they wanted Britain to be in or out, as the only referendum on EU membership had been the EEC referendum in 1975, which had recorded a result of 2:1 in favour.

The truth was, however, that he adopted Davey's proposal as something of a damage limitation exercise, and it proved a messy compromise, as many Lib Dems felt duty bound to support a referendum on the Lisbon Treaty, as they saw this as consistent with their election commitment demanding a referendum on the adoption of an EU constitution. So when Clegg tabled an amendment to the Lisbon Treaty Bill calling for an 'in or out' referendum, and called on his MPs to abstain on the Conservatives' call for a Lisbon Treaty referendum, the party split three ways. Fifteen Lib Dem MPs backed the call for a Lisbon referendum, which made the Lib Dem position on Europe seem shambolic. And coming so early in his leadership, Clegg had to play the disciplinarian, sacking a number of MPs from their positions, including David Heath, Tim Farron and Alastair Carmichael. Ultimately the storm blew over, and the issue of Europe didn't figure prominently in the 2010 general election campaign, largely because talk of immigration caps and a possible amnesty for immigrants who had a job and a clean record took over the space that the EU might have occupied in the campaign. But it was a warning to the new leader how problematical an issue that for him was fairly clear cut could prove.

There was another story at that time from which Clegg emerged with his reputation enhanced. It involved the right of Gurkha soldiers who had served in the British army to live in Britain. The issue was not without political risk, but his internationalist outlook told him that going in to bat for the Gurkhas was the right thing to do.

The Gurkhas are a people from the north of the Indian sub-continent, mostly today's Nepal, known for their immense bravery and lack of fear of dying. They played a significant role in the British army in the twentieth century, and remained part of a British army unit in Hong Kong up to the handback of the colony to China in 1997. At that point the unit was moved to Britain, but once they retired or otherwise left the regiment, Gurkha soldiers had no right to live in Britain, and many faced immense hardship if they returned to Nepal.

In 2004 the British government changed the rules, allowing any Gurkha soldier who had retired since 1997 to stay in Britain, but those who had retired earlier were still excluded. This new situation was challenged in the High Court, and in 2008 it was ruled unacceptable. So the government proposed changing the law, this time to allow any Gurkha who had served for twenty years to stay in Britain. This still caused outrage among the Gurkhas and their supporters, as pretty much the only Gurkhas to have served for twenty years were the officers, so it was seen as a rank-based decision that discriminated against the common soldiers.

The cause was taken up by the actor Joanna Lumley in a high-profile campaign outside Parliament. She played a superbly effective role in a campaign that tickled the nation, as much because she took the initiative right away from Gordon Brown and his immigration minister, Phil Woolas. But Lumley needed a partner within Parliament, and she found a friend in Clegg, who in April 2009 used an Opposition Day parliamentary opportunity to propose a motion censuring the government's plans. The government was defeated, and Clegg and Lumley celebrated a remarkable victory. The law was subsequently changed to allow any Gurkha who had served for four years or more to stay in Britain.

With immigration and population levels always a political hot potato, Clegg was not guaranteed an easy ride, nor was he ever going to get the lion's share of the credit when his co-campaigner was such an iconic and fragrant star. But he was insistent on his course of action: 'These are people who are willing to lay down their lives for our country,' he said after the victory, 'so we simply could not tolerate a situation where they are not allowed to live in our country.'

A feature of this period is that those who engaged personally with Clegg speak very highly of him, but he still wasn't widely known. Apart from at election times, the political world seldom permeates deep into the mainstream British consciousness, so it was a slow build-up of what one might term low-level decency.

His utterances were subjected to a higher level of scrutiny than they had been before, but he clearly tried to avoid saying simply what people wanted to hear. 'One of the things I've learned over the last couple of years,' he said in an interview with *The Telegraph* magazine in March 2010, 'is that it really is better to say something that people might not agree with, but say it because you really mean it, rather than constantly tip-toeing around what the latest focus group has told you. And I don't think I've resiled in any way. This is the thing that does happen in politics, of course – you start stepping back from the things you believe in.' He also took care not to get personal with Gordon Brown or David Cameron, however much he disagreed with them, and a feature of the first televised debate in April 2010 was that Clegg constantly referred to them in 'First name Surname' format rather than 'First name only' or 'Mr Surname'. 'If you make it personal, you lose your sense of judgement,' he said.

Avoiding the polemics runs the risk of not making yourself interesting enough for the media, and it was a problem for him at a time when the third party of British politics needed the oxygen of publicity. It was perhaps his cross to bear that his inherent optimism didn't always make for the best headlines, a syndrome illustrated when asked whether Britain was 'broken'. 'I think it's both patronising and pessimistic to just dismiss the whole country as broken,' he said in early 2010. 'I know lots of families in my constituency who have a very difficult time; they worry about their children's education, they struggle to pay the bills, they worry about anti-social behaviour on their doorstep, whether their elderly relatives can afford to stay in their home. But is that a broken Britain? No. I am actually on the whole constantly amazed by the resilience and generosity of people. I think that people are basically born good. I look at the innocence in my own children – and they can be an absolute pain, of course – and I don't see how anyone could say that a little child can be born bad. Things can happen to them that have devastating effects, but taking this grim view, writing people off – "It's all broken" – I can see why people do it for political effect, but it doesn't reflect the Britain I either inhabit or want to live in.'

If the Lib Dem manifesto for the 2005 general election had been a shopping list, the 2010 manifesto promised less but told more of a story. Exactly what story it told was to be the subject of much deliberation, especially after the Lib Dems had made certain concessions on second-tier manifesto pledges that were then labelled 'U-turns'.

In 2005 there had been about a dozen loose promises, whereas now there was to be a platform based around four headline ideas that could be sold to the electorate on a poster or in a twelve-second sound bite. There was a major battle within the party's democratic structure about what the headline policies should be, and in particular whether the Lib Dems' stance on a local income tax and abolishing tuition fees should be among them. Once the four had been agreed – raising the income tax threshold to £10,000, a programme of economic stimulus based around 'green' jobs, more money for education through a 'pupil premium', and reforming and cleaning up the political system – they were splashed on the front of the Lib Dems' manifesto, and were the party's red-line issues when it came to drawing up a programme for government in coalition with the Conservatives.

It's easy to see the difference between the 2005 and 2010 Lib Dem manifestos as a triumph for the *Orange Book* brigade. Clearly there were fewer spending promises, and the fingerprints of Vince Cable and David Laws were to be found throughout the 2010 manifesto. But to see it as a lurch to the right misses three important aspects. Firstly, the economic situation was vastly more dire in 2010 than in 2005, so any Lib Dem manifesto would have promised less. Secondly, most of the Lib Dem spending pledges in 2005 were based on the revenue from a 50p top rate of income tax, whereas by 2010 that had been introduced by Gordon Brown as part of his efforts to fund the bailout of the banks in 2008 (the fact that the Lib Dems had abandoned their commitment to the 50p tax rate under Ming Campbell's leadership *was* a victory for the *Orange Book* tendency – perhaps a case of listening more to the views of millionaire donors than those of average voters). And thirdly, the Lib Dem membership has a major say on the content of the party's manifesto, and the leadership doesn't dare stray too far from ideas that the membership holds dear. As a result, the road to Clegg's first manifesto was a very bumpy one. It had three basic drafts: a paper called 'Make It Happen' in July 2008, a follow-up pre-manifesto that went to the party's autumn conference in 2009, and the manifesto itself.

In July 2009, the party's Federal Policy Committee (the Liberal Democrats' belief in decentralisation and localism means that anything within the party that is nationwide in a British sense is termed 'federal') discussed the draft pre-manifesto document. The FPC is a high-level internal think-tank charged with turning the party's various ideas into coherent policy; it meets once a month, is made up of a handful of MPs and party activists elected by the membership, and the party leader is allowed to chair it if he/ she wants to. Ashdown, Kennedy and Campbell had all done so, and Clegg chaired most meetings of the FPC until the election campaign got seriously under way in late 2009, when the chairmanship passed to his closest political ally, Danny Alexander. And Clegg was in the chair when the committee discussed the pre-manifesto at Westminster on a day when there were important Commons votes happening.

The atmosphere in the meeting wasn't helped by the MPs on the committee continually having to leave to vote in the House, and Vince Cable was in a particularly tetchy mood. The meeting, which was expected to last three hours, ran to five, as the committee debated whether the party's commitment to a local income tax to replace council tax should be one of its front-line policies. Cable was keen for it to take a back seat, and Clegg was happy to support him, but the committee members felt it should be a headline policy. Eventually Cable's patience snapped, he uttered an acerbic comment insulting the competence of the FPC's members, and stormed out. He eventually got his way, as the local income tax became very much a walk-on part of the Lib Dem manifesto, but not everyone was impressed with Clegg's chairmanship that day, even though the general view is that he chaired FPC meetings pretty well.

Another difficult issue between Clegg and his party was the environment. To many in the party, the environment is a central issue; a number of Lib Dems are motivated primarily by environmental issues, and feel the party's biggest battle is as much against the Greens as against Labour or the Conservatives. Clegg certainly recognises the environment's importance, and had spent the best part of a year studying the environmental movement in Minnesota in his early twenties (see page 70). But in the run-up to the general election he left a lot of his senior party wondering whether he really got it.

At an 'awayday' for Lib Dem MPs in the months after the 2005 election, all sixty-two MPs were asked to list their top three priority issues. Clegg is believed to be the only one not to have listed the environment. And some of the 'greener' members of the FPC were consistently disappointed by the lack of prominence for environmental pledges in the three documents leading up to the 2010 manifesto. As one FPC member put it, 'All three were weak on environment, and some of us wrote lots of amendments to them, which the manifesto team were quite happy to accept – it wasn't like they were objecting to them, but time after time the next draft emerged and was still poor on environmental stuff. It was as if the manifesto team, led by Danny Alexander, understood intellectually that environmental politics were important for us but they didn't really grasp what it meant.'

In many ways, Clegg didn't need to do much on the environment at the 2010 general election, because his defeated leadership rival, Chris Huhne, had done it all for him. Under Ming Campbell's leadership, Huhne had produced an impressive Lib Dem policy document that mapped out the route for Britain to become carbon neutral by 2050. Inevitably it contained various assumptions that one could question, but it allowed Lib Dem candidates up and down the country to claim the party had a platform on the environment to match the Greens. Yet Clegg and his manifesto team seemed strangely reluctant to run with Huhne's work.

Even Clegg's strongest supporters within the party accept that the environment is 'not what he gets him out of bed in the morning'. David Boyle says, 'It's the one really important area that he didn't have a natural interest in. There was a group of us around Nick who began talking about the leadership when he was elected to Parliament, and there was someone who had a green background who got very angry about his failure to grasp this issue. I think his approach – and this is true of other issues too – was always to worry away at it until he found something about it that excited him. He wanted to be intellectually excited about environmental issues, and unless he could be, he just wasn't terribly interested in the thing as a whole. He's always been keen not to have the same tone of voice as the traditional left, which can come across as rather worried and puritanical, and that's why he sometimes looks uninterested in some of the traditional left-wing themes.'

Danny Alexander also says Clegg's apparent lack of interest

in the environment is due to his uncertainty about how to make it 'compelling to a much broader section of the population'. The man who drafted the Lib Dem manifesto adds, 'That's the hard bit. It doesn't mean Nick doesn't care about the environment. He clearly does – the green economy and renewable energy are things Nick is very motivated by and we had a lot of environmental tax proposals in the manifesto. But as a party, when you're designing a manifesto and a message for a highly competitive election in which you have to make sure your policies are crisp and comprehensible, we felt we had to build the environment into the economy and it wouldn't have carried more weight in the manifesto if we'd given it a bigger mention.'

Norman Baker, another Lib Dem for whom the environment is a motivating force in getting him out of bed in the morning, says, 'I don't think it runs through his blood, but I think he understands the importance of it, and more to the point, he's never stopped me doing something I want to do on the environment. If you look at our manifesto for the 2010 election, there was a whole lot of stuff in there that I wanted, such as road pricing and quite radical proposals on railways. Nothing I have ever wanted to do has been stopped; in fact, under Nick's leadership it has been encouraged.'

Even Huhne himself, who could have been forgiven for feeling the work he had done (with Neil Stockley, who had chaired the Lib Dems' environment policy review group) was being kicked into the long grass, feels Clegg's approach wasn't wrong. 'The sad truth is,' Huhne says, 'that the green agenda is important for the party but it doesn't reach out to great swathes of the electorate. The policy [of being carbon neutral by 2050] worked from the point of view of giving us street cred with groups we needed to have street cred with, because it was doable, and that has been of great value now that we're in coalition. In fact one of the reasons I can be so relaxed doing the job I'm doing [energy and climate change] is because we did all the spadework while in opposition. But I don't think we were wrong to give it only moderate prominence in the campaign.'

The third clash between Clegg (and Cable) and the Federal Policy Committee came on university tuition fees. Not only was this the incendiary issue that blew up in the autumn of 2010, but it reflects the difficult transition the Liberal Democrats are undergoing in moving from a party that feels good about its programme to one that has policies that are credible in the sense that they will work in government and can be sold through the media. The way the issue played out in government is discussed in Chapter 12, but the story of how the policy came about is worth recording.

The Lib Dems had opposed university tuition fees when David Blunkett introduced them in 1997. The party campaigned against tuition fees at the 2001 and 2005 general elections, and Charles Kennedy was very much against them – in large part because he could see the political potential of having a magnet with which to attract the student vote. But with more than 40 per cent of British young adults going to university, the pledge was a very expensive one (especially without the 50p income tax band to fund it), and would have been hard to implement even if the Lib Dems had got into government on their own.

Between 2005 and 2010, the dilemma between opposing an unpopular government policy and putting forward a credible – and fundable – alternative became the subject of increasing discussion within the Lib Dems, as the ambitious MPs tried to prepare the party for a role in government. At a parliamentary party debate in 2008, Vince Cable, who with David Laws had been agitating to get rid of the commitment to abolish tuition fees, said he thought what the government was doing was generally pretty good. Yet the issue of education is central to the liberal mindset, as equality of opportunity is perceived as being the route to a fairer society, and there was therefore vehement support from some sections of the party to maintain opposition to tuition fees.

'I had been encouraging our higher education spokespeople – basically David Laws, Sarah Teather and Stephen Williams – to drop it,' says Cable, 'but a group of people had been elected to the Federal Policy Committee for whom this was the big issue;

they saw this as the battle they had to fight against the wicked *Orange Book* people.' That last part of Cable's comment is a little unfair but quite revealing. There were indeed many who had stood for election to the FPC specifically because they wanted to maintain Lib Dem opposition to tuition fees, but did that make them soldiers in a holy war against *The Orange Book*? Cable was clearly irritated at how strongly his party was attached to free higher education, but many who defended the party's 2005 opposition to tuition fees would claim they were not specifically antagonistic towards the *Orange Book* people, though they may have been antagonistic towards many of the *Orange Book* policies.

Clegg had come to the leadership convinced that the party's commitment to funding higher education courses was highly desirable but simply unaffordable. Unsurprisingly for a man who had studied at three higher education establishments, he was emotionally committed to furthering university education, but couldn't square the numbers in an increasingly harsh public spending climate.

Matters came to a head when drafting began on the manifesto for the 2010 election. Stephen Williams had come up with an idea to help students from poorer backgrounds with better bursaries, which would allow the party to get away from its commitment to abolish tuition fees without losing its commitment to social justice. But the FPC were very keen to continue the Lib Dems' commitment to state-funded higher education, and Lib Dem MPs were also split on the issue. The upshot was a compromise negotiated by Clegg and Alexander with the FPC that committed the party to phasing out tuition fees for first degrees (mostly the three-year undergraduate degrees that students take between eighteen and twenty-two) over a period of six years. 'The ideas put forward by Stephen Williams that had the support of Nick and Vince were closer to what the government has done on tuition fees than what was in our manifesto,' says Alexander, 'but we're a democratic party, and we took the ideas through the FPC and debated them at conference. In the end the change to our policy didn't go as far as had been suggested. We ended up with a more financially responsible policy than we might have had, but one that in any circumstance other than a Lib Dem majority government could not be delivered, because both Labour and the Conservatives were in favour of putting up tuition fees.'

Having agreed the compromise policy, there was then the question of whether it should be one of the party's headline policies for the election campaign. The FPC wanted it to be, but Clegg and Alexander didn't, and they got their way. That at least allowed Clegg some logical justification when he later claimed the Lib Dems' agreement to tuition fees in government was not a U-turn – not that this argument did him much good, such was the perception that a U-turn is very much what it was.

How much of a U-turn it was in reality depends on how strongly one thinks the Lib Dems campaigned on their tuition fees policy in the 2010 election campaign. The compromise policy, which Cable hated, allowed the party to woo the student vote; indeed, one of Clegg's great successes in the 2010 campaign was in energising the student populace. But the party did something that in retrospect looks like an own goal. In the run-up to a general election, all candidates of all parties get bombarded with campaigns asking them to sign up to certain pledges. It's no doubt good campaigning, and Lib Dem HQ gave out advice on which pledges it was safe for Lib Dem candidates to sign up to. One of the green lights was given to a pledge drawn up by the National Union of Students that required candidates to undertake that, if elected, they would not vote to raise tuition fees. Ironically, the NUS says the primary aim of the pledge was to try and get Labour candidates to sign up, so that Labour's commitment to the anticipated recommendations of the Browne report (to allow tuition fees to rise) could be challenged from within the party, but it was Lib Dem MPs who were ensnared by it.

Clegg was not the first Lib Dem MP to sign the NUS's pledge, but he says he signed without any qualms. 'It conformed with our party policy,' he says, 'so I thought it would be rather odd not to sign a pledge that said I'm pledged to a policy we had in our manifesto.' But others were less enthusiastic; Vince Cable still tells the story as if it's a bad dream that's just got worse. 'I didn't like the policy we came up with, but I was happy to accept it, and if it had just gone in our manifesto, that might have been OK. But then we had this business of the NUS pledge. Whoever advised Nick to sign probably did so on the basis that, if we have this potty policy, at least let's get some credit for it among the students. I was adamantly opposed to signing the pledge, as was David Laws. But one day we were told Nick had signed it, and I was confronted with the situation that the leader had signed it but I hadn't. At that time, I was being accused of overshadowing Nick, so I very reluctantly signed. To be frank, I was embarrassed by it, and I avoided making any mention of it in any of my campaigning.'

Within six months of the coalition government taking over, Cable as Secretary of State for Business, Innovation and Skills had to confirm the rise in tuition fees, unleashing major wailing and gnashing of teeth both within the party and among those who had voted Lib Dem on the basis of the tuition fees pledge. Much of the anger was directed at Clegg and his family (see page 245). 'When we signed the pledge,' says Cable, 'it probably didn't occur to anybody that it would be such a millstone around our neck. Although we had costed the option we put in the manifesto, it was a leftover contradiction between our being the nice protest party and being a realistic, ambitious party. For a while these contradictions didn't matter, but when you get close to government they do, and the contradictions become painfully apparent.'

But Clegg remains unapologetic. 'The pledge is not the controversy,' he says; 'the controversy is that people don't seem to accept that, just because you sign something, it doesn't mean you can necessarily deliver it if you're not in power on your own. We had a policy that we would have delivered with a Liberal Democrat majority government, but the moment we failed to get that majority, we were stuffed because Labour and the Conservatives didn't agree with us. I'm not going to apologise about that.'

There's an inherent logic to what Clegg says, but given that the Lib Dems were never going to get an overall majority, given the compromise on the manifesto policy on tuition fees, and given the other two major parties' intention of raising fees, it was perhaps a rash thing to promise. The Lib Dems' role in the background to the great tuition fees controversy of 2010 will probably be seen in a more benign light in years to come, but when campaigning begins in earnest for the next general election, the leadership may well be a little less quick to encourage its candidates to sign pledges on issues it has itself compromised on.

In the fourteen months leading up to the 2010 general election, Clegg gained a friend from an unlikely source, who proved something of an inspiration and a source of some useful coaching.

Howard Dean was the governor of Vermont, who had stood as a radical candidate in the race to be the 2004 American presidential candidate for the Democrats, and at one stage early on was the front-runner. He failed, but became chair of the Democratic National Committee, and was a key figure in the successful Barack Obama campaign in 2008. Lib Dem contact with Dean was established through the long-standing friendship of the Lib Dems' chief executive, Chris Rennard, and a US-based political consultant, Rick Ridder, who had been Dean's campaign manager in the early (and successful) stages of his presidential bid. Rennard and Ridder had kept up a Lib Dem–Democrat relationship since the late 1980s, swapping notes on campaign techniques, and Ridder arranged for a number of Lib Dems to spend a few weeks looking at the Obama campaign in Ridder's home state of Colorado. As a follow-up, Dean was invited to the Lib Dems' spring conference in Harrogate in March 2009.

There is a tacit understanding between the American Democrats and the British Labour Party that they help each other – not to the point where a Labour prime minister can't get on with a Republican president, or where a Conservative prime minister can't survive with a Democrat in the White House, but as a recognition of mutual shared philosophies. Yet Dean had never forgiven Tony Blair and Labour for their backing of George W. Bush over the Iraq War of 2003, so when Clegg asked Dean to help the Lib Dems, his invitation landed on fertile ground. Dean spoke – in a personal capacity – to considerable acclaim to the Harrogate conference, as part of a whirlwind series of meetings which Rennard arranged so that Dean could meet the party's major donors and address meetings with party staff and parliamentary candidates. One of them was the Hampstead & Kilburn candidate, Ed Fordham. 'Howard was always keen for the Lib Dems to be bolder,' Fordham recalls, 'and he was quite open. He told us, "You all seem content to win a few more seats, yet you have a leader who could be a national leader, and surely that's the goal. Support Nick, push Nick, urge him to be bolder and don't accept that you are the third party – you are playing for high stakes and you have a leader who can sit at that national and international table. Use him!"'

Dean returned to the UK for a second visit in November 2009, and had a series of private meetings with Clegg and some of his closest personal advisers. He told them about the presidential TV debates in America that were 'game changers' and had the ability to make or break a candidate. Fordham adds, 'For most of us who met Howard Dean it was clear that he was onto something. Here was a very senior Democrat, the chair of the Democratic National Committee no less, backing Nick Clegg. Effectively he had rejected Blair and Labour over Iraq, he was looking for something new and fresh, and had found Nick Clegg and the Liberal Democrats. I have subsequently kept in touch with Governor Dean, and his interest and enthusiasm have not gone. He recently told me, "I told you Nick was destined for office, and it worked – maybe not PM this time, but DPM is pretty good considering where the Liberals have been for eighty years." He remains interested, keeps in touch, and follows the UK elections.'

By the time of Dean's second visit to Britain, it was clear that Britain would have its first televised leaders' debate. In September 2009, the three leading news broadcasters in British television – the BBC, Independent Television and BSkyB – wrote to the three party leaders asking them to take part in a series of televised debates in the run-up to the general election that, at the time, could be no more than nine months away. The idea of TV debates had been on the agenda for several years, as they are part of the landscape in several other countries, notably the United States. But until the 2010 election, unanimity among the two leading parties could never be achieved, as one of them always felt they had more to lose than to gain.

The Liberal Democrats have always been up for it, and Clegg was the first to agree. David Cameron was almost as quick to say yes, and a month later, Gordon Brown signalled his willingness. In many ways, Cameron's decision was the deal maker. The received wisdom has always been that the front-runner has most to lose, so should always say no for tactical reasons, and indeed many within the Conservative party criticise Cameron's decision to agree to TV debates. But the broadcasters had got their timing right, as all three party leaders sensed that the political world had to work hard to regain the public's confidence after the expenses scandal. Also, although Cameron was the front-runner in the early autumn of 2009, he was not guaranteed outright victory, so his decision to say yes to the debates was based on a calculation that he had more to gain than to lose.

The opportunity for the Liberal Democrats was massive, and they knew it. They began preparing as far back as the end of 2009, as there was a fear that Gordon Brown might call the election a few weeks earlier than the widely predicted date of 6 May 2010. While much was made of the media coaching allegedly being given to Brown and Cameron, Clegg's coaching was done largely in house, with only small bits of help from outside.

There were two Lib Dem teams. One worked with Clegg on preparing him for the debates, the other negotiated with the other two parties and the broadcasters on the rules of engagement; and obviously they worked closely with each other. The latter team was made up of two of Clegg's closest day-to-day advisers, Jonny Oates and Lena Pietsch, plus the man to whom he had delegated the management of the general election campaign, John Sharkey. The brief from Clegg was just to go into the negotiations and make the debates happen, not to worry about every single rule. The worst-case scenario for the Lib Dems was that the talks might collapse and the debates simply not take place, but there was never any serious danger of that, as it would have meant a damaging climb-down by someone. The main demands of the Lib Dem team were that the moderators (Alastair Stewart of ITN, Adam Boulton of Sky News, and David Dimbleby of the BBC) should not play too much of a role – the team worked on the basis that Clegg would score highly if the audience–politician interaction was at a maximum. Those involved describe the negotiations as good-natured and fun, and in early March, a 65-point plan determining the rules of engagement was agreed by all six participants.

Meanwhile, the Clegg team began rehearsals. They brought in the former Sky News anchorman Scott Chisholm as principal adviser to the Lib Dem leader. Chisholm, a larger-than-life bear-like New Zealander with years of broadcast experience, was an old friend of some of the team and had given a lot of advice to party figures, so his value was as someone who didn't work with Clegg on a day-to-day basis who could give him some tips and generally oversee the early rehearsals. Some credit Chisholm with three of the techniques that won Clegg so many plaudits in the first debate: the casual hand-in-the-trouser-pocket gesture that made him seem more relaxed than Brown and Cameron, mentioning the question-ers' names in his answers, and looking directly into the camera. Others say Clegg succeeded because he is genuinely engaging, and that Chisholm's biggest asset is that he and Clegg get on so well. Both are probably true, but the closeness and fun enjoyed by the Clegg team should not be underestimated in his success in the first debate, nor should the fact that everyone on the team felt able to tell Clegg how bad he was at something without fear of having offended the hierarchy.

The early rehearsals unveiled two of the undiscovered actors in British politics. Chris Huhne was charged with playing Gordon Brown, while David Laws was assigned the role of David Cameron. 'It became very clear how well Laws and Huhne had played

Cameron and Brown,' says Neil Sherlock, a Clegg confidant who was a member of the debates preparation team. 'There were some fiery exchanges between Laws and Huhne, and that helped Nick see the dynamic of Cameron and Brown having a go at each other; it made it clear that Cameron and Brown just couldn't get on, and that in turn showed up opportunities for Nick. The homework that had been done on both the questions that would be asked and the likely responses of Cameron and Brown was very thorough. In the first debate we had anticipated all the questions, and we had predicted most of Cameron's and Brown's answers too. At one stage I found myself saying "Blimey, that sounds familiar" when Cameron said something, because we had listened enough to him to work out what he was likely to say.'

Laws says he and Huhne had a clear strategy for the rehearsals. 'Chris and I were very determined to try to box Nick out of it as much as possible. So I, as Cameron, would agree with what Nick was saying, but be slightly patronising by saying I agree with all this and marshalling Nick on my side against Gordon Brown; and Chris's Brown would tend to ignore Nick completely, so the debate would just go backward and forwards between us – being ignored is the worst thing in those debates.'

Clegg's preparations really were thorough. He had not prepared in some dusty village hall but in a TV studio in circumstances that were likely to be similar to those of the debate. Most of the practice debates were filmed, so the team could look at it all afterwards. (The tapes probably still exist in some archive, though no-one among Clegg's advisers admits to knowing where they are.) The day before each of the real debates, the team met up and did rehearsals in the afternoon and the following morning.

When it came to the real thing, the ITV-hosted debate in Manchester on 15 April, Clegg's lieutenants all had their roles to play, some of them in the ludicrously though accurately named 'spin room', where the press were following the debates and could question senior members of each party whose job it was to say how well their man had done. Some members of the Clegg team say they didn't realise until a good half-hour in that their man was doing well, while others claim to have got a sense early on.

One very interested spectator was Laws, who found himself looking at the debate as much from Cameron's perspective as Clegg's. 'Cameron was a lot less comfortable in the debates than I'd expected him to be,' he says. 'I thought he'd perform very strongly. I'd been in his shoes in the practice, and I felt he had some very resonant themes and narratives that he could use, themes he was quite passionate about publicly, and I expected that to come out in the debates. But particularly in the first one, he looked like someone with most to lose, which, in fairness, he was. It was very safety conscious and safety first, so I felt I'd done my job in being a testing David Cameron. Our fear that Brown and Cameron would box Nick out of it didn't happen, both because of the way Cameron and Brown played it, but also because Nick was very effective and had learned all the lessons from the preparation.'

After an hour and a half it was all over. While the spin room raced to top speed in analysing the historic moment, Clegg greeted a few people – among them David Blunkett, who observed that Clegg was 'walking on air' – and then retired to his hotel, somewhat unusually, on his own. While his staff were making their way back (one taxi carrying two of them exploded and ended up in a ditch; no conspiracy theory has ever been advanced) Clegg phoned his mother. 'Yeah, you did well – well done,' was apparently her comment to him. It was to prove something of an understatement.

Eventually everyone in Team Clegg ended up sitting in the bar, drinking wine and relaxing after the intense build-up. One by one they all gave him a big hug as they arrived. One close adviser says she felt the sense that he had 'rocked the establishment' that night, while another says he remembers thinking 'This has massively changed things'. Clegg himself kept muttering 'This is massive, this is massive'.

It was massive, and within days the Lib Dems were up to 32 per cent in one opinion poll. But a note of caution was sounded by Paddy Ashdown. He had adopted the approach of talking Clegg up in public and talking him down in private. His advice that night was that Clegg was now a marked man, and the party had better be ready for it.

The initial outbreak of 'Cleggmania' was largely positive, if somewhat intrusive. He was all over the following day's papers, and when he next took a train, he was asked for his autograph five or six times on the platform, and on the train itself people constantly wanted their photo taken with him. Wherever he went, there were people wearing T-shirts emblazoned with 'I agree with Nick', a reference to Gordon Brown's much-used phrase from the debate that had been intended to cement Lab–Lib relations but in reality backfired. The press corps following Clegg grew in number, leading to some comical scenes. A few days after the first debate, the Clegg battle bus was running early for an appointment, so it pulled into a lay-by to allow all on board to stretch their legs. Clegg jauntily bounced off into the woods eating an apple, preceded by a phalanx of snappers keen to immortalise his every bite. 'It's a good job he's not eating a banana,' one political journalist muttered to Clegg's press officer Lena Pietsch, a reference to the grief David Miliband had endured eight months earlier after being photographed doing just that. 'Yes,' replied Pietsch, 'we don't do bananas.'

While anticipation was growing about the second TV debate scheduled for a week later, in particular over whether Clegg could repeat his performance from the first one, knives were being sharpened elsewhere. Perhaps the biggest thing the first debate did was bring to an end the period where Clegg was, in many people's eyes, play-ing second fiddle to Vince Cable. In the first week of the campaign, not only could he walk down most streets and go unrecognised, but almost every interview started with a variant of 'Nobody knows who you are; shouldn't you step aside for Vince Cable, who's better known and more popular?' All that ended, and it changed the dynamic of the election. Lib Dem candidates who had assumed they had no chance – and in reality didn't – were suddenly confronted with opinion polls that suggested they might get in.

That, of course, represented a threat to the two biggest parties, in particular the Conservatives. The *Daily Mail* ran a headline, 'Is there anything British about Nick Clegg?', which not only focused on his multinational heritage but even cited his German press officer as a sign that he couldn't possibly be very patriotic. But the *Daily Telegraph* had the biggest retaliation in store.

On the morning of the second debate, it ran a story that Clegg had put money that had been given by three supporters to fund his office into his own personal account, rather than his office account. The front-page headline was 'Clegg Accused', and said he had received 'up to £250 a month' from party donors intended to fund a second researcher in his parliamentary office, money that went into the wrong account. Clegg instantly responded by saying 'I received money from three friends which was properly given, properly received, properly declared, and properly used to pay for part of the salary of a member of my staff. Any suggestion I did anything wrong is out of order, and I'm going to publish the figures to prove it.'

The three people who had funded his office – Neil Sherlock, Ian Wright and Michael Young (see page 162) – gave the money to Clegg, who pooled it in his own account and then transferred it all, along with a top-up sum of his own, to his political account, and declared it all. Pooling it in his own account may have been convenient, but it was also somewhat naive, and the convenience was rather lost when he had to reveal his own personal bank statements in order to publish the figures and thus show that there had been no misuse of money. But did the use of his own private account really justify the magnitude of *The Telegraph*'s story? The paper had gone massive on it, and many in the Lib Dems smelt a rat. 'It was a deliberate attempt to smear him,' Wright says. '*The Telegraph* used a typesize for the "Clegg Accused" headline that they've only used once before, that was for 9/11, which was somewhat disproportionate but showed the extent to which they were worried about him. It was interesting and indicative of how far he'd come so quickly, that someone who had had to fund one of two staff members in his office out of donations from three friends just a few years earlier was now leader of a party that was rocketing in the polls.'

For its part, the *Daily Mail* dredged up an article Clegg had written for *The Guardian* in 2002 about the legacy of the Second World War. In it Clegg had said the British were still carrying the scars of the war through 'a misplaced sense of superiority, sustained by delusions of grandeur and a tenacious obsession with the last war'. The *Mail* described it as 'an astonishing attack on our national pride' and even 'a Nazi slur'. That allowed Clegg, whose popularity had been compared with Winston Churchill's just a few days before, to claim that he'd 'gone from Churchill to a Nazi in less than a week'.

The vehemence of the attacks on Clegg in newspapers sympathetic to the Conservatives led the Lib Dem high command to suspect a coordinated campaign. For three or four national papers all to have smear stories on the Lib Dem leader, in the week after he had impressed in the first TV debate, pointed to a leak from the Conservative camp. No-one has been sure enough to mention any names, but there are still many people in Lib Dem HQ who suspect Tory HQ was behind the stories.

Such extreme reactions produce their own counter-reactions, and one satirical Twitter hashtag called '#nickcleggsfault' sprang up, which sarcastically blamed Clegg for a catalogue of misdemeanours. Among them were allegations he had tampered with the brakes on Princess Diana's car, lived in the same town as a seriously ill man without ever visiting him or offering him a spare kidney, poked the volatile Icelandic volcano Eyjafjallajökull with a stick, and not fought in either world war.

In the early months of 2011, when Clegg's profile had sunk to the point where he was given only a modest role in the campaign for a change in the voting system, it became fashionable to compare his fall from the heights of Cleggmania in April 2010. Cleggmania certainly put a spring in his step, yet those close to him say he never got carried away with it. Lena Pietsch says, 'I remember saying to him, "This is weird for all of us who travel with you, but what's it like for you?" and he said, "This is not really about me, it's people projecting ideas onto me." He was detaching himself during Cleggmania, separating the public perception from the perception he has of himself. Looking back, I sometimes think that, in that sense, those three weeks were a good preparation for what was to come.'

He was also coming down in the remaining two weeks of the campaign. Some of the Clegg effect from the first debate had come from the fact that few people knew him; by the second and third debates they did, and his impact was less great. After the dust had settled on the first debate, his dad called and told him ten things he'd done wrong, and there were other pieces of input that suggested there was room for improvement. But Brown and Cameron had much more room for improvement, and while Clegg performed creditably in the second and third debates, he was unable to build on the Cleggmania surge. The Liberal Democrat campaign also seemed to fizzle out in the final week – there seemed to be no slogan or issue to provide an extra push, and the opinion polls that had put the party's popularity in the low 30s the weekend after the first debate began recording mid-20s again. It wasn't bad for a party that had spent most of the previous five years between 11 and 18 per cent, but it was a dip from the dizzy heights.

Still, the BBC's exit poll at 10 p.m. on election day seemed utterly implausible when it predicted 23 per cent for the party but a drop from sixty-two seats to fifty-nine. Pundits and figures from all parties thought it had to be wrong. And it was – the Lib Dems were not three down but five down, finishing on fifty-seven seats to the Conservatives' 306 and Labour's 258. But the Conservatives had fallen twenty seats short of an overall majority. The UK had only its second hung parliament since the Second World War, and this time the third party did hold the balance of power.

Chapter 11

'MIGHT BE SHOT IN FOUR OR FIVE YEARS'

IT'S PERHAPS remarkable that a group of people can spend decades campaigning for something, tell their mates and supporters that they're on the verge of the breakthrough, and then be utterly gobsmacked, if not traumatised, when they actually get what they want.

That was, by and large, the reality that hit the Liberal Democrats within days of the eagerly awaited 2010 general election. While there was a palpable sense of history in the making when, on the Tuesday after the election, David Cameron and Nick Clegg announced that they had reached agreement on a programme for five years of coalition government and then appeared in the rose garden at 10 Downing Street the following day, the party went into something of a spasm. This took two forms: the shock to the system arising from the fact that many of the people who had campaigned for the Lib Dems and voted for them had done so because they wanted to keep the Conservatives out; and possibly more importantly because the party 'lost' its five most senior and capable figures to their new roles in government. Even several months later, a figure close to Clegg was talking about the party suffering an organisational trauma.

The possibility of no single party getting an overall majority had been in the air for some time, and the Lib Dems had prepared for it to a certain extent. But there had been an alternative line of thought within the party, shared to a degree by Clegg and his leading associates, that the Lib Dems would achieve a sizeable share of the seats in 2010, but not have a hung parliament in which to wield their influence until the next election in 2014 or 2015. While the party had to prepare for a hung parliament in 2010, the belief among many was that, while the total number of Lib Dem seats would go up, the Conservatives would achieve an overall majority, albeit a smallish one. The Tories would then get blamed for the unpopular measures needed to counter the recession, and the Lib Dems and Labour would clean up at the following election and form a progressive centre-left government.

The best-laid plans are, of course, never guaranteed to give the desired result, especially in politics. And so it was that the Lib Dems achieved their breakthrough one election earlier than many expected, and ironically with a drop in seats. Worse still, the apparently obvious party to coalesce with, Labour, had too few seats to make an overall majority. Nick Robinson, the BBC's political editor, quoted an unnamed senior Lib Dem on the morning after the election as saying, 'The electorate has created an excruciating instrument of torture for us Liberal Democrats – our hearts went one way, but the mathematics went the other.' That quote came from Paddy Ashdown, who was to play a remarkably crucial role in the days to follow.

The minutiae of the machinations that went into forming the Conservative–Lib Dem government – and that went into exploring, but ultimately rejecting, a Labour–Lib Dem coalition – have been well documented elsewhere. David Laws, a member of the Lib Dem negotiating team, has written *22 Days in May*, which is the insider's account of the process, while another MP, the Conservative Rob Wilson, has written a similar book, *Five Days to Power*, which has a wider range of sources than Laws's but is more outside the actual process. Peter Mandelson covers the post-election machinations in the final chapter of his memoirs, *The Third Man*, and there have been other analyses in written articles and radio and television documentaries. As there is no need to reinvent the wheel, this book concentrates largely on the role played by Clegg in the days after the election, a role that was largely at arm's length from the detailed negotiations carried out in his and his party's name.

So were the Liberal Democrats, as some have suggested, unprepared for their role as a potential government party in the post-election negotiations? The answer is clearly no. Some in the party believe the leadership should have seen a hung parliament coming more clearly than it did, but preparations had been in progress for six months and, perhaps astonishingly in a world of leaks and media speculation, they had been kept out of the public domain.

At the suggestion of Danny Alexander, Clegg had secretly set up a negotiating team in late 2009 to prepare the ground for a possible coalition if the election delivered a hung parliament. He had deliberately sought to keep the existence of the team quiet, as he knew he would have enough difficulty ploughing the Lib Dems' own furrow in the election campaign to come without the distraction of the world knowing he was preparing for coalition talks. He also didn't want the party to be accused of hubris when, in reality, no Lib Dem parliamentary seat is truly safe.

Clegg's negotiating team consisted of four leading Lib Dem MPs and was carefully constructed. Alexander was its chair – he had become Clegg's closest political ally; in fact, some people familiar with the Lib Dems in Parliament call Alexander 'Clegg lite' because he is so close to the Lib Dem leader. There was Chris Huhne, who had courted the left-wing vote in the 2007 party leadership election and was a keen advocate of coalition government (as opposed to less formal arrangements whereby the Lib Dems might support one of the main parties without having government positions); he had done a lot of research on coalitions in other countries. There was David Laws, the party's leading authority on economics, and a trusted Lib Dem among the Conservatives – so trusted that he was specifically head-hunted by David Cameron and George Osborne in 2006 and asked to defect to the Tories (Laws rejected the offer, saying 'I am a liberal, not a conservative'). And the fourth member was Andrew Stunell, whose strong speciality was local government and was in the mix to ensure the realities of the Lib Dems' numerous local councillors were taken into account in any talks. Vince Cable was also part of the group, but did not take part in direct talks when the group became the Lib Dem negotiating team after the election.

The group met on four or five occasions, and eventually reported back to Clegg and a couple of other senior party figures on 17 March, six weeks before the election. They basically said that if the election produced a parliament with no party enjoying an overall majority, the Lib Dems would need to act decisively and constructively if they were ever to achieve their aim of reforming the voting landscape. The cherished Lib Dem dream of a proportional electoral system – one that gives each party a percentage of parliamentary seats similar to the percentage of votes it polled – would inevitably create more hung parliaments than not, so the party needed to ensure that the public got a good picture of a parliament with no overall majority and not an impression of weakness and chaos. Various options were discussed, including an informal 'confidence and supply' arrangement in which the Lib Dems would back a minority Conservative or Labour government on important votes in return for concessions in certain policy areas. The committee was largely united, though Huhne did insist on submitting his own conclusions, which reinforced his belief that only a full-blown coalition would serve both the party and the country in the post-election period.

Reading both Laws's and Wilson's accounts of the post-election negotiations, two factors stand out. The first was that this was a government formed amid great sleep deprivation. That was partly a Lib Dem sensitivity; the country was unused to being without a clear winner the morning after an election, so the last thing leading Lib Dems wanted in their hour of power was the media broadcasting that they had gone to bed to get some sleep. As a result, tired politicians who had powered through the previous three weeks of campaigning on adrenaline forsook their beds for the immediate task of negotiating a stable government.

The second factor was an undercurrent of fear that ran through all the negotiations about how the stock and money markets would react if a solid government wasn't put together in the shortest credible amount of time. Cynics could argue that too much heed was paid to the markets – after all, hung parliaments are nothing new in most mainland European countries, and coalitions frequently take two or three weeks (or over a year in Belgium's case) to form. But the Greek economic crisis had erupted just two days before polling day, triggering a collective firestorm within the eurozone; Clegg was deeply worried that Spain, a country he knew well through his in-laws, could be the next to tumble; and there were rumblings that even the British economy could not assume it was immune from a similar collapse in confidence. Whether exaggerated or not, fears that billions of pounds could be wiped off the value of British industry were an ever-present feature of the post-election negotiations.

Clegg had made sure all his options were open. His dislike of Gordon Brown was well known in Westminster circles – he could never work out how someone with so few social airs and graces had made it to the top job in Britain – and he could surely not have imagined forming a coalition with a Brown-led Labour party that had just lost the election. But when Laws put it to him in late 2009 that he should rule out working with Labour as long as Brown was the party's leader, he rejected the idea. This was largely because he didn't want any public discussions about who the Lib Dems would work with and who they wouldn't, but also because he knew that all routes had to remain open.

One tactical decision that was taken when it was clear that the Conservatives were likely to have the largest number of votes and seats was to put Simon Hughes in charge of media responses from the moment the polls closed on the Thursday night. In the run-up to the election, Clegg's chosen way of dealing with talk of hung parliaments and possible post-election deals had been to say that the party with the biggest mandate should have first go at forming a government, even though it could be argued that constitutional convention dictated otherwise, given that the sitting prime minister remains in office until he/she resigns. Once it was clear that the right-wing main party had earned the first go, the leading figure from the left of the Liberal Democrats became the party's immediate spokesperson. 'The thinking was', says Hughes, 'if the party saw me there saying it was all alright, they would probably think that it couldn't be all that bad. I was coming from the opposite side of the party from Nick, but I wasn't a threat because I'd stood twice for election and hadn't made it. And I was committed to the coalition working.'

When the exit polls announced the extreme likelihood of a hung parliament, it meant Clegg would have to deal with a situation in which his moment of massive opportunity came amid massive disappointment. The Lib Dems may have held the balance of power, but they were shattered that the Clegg bounce had delivered fewer seats and only a small increase in votes, and they were mourning defeats for some valued parliamentary colleagues and the failure to win some target seats. When Clegg arrived back at Lib Dem HQ from his vote count in Sheffield, television helicopters having followed his car all the way from St Pancras station to Cowley Street, he looked drained and demoralised. Outside the Lib Dems' office, a phalanx of cameras and reporters awaited, along with what looked like a crowd of supporters. They were supporters, after a fashion – they were office staff who had been asked to go outside to give the party leader a backdrop for a comment that was likely to be broadcast all day (morale within 4 Cowley Street was very bad that morning, but Paddy Ashdown had come in to rally the troops and make everyone feel much more positive by the time Clegg and the cameras arrived). Clegg mustered the effort for a brief comment, restating his position that the Conservatives, as the largest party, should have first bite at forming a government and that the Lib Dems would talk to them first. He then went in to thank party workers for their efforts during the election campaign. As he finished his speech, he was given warm applause, and Laws says he was 'visibly choking back the tears and emotion' as he left the Lib Dems' so-called War Room. 'That was the toughest speech of my life,' he told Laws.

The first talks between the Conservative and Lib Dem delegations happened on the Friday evening, but before then Clegg had been phoned by both David Cameron and Gordon Brown. The conversation with Cameron is reported to have lasted twelve minutes, and involved a discussion about going into negotiations with a positive attitude and good faith. The conversation with Brown lasted twenty-three minutes, of which about twenty-two were Brown talking at Clegg from what sounded like a prepared script. Brown was clearly desperate for a deal. He tried to get Clegg to renege on his promise to give the party with the biggest mandate the first chance to form a government; the Prime Minister wanted the Lib Dems to negotiate in parallel with Labour and the Tories. Clegg tried to politely refuse, but kept getting steam-rollered by Brown (who as prime minister did have constitutional convention on his side, but was making a hash of using it to his advantage). Even Peter Mandelson, who was sitting with Brown when he made the call, admits in *The Third Man*, 'I was a little worried that Gordon might have come across a bit too heavily, telling Nick what he should think rather than asking him what he thought. I told him this, but he was excitedly focusing on the negotiating team he wanted to handle the detailed talks with the Lib Dems.' The call certainly did nothing to encourage Clegg in the belief that he could work with Brown, yet he knew that his party's hand in negotiations with both the major parties would be stronger if a deal with 'the other lot' was always plausible.

The Lib Dem team went into the post-election negotiations with four options: doing nothing and taking each parliamentary vote on its merits; a 'confidence and supply' arrangement with the Conservatives; a full-blown coalition with the Conservatives; or a coalition with Labour that included informal support deals with smaller parties (known by various names, but mostly a 'rainbow coalition'). Clegg and his negotiating team had rejected a 'confidence and supply' deal with Labour even before the election, as it would have meant sustaining a losing party in power without any sense of it being a new government, but some senior figures in the party privately considered that option over the weekend after the election.

By Saturday morning, the four options were down to three, as a meeting of the parliamentary party – Lib Dem MPs and peers – rejected the first one, the 'do nothing' option. The meeting was originally announced for 10 a.m., but had to be put back to noon because Clegg had to join Brown and Cameron for a wreath-laying ceremony at the Cenotaph. It was the sixty-fifth anniversary of VE Day, and the presence of the three party leaders looking very sombre in dark suits and dark ties, just thirty-six hours after the country had effectively said it wasn't bowled over by the thought of any of them becoming prime minister, was one of the more surreal images of the post-election theatre. 'It was fantastically British,' Clegg says with an almost disbelieving smile. 'We were standing there talking about everything except what was on our mind. I don't know if we did talk about the weather, maybe we did, it was a bit patchy, so we'd say "Oh, it's drizzling today" in mock jocularity, when actually everyone knew that that very day discussions were continuing in one way or another between us.'

In his account of the negotiations, Laws gives full vent to his frustrations at the difficulty of getting decisions out of Liberal Democrats, because they love to throw around ideas and sometimes debate them *ad nauseam*. Hence his, and others', delight when the party's leading representatives, at their delayed meeting, proved to be pragmatic, realistic and ambitious. 'What had happened', Laws wondered, 'to my colleagues' reputations for truculence?' They all made it clear that doing nothing was not an option and would only land them with another election in the autumn. So that option was off the table.

It soon became clear that there was only one serious obstacle to doing a deal with the Conservatives: electoral reform. There was plenty of common ground; the Tories were happy to go along with three of the four Lib Dem headline manifesto pledges, and the Lib Dems were even willing to concede some ground on one of their campaigning themes: the idea that action to cut the budget deficit should not start too quickly for fear of endangering the economic recovery. The Greek crisis, coupled with a sense of urgency communicated by the Bank of England, had led to a change in emphasis in the Lib Dem position. But the Conservatives were not willing to offer anything on changing the voting system that the Lib Dems felt was worth having.

The problem for the Lib Dems was that, privately, they didn't want a 'confidence and supply' deal, as they believed that would have led to an autumn general election as well as all the blame for the government's actions. But they knew they could never sell a coalition with the Tories to Lib Dem members without at least a referendum on changing the voting system. Labour was offering that, or at least had done so in its manifesto, but the arithmetic didn't give Labour plus Lib Dems an overall majority in Parliament.

Clegg had a long meeting with Cameron on Saturday night, essentially to see if they could get on with each other – they had had very little contact outside state formalities up to that point. At the same time, the Lib Dem negotiating team met for informal and secret talks with the Labour delegation sent by Gordon Brown. The Labour team consisted of Peter Mandelson, Andrew Adonis (a former Lib Dem who had defected to Labour and had been education minister and transport secretary), Ed Balls and Ed Miliband. Adonis was certainly trusted by the Lib Dems, and Mandelson was known to be keen on cooperation among progressives in British politics. But the inclusion of the two Eds ran counter to Brown's apparent enthusiasm for a Lib–Lab deal. As putative candidates in a forthcoming Labour leadership election, they were both reticent about becoming too associated with the Lib Dems, whose status in some Labour ranks was pretty low. Laws reports detecting 'a lack of urgency' among the Labour team, certainly compared with the Conservatives' delegation.

There was also an elephant in the room. The Lib Dems just could not envisage doing a deal with Labour if Brown remained prime minister. For a while this was left out of discussions, but then Chris Huhne said, 'We have yet to discuss how we deal with the Gordon Brown problem.' He was slapped down by Danny Alexander, who said, 'No, Chris, that is not a matter we are discussing.' Alexander had apparently been in contact with Mandelson, and while the Brown problem had been acknowledged, it was considered too sensitive to debate at this early stage. In *Five Days to Power*, Rob Wilson makes a comment about the Lib Dems' attitude to Brown which reflected how many Labour and Conservative supporters felt at this stage of the negations: 'With as little as 23 per cent of the vote and 57 MPs, Clegg and his team had concluded that it was right for them to choose who should not be the leader of the Labour Party and who should not be prime minister of the UK.' That is one way to look at it; the Lib Dems saw it as a question of what price someone is willing to pay for a service – they were simply saying they would not be willing to go into a deal with a Brown-led Labour party, and were having difficulty understanding why Conservatives should have any difficulty accepting this. In the language of economics, the thinking was that business happens when both sides are happy with the deal, and the Lib Dems were setting out their terms. Wilson's phrasing perhaps reveals a lot about how the Conservatives felt on that Sunday night – that power was gradually slipping away from them.

Indeed a feature of this whole post-election period was that the Liberal Democrats – from Clegg, through his negotiating team and his shadow Cabinet, to the party's MPs and peers – proved to be remarkably sanguine and hard nosed. That may sound a somewhat biased assessment, but Laws's frustrations about the impractical elements of a party that is liberal and democratic to its core were shared by many others, both inside and outside the Lib Dems. Yet it was almost as if, faced with both an opportunity and a tremendous responsibility to the country, the party grew up, at least in Westminster terms. This clearly upset some traditional liberals, who would always have put their concept of liberalism ahead of any tactical considerations in forming a government. But the Lib Dems knew what they needed (a deal that delivered some meaningful progress on electoral reform), they all pulled by and large in the same direction, and they worked their tactics in a way that led to the desired outcome. Growing up, or an end to innocence? Both, probably, although some Labour and Conservative activists who had worked with the Lib Dems at council level would laugh at the idea that the party was still innocent by 2010.

This new hard-nosed approach was evident in Clegg's bluntness to Brown. By Sunday night, negotiations with the Conservatives had been largely completed except for the hoped-for concession on electoral reform. The position they had reached might be enough for the Lib Dems to accept a 'confidence and supply' deal, but certainly not a full-blown coalition. The Lib Dem negotiating team had therefore begun formal negotiations with Labour, and on Sunday evening Clegg and Alexander met Brown and Mandelson. Brown had indicated earlier in the day that he was willing to stand down if it smoothed the way to a Lib–Lab deal, but by the time he faced Clegg across the table in his House of Commons office, he was talking about staying on to usher in a new constitutional era.

This frustrated Clegg, who felt the issue of 'personnel' could no longer be avoided. He told the Prime Minister, 'Please understand I have no personal animosity whatsoever, but it is not possible to secure the legitimacy of a coalition and win a referendum unless you move on in a dignified way. You have said you don't want to be a barrier. You've been an incredible catalyst in reshaping politics, but we cannot persuade the public of renewal unless you go in time.' Brown still resisted, saying he wanted to see the referendum through, to which Alexander retorted, 'But we can't win this referendum with you as prime minister.' Those present say this was the moment when the air went out of Brown's balloon and he realised the game was probably up. 'It was a hard message to deliver,' says Alexander, 'and Nick found it very hard; Gordon Brown was very taken aback.'

Clegg later told Rob Wilson, 'I remember thinking that perhaps it was unfair that I said all this about Brown in front of other people, because he is a proud man and I felt for him. Afterwards I apologised that I had been so blunt with him in front of other people, and that I should have said it one to one. I didn't want him in any way humiliated. I said to him, if he were to go he should go with dignity. I felt no animus towards him, but he was clearly taken aback by what I'd said.'

A year on, Clegg offered this assessment: 'The discussions with Gordon Brown were very intense. He's a very intense man, and in many respects an admirable man. I didn't know him at all, and I guess what stands out in my mind is the extraordinary, almost bizarre ability he had to speak with admirable clarity and passion and conviction about things that were important to him – I remember having a fascinating discussion with him about forming an international financial system, and honestly I was totally engaged. And then the next moment he would show a kind of anger and bitterness and complex fury about domestic politics. So at one moment he made me think "This is someone I share things with", and at another moment I felt this was a person I could never work with.'

So the Lib Dems had said it straight, but there was still no guarantee that Brown would go. Without Brown going, the Lib Dems couldn't see themselves doing a deal with Labour. The Conservatives could see that, so with Brown still in situ, they had no need to offer anything substantial on electoral reform. It was a dilemma for the third party at the height of its supposed powers of leverage.

The way the dilemma was got round was almost comical, and gives the lie to the idea that retired British politicians fade gracefully into the middle distance, to be dredged up only for the occasional media interview.

Paddy Ashdown, still a member of the Lib Dem parliamentary party, had been given Clegg's blessing to talk up the prospects of a Lib–Lab deal. He was trawled around the media on Sunday night and Monday morning. He says, 'Somebody had got to make this very fragile deal with Labour look as though it was a possibility, otherwise how would we have any bargaining power with the Tories? Somebody had to go round pumping this thing up, and I was the person to do that. I said the grand panjandrum that would involve all the Scottish Nats, the Welsh Nats, would never work, but we might be able to give some sort of a verisimilitude to the idea of a Lib Dem–Labour minority government against whom there was a mathematical majority but one that would never be politically assembled. Did I emotionally feel more comfortable with that? Yes. But did I know I was doing something that was very unlikely to succeed? Yes. And at one stage that was pretty cruelly exposed when I was on the *Today* programme and was interviewed by Nick Robinson, who said I was pushing a tactical line; I said I wasn't, but it was pretty obvious I was. It wasn't my best interview ever.'

Ashdown is probably being a little too self-effacing here. The fact was that he and more than a few in the party were serious that if such an arrangement with Labour could work, then an effort should be made to try to see if it was possible. Ashdown got Chris Rennard – now retired from the role of party chief executive but, as Lord Rennard, still a member of the parliamentary party – to work out the Commons arithmetic. It showed that a rainbow coalition was possible, but only if Labour MPs were united behind it and the commitments to electoral reform that a Lib–Lab deal would have to carry. They proved not to be, as the coordinated anti-Lib–Lab interventions of David Blunkett and John Reid demonstrated on the Monday evening and Tuesday morning.

With the news media having concentrated on the growing likelihood of a Conservative deal with the Liberal Democrats for most of Saturday, the tone of Monday's stories had changed to the distinct possibility that Labour and the Lib Dems would do some deal. This also changed the nature of Lib Dem MPs' and defeated candidates' mailboxes. Over the weekend, left-leaning Lib Dem supporters had deluged their MPs and candidates with 'Don't do it!' messages. By Monday morning, the 'Don't do it!' messages were coming from the right-leaning Lib Dem supporters. Such was always going to be the reality for a party that had taken votes from Labour, Conservatives and strictly non-aligned people – a coalition with either major party was going to leave two of the Lib Dems' three constituencies severely cheesed off.

The shift from a likely Con–Lib deal to a Lab–Lib deal also unleashed severe anger among Conservative supporters. The following, sent by a former Tory parliamentary candidate to a friend who had just stood for the Lib Dems, encapsulates the strength of feeling: 'I have never been as angry as I feel this morning and I now regard Clegg as a duplicitous bastard who, while publicly negotiating with the Tories, was secretly negotiating with Labour, including the resignation of Brown. So now it seems that we will have a coalition of two parties who lost seats at the election, led by someone who was not a candidate for prime minister. Even so that coalition will need the support of the Nationalists who will no doubt demand that England, and not their countries, bear the brunt of the inevitable public spending cuts. If that happens, I cannot believe that the English, who overwhelmingly voted Conservative, will not rise up and demand fair treatment. I can see all this leading to the break-up of the United Kingdom, and if that happens this proud Brit will never forgive your party.'

Again, the anger is understandable, especially in a party that had spent thirteen years in opposition and had fallen agonisingly just short of an overall majority. But were the Lib Dems really doing anything different than the Conservatives would have done in the same circumstances? If there is a moral stick with which to beat the Lib Dems over their negotiating tactics, it would more reasonably be the fact that the party had campaigned for a 'new politics' but had taken to hard-nosed negotiating tactics to achieve the best deal it could get for its 23 per cent of the vote (which, after all, had yielded less than 9 per cent of the seats). This was the difference Clegg and the new generation of Liberal Democrats had brought about – theirs was no longer a cuddly philosophising-and-protest-vote party but one that was determined to use its leverage to get as many of its policies put into practice as it could.

The other thing Ashdown did was also a crucial bargaining manoeuvre, and again it had Clegg's tacit blessing. That evening, the former leader had hosted one of his many dinner parties, in which his wife Jane cooked dinner for a handful of Lib Dem MPs not part of the negotiating team. That evening's guest list included two heavyweights from north of the border, Ming Campbell and Alistair Carmichael. David Laws had been nominally invited, but had negotiations with the Labour team to go to. Ashdown told Laws to phone him after the talks had finished, whatever the hour.

During the evening, while the negotiations were happening, Ashdown and guests consumed 'a bottle of wine or three' and took some interesting phone calls. Gordon Brown rang Campbell, and the Scottish Nationalists' leader, Alex Salmond, rang Carmichael. Ashdown recalls all this with a bemused pride, as if his living room were the central switchboard for the various peripheral negotiations.

Around midnight, the guests left Ashdown's flat in Kennington, at which point Paddy and Jane left all the washing up to go to bed. But at around 1 a.m., Laws phoned sounding very demoralised. Ashdown ordered him round and put the kettle on. Laws explained that Brown had gone back on his apparent willingness to stand down, and the Lib Dem team couldn't see how they would be able to do a deal with Labour.

'Leave it to me,' the man nicknamed Action Man said. 'Tell you what, I'll ring Blair.' So Ashdown rang Tony Blair's home number and got Cherie out of bed. 'Where's Tony? I need to speak to him,' Ashdown said, only to be told Blair was in the Middle East. 'OK, give me his number.' Cherie duly obliged, and Ashdown rang a number in the Middle East and left a message for the former prime minister to get back to him as soon as possible. An hour or so later, Blair phoned back. Ashdown says, 'So I said to him, "Tony, I don't know if this progressive coalition of the left is going to work, but if it is, Gordon's got to go." He said "Fine, leave it to me", and the next morning there were lots of conversations, no doubt involving him, Mandelson and Alastair Campbell, and Brown went.'

It wasn't quite that simple. Blair did phone Brown, and tried to persuade him to go by saying a long-term recovery of the left would be more achievable if the Conservatives got into government at the height of the recession, when they were bound to make themselves unpopular. That wasn't quite the message Ashdown wanted to have imparted, but the Ashdown–Blair axis, which had looked like delivering some form of Lib–Lab cooperation in the late 1990s until Labour's landslide victory meant it didn't need the Lib Dems, was playing a significant part in the post-election negotiations of 2010.

After further discussions with Clegg, Brown made a statement in Downing Street on the Monday afternoon, saying the election had been something of a verdict on him, that he didn't want to be an obstacle to a deal between Labour and the Liberal Democrats, and that he was therefore asking his party's officials to make preparations for a leadership election to deliver a new Labour leader by the autumn.

With Brown looking like he would soon be out of the way, a Lib–Lab deal was suddenly a much more realistic option. Within a couple of hours, the Tories' chief negotiator William Hague had announced that the Conservatives were willing to offer a referendum on the alternative vote. That was the concession the Lib Dems were looking for and, in retrospect, it was the turning point in the negotiations. The Lib Dem team carried on negotiating with Labour until Tuesday morning, but their heart wasn't in it, as Peter Mandelson accurately observes in his book. In fact, having got the concession on the referendum, the Lib Dems' entire focus was thrown back into getting a deal with the Conservatives.

Brown, however, had one more card up his sleeve. On the Tuesday morning, he met again with Clegg to make an offer of the alternative vote without a referendum, a referendum on proportional representation, and a 50:50 split of Cabinet positions between Labour and the Lib Dems. On paper, this was an impressive offer for the Lib Dems, but Clegg found himself unable to trust such a good offer from a man clearly trying to save his own skin. And it was badly timed. Only that morning, David Blunkett had had an article published in *The Guardian* opposing a Lib–Lab deal, and the previous evening, another former Labour Home Secretary, John Reid, had gone on BBC TV's *Newsnight* with a similar line. Reid had phoned Blunkett on Monday afternoon to say he was going on television that night and asking for Blunkett's support in saying no to a Lib–Lab deal. As Blunkett's *Guardian* article was already submitted, he had no difficulty supporting his former Cabinet colleague.

All this, coupled with the Lib Dem negotiating team's reports of the Labour team's half-heartedness, convinced Clegg that Brown's offer was just too good to be true, and he rejected it. The offer was thought to be too implausible for the Lib Dem high command to have even canvassed it widely among the party. As Brown tried to persuade Clegg by talking about the chance of a realignment of the left being lost for at least a generation if the Lib Dems went in with the Tories, Clegg replied brutally, 'The reality is that your party is knackered after thirteen years in power.'

That perhaps should have been the final word, but Clegg clearly believed that Brown couldn't yet resign as prime minister because there was no alternative government. But Brown had had enough, and forty-five minutes later he told Clegg by phone that he was going. As Mandelson describes it, 'Gordon was serene in telling Nick "The public has run out of patience, and so have I ... You are a good man and you have to make a decision, I have made mine. It is final. I am going to the Palace. Goodbye."' It took another few hours before the Browns were ready to leave their home of the previous three years at which point, Gordon Brown made a brief statement outside 10 Downing Street, and then walked down the road with his wife and two young boys, departing his office with a warmth and dignity that moved many, and left even more wondering why it had taken him until his parting moment to look so human.

By seven o'clock on that Tuesday night, Brown had gone. At 8.40 the same evening, David Cameron stood outside 10 Downing Street announcing Britain's first coalition government since the Second World War. It was a momentous announcement, and even the most flowery of political commentators found their hyperbole to be justified on this occasion.

Clegg had had to overcome some severe reservations before agreeing to the coalition. 'Do you really think the party membership will wear a coalition with the Conservatives?' he had asked his senior lieutenants. His political nose was clearly working, as the fallout from the coalition announcement was to confirm, but ultimately the party had no real alternative. As Paddy Ashdown colourfully put it, 'We had three choices: we could be shot in the morning if we went in with Labour, we could be shot in the autumn if we let the Tories govern on a minority basis, or we *might* be shot in four or five years if we went into coalition with the Conservatives. So it was the only thing to do.'

Clegg himself was never in doubt that going into coalition with the Conservatives carried massive risks for his party. 'There was a moment late in the process when the negotiations were going in the wrong direction,' he says. 'We and the Conservatives couldn't agree on some crucial issues, so we said "Let's have a minority government". I had a phone call with David Cameron in which we said, pretty well at the same time, "That's just not good enough, it won't last, it'll be unstable, the country won't like it, we won't be able to do the difficult things, we've got to go further". That was a very crucial moment, because I realised we'd got to take an even bigger risk. It is a hugely risky thing to do politically, particularly for the party that's smaller. When I put the phone down, I just felt I had thought it all through and there were no other easy options.'

The test of the parliamentary Lib Dems' new-found lack of truculence was to come on the Tuesday night. The parliamentary party and Federal Executive met to vote on the coalition agreement. A majority was expected to vote in favour, but how many would abstain or vote against? The higher the number of dissenters, the rougher the seas for the junior coalition partners were likely to be. Of all the MPs and peers, no-one voted against. There was one objecting voice among the Federal Executive members – that came from David Rendel, the former MP for Newbury. Among the MPs there were two abstentions, not a bad vote of confidence, except that one of the abstentions was from a former leader, Charles Kennedy.

Kennedy had phoned Clegg that afternoon to tell him where he stood on a Con–Lib deal. 'I was quite supportive of him personally,' Kennedy says, 'and he appreciated where I was coming from. I abstained, visibly so, but I didn't look around the room to see if there were other abstention hands. I didn't feel as a former leader that that was fair – I don't like abstentions as a rule, but I think on this one, it wouldn't have been right for me to go against Nick, and everybody else for that matter. We didn't have a full house of parliamentarians, so there may be someone who didn't endorse it who wasn't there.' (The other abstaining MP was John Leech.)

Kennedy says his reservation was of a long-term strategic nature rather than because of the deal itself. 'The coalition agreement is excellent. You're never going to get everything you want, but as deals go, that was fine. My concern is more historic, that if you look back at the Chamberlain period or the National Liberals, every time the Liberal tradition has hooked up with the Conservative tradition, funnily enough the long-term gainers tend to be the Conservatives, and that remains my strategic anxiety.'

The risk Clegg took was in taking a party that had spent the previous twenty years with a picture of itself as the more free-thinking and less cloth-cap end of the progressive movement in British politics, into a coalition with its traditional enemy. Indeed even in the latter years of the Liberal Party – before the Social Democrats and the Liberal Democrats came along – the growing mindset was that Labour was the competition and the Conservatives the opposition. While Liberal fortunes suffered immensely during the Lib–Lab Pact of 1977–8, when David Steel's thirteen Liberal MPs propped up an increasingly weak-looking Labour government under James Callaghan, most Liberals felt it was the right party to be doing business with. Although Clegg believed the Con–Lib coalition would work, he couldn't be sure his party would feel the same way. He had seen through changes in how Liberal Democrats would try and achieve their aims; he had also seen what he thought were changes in the Conservative Party that the grey heads of the Lib Dems hadn't; and he had decided that he could work with David Cameron. But he knew the average Lib Dem member was more likely to feel the party was supping with the devil than forming a progressive alliance. Hence his mixture of relief and delight when a pre-planned but hastily convened special federal conference of the Liberal Democrats in Birmingham the following Sunday overwhelmingly approved the coalition. There were a few objections, but the mood and the vote were massively in favour.

Looking back on that period, Clegg says, 'I had a profound sense of pride in our party, that we had made a very difficult decision in the national interest, and most importantly that we had made it collectively. We started out disappointed at our own result, and as a party naturally with great scepticism about going into government with the Conservatives. But throughout many long, often late-night meetings, we developed a maturity, a team feeling, which extended to the whole party at the conference in Birmingham. We are such a diverse bunch at times, but when it came to the crunch, when it came to providing government for the nation at a time when both the country and the markets were craving stability, we had a room full of MPs with various shades of liberal opinion willing to come together to make a very difficult decision. Some knew that the moment they went into coalition with the Tories, it would be difficult for some of our reporters, so to still take that decision in the national interest was something that was very impressive.'

Part of his confidence that his party would buy the Con–Lib coalition stemmed from his belief in the importance of civil liberties, which the Lib Dems felt had taken a hammering under Labour and which helped send out the message that Labour could not be trusted on all the issues dear to liberals' hearts. And his European background may well have played a part. 'Liberals just assume that being on the left of centre is the morally right place to be,' says the Lib Dem MEP and former close confidant of Clegg, Chris Davies, 'so to go into coalition with the Conservatives is seen as a betrayal of everything that's natural, and it's nonsense. As D66 [one of the two Dutch liberal parties] learned, you're standing up for your liberalism, and that forces you to be more liberally distinctive in your own identity and be more confident about your liberalism. We are not supposed to be aiming to be some adjunct to the Labour Party, or the Labour Party's conscience.'

The completion of the coalition deal less than five days after the polls closed was a remarkable achievement, something that is largely unappreciated in a British political culture not used to coalition-forming. 'It was remarkably untortuous,' says the Lib

Dem MP Norman Baker. 'In fact our European neighbours would be astonished that we could put a coalition together in such a short space of time, especially with such a detailed programme – it's almost incredible. There was an intellectual acceptance within the party that this was our chance, helped by the numbers, and by the fact that Tories were offering quite a lot and the deal was a good one. My heart said no but my head said yes, and that's where we ended up.'

Perhaps inevitably, it is the bounding figure of Paddy Ashdown who most colourfully sums up the Lib Dems' dilemma and their attitude to resolving it. 'When Nick and the guys took the decision to go with the Conservatives, I was very upset, extremely upset emotionally,' he says. 'I walked into the parliamentary party meeting and I was going to say, "Look, guys, you've probably taken the right decision but I can't go along with it." My speech was that I've spent all my life fighting the Tories, I didn't come into politics to put the Tories in power, and I don't see that the party should be used as a prop for Mr Cameron to reform his party and be the new Disraeli. I've spent thirty years getting Labour out of the south-west and now they'll have a chance to get back, and we're left with a strategy that's no longer the realignment of the left but confines us to being the FDP [the centre-right German liberal party], always the bridesmaid and never the bride. But I read the coalition agreement as I sat there, and my response changed to "Fuck it, I'm always up for a fight, and if this is what you're fighting for, count me in". So I was wrong for about an hour.'

The subject of 'personnel' had revolved so much around the figure of Gordon Brown that it totally left out the question of who would take up the ministerial posts in the new coalition government. Indeed the Lib Dems' preparations had been focused on policy rather than on who would do what jobs.

The distribution of responsibilities was left to Cameron and Clegg to work out, and Cameron made it clear he wanted Conservatives in the three major offices of state (Foreign Office, Home Office and Treasury). That scuppered Vince Cable's hopes of becoming Chancellor of the Exchequer, a job he says he was 'mentally prepared for, and it was a job I think I could have done well, but it didn't happen, and I accepted it with good grace'. With Clegg as the Deputy Prime Minister, with a much more defined role than previous incumbents of that office, it would probably have been a concession too far for Cable to take on the role of principal finance minister. So it was that George Osborne was the first Cabinet minister to be named after the two party leaders had announced the coalition deal.

There is a view in some Lib Dem circles that Cameron outfoxed Clegg by giving the departments of Energy & Climate Change and Business, Innovation & Skills to Lib Dem ministers, Chris Huhne and Cable respectively. The thinking goes that the Lib Dems had campaigned against nuclear power and tuition fees, and the two ministers would have to implement a pro-nuclear energy policy and a raising of tuition fees. There may be something in that, although Huhne is a Liberal for whom the environment is a primary issue, and Cable was more concerned with banking reform, something he could do as Business Secretary, than with tuition fees, which he felt were inevitable.

The other two Lib Dem Cabinet members were also naturally placed, Danny Alexander going to the Scottish Office, and David Laws taking the role as Osborne's second in command as Chief Secretary to the Treasury. Despite their inexperience in government, the Lib Dems had provided five ministers who seemed genuinely qualified for their roles. But the coalition's first personnel snag erupted on 28 May, just a fortnight after the ministers had been sworn in.

A week after taking up residence in the Deputy Prime Minister's office, overlooking Horse Guards Parade, Clegg took a few days' holiday with this family in France. That holiday came to a premature end when David Laws phoned him to say he wanted to resign from the Cabinet over a story the *Daily Telegraph* had run about him having claimed £40,000 of taxpayers' money to pay rent to his partner, James Lundie.

The case was a somewhat unusual one, in that Laws's motivation in what was a breach of the rules that had changed in 2006 (five years after he became an MP) was not financial but a wish to keep the relationship with Lundie private. The Parliamentary Standards Commissioner's report accepted this. The relationship and the nature of his sexuality was unknown to family and friends until made public following questions by the *Daily Telegraph* about his expenses claims. While being 'outed' would not have caused many waves politically given that both Labour and Conservative front benches featured several openly gay figures, Laws felt that making his relationship public would have caused distress to people close to both men. Ironically, if Laws had had a wife in Yeovil, but spent most nights with a mistress in London and paid rent to her, this would have been within the rules. In addition, Laws could have legitimately made much larger claims for a mortgage on his constituency house in Yeovil, and Lundie paid 40 per cent tax on the rental payments. But they broke parliamentary rules, and Laws was forced to apologise. Among the comments he issued in resigning was, 'I cannot escape the conclusion that what I have done was in some way wrong, even though I did not gain any financial benefit from keeping my relationship secret in this way.'

Because Laws had apologised, agreed to pay back the £40,000 he had claimed, and had referred his own case to the Parliamentary Standards Commissioner, Cameron's and Clegg's initial reaction was that he should stay in office while the House of Commons authorities investigated his case. 'He was very supportive and helpful,' Laws says of his phone conversation with Clegg. 'He tried to encourage me to continue and see things through, which was nice to have, but when he was clear that I was very certain what I wanted to do, he accepted it.' Cameron's and Clegg's willingness to see Laws given a chance to ride out the storm probably says more about the esteem in which the two men held him, than about the political reality. Less than three weeks after the election that was supposed to bring to an end a discreditable era in the finances of British politics, there was no way Laws could remain in a job that was all about restoring confidence in public finances. In the ensuing months, there was much speculation about the MP for Yeovil returning to the Cabinet, but Laws doesn't given the impression of a man bursting to get back; indeed, his talk of needing to 'redress the balance' of his political career and 'the interests of those I love most' suggests that he would not wish to reignite the controversy.

His resignation required a reshuffle in the Lib Dem component of the Cabinet, with Danny Alexander moving to Chief Secretary to the Treasury, and Michael Moore coming in to replace Alexander as Scottish Secretary. Although Alexander had less of an economic track record than Laws, the move probably suited Clegg very well, given that his close friend was now in the second most powerful financial role. Three weeks after the general election, the personnel of the new government were finally in place.

Chapter 12

'THE LIGHTNING ROD'

THERE'S A lovely perception about Britain that our politics is very harmless and genteel. People make fun of it, and these days hold their politicians in fairly low esteem, but there's a sense that British politics is civilised, because you can say what you want. It's true that you don't get thrown into prison for your beliefs (unless they're likely to cause civil unrest or compromise national security), but the idea that you can say what you want and the worst that will happen to you is a bit of gentle ridicule is not one those close to Nick Clegg would share following the autumn of 2010.

As protests about the government's Bill for funding higher education reached a peak in October 2010, Clegg's family and constituency workers came under increasing attack. Initially, security around his family home had been modest, indeed there was even talk within security circles that it wasn't warranted – the custom is that only the Prime Minister and the Home Secretary have police guards. But Clegg's staff continued to argue for police presence, and when demonstrators staged noisy protests, and dog excrement was put through the letter box of Clegg's constituency office in Sheffield, the protection was made full-time. On one occasion, his eldest son, Antonio, came home from school upset because he couldn't work out why the other kids were giving his dad so much stick. 'Why are the students so angry with you, Papa?' he asked him. On the occasion when Clegg gave the annual Hugo Young memorial lecture in London, demonstrators held a mock execution outside the building, burning an effigy of him, with the protest leader hailing repeatedly through a megaphone 'Nick Clegg must die'. Nice, harmless, civilised politics.

'I think it's been very, very painful for him,' says Vince Cable of the stick Clegg took in the autumn of 2010, 'and he's shown a lot of courage. A lot of people would have just crumbled under the relentless hate. The Labour people have been unbelievably tribal, mainly towards him. It may be the Sheffield thing, maybe because he's leader, but they've really targeted him with absolutely concentrated hatred, and that's been communicated at a grass roots level, and the burning of the effigy is part of that. That, the tuition fees, the talk of betrayal, the endless propaganda from *The Guardian* – to have that relentlessly thrown at him day after day, and he's had ridicule too. There's obviously some inner steel that's keeping him going, but it's not pleasant. Although a lot of this is very hurtful, he's sufficiently self-confident and professional that he can carry on and, even after a bad day, can perform well in a Cabinet discussion.'

Even those who have the highest regard for Clegg felt, when he became Deputy Prime Minister, that the one thing he had not proved was his ability to fight against adversity. He had had a few setbacks, but essentially had enjoyed a steady and uninterrupted progression through his three degrees, working for the European Commission, becoming an MEP, then an MP, and ultimately party leader. One of his biggest advocates is Lord Brittan, but even he mused in the autumn of 2010, 'Does he have the resilience to cope with a serious setback? You don't know until you have one, and he hasn't yet. I think he's developed enough experience and character that it's reasonable to hope that if he had a major setback he would have the necessary resilience, but until he's in that situation, you can't be sure. I personally think he would have it, but he has been lucky not to need to show that particular quality up to now.'

The word that those around Clegg use most often to describe how he handled the first year of the coalition is indeed 'resilient'. His principal coping mechanism was to see the person 'Nick Clegg' that the public and media continually whipped into a hate figure as a different person to the man he sees himself as. One staff member (his office staff cannot be named as they are on the government payroll and are therefore not allowed to make public pronouncements by name about matters to do with government) said, 'We'll come in glum because someone has given him a kicking in the press, and then he'll come in cheerful despite knowing about it. There's a public image that he's beaten down by it, but that's not what he's like – he's the one who comes in and makes the banter and the jokes, and takes the mickey out of what's in the papers. When he finds he's criticised, he asks whether it's of great importance, and if it is, he'll deal with it, but if it isn't, he just doesn't get involved with the myth. It stuns me how resilient he is.'

His friend Neil Sherlock says, 'He gets up every morning with his armour on, but it's almost liberating in that it allows you to do the right thing, because the media will say what they want anyway, so you may as well do what you think is right. People say he doesn't read the papers, when he self-evidently does. But he has a very powerful home life, and some very supportive friends, so that gives him a break from it all.'

Such plaudits suggest his resilience comes from a head-in-the-sand approach, but it's probably more constructive than that. Danny Alexander says, 'I think you wouldn't be human if it didn't register, but Nick is someone for whom the effect was to stimulate him to go out and make the argument and confront people head on. The most famous saying attributed to Jo Grimond was that, in times of crisis, you should not run away from trouble but "march towards the sound of gunfire", and Nick's done that. He's kept up his regular town hall meetings and discussions with students as a way of getting out there, confronting the critics, and trying to persuade them. He's someone who believes very strongly in the power of reason and persuasion. The barracking has had the opposite effect to the one you might think. I don't think it affected him personally, but it definitely spurred him on to take on the debate as opposed to shrinking from it.'

There's a belief among many of his staff that it's much better to be demonised than ignored. They remember the time when they were fighting for publicity for him, when the media viewed him as a figure who added a bit of colour to the political spectrum but wasn't taken seriously, perhaps not even within his own party while Vince Cable's star shone so brightly. In publicity terms there may be something in that, but in electoral terms it's much more hazardous. Clegg's Lib Dems did very well when there was less scrutiny on them, and the hammering they took in the May 2011 elections after a year of Clegg-bashing by the media suggests that being demonised does seep through to many voters.

Clegg's view now is to play down the abuse. 'I think it's been exaggerated,' he says of the battering he took. 'Maybe I've been responsible for that. There were a couple of occasions when we had students shouting outside the house in London, and then there were some environmentalists who left something at the door at five in the morning, which rather alarmed Miriam. We had some people demonstrating in my constituency office in Sheffield who wrote graffiti on a wall there, but on the whole we've been very lucky that the kids have been relatively insulated.'

A strong motivating factor behind such statements is that Clegg would not want to be seen to be wallowing in self-pity (not that self-pity is part of the Clegg personality, but the wrong utterance could easily be construed that way). But his chief parliamentary and political adviser, Norman Lamb, says it has been very stressful. 'If you imagine what it must have been like in the autumn, he'd been in Parliament for five-and-a-half years and DPM for a few months – suddenly you're into the student protests with burning effigies and people gathering outside your home in an aggressive way, and you've got small children. It's staggeringly tough, and he's demonstrated an extraordinary resilience. But he is acutely aware of the responsibility he carries, both for the party and the country, and he has a considerable self-confidence, a lot of political skills and the confidence to go for it.'

As befits someone keen to play down the unpleasantness, he has talked very little about it to his parliamentary colleagues, but one middle-ranking Lib Dem MP believes it could have long-term consequences. 'I think it has hardened his opposition to Labour,' says junior transport minister Norman Baker. 'He's getting himself potentially into a position where it's more difficult to do a deal with Labour after the next election, if that's an option. He's probably seen the worst of the Labour Party in action in Sheffield, on the doorstep, and that's coloured his judgement. If the objective of those people from the old left has been to try and separate the Lib Dems from the Tories, it may have had the opposite effect, because it makes the Tories look sympathetic and pleasant, and Labour look like a bunch of vandals and hooligans. Nick has become the lightning rod for those people who cannot accept the logic of a coalition with the Tories. These are people who hate the Tories, who believe that any Tory government is a reincarnation of Thatcher, and feel that somehow anybody who does business with them to keep them in power is betraying that opposition that we all feel. That's the emotional response – it works off a mindset that the Tories are expected to be horrible, so people get furious that nice people like the Lib Dems keep the Tories in power. Thus Nick Clegg becomes the lightning rod for this attack that comes from the old left and *The Guardian*.' (It should be noted that Baker made those comments before the campaign for the alternative vote began in earnest, and that once it did, Clegg felt as disgusted by the scale of the Conservatives' attacks on him as he had by Labour's response to the Lib Dems going into coalition with the Tories.)

The first year of the coalition was always going to be tough. The government had to take decisions about the economy that were bound to be unpopular. The idea of coalition was new, and subject to quick judgements by press and public alike. The Lib Dems were brand new to the big bad world of national government, and in bed with the party that was thought to be further away from their ethical point of reference than the other major party. In addition, Clegg was coming off the unsustainable high of Cleggmania. Yet what was remarkable about the first electoral test of the new government a year later was that the Conservatives escaped largely unscathed, despite the fact that they were shaping the hard-line approach to getting the economy back on track, while the Lib Dems, who thought of themselves as the socially moderating influence in government, took a pummelling, as their leader suffered a backlash of hate, ridicule and vilification.

Could Clegg and his party have done anything different to ward off the resentment that grew out of the way the public began to see hopes of the Lib Dems offering something different coming to nothing? Leon Brittan makes an interesting point in this context. 'It's quite something to be flung in to be Deputy Prime Minister,' he says. 'My first job in government was being minister of state at the Home Office, and I crawled my way up from there, so to be thrown in at the deep end, and also having to lead a party that at best is unsure about this whole thing, it's not easy.'

It's worth remembering the context, something that easily gets forgotten with hindsight. The economic context was one of a major fear that, without a stable government, the British economy could at least be badly harmed, if not go into a Greek-style meltdown. Clegg's personal context was that his rise up the political ladder had been so rapid that he couldn't possibly be fully prepared for the reality that awaited him. His first political election was in 1998 when, at the age of thirty-one, he stood for the Lib Dem European Parliamentary nomination in the East Midlands and topped the poll. He was elected first time to the European Parliament. He was elected first time at age thirty-eight to Westminster. He was elected leader of Britain's third party a few weeks before his forty-first birthday. And he was Deputy Prime Minister at forty-three. In fairness, David Cameron had had no governmental experience when he became Prime Minister, but he had been elected to Parliament four years before Clegg, and came from a party that was used to governing and thus dealing with all the sideshows that come with it. By contrast, Clegg led a party that had not had a share in national government for sixty-five years. Being in government may have represented a remarkable rise, but it left both him and his party brutally exposed when the harsh realities of government started to bite.

As a result, he and his party were always going to make mistakes, some due to inexperience, some to naivety, and some purely self-inflicted. Yet this was simply inevitable given the unpopularity of the measures the government would have to take, while the seeds of some of the Lib Dems' difficulties were sown before the election. What made matters worse was that the party was also slow to respond to the staffing needs that the Prime Minister's office had no qualms about demanding. It was a massive learning curve, and opinions differ as to which of the difficulties Clegg should perhaps have foreseen and which can reasonably be written down to the inexperience of both a leader and his party who were in some ways out of their depth when they first entered government.

Before the issue of university tuition fees became a blazing political inferno, there were other controversies.

One of the differences between the Conservatives and Liberal Democrats in campaigning for the 2010 general election was that the Conservatives were proposing an immediate package of cuts totalling £6 billion. The Lib Dems conceded on this, partly because they were the junior party in government so had to make more concessions than the Conservatives, and partly because the Greek economic crisis had heightened the need for a significant gesture to be made to calm the stock and bond markets. But when George Osborne presented his first Budget in June 2010, the first round of cuts was a rough start for the Lib Dems, who had to explain why they were voting for something they had campaigned against.

A feature of Osborne's first Budget was a rise in VAT from 17.5 to 20 per cent, albeit delayed until 1 January 2011. This was a big embarrassment for Clegg. In the early stages of the election campaign, he had wanted to make his mark on the economic debate, perhaps in part because he was still somewhat in the shadow of Vince Cable. The result was a photo opportunity depicting the Conservatives' '20 per cent VAT bombshell', despite the fact that Cable was warning behind the scenes that putting up VAT might prove inevitable. When the coalition agreed to the rise to 20 per cent, it was portrayed in the media as a big Lib Dem 'betrayal'.

Of greater concern for Clegg at constituency level was an issue involving one of Sheffield's iconic firms. Three days before the election, Labour's Business Secretary, Peter Mandelson, had announced a £80 million loan to help Forgemasters, a Sheffield company employing 700 people which had been the subject of a management buyout when threatened with closure. The company was hugely symbolic for a former steel-manufacturing city such as Sheffield, and the news was greeted locally with delight. The problem was that the £80 million came from a budget that didn't exist, so it wasn't even a sum that could be cut – it just wasn't there. Cable and Osborne therefore had to announce that Forgemasters would not be getting its loan. Labour used this to send out the message that the Liberal Democrats didn't care about Sheffield, and Clegg took a lot of criticism from Sheffield's two most prominent Labour MPs, David Blunkett and Richard Caborn. Cable is scathing about Mandelson's promise to Forgemasters. '£80 million is not a huge sum in financial terms,' he says, 'and the firm could have got the money on the financial markets, but it would have cost the equity. So the money was effectively to save a capitalist the cost of the original equity. It couldn't be justified.'

The Forgemasters issue is just the latest chapter in a catalogue of antipathy between Labour and the Liberal Democrats in Sheffield. In parliamentary terms, Sheffield is a Labour stronghold in five of the city's six constituencies, with the Tories holding the sixth, the well-to-do area of Hallam, until 1997. When the Lib Dems took Hallam, they became the Sheffield Labour Party's enemy number one, and the local Lib Dems complain that Labour is forever peddling a 'What has Nick Clegg ever done for Sheffield?' line.

Not surprisingly, Blunkett doesn't see it quite so simply. He admits that the Lib Dems' success in edging out the Conservatives in Sheffield has caused Labour to view them as 'surrogate Tories', but says he has no personal problem with Clegg, and has frequently rubbed shoulders with him at local events, as the two men's constituencies share a short common boundary. But the former Labour frontbencher, who hails from Sheffield, believes Clegg has misjudged his own city. 'I feel he didn't necessarily embed himself sufficiently in an understanding of how Sheffield people tick,' says Blunkett. 'That's partly because he is, in the best sense of the word, an internationalist, but he never instinctively understood what the anger was about. Sheffield has a very fierce sense of identity and sense of belonging, it's known as the biggest village in England – it's a welcoming place, but it's also very fierce in its defence of itself. So you've got to be on the side of Sheffield, and if you're a senior minister, you've got to be able to manage that balance without being accused of favouritism. It isn't easy, but it is manageable.'

Blunkett's attitude towards the Lib Dems has to be seen in perspective. His name is mud to many Sheffield Lib Dems for reasons going back to his time running the city council in the 1980s, when he saw South Yorkshire as a battle front against Thatcherism, and for more recent skirmishes. In the last couple of years, Blunkett's view of the Lib Dems has mellowed, in part because in 2009 he remarried, and his second wife, Margaret, is from a liberal family. In fact, her house was in Clegg's constituency, and her parents have delivered campaigning material for Clegg in Hallam. But on Forgemasters, the two are never going to agree.

'Forgemasters wasn't a hiding to nothing,' says Blunkett. 'Had Nick gone to see them and tested the water, he might have been able to say to Vince Cable and David Laws "You might want to cut the £80 million loan, but can't we underwrite the investment", and I don't know to this day why they didn't do that. I think if he'd had a bit more experience, he'd have done that. Maybe he was diverted, because the workload as Deputy Prime Minister is so big that you do get diverted – sometimes as Education Secretary I even had days when I had a job ringing my own family.'

At the level of political tactics, Blunkett has a point, but Clegg was furious with Mandelson for having made an offer to Forgemasters that he felt was pure electioneering. Moreover, he never saw any realistic chance of getting Forgemasters its £80 million. So while he could have strung the company along for a few weeks, saying he was trying to secure some form of underwriting guarantee, he felt it would have been a symbolic gesture with no substance, which people would almost certainly have seen through. The outcome would have been the same, or possibly even worse as some folk would have felt resentful towards him for giving Forgemasters false hope.

But it wasn't all cuts and cut-throat politics. Clegg had two foreign trips on which he was able to shine. The first was just four weeks into the new government's tenure, when he went to Berlin for a meeting with his opposite number in the German centre-right coalition government, the vice-chancellor and FDP leader, Guido Westerwelle. Clegg was accompanied by the Foreign Secretary, William Hague, but Hague was rather eclipsed by Clegg's linguistic dexterity. In a press conference, Clegg was very happy to speak German, and even cracked a couple of jokes in the language with the assembled German media. He and Westerwelle had spoken German, and Westerwelle was quick to mention Clegg's 'excellent German' at the start of the press conference. Clegg in turn praised Westerwelle's English, a diplomatic nicety that everyone saw through as Westerwelle's English is something of a running joke among the German press corps.

Hague played his part with great dignity. He could easily have been the fall guy, but he just listened through headphone translation to what his colleague was saying, and let Clegg do the talking. Some commentators suggested the British government was trying to drive an imperceptible wedge between France and Germany, the historic axis behind the European Union. That may be stretching a point, but having the British Deputy Prime Minister speaking German on national television news bulletins certainly did no harm to Britain's standing in Europe's most successful economy. It also enhanced the street cred of British politicians daring to speak foreign languages, something Tony Blair had boosted when he addressed the French Parliament in French. Clegg's rock-solid German gave him the confidence to know exactly what he was saying, and thereby avoid the pitfall once ascribed to Blair – he (Blair) apparently wanted to say 'I like your prime minister in many different ways' but used a formulation in French that amounted to 'I desire your prime minister in many different positions'.

Three months later, Clegg made a major speech about British foreign policy to the United Nations General Assembly in New York. It could have been problematical, as the Lib Dems and the Conservatives had taken diametrically opposed positions on the Iraq War seven years earlier. But his speech was cleared with David Cameron and Hague, and was widely seen as a repositioning of British foreign policy. Clegg promised 'a hard-headed foreign policy based on liberal values' and called for a radical overhaul of the UN that included permanent seats in the Security Council for certain developed and developing countries. 'The UN cannot speak for the many if it only hears the voices of the same old few,' he said.

Clegg's appearance in New York was a source of immense pride to the British Liberal Democrats. Soon after the trip, a photo of him addressing the General Assembly was given pride of place in the reception of Lib Dem HQ in Cowley Street, and those close to Clegg felt it was a massive personal achievement to have delivered a speech on Britain's foreign policy that included several significant uses of the word 'liberal'.

One other trip abroad was his now annual pilgrimage to Spain to say hello to the in-laws. That holiday also allowed time for him to do some of the feted walk to Santiago di Compostela along the northern Spanish coast.

Clegg's new modus operandi as Deputy Prime Minister took some time to bed down; indeed, it took several months for him to get anything like the support he needed. He was by no means the first person to hold the title, but whereas previous incumbents had been glorified ministers of the governing party who had the right to stand in for the prime minister when he (or she) was away, Clegg's role was much more defined, given that it was the position held by the leader of the junior coalition party.

His main job is chairing the Home Affairs Committee, the body that reviews all the legislation to do with Britain that goes through Parliament (effectively all legislation except foreign affairs). In that role he can put a Lib Dem slant on legislation, though sometimes policy differences have to be resolved in the 'quad', a four-man committee involving David Cameron, George Osborne, Clegg and Danny Alexander. His chief parliamentary adviser, Norman Lamb, says, 'He basically has to perform the same role as the Prime Minister. He has to make all the critical judgements Cameron has to make and negotiate solutions. It's not like the role Michael Heseltine or John Prescott had when they were DPM. It's a very big burden on his shoulders – he described it at one event as "existential for the party", given the challenge and the threat we face that the party could be destroyed by being in government, so he was acutely aware of the responsibility he carried.'

It leads to a daily routine that's a model of variety. He might have half an hour put aside to speak on the phone to a foreign leader or deputy leader, the next slot he could be meeting a delegation from an eastern European country, then he might be trying to sort out and negotiate some financial matter in the 'quad' and defending Lib Dem interests, and then he could be dealing with an aspect of the health reforms – all in thirty- or forty-minute slots. 'He likes that kind of brain activity,' says one of his long-standing aides, 'even though most mere mortals would find it utterly exhausting. He's got a very curious mind, so he'd hate to be bored. He's very good at acquiring and digesting information, and strategically implementing what he wants to do.' He also insists on taking his kids to school at least once a week. 'There's a regular morning meeting at 8.30 a.m., but sometimes he arranges to arrive late because he's taken the boys to school, and he's quite disciplined at the weekend to devote time to his children, in particular taking the older two to football.'

The problem was that, in the early weeks of the coalition, he didn't have anything like the back-up that the prime minister has. Clegg has a very grand office overlooking Horse Guards Parade in the Whitehall building that houses the Cabinet Office, but he suffered from a distinct shortage of staff. 'We needed to make sure he had more civil service support,' says one of the Lib Dem staff members who now works for the government, 'because the civil service wasn't prepared for a Deputy Prime Minister who had a much bigger responsibility than any previous DPM.' Norman Baker says very little has changed since the Lib Dems were in opposition, as they still have to keep up with the two big parties but with vastly fewer resources. 'He's hopelessly overstretched,' says Baker. 'We've penetrated the centre of government like a rapier, but it's a bloody thin rapier.'

The result is that Clegg frequently works off less sleep than he should ideally be getting. That goes for most government ministers, but it hasn't helped Clegg that his third son, Miguel, hasn't been the best sleeper through the night. One close colleague says he doesn't stop to think about getting tired, he just keeps on going. However, he does have access to the Foreign Secretary's grace-and-favour mansion, Chevening, which he makes some use of to relax and unwind.

The coalition meant a major adjustment for the party, as well as for its leader. Although the Lib Dems' chief executive, Chris Fox, had planned for a possible role in government when he took over from Chris Rennard in mid-2009, he admits he didn't have a blueprint for the organisational upheaval that would be necessary. 'Organisationally, we had a large number of people who worked for the party who started working for the government,' Fox explains, 'and we lost £2 million on Short money [public money given to opposition parties for the purposes of furthering democratic debate], so I had to remove £1 million from the payroll. In that sense we lost control of who and where we were, simply because many people left the employ of the party. We had to make 20–30 redundant out of a staff of around ninety; thirty-eight people left the employ of the party, some going into government, others were laid off. We had a blueprint for the coalition negotiations but not for the organisational impact, but then that goes for the civil service too.'

There were other adjustments of style. As the Deputy Prime Minister, Clegg sat alongside David Cameron at Prime Minister's Questions and major parliamentary debates and statements, so slipped into the practice of agreeing visibly with his government colleague. After a few months, word had seeped through that Lib Dem members found this uncomfortable, and on some issues even distasteful; Clegg had slapped George Osborne on the back after the Chancellor had delivered his statement on the comprehensive spending review, which went down very badly with activists. So he agreed to sit alongside Cameron and Osborne with minimal facial expressions. That then led to a rush of 'why do you look so glum?' comments. Addressing the Lib Dems' spring conference in Sheffield in March 2011, Clegg used this as an example of how, on some matters, he was damned if he did and damned if he didn't.

Since the coalition was founded, Clegg has attended most of the meetings of the parliamentary Lib Dem party, but his contact with the wider party has been more complicated. He only spent a short time at the 2010 party conference in Liverpool (largely because of his appointment with the UN General Assembly), though he did make two appearances on successive days at the 2011 spring conference in Sheffield. He has political time built into his diary, and if there are any expenses resulting from what he does in that time, the party pays them because it has to keep government and party separate. But as Deputy Prime Minister, such time is limited, which puts added pressure on party organisers to use it more efficiently than they did before.

Although the first round of cuts and the raising of VAT to 20 per cent had been embarrassing Lib Dem concessions, the issue that did Clegg and the Lib Dems such harm was tuition fees for higher education courses. Looking back on the couple of months in the autumn of 2010 when the issue was regularly topping the news agenda, much of it makes very little sense, and some of the participants may well look back at their own involvement with a mixture of puzzlement and embarrassment. But it was the issue that taught Clegg and the Lib Dems that, in politics, perception is often vastly more powerful than what you say in the small print, or even the large print.

Reduced to its simplest form, Labour and the Conservatives went into the 2010 general election with a pledge not just to keep tuition fees but to raise them in line with the recommendations in a report by the former chief executive of BP, Lord Browne of Madingley, which had been commissioned before the election but had not yet been concluded. The Liberal Democrats went into the election pledging to phase out tuition fees for first degrees over a period of six years. The National Union of Students seized on this by calling on all candidates to sign a pledge not to vote in favour of higher tuition fees if elected to Parliament, a pledge which all fifty-seven Lib Dem MPs elected in 2010 had signed.

So when the Conservative–Lib Dem coalition came into being, it was always going to be well-nigh impossible for the junior partner to carry through its promise to phase out fees. One could argue it lacked the stomach for the fight, and Vince Cable's scepticism about the Lib Dems' six-years policy adds weight to that argument, but Clegg and Cable went in to bat for a better deal for students than would have happened if the government had implemented all the recommendations of the Browne report. The question was how strongly to push on an issue that had clearly been part of the Lib Dems' 2010 general election campaign but had not been one of the four 'headline' issues trumpeted on the front cover of the party's manifesto.

Clegg and Cable gained four important concessions in the resulting bill: an end to up-front fees (which still existed for part-time students); a rise in the threshold before which graduates have to start paying back their loans from £15,000 to £21,000, with the new limit to rise ahead of inflation; a cap of £6,000 or £9,000 for annual tuition fees when Browne had called for no cap; and a time limit for a graduate's outstanding debt that would mean most ex-students would never pay back the full amount they had been loaned. The annual cap became a crucial political issue: Cable had proposed £6,000, with scope for universities to go up to £9,000 if they could justify the additional £3,000 through making provision for students from poorer backgrounds, but it gradually became clear in the ensuing months that universities would make £9,000 the norm rather than £6,000. The ease with which the media and public picked up on '£9,000' as a term that appeared to encapsulate the burdening of the next generation with debt became a knife in the back of Clegg and the Lib Dems, often wielded by those who would have faced unlimited fees without Clegg's and Cable's efforts.

Cable says the full complexity of his task has never been fully appreciated. 'When we took over in government,' he says, 'the civil servants hadn't been in this world, they'd been used to spending money for years. So when we set about the first round of cuts and then the comprehensive spending review, they just presented me a list of things that could be cut. Taking over BIS [the Department for Business, Innovation & Skills] was a bit like inheriting an archipelago like Indonesia, with a civil war taking place on every island. By far the biggest island was higher education, with universities taking up about 70 per cent of my department's available funding. Other significant islands were further education [aimed at 16–18-year-olds] and scientific research funding. I had to save 25 per cent of our total expenditure. The Treasury wanted to savage further education, but I felt this was wrong – what the country needs is good training, apprenticeships etc., and I was alarmed at how many sixteen-year-olds leave school with a reading age of eleven for whom further education acts as a safety net, so we have to protect the 16–18-year-old sector. We therefore knew we needed a cut in higher education: we could have done this by drastically reducing the number of students, by taking the money away from universities and letting some of them sink, or giving them an alternative source of income. We felt the first two were unacceptable, so we were back to tuition fees. We looked at all sorts of mechanisms, but by September it was abundantly clear that we had no alternative, so we had to design a system that was as progressive as possible – better than the current one, and better than what Browne was proposing. I think we did produce a policy that was significantly better; indeed, it was a time-limited graduate tax in all but name. But what we weren't ready for politically was the murderous assault from the opposition and the NUS, centring not on the policy – they weren't interested in the policy, Labour would have done pretty much what we did anyway – but on the pledge. We were hung out to dry as a result of that single thing.'

As Clegg said, 'We were stuffed,' a comment he meant not as some vernacular joke, but because the Lib Dems, with 23 per cent of the vote, could do very little to pursue the abolition of tuition fees when the biggest two parties had both been in favour. 'I had signed the NUS pledge in good faith, but the numbers meant we just couldn't deliver. So we worked very hard to do the next-best thing, which was to build into the funding proposals safeguards for students from the poorest families.'

A logical development of the political scenario would have seen the NUS giving the new deal for students a guarded welcome, perhaps criticising the emphasis on burdening future generations with debt, but blowing its own trumpet about its success in forcing the Lib Dems to fight the students' corner in government. Instead, the NUS turned against the Lib Dems for breaking their promises, demonising Clegg and Cable, which in turn deflected attention from the Conservatives – and indeed Labour – who had campaigned at the election for higher tuition fees. As a way of turning on those who had fought the NUS's cause, it could easily be seen as either an act of crass ingratitude or gross stupidity – possibly both. It was certainly a crazy state of affairs for the national student body and the party it had persuaded to fight its cause to have reached.

So why did Clegg and the Lib Dems become the whipping boys over tuition fees? There are several reasons, and it's hard to ascribe any of them a definitive weight in the absence of more research.

The obvious one is that the Lib Dems were now in government for the first time in living memory, and were getting their hands dirty, so they were no longer an untarnished brand of philosophical or protest vote. Hand in hand with that goes another reason: people were expressing their disappointment. Many had voted Lib Dem because of the tuition fees issue – or to keep the Conservatives out – and couldn't see why the party they had put their trust in was suddenly doing the opposite of what it had campaigned for. The fact that coalitions mean compromises, to the extent that not everything in a party's manifesto can be put into practice, clearly needed more explaining to the British public than many in the Lib Dem high command had realised.

The media played a major part in this too. The media's role is discussed more fully in Chapter 13, but what was remarkable about the coverage was the delight correspondents took in not only calling the Lib Dems' stance a U-turn, but a 'dramatic U-turn', a 'spectacular U-turn' and other hyperbolic descriptions. This went even for some of the more respected political correspondents, including those who generally go out of their way to be fairer to the third party than more tribal political commentators.

The use of the term 'U-turn' shows what can happen when a story gathers a momentum of its own. On tuition fees, Lib Dem MPs certainly found themselves having to vote for a policy that was the opposite of what they had campaigned for (and not all did vote for it), so in that sense it was a U-turn. But was it any more of a U-turn than accepting the first £6 billion of spending cuts, or a rise in VAT to 20 per cent, or accepting a role for nuclear power in the government's energy strategy after being hostile towards it in the manifesto? These were also issues on which the Lib Dems had compromised as part of the coalition agreement, yet there was no cry of 'U-turn' on those. The Conservatives also made concessions in the coalition agreement, notably on inheritance tax, immigration, the Human Rights Act and their general attitude towards the EU, but these were never portrayed as 'U-turns', whether 'spectacular', 'dramatic' or whatever. Leaving aside the issue of whether being persuaded to change direction is really such a heinous crime, why should the Lib Dems' concession on tuition fees be considered a 'U-turn' more than any other? And there have to be concessions – if parties campaign at an election for different policies, which they always do (if they didn't, all politicians would be in the same party), and no single party gains an overall majority, there have to be discussions on forming a cooperative programme, and those discussions inevitably involve some concessions on both sides. A coalition government without some concessions that can be portrayed as U-turns is arguably a logical impossibility.

A more reasoned defence for calling the Lib Dems' acceptance of tuition fees a 'U-turn' would be if tuition fees were what's commonly known as 'a red-line issue' for the party. Interestingly, both the then NUS president, Aaron Porter, and various political correspondents say tuition fees were a red-line issue for the Lib Dems. If they really believe that, then their claim of a U-turn at least has some logic to it. In the absence of a definition of 'red-line issue', or even a reliable measure of how much the party campaigned on this subject rather than other subjects, it's hard to know whether tuition fees were a red-line issue or not. Clegg and the Lib Dems argue clearly that they weren't, and this is perhaps the key to the lack of comprehension Clegg showed for the demonising of the Lib Dems over tuition fees. One of the changes from the 'shopping list' Lib Dem manifesto of 2005 was that the 2010 manifesto was based around a narrative involving four core issues: raising the income tax threshold to £10,000, a programme of economic stimulus through investment in 'green' jobs, a 'pupil premium' to help the most disadvantaged schoolchildren, and reforming/cleaning up politics. On all four issues, the Lib Dems gained concessions in the coalition agreement, along with other Lib Dem policies that tallied with Tory thinking such as index-linking the state pension and scrapping both ID cards and the proposed third runway at Heathrow airport. They therefore say they made absolutely clear that the plan to phase out tuition fees, although genuine, was not one of their headline policies, so can't be seen as a red-line issue. Their argument concludes that it is thus impossible to justify a serious charge of the concession on tuition fees being a U-turn.

Yet in politics, perceptions are often worth more than the wordings of manifestos, and the Lib Dems were strongly perceived to have made such a strong thing of signing the NUS pledge – Clegg was even photographed signing it alongside a Lib Dem candidate – as to make the public outcry over the rise in tuition fees at least understandable. Aaron Porter makes an interesting point: he says, 'In my eyes, and I believe in the eyes of young people, the three things the Lib Dems stood for were electoral reform, no tuition fees and no replacement of Trident. As I watched the election results come in and it became clear the Lib Dems would be in government with either Labour or the Conservatives, I thought the presence of the Lib Dems in government would mean fees wouldn't go up, because free education was such a strong Lib Dem policy. I think Clegg was politically naive on this. The reason students are angry is because the Liberal Democrats secured a reasonable number of votes off the back of their pledge and then didn't make enough of an issue about it. We accept that compromises have to be made across government, but in my eyes tuition fees should not have been one of them.'

Porter has an interest in student fees, so that final comment has to be taken with a pinch of salt. He is also a member of the Labour Party who clearly has political ambitions, so that must also be taken into account, and he recognises that Clegg and Cable burned large amounts of midnight oil fighting for the interests of students from poorer backgrounds. But if there is even a modicum of truth in Porter's assessment of what most people felt the Lib Dems stood for – and his perception is backed up by independent research – that does indeed suggest there was a certain amount of naivety in Clegg setting greater store by the front cover of the Lib Dem manifesto than on how the public perceived the party's main platform. He still says he 'didn't spend that much time campaigning on tuition fees', which may be strictly speaking true. But the Lib Dem negotiating team for the coalition agreement did, after all, secure the right for

Lib Dem MPs to abstain from the tuition fees vote, so they were clearly aware of the potential for their coalition compromise to be seen as a broken promise. (That right of abstention actually proved something of a poisoned chalice, as Clegg explored the idea of all Lib Dem MPs abstaining, but it wasn't realistic as it would have created the laughable situation of having the minister presenting the legislation not supporting it; and simply exploring the abstaining option allowed the media to portray the Lib Dems as indecisive in government.)

Another reason for the uproar was that the students had three prerequisites for an effective campaign: eloquence, time and money. Their protests were generally well organised (it would be wrong to blame the students for the infiltration of their demonstrations by renegade elements that led to much of the newsworthy violence), the NUS president had the oxygen of a lot of media coverage time, including an appearance on the high-profile BBC programme *Question Time*, and they had friends in the wider media to make their case – no doubt many journalists and leader writers aged 40–60 with teenage children, who could see a big bill coming when their offspring reached university age. By contrast, there were no orchestrated protests or media campaigns on behalf of further education students or those who could benefit from apprenticeships rather than degrees. It allowed the students to create the impression that they were seriously hard done by.

Throughout all this, senior Lib Dems bowed their heads apologetically. On *Desert Island Discs*, Clegg said, 'I made a pledge which I now find I can't keep,' while on *Question Time* Norman Lamb said, 'This is a very tough judgement. We made a pledge, I signed the pledge, I accept I shouldn't have done, I made a mistake, and I think it's best to fess up to that.' Perhaps the most striking thing about this whole period is that no prominent Lib Dem felt confident enough to take the fight to the students by pointing out that they were supposed to be the nation's academic elite but were displaying something of a lack of intellectual rigour by saying 'poor me' rather than looking at the wider educational picture.

Another point that was barely made was that the only thing that seems to get most students out on the streets these days is a threat to their own pockets, rather than wider social, environmental and human rights issues – quite a comedown from the heady student idealism of the 1960s and 1970s. The NUS maintains students would be more ready to show an interest in wider issues if they weren't so weighed down by debt, which may be true but may also be self-serving.

The reason for the Lib Dems' bowed-head apologia lies partly in a decision that Clegg took at the start of the coalition and was cemented at a meeting of Lib Dem MPs, peers and MEPs in November 2010. He said that the key to a coalition working was shared responsibility, so the Lib Dems had to stand behind what the government did, even if it was doing things the party had campaigned against in the election. If the party wanted to secure electoral reform, which in any meaningful form would mean an increased likelihood of more coalitions, it had to show that coalition government works. Clegg therefore ordered a strategy that has become known as 'owning everything'.

It came as something of a shock to Lib Dem supporters (and some MPs), who seemed to have got their heads round the idea of working with the Conservatives but had expected to hear their ministers saying that, while they had voted for or against a certain measure, it was only because it was in the coalition agreement and thus they had voted with a heavy heart. Clegg effectively banned that sort of language. He said that if you knocked your own coalition, you would never be seen to have any pride in it, which was hardly a positive messge to send out to the electorate.

This was reinforced six months into the new government when Clegg held a meeting of the parliamentary party in Church House, just round the corner from the Houses of Parliament, to which he invited not only a healthy selection of British Lib Dem MEPs but also parliamentarians from Belgium, the Netherlands and Sweden. The foreign delegation was led by Clegg's old friend from Brussels days, Lousewies van der Laan, the former leader of the Dutch liberals

D66. She presented a memo to the meeting entitled 'Everything You Need to Know about Coalition Politics You Already Know from Your Marriage'. It was also written in the jargon of marriage – it talked about the pre-nuptial stage, the honeymoon, how to set up a home, and even had a section on the irritation of living together. Its main message was that disagreements are perfectly legitimate, but you don't want them in public, or your marriage quickly begins to look very shabby. 'Let each other shine,' van der Laan wrote, 'grant each his moment of glory ... don't begrudge the other half's victories ... don't gloat when the others stumble,' and the hard-hitting 'Stay relaxed, even with bad opinion polls, it's par for the course – don't govern if you are afraid of losing popularity'. Whether van der Laan was quite the best person to present such a paper when she had made some pretty disastrous decisions that had led to the collapse of one Dutch coalition is another matter, but the message was clear, and Clegg was happy to endorse it.

The policy of 'owning everything' was a case of Clegg exercising firm leadership, so firm that no-one in the parliamentary party seriously questioned it, at least not at the time. The party's Federal Executive questioned it in January 2011, and the March 2011 party conference called for it to be abandoned. By then, the drawbacks, especially in a country unused to coalition government, had become apparent.

The idea of 'owning everything' may be good for occupying the moral high ground, it is useful for claiming credit for things that go well that you haven't advocated, and it looks good in the halcyon days of a coalition's novelty, but it has one serious flaw, especially for the junior partner: the bigger party can drown out the smaller one. And indeed after several months of the coalition, the Lib Dems began sinking rapidly in the opinion polls, as they were associated with the government's cuts in public spending but were doing very little to highlight what they had brought to the coalition. Since they had campaigned for certain things that were now not happening, and against things that were, what the public saw was the Lib Dems smoothing the way to the unpopular measures and getting

nothing in return. The reality was very different – an analysis by
University College London's School of Public Policy concluded that
75 per cent of the Lib Dem general election manifesto found its
way into the coalition programme, as opposed to just 60 per cent of
the Conservative manifesto – but this wasn't being communicated
to the public, largely because of the 'owning everything' approach.
UCL also made the point that the Lib Dems had taken over the
constitutional reform and climate change agenda and were seriously
influencing government policy, but that these were areas that didn't
score highly with the public or the news media.

There were Lib Dem successes as part of the tuition fees issue
too, but again little was publicised. One of the major achievements
of the Lib Dems has been in protecting the funding for further
education, but this is barely known. Aaron Porter, whose job is to
fight for higher education rather than further education, says, 'To
govern is to take the decisions that you think are right, and I think
in this area [further education funding] they have taken the right
decisions. You could argue that this is a classic example where Lib
Dem influence in government has actually had a positive impact,
but it has not been communicated to the population at large. I'm
not saying that is political naivety, but it might be the difference
between a party that spent five years preparing for government, and
another that spent five weeks thinking "Oh crumbs, we might be
in government".'

Vince Cable, who of the five Lib Dem Cabinet ministers
looked the least comfortable with the coalition, sympathises with
the dilemma of whether to own everything or not. 'Where do you
start and where do you stop?' he says. 'Nick's view was a more
far-reaching one. He brought four or five European liberals to our
meeting, and their message was unequivocal – once you start doing
a pick-and-mix approach to policy, you get into terrible trouble.
We had the experience of the German FDP, who were in desperate
political trouble because they'd followed the strategy of saying "We
like this but we don't like that". Nick set out at our party conference
that we needed to own the coalition. I do disagree somewhat with

Nick on this, but it's a difference of emphasis. I felt we could have differentiated a little more. There's no harm in saying the measures we're having to take are painful and difficult, and we don't agree with other things. We can't dissociate ourselves from broad government policy, you really can't do that, but I believe we could make it fairly clear that we feel it's uncomfortable. Nick's view was complete ownership: take pride in decisions, even if they're not ours.'

Clegg did allow more publicity for Lib Dem successes in the early months of 2011, but by then some serious damage had been done to his and the Lib Dems' standing, and he also made it clear that publicising Lib Dem successes was not to reach into the realms of publicising what the Lib Dems had stopped the Conservatives doing. This became a serious problem for his party, because much of the Lib Dems' effectiveness in coalition has been in largely silencing the 30–40 right-wing Tory MPs who had hoped to hold a Conservative government to ransom by bringing anti-EU and anti-immigration stories to the table at regular intervals. Lib Dem MPs were happy to talk about such achievements at party dinners, but not through the media. The failure to highlight such successes was part of the reason the party found it so hard to counter the anti-Lib Dem feeling that led to such a shattering set of election results in May 2011.

At the end of the day, the tuition fees issue was probably a battle by proxy, as well as being of genuine concern to students, potential students and parents of potential students. The numbers in higher education had risen markedly in the previous three decades, to a point where higher education had to be funded differently in some way, so something radical had to happen at a time when Britain had a record deficit. The decision of the Liberal Democrats to go into government with the Conservatives had inflamed a lot of people who had voted Lib Dem for progressive reasons, so tuition fees provided a suitable stick to beat the third party with. And some people just like bashing the government. Ultimately the blood-letting had to stop, and even Porter, who had said on *Question Time* that he could 'never trust Nick Clegg again' was, by the spring of

2011, building bridges between the NUS and the Lib Dems, and saying that elements of the new higher education funding deal were better than the one it replaced. He also recognised that improving relations with the Lib Dems was the only way for the student body to make progress on other issues, such as improved social mobility, a government initiative that clearly came from the Lib Dem side of the coalition.

In time, the tuition fees issue will probably be judged as part of the rapid learning curve of a party that was so inexperienced in government. Those in the party who felt the policy of abolishing tuition fees was too populist and not the thinking of a credible party of government will see themselves vindicated, while others will feel that the Lib Dems did nothing wrong in using their signing of the NUS pledge to reform a piece of legislation that could have been much worse, and were undone by what the public thought were their main priorities rather than what those priorities really were. The perceived U-turn clearly damaged Clegg and the party, but whether that damage is long term will depend to a large extent on what choices the electorate have in 2015. The lesson for Clegg is that what the public thinks it sees is often more important than what you say are your main aims.

At least the tuition fees issue had been in the coalition's programme. An issue that had the potential to create much greater problems (and that was still producing aftershocks as this book went to press) was the government's proposed reforms to the National Health Service.

The reforms were set out after a fashion in the Conservative Party's manifesto for the 2010 general election, though not with the kind of emphasis that could undermine the crucial message David Cameron was trying to put out in the election campaign: that the NHS would be safe with the Tories. Those with memories of Margaret Thatcher's attempts to cut it back in the 1980s were reluctant to trust him, and he and George Osborne knew that successfully protecting the NHS was part of detoxifying the Conservative brand after the bruising it took in the years leading up to Labour's victory in 1997. The fact that Cameron had experienced the state's medical service at first hand over the six years of his disabled son Ivan's life was a powerful argument for the Conservatives to use in pushing their line that the NHS would not be dismantled under the Tories. Yet in July 2010, just a few weeks after the new government had taken office, the Health Secretary, Andrew Lansley, announced his proposed restructuring, with its flagship elements of abolishing primary care trusts and allowing GPs to buy in the services they need as leaders of consortia.

The reforms were quite clearly not part of the coalition agreement; in fact it specifically rules out top-down restructuring of the NHS. According to the agreement, primary care trusts were not going to be abolished, and they were not going to have elected boards, so Lansley's proposals denoted a distinct straying from the specific Con–Lib contract. The agreement is also supposed to preclude surprises for one side dished out by the other, although that is not really applicable in this case – the 'no surprises' clause prevents ministers announcing policy on the hoof without both parties having been notified; Lansley had at least notified the Lib Dems, who had the right to refuse, but gave it the benefit of the doubt. The reform package was therefore published, and both Cameron and Clegg signed the foreword to it. It all seems a little odd in retrospect, as this put both leaders in a rather difficult position. The whole issue serves to highlight that decisions were taken in the first weeks of government which betray both Conservatives and Liberal Democrats as having not yet attuned their political senses to the implications of governmental decisions.

One of the recurring reactions from Lib Dem circles about the NHS reforms is why the party didn't just say no, as it had every right to under the coalition agreement. There are two answers to this.

Firstly, the tone set by Clegg at that time was to prove that 'coalition works', so when the senior partners suggested something, he didn't want the junior partners – the ones with the long-term interest in showing that governments of more than one party can be a good thing – to be depicted as simply saying 'Can't be done, mate'. More to the point, the Lib Dems simply didn't have processes in place that would kick in when they had disagreements with the Conservatives on issues that went beyond the coalition agreement. The agreement provided for a 'coalition committee', albeit without setting out when or how often it should meet (and in reality it has barely met since the government took office). As one senior Lib Dem put it, 'The coalition agreement was very good, so we rather overlooked the need to protect ourselves, and it took the NHS issue for us to put processes in place that allow us to deal with matters the Tories want to pursue that we're not bound by and not sure about.'

Secondly, Clegg was open to at least some of the ideas Lansley was putting forward. Intellectually, he saw the proposals as a development of some of the ideas Lib Dems had discussed in opposition in the mid-2000s. For example, localism and decentralisation are core tenets of liberal thinking, and the idea of giving the doctors, who are most patients' first port of call, a greater say over what services their patients get seemed a liberal idea (even if he and David Laws had spoken out against 'producer interest' in speeches made in opposition). In addition, a central aim of the reforms was to lessen the involvement of Whitehall, which appealed to Clegg's anti-statist instincts. He was also happy with the broader principle behind Lansley's reforms – that Britain has an ageing population and money is short, so in order to deliver the same level of NHS service, you have to change it. This does not run contrary to Lib Dem ideas, or indeed aspects of the party's 2010 manifesto, so Clegg was happy not to reject Lansley's proposals out of hand.

His problem was with the detail and the delivery of the reform package, but even that took a while to filter through, by which time there was much disquiet in Lib Dem ranks. The deal struck between Lansley and the Lib Dems' health minister, Paul Burstow (there is one Lib Dem minister in most government departments, even if – as in Burstow's case – not a Cabinet minister), involved getting rid of primary care trusts and giving more power to local councils. Clegg saw the attraction of giving more power to local government, but didn't have the staffpower to scrutinise the proposals to an adequate extent, so the white paper was published with a number of elements that caused Lib Dem eyes to widen and jaws to drop open.

The NHS is a highly complex organism that will never be able to satisfy all demand as new drugs and treatments are being patented all the time, so its potential to swallow up large sums of public money and still leave great numbers of people dissatisfied is immense. The dilemma for all politicians is whether to mess with something that clearly occupies a massive part of the nation's emotional make-up (Clegg has described the NHS as 'a national religion'), because even the best ideas will be painted as villainous if they are not sold carefully to a highly suspicious public. Inevitably, many on the political left – including many Lib Dems – wondered whether it was part of a secret agenda to dismantle the service, or an ideologically driven scheme to boost private enterprise. In addition, at a time of great austerity, the chancellor, George Osborne, was clearly interested in any measures that could save money and boost opportunities for businesses of all sizes.

By the end of 2010, the proposals were in serious trouble, largely because the NHS and the broader medical profession were vehemently against them. There were people within the medical ranks who felt the idea of GP commissioning was a logical development for the NHS, but there were many more who felt the idea of having different companies competing to provide the same services was a recipe for disaster for those people the NHS was primarily designed to protect. Medical unions and professional associations came out strongly against the proposals, largely because they felt they were wrong, but also because the medical profession felt it had barely adjusted to the last round of deep-rooted NHS reforms in the mid-1990s and just couldn't face another series of upheavals.

Inevitably, the debate became somewhat emotional, with only a select group of health professionals and experts even remotely aware of the full implications of what was being proposed. At the height of the debate, David Laws said, 'The NHS reforms that are being proposed have issues of accountability, management capacity, constraints to budget, and some of the involvement of the private sector. There are some big complex issues there. But there's a lot of sentiment and gut reaction that's going into the protests, and there are a lot of people who are not even looking into the small print of what the government is proposing but saying "private", "markets", "America" and aren't actually thinking. Of course we must subject this to rigorous scrutiny, but let's do it on the basis of substance, not gut reaction.'

All very reasonable, no doubt, but the inexperience of the Lib Dems as a party of government, and their lack of resources to digest the implications of what they were doing, are apparent. Clegg seems to have set too great a store by the detail and paid too little attention to how the issue was playing out in public. One could praise that for its adherence to firm government and a refusal to succumb to the dictates of populism, but there seemed to be an initial failure to recognise that in politics you have to take people with you, at least to a certain degree. More importantly, there was a core group of health experts within the Lib Dems who were screaming for the party to take a tougher line against the NHS reforms. These included the MP and backbench health spokesperson John Pugh; the man Clegg had appointed as his health spokesperson in opposition, Norman Lamb; the former MP Evan Harris (a medical doctor and now vice-chair of the Federal Policy Committee); the former Labour Cabinet minister Shirley Williams; a former national medical director of the NHS, Graham Winyard (now chair of Winchester Lib Dems); and a Shropshire GP and Lib Dem parliamentary candidate, Charles West. Lamb even offered to resign his position as chief parliamentary and political adviser to Clegg so he could speak freely about his concerns on what he saw as a 'wholesale rush to the untried and untested concept of GP-commissioning', though Clegg said resignation wasn't necessary.

At the Lib Dems' spring 2011 conference, Paul Burstow put forward a motion broadly agreeing with the government's proposed NHS reforms. This would have been roundly defeated if the conference had been asked to vote on it, but the party was spared that embarrassment when the leadership accepted an amendment calling for significant changes and safeguards, and the heavily amended motion was passed in its place. If not a full-blown embarrassment, the fact that the amendment had to be accepted to avoid a heavy defeat was a serious slap across the face handed out by the party to the Lib Dems in government. Faced with the potential of 'Lib Dem split' stories, Clegg responded by saying that afternoon that it was a sign that 'Conference is playing its part', and promising to take the amended motion back to his discussions with David Cameron. In many ways, Clegg was very lucky, because many Lib Dems with a knowledge of NHS issues wanted to kill the NHS reform bill completely. Indeed, the Cornish Lib Dem MP Andrew George spoke at the conference in favour of throwing the whole thing out. In effect, the amendment threw Clegg a lifeline. He was given a strongly critical motion to take back to the 'quad', but one which stopped well short of saying that there should not be any reform at all. That strengthened his hand in the negotiations, and the *Daily Telegraph* later said in an editorial that the turning point in the whole process was the vote at the Lib Dem spring conference in Sheffield.

There was a view put about in the press that the turning point in the NHS reforms was actually the Lib Dems' horrendous election results in early May 2011. The line of argument goes that the results highlighted the need for the party to show its supporters that it was having some influence in government, which in turn made Clegg push for a harder deal than he might have done a couple of months earlier. The timing doesn't bear that out. More than four weeks before the elections took place, the government ordered a 'pause' and announced it would be setting up a doctor-led body called the NHS Future Forum to look at the reform proposals. More importantly, the government set a test that the NHS, the clinicians and others involved in the medical world needed to be on board with proposed reform. Therefore, there is little substance in the argument levelled at the time that the 'pause' was cosmetic – if anything it was the opposite: designed to create a justification for the kind of climbdown that both Conservatives and Lib Dems had realised was necessary. Of course the Lib Dems were keen to assert their influence after the drubbing they had taken at the polls and the AV referendum, but by pushing for the requirement for the medics to be happy with the reforms, they had effectively exerted their greatest influence before election day. As such, if there was a turning point in the process, it occurred in the period between the Sheffield conference in mid-March and the negotiations setting the terms of reference for the NHS Future Forum in early April. Pressure to make the changes had actually come from within both coalition parties. The Conservative hierarchy were fearful of alienating public opinion on the NHS in the way that the last Conservative government had done, and there was the campaign by Lib Dems largely outside Clegg's leadership circle that felt it was necessary to alert the party's leadership to the policy and political dangers.

When it reported, the NHS Future Forum did indeed make recommendations that provided cover for a major government climbdown. NHS organisations had been overwhelmingly hostile to the reforms, but even those who talked most about reform of the NHS hadn't espoused the changes that were initially proposed as the right sort of reform. In addition, the political reality meant that Lib Dem votes were needed to get the Bill through the House of Commons. Even if Lib Dem MPs didn't block the Bill, then Lib Dem peers together with Labour, crossbench and rebel Tory peers may well have blocked it in the House of Lords. So there was no real alternative but to change the reform package significantly.

The outline of the 'reform of the reforms' was announced in mid-June, and it showed a number of compromises. The idea of reshaping the NHS remained intact, and there seems little doubt that the system will be considerably different in a few years. But the changes will not come about as quickly as originally announced, and the deadline of 2013 set for the process of GP commissioning to kick in has been removed, with an 'able and willing' clause added which effectively makes it voluntary. For those areas where GP commissioning does not happen immediately, primary care trusts will remain. Additional changes mean that other clinicians, such as hospital doctors, will also be part of the consortia; the consortia will have to meet in public and consult publicly; and the proposals lay down that competition will not be based on price but on 'managed competition', a term designed to guarantee quality and uphold professional standards in the arena of competition. These are indeed significant concessions, though there are numerous Lib Dems who are left wondering whether even this package risks going further towards the marketisation of the NHS than the party should ever have allowed.

In a joint press conference with David Cameron and Andrew Lansley, Clegg's phrasing was careful and only partly triumphalist. 'Where we all agree is that the NHS needs to change,' he said. 'For all the reasons David talked about, the question has never been whether to reform, but how to reform. We didn't get that right straight away. But you told us what to do differently. We listened. And now we have a plan I hope we can all get behind. You told us you were worried about privatisation through the back door, so we have made that impossible. Yes, diversity can drive up quality and increase choice. And the NHS has always had a mix of providers. But competition will not be encouraged for its own sake, only where it clearly benefits patients.' He also made the point that he had delivered eleven of the thirteen concessions that had been demanded by the Lib Dems' March 2011 conference.

The concessions were presented by the Lib Dems as a victory for their influence on government. Baroness Williams wrote in *The Independent*, 'Liberal Democrats, from our party's grass roots to its leadership, can be proud of the influence we have exerted to change the government's NHS plans. It is clear now that the proposals that will be taken forward are dramatically different to those originally proposed.' Some were more subdued in their welcoming of the changes. John Pugh declined to maximise media opportunities for saying the Lib Dems had made the difference, and Evan Harris's utterances were limited and cautious. 'The changes have delivered three-quarters of what we asked for,' Harris said, 'but there is scope for about a third of it to be put back by other routes. The role of Monitor [a government body that would have had the job of promoting competition] may have been put back in its box, but more competition hasn't. We have to watch to make sure that the Tories don't introduce the same reforms through the back door.' Harris believes some of the original proposals have indeed been 'smuggled' back, and he is likely to remain one of Clegg's fiercest internal critics in the battle to protect the NHS from what the Lib Dems see as increasing marketisation.

Not everyone, however, was quite so sceptical, and an interesting perspective comes from Graham Winyard, who was one of the biggest critics of Lansley's reforms from within the Lib Dems. 'We need to recognise that Nick, Paul [Burstow] and others have, with our prompting, secured a major victory with the changes announced to the NHS bill. These do not include everything we would have liked, but I don't think the omissions are as threatening as has been suggested, and can and should be sorted in committee and in the Lords without further prompting from us. Allowing the privatisation of the commissioning function may be bad politics, but it's not necessarily bad for patients given the mediocre commissioning performance of many PCTs. The NHS needs fresh approaches and should not be prevented from seeking these. We need to recognise that many of those who argued for more competition are not rabid private sector marketeers but people who believe in the NHS but are deeply concerned that many NHS services are still mediocre, even after a decade of record levels of investment, and very resistant to change. However, the sad reality about reversing the Lansley bill is that this has only ever been damage limitation. We are left, as a party of government, with the challenge of managing successfully an NHS that has to live on flat funding for the next four years. There is great potential in the revised bill to define a proper Liberal Democrat approach to the NHS that we can get behind.'

The appearance in the media of the junior partner fighting for and gaining concessions on a piece of legislation eliciting great public concern was essential for Clegg and the Lib Dems, especially after the very poor election results just a few weeks before. Interestingly, the Lib Dems had found an unlikely friend behind the scenes. Private polling for the Conservatives had suggested the NHS reforms as presented by Lansley were very unpopular, and threatening to retoxify the Tory brand, so George Osborne went into battle with Cameron's director of strategy, Steve Hilton, a strong advocate of public sector reforms, to encourage a scaling down on the NHS plans. But even the spectacle of Osborne pulling in the same direction as the Lib Dems was helpful for Lib Dem influence. After the setback to the chances of electoral reform, and the heavy losses in council elections, the party was finally able to present the public with the image of two different parties compromising on a contentious piece of government work. If only for the sake of appearances, it was a vital step forward for Clegg and his party in government.

One consequence of the NHS reforms was the beefing up of the 10 Downing Street policy unit. If there was a perception that Tony Blair had gone too far in his policy unit, that he had created the undemocratic idea of 'sofa government', Cameron and Clegg saw that in government you do nevertheless need a strong policy unit in No 10 to scrutinise what comes from the departments. As one leading Lib Dem put it, 'On the Tory side there was a sense that "Lansley knows the NHS so we'll trust him on that", but neither governmental party had either the people or the processes to analyse properly what was being proposed.'

The lesson Clegg took from the NHS 'reform of reforms' was that the 'why' is just as important as the 'how'. His staff felt they did explain the 'why' on the cuts, setting out to the public that there was an overriding need to reduce the deficit, and that this created a greater willingness to accept the 'how'. 'If you want to do something which is reformist or radical,' said one of Clegg's close aides, 'you need to take people along with you and explain to them why you need to do that. With the NHS we never communicated why. Most people's experience with the NHS is a positive one; we had to explain to people that the population is ageing and that for the NHS to stay at the same level it had to change – that came far too late.'

No doubt it did, but there was probably a little more to it than that. In the heady days when it was getting its feet under the desk of national government, the Lib Dem leadership team allowed itself to accept a package of reforms that the various health think-tanks felt, almost unanimously, was misconceived. Some will put that down to naivety and inexperience, others to too strong a right-wing or free-market leaning within the leadership. Time will tell whether lessons have been learned. Time will also tell whether Lansley's efforts will indeed protect the NHS on flat funding with quality and standards of professionalism maintained, or whether they will lead to the kind of NHS that many Lib Dems, and indeed progressives on the left of British politics more generally, have long feared.

The degree of ridicule that Clegg was subjected to over the first nine months of the coalition was at times ridiculous. Even an enquiry he made about joining his local tennis club became a story in a gossip column, presented not for what it was (an enquiry about joining) but as a rejection because the club concerned quoted him its rule that it subjected all new members to a 'play-in' test with an established member to determine the applicant's playing level. Such was the lack of attention to detail that even the term 'play-in', known to many club tennis players in Britain, was presented in the story as 'playing'.

Perhaps the ultimate was a story that implied he was lazy, as he didn't want to work after 3 p.m. The source of the story was a tag line at the bottom of all emails sent out by Shelley Williams-Walker, his diary secretary at the Deputy Prime Minister's Office, and which is used in most ministries. It reads, 'Box deadline for routine submissions is 15.00 on Monday–Thursday and 12.00 on Friday.' This was seized on by the *Sunday Telegraph* as proof that Clegg doesn't want to work after three in the afternoon. The paper even quoted a Labour MP as saying that while the rest of the country needed to work harder for less reward, Clegg was 'clocking off after lunch and putting his feet up'.

'Of all the silly stories I've heard, this is the silliest,' Clegg responded. 'I may have many flaws, but not working hard enough? – even my strongest critics wouldn't say that's one of them.' They wouldn't indeed. One close aide says 'he works like a horse'. Many talk about how he works late into the night when his boys are in bed – fifteen-hour days are the norm rather than the exception – and Norman Lamb says, 'I've texted him at night and got responses at night. The idea that he doesn't work hard is just ludicrous.'

Such working days rob him of time with his wife and boys. In an interview Miriam González gave in 2010, she said she never gets to see her husband. The piece, which *The Times* trailed as 'her first interview', was actually about a sustainable and ethical fashion venture called EcoLuxe she was involved in promoting, and clearly was intended to feature little or nothing about her role as the Deputy Prime Minister's wife. But inevitably the question about her relationship with Nick was slipped in, and her only comment was 'I see very little of my husband, I talk about our children mostly'. Clegg responded, 'I saw that and rang her straight afterwards and said, "What do you mean? I'm seeing you in a minute."' Doubtless he was, but the idea that he is putting up his feet by 4 p.m. to have a nice cup of tea with his wife and kids is little more than wishful thinking.

When the world is out to get you, anything gets seized on. Clegg's easy manner with people means he's always cracking jokes, but that can be a dangerous business. A journalist from the *Metro* free newspaper in London carried out an interview with him, and on packing his bag to leave, asked whether Clegg was in charge while David Cameron was on a trip to the Middle East to drum up business for British businesses, including arms manufacturers. Clegg joked, 'Yeah, I suppose I am. I forgot about that.' Those that know him recognise the Clegg humour, but the journalist made it out that the Deputy Prime Minister had forgotten that he was, well, Deputy Prime Minister. And on leaving a question-and-answer session with Cameron in Nottingham, Clegg muttered, 'David, we won't find anything to bloody disagree on in the bloody TV debates,' forgetting that his microphone was still on. Coming less than a year after Gordon Brown's faux pas with a lapel microphone he had forgotten was still attached to his jacket during the general election campaign, in which he described a Labour supporter as 'a bigoted woman', it was a silly mistake to make, but again the sense of humour is recognisable to those who know Clegg. In fact there are many close to him who feel that those who took his comment literally were guilty of missing the inherent irony in it.

The tuition fees issue had also spawned a rather poor joke that did the rounds of school playgrounds: 'Why did Nick Clegg cross the road? Because he said he wouldn't.' British politics would be the poorer without its humour, and Clegg was perfectly able to laugh off such digs at him. But such digs can penetrate the psyche of voters; Lib Dem members and political commentators often wonder whether David Steel's credibility was irrevocably damaged by a sketch on the satirical puppet programme *Spitting Image* depicting him getting completely stitched up by David Owen over the Liberal–SDP merger as the two men worked out the deal in bed. It may be better for people to be talking about you than not talking about you, but not when it undermines your basic credibility.

How much the backlash over tuition fees and the Lib Dems' standing in the coalition had influenced the electorate was to be brutally exposed when the country voted on 5 May 2011 in elections to the Scottish and Welsh assemblies, English local elections, and the Lib Dems' cherished dream of voting reform.

Chapter 13

'THIS IS A BITTER BLOW'

A**T THE** end of April 2011, a group of satirists staged a one-off musical production in Suffolk called *Nicked*. It was sub-titled 'The rise and fall of Nick Clegg'. Less than a year after getting into government, people were already talking about the fall – in many ways the dramatic fall – of the bright hope of the previous year's election.

There's a syndrome in British sport whereby a rising star is put on a pedestal and feted as a hero, then shot down after a relatively short time. Inevitably it will also apply to politics, but both the beatification and demonisation of Clegg were risible in their extremes. The rise was so dramatic that the disappointment when Clegg couldn't live up to the expectation that went with the hype was always going to be great.

On the eve of the 2010 election, the steps of Sheffield city hall had seen 2,000 people who turned out to see the local hero, Nick Clegg. The then leader of Sheffield City Council, Paul Scriven, had to hold the fort for twenty minutes while Clegg's bus was delayed. Ten months later, when the Lib Dems held their spring conference in Sheffield (it had been booked well before the general election), concrete blocks and extra police formed a cordon around the building, while Clegg was barricaded inside, having to take police advice because of a thousand or so noisy protesters. Some of the demonstrators were Labour activists who would have turned out anyway, and some were to the left of Labour, but the contrast made the point that the hero had turned villain in many people's eyes.

'I think it's been one of the most extraordinary rises and falls that any of us have seen,' says Isabel Oakeshott, the political editor of the *Sunday Times*. 'To go from a position where no-one was taking him seriously as the leader of the third party, to then go stellar with the debates and the Cleggmania, and then a few months later absolutely rock bottom. His reputation in the lobby has definitely suffered. The lobby is a funny place, it's full of people who are very grand, they've seen so much, and in the lobby you are free to criticise without having to have an alternative. There a lot of people who have been very scathing about Clegg who feel only too glad that their judgement has been vindicated. I don't think you can overestimate just how damaged he is now.'

Oakeshott's assessment is legitimate, but journalistically short term. Whether such 'damage' is long term remains to be seen. Some politicians do indeed suffer damage to their reputation that they never recover from, but some bounce back. Which camp Clegg falls into won't be known for several years.

Throughout both the Cleggmania period and the vilification of him in the first year after the coalition was formed, Clegg kept a detachment from it all. He never felt it was about him the person, but about what the image of him projected through the media meant to people; and the more people admired or loathed him, the more the distance grew between who he really was and the 'cardboard cut-outs' the public saw. But could he have avoided the extent of the plunge in his and the Lib Dems' fortunes after the novelty of the new coalition began to wear off? To answer this, it's important to look at how the Lib Dems viewed the media in the early months of 2011. There is certainly evidence that the party badly underestimated the power of the media in toxifying a political brand.

The media are a section of British society with which the public has a love–hate relationship. People love moaning about journalists and their publications, but couldn't do without them; they castigate the lies and bias, but rush to the media whenever they sense any wrongdoing that needs to be exposed. It's the same with politicians. They hate the fact that their policies and utterances are largely seen through the prism of newspapers, radio, television and internet media, but know that without coverage in the media they wouldn't communicate with many of their voters. Hence the need to be both media savvy and thick skinned. 'If I bridled every time I felt we weren't getting right or fair coverage,' Clegg says, 'I'd have been driven round the bend a long time ago.'

There's another element about the media that the Lib Dems find harder to deal with than the other two major parties. The need to fight 'air wars' (political campaigning through the media) as much as 'ground wars' (political campaigning through leafleting and knocking on doors) has turned politics into a game of media manipulation. Summarising a policy or a response to a breaking issue in a twelve-second sound bite is absolutely vital, as is the use of a few carefully chosen slogans. Margaret Thatcher's 'The lady's not for turning' and 'There is no alternative' arguably did more work for her than any political philosophies formulated in smoke-filled rooms with the likes of Milton Friedman, Keith Joseph and other advisers. And Tony Blair's career was launched as much through his 'Tough on crime, tough on the causes of crime' slogan as by rapid rebuttal units and the addition of the word 'New' to 'Labour'.

For a party like the Liberal Democrats that prides itself on being a refuge for the thinkers, and with its *raison d'être* based more on philosophy than the remnants of class-based allegiances, having to distil everything into media-sized chunks goes somewhat against the grain. Many of the most loyal and long-standing Lib Dems enjoy thrashing out ideas *ad nauseam*; indeed, that's why they are in politics: to debate. It therefore comes as a harsh reality check to find that political effectiveness has little to do with debates, and much more with how well you can play a media game. The best arguments in the world are no good if it takes longer to explain them than the media allows you, or if they can be shot down by some carefully crafted opposing slogans.

When the Lib Dems' then chief executive, Chris Rennard, reviewed a party debrief on its 2005 general election campaign, he ended his paper by stressing the need for good slogans that reflected what the party stood for, which were then road-tested before being put to widespread use (and reuse). He loosely recommended 'Lib Dems – fairer, greener and more democratic', but that was never

widely adopted – except perhaps the word 'fairness', which played
a big part in the Lib Dems' 2010 general election language. Indeed
the only slogan used by the Lib Dems between 2005 and 2010 that
could be considered to have found any resonance among the public
was the idea of a 'new politics', and that came about more by evolution than design.

It's possible to argue that Clegg too has never had a slogan that
has really captured the political agenda. The closest he has come was
his line from the 2010 election campaign 'No more broken promises'. It was designed to complement the Lib Dems' pitch for a 'new
politics', one that neatly tapped into public anger about the MPs'
expenses scandal of 2009. It dovetailed nicely with his performance
in the 2010 television debates, but it came back to bite him when the
compromises the Lib Dems had to make in coalition were seen by
the public as broken promises. Did Clegg and the Lib Dems really
not see that coming? There are two possible explanations: either
they underestimated the task of explaining to the British public
that certain electoral campaigning themes they had used to attract
votes had to be jettisoned as part of the give-and-take of forming a
government; or they thought the 2010 election would not deliver a
hung parliament, and therefore their campaign promises would not
be subjected to the scrutiny of government. In either case, it could
be construed in retrospect as somewhat naive, and perhaps reflects
the inevitable lack of streetwisdom in a party unused to being in
government at national level.

But by the spring of 2011, Clegg had another problem that was
only peripherally related to the media. He had staked everything in
the months following the general election on showing that 'coalition works', yet by early 2011 he was becoming aware that the Lib
Dems needed to show the public what they were bringing to the
governmental table. Out of this emerged a slogan, 'alarm clock
Britain', aimed to show the people the Lib Dems were batting
for in the coalition. But the term was never properly developed,
and was accompanied by a well-meaning but ill-conceived initiative to get interns to be paid. The idea that unpaid internships are

an abuse of young adult labour is perhaps a viable argument, but Clegg overlooked two rather glaring Achilles heels: he himself had benefited from an unpaid internship in Finland as a teenager (see page 57), and the practice of unpaid internships is in widespread use in the Liberal Democrat administration. The need he perceived to acquiesce with those calling for better differentiation for the Lib Dems had led him to a knee-jerk policy that brought some low-level ridicule on him and his party.

Clegg's approach to the media remained unaffected by the poor opinion polls. He denies it was a deliberate strategy to be himself and not pander to media agendas, but he did continue to be himself. He agreed to give an interview to Jemima Khan in the week she guest-edited the *New Statesman* magazine, in which he talked candidly about life, emotions and – to a limited extent – his family, even inviting Khan to have dinner with Miriam and their three boys. He admitted to feeling 'quite miserable' when he doesn't get his work–life balance right, that he worries when his nine-year-old son Antonio starts to sense some of the public anger aimed at his dad, and admitted – not for the first time – that he 'cries regularly to music'. To those who read the full interview, Clegg came across generally very well, and Khan – who herself was married to a high-profile figure, the Pakistan cricketer turned politician Imran Khan – wrote highly of him as a person. But once again it was the quotable bits that became the hostages to fortune, with one newspaper even taking issue with the fact that his kids call him 'Papa' rather than 'Dad'!

The interview also featured another example of Clegg's mild discomfort at being associated with the landed and moneyed classes. When asked about a lunch David Cameron had had with the former News International executive and former *Sun* and *News of the World* editor Rebekah Brooks at her home in Oxford, Clegg was quoted as saying, 'I don't know anything about Oxfordshire dinner parties ... I don't hang out in Oxfordshire at dinner parties. It's not my world. It's never going to be my world.' As an attempt to distance himself from the kind of Home Counties affluence that turns many Lib Dems off, and to emphasise that he'd rather be dining at home rather than on a dinner party circuit, it was understandable, but perhaps an odd comment from a man whose parents live in Oxfordshire.

Hearing Westminster journalists speak, it's easy to get the impression that the media are the kingmakers of British politics – that what the lobby decides is what the reality will be. Yet in the two decades since the 1992 election result was thought to have been influenced by a front page in the *Sun* that read 'If Kinnock wins today, will the last person to leave Britain please turn out the lights', there has been ample evidence that people are remarkably impervious to the voting advice they're given by the newspapers they read. There have been suggestions that coverage of David Cameron's speech at the 2005 Conservative Party conference, the speech that won him the party leadership, was strongly influenced by an informal decision by a group of editors that Cameron would be a better party leader than David Davis. Whether that's true or not, Cameron was certainly given a reasonable ride by the British press in the run-up to the 2010 election, yet still failed to win a majority against a tired government led by a socially limited prime minister.

Such considerations led those high up in the Lib Dems to believe the demonisation of Nick Clegg was largely a media construct. They had reasons to believe this. In an aggregate of council by-elections that had taken place since the 2010 general election, the Lib Dems had done much better than their opinion poll ratings suggested. In the 113 principal local by-elections that took place in England, Scotland and Wales in the first year of the coalition, the Lib Dems had gained twelve and lost five, while the Conservatives had lost sixteen and Labour had gained sixteen. Party membership also showed a net gain. Although some members had left, others had joined, and at the start of 2011 the gain was healthy, though it tailed off after that (but then break-even would have been seen as a success).

In late March 2011, the Lib Dems' chief executive, Chris Fox, accompanied Clegg on a trip to Wales. 'No-one mentioned tuition fees,' said Fox, 'and this was a day after the Jemima Khan interview. They wanted to talk to him, they wanted to tell him about what they were doing, and they warmed and really wanted to be there. That was hundreds of people in five visits. He's still the party leader people would most like to have a drink with. Whatever the media or the Whitehall bubble is telling you, it's very different to what real people are saying. The party membership's frame of reference is *The Guardian* or *The Independent* – members have to go canvassing or they will be dragged into this extremely narrow and wrong framing of where we are, where Nick is and what people really think.'

Out of this was born an internal slogan, 'Where we work, we win', which was the Lib Dems' mantra going into the Scottish, Welsh and English council elections in May 2011. Although not a conscious challenge to the media, there was an element of wanting to show them that Lib Dem support on the ground was much better than a few thousand respondents phoned by opinion polling companies would have people believe. Yet there were three problems with this approach. Firstly, Clegg may have impressed people he met, but he was never going to meet enough to counter the perception of him spread by the media. Secondly, by no means everyone thought Clegg was the devil incarnate, but enough did to swing a few seats in council elections – the Lib Dems know this; indeed, one of their primary objections to the first-past-the-post voting system is that it leaves the outcome of elections in the hands of very few voters. Thirdly, there were never going to be enough activists to win a whole host of elections – the Lib Dems have thrived on flooding activists into by-elections, which by their nature are one-off events, but that only works when the same activists don't have their own elections to fight. Private polling conducted a couple of weeks before the May 2011 elections dented even Clegg's normally unshakeable bonhomie. When presented with news that returns on the doorsteps were reasonably good, he tended to respond that this was all well and good where the Lib Dems were up against the Conservatives but was unlikely to help in the north of England, where many of the fights were with Labour.

'I was really struck by the strength of the anti-Tory sentiment in the North,' he said, 'it was very apparent on the doorsteps when I went out campaigning. A lot of people see any vote for the Conservatives, and so by association for us, as basically a return to Thatcherism and a return to the 1980s. Even though circumstances are completely different and things will turn out quite differently to the 1980s, it still remains an easy message for Labour to sell.'

In many ways the 'where we work, we win' strategy proved accurate, certainly in Lib–Con battlegrounds. The Lib Dems did well in the Hampshire borough of Eastleigh (Chris Huhne's constituency), and reasonably well in areas where the Lib Dems had a sitting MP who had beaten off a Tory. But in the north of England and Scotland, the party was hammered. It lost control of nine English councils, suffered a net loss of 748 councillors, and saw its overall share of the vote fall to 15 per cent from the 23 per cent it had polled at the general election a year earlier.

Clegg had been prepared for bad results at some stage in the coalition adventure. He knew it was a five-year project that at various stages could look very bad. And he knew that even the hardest-working and most respected councillors can be thrown out of office because their party is out of favour at national level. What he was not prepared for was the scale of the defeat for the Lib Dems' cherished hopes of changing the voting system used for Westminster elections.

It is difficult to overstate the sense of betrayal Clegg felt by the actions of both David Cameron and Ed Miliband in the campaign for the referendum on a limited measure of electoral reform that took place on 5 May 2011. He felt a sense of despair when Miliband declined to share a platform with him, despite both men campaigning for a Yes vote. And he felt betrayed by the scale and style of Conservative involvement in the 'No to AV' campaign, an involvement that changed in subtle ways the nature of both the coalition and his own relationship with Cameron. Such changes would probably have happened anyway, but instead of a gentle metamorphosing, they came with a massive resentment on the Lib Dem side, one which left many feeling Clegg had been conned by the ruthlessness of the Conservatives' electoral machine and undermined by Labour short-termism.

When the coalition was formed, Cameron had volunteered the promise that he would not take a high-profile role in the referendum campaign. Clegg reciprocated, and it became an understanding between them. In the summer of 2010, most of the opinion polls were suggesting that the Yes camp would win, but campaigning had not begun in earnest. By the time the referendum bill was approved and it was clear the vote would happen, the polls were as close as to suggest the outcome was on the line. By and large, the No camp were ahead, but a few polls favoured a Yes vote, and the propor-tion of don't-knows was sufficiently high to make the outcome very much all to play for.

Many political commentators believe it was Cameron's interven-tion that swung the referendum. Whether one factor can be cited for a vote that was more than 2:1 for one side is questionable, but pictures of Clegg that appeared in No literature alongside slogans such as 'more broken promises' became a central feature of the No campaign. There was even one photo of Clegg entering 10 Downing Street with Cameron, looking back at the cameras with a shifty smile and patting Cameron on the back, which was accompanied by the slogan 'AV would lead to more hung parliaments, backroom deals and broken promises'. One unnamed Lib Dem told the *Independent on Sunday*, 'It beggars belief that they had a leaflet attacking Nick Clegg for breaking his word on increasing VAT, when we only did that to sign up to their economic strategy.'

According to the ConservativeHome website, a major battle had raged between Downing Street and the Labour element of the No campaign. It says Downing Street was worried about the Deputy Prime Minister's photo appearing on the No literature, and Conservative HQ repeatedly asked that photographs of Clegg be removed from leaflets. But the leading Labour personnel in the cross-party No campaign were so determined that images of Clegg and the language of 'broken promises' should feature that they threatened to pull the plug on the whole campaign if Clegg was off limits. This explains Cameron's decision to distance himself subtly from the cross-party campaign and defend only the Conservative Party's own campaign, which was largely invisible, certainly compared with 'No to AV'. In a bruising interview with John Humphrys on BBC Radio 4's *Today* programme, Cameron refused to engage in any questions to do with the 'No to AV' literature, saying only that he would defend the Tories' own No campaign. The Prime Minister appears to have been genuinely concerned about using his deputy's unpopularity in the run-up to the referendum, but more concerned that a Yes vote would damage his own position, hence his willingness to break his gentlemen's agreement about a low-profile campaigning role. Cameron's distinction between the cross-party 'No to AV' campaign and the Tories' own campaign cut no ice with the Lib Dems, whose bitterness was based on the fact that hostile images of Clegg appeared in literature funded by Conservative Party donors. Ultimately, the Conservative Party had forced Cameron's hand in coming out vociferously for the No campaign.

Aides of Clegg say Cameron told him what he was going to do in terms of taking a high-profile role in the No campaign. As it was a gentlemen's agreement, there was nothing Clegg could do to stop Cameron, but even he was taken aback by the vehemence of the attacks. In particular the Lib Dems were aghast at the fact that Cameron had promised to fight a constructive campaign in favour of first past the post, yet the driving force behind the No campaign was the recurring image of Clegg appearing on almost all the No literature.

Passions boiled over in Cabinet during the campaign, when Chris Huhne verbally attacked George Osborne for the negativity and hostility of the anti-AV campaign. Clegg knew nothing in advance about Huhne's attack, nor did he intervene – he just let it run and observed the spectacle. He has never spoken about the incident because it was a Cabinet meeting and all attendees are bound by Cabinet confidentiality (which raises the question of who leaked news of Huhne's attack). Osborne apparently put down Huhne by making the point that the Cabinet is not the appropriate place for such outbursts. It is perhaps reassuring in an era of safety-conscious politicians to know that Huhne behaves with the same anger and passion behind closed doors as he does in public.

Two weeks before the referendum, Clegg stepped up his attacks on the Conservatives, but it was the Conservatives rather than Cameron. 'This nasty No campaign', he told the *Independent on Sunday*, 'will, I hope, prove to be the death rattle of a right-wing elite, a right-wing clique who want to keep things the way they are. That's why they're lashing out.' The paper asked Clegg if he was referring to the Prime Minister. 'I include all those, and of course it includes the Conservative Party, who like this nice little racket.' One can interpret this refusal to condemn Cameron as a case of either a loyalist standing by his coalition partner, or a lack of political ruthlessness. There were suggestions that an attack on Cameron might have been the Yes campaign's most effective weapon, but Clegg clearly felt it was too risky to the coalition for him to make such a personal attack.

With hindsight, it looks like Clegg got his timing wrong in insisting that the referendum take place on the first anniversary of the general election, but that would be a simplistic view to take. He was never going to be able to persuade his party to go into coalition with the Conservatives without a meaningful promise on electoral reform, and having secured the promise of a referendum from a reluctant Conservative Party, he then had to fight off various legal and parliamentary attempts to stop the referendum taking place. If he had said to his party, 'We're likely to be unpopular twelve months from now, but people will have seen the benefits of coalition government by 2013, so let's have the referendum in three years,' he would have lost credibility with it. To have backed down on having the vote at the first reasonable opportunity would have been a massive concession that might have brought down the coalition, and possibly himself. More importantly, Clegg had ordered private polling back in the summer of 2010 to test out the proposed ballot paper – the results were strongly in favour, which told him the referendum was eminently winnable.

And yet the No campaign polled more than 68 per cent while the Yes vote was less than 32 per cent, a resounding defeat for hopes of electoral reform. Why?

At least part of the result was down to an attack on Clegg himself. For reasons still not fully explicable, the Lib Dems took pretty much all the flak for the unpopular measures enacted by the coalition government in its first year. Some of this can be put down to political naivety, and some to the newness of a coalition that made voters blame the Lib Dems for what were perceived as 'broken promises' rather than blame the Conservatives for doing largely what they said they would. Ed Miliband justified his decision not to share a platform with Clegg on the grounds that Clegg was so unpopular that it would have undermined the Yes campaign that Miliband was committed to. It left Clegg in a difficult position – he was quite happy to take a low profile in the campaign, but he didn't want to put himself in the position where he could be accused afterwards of not fighting for what he believed in and what was something of a holy grail for his party.

Clegg himself put the resounding No vote down to the difficulty of selling change at a time of economic insecurity. 'At a time when people feel insecure about their jobs, about cuts, about their children's future,' he said, 'changing things feels like a very tricky and risky thing to do, and it's not a time for risk-taking – and that's probably what it felt like.' Although possibly true, that may not be Clegg's most convincing argument. At a time of economic insecurity, people like to lash out – it's when extremist parties tend to do best – and to many voters Clegg seemed as good a person as any to lash out at.

Some say he failed to convince Cameron that the Conservatives had little to fear from AV – that it would have made very little difference to the Conservatives' fortunes at almost all post-war general elections. Although factually true, Cameron was never going to be convinced. While AV was not a threat to the Conservatives, its role as a possible gateway to proportional representation was a threat, and the Conservatives were always going to mobilise all their support to oppose a change in a voting system that had served their own interests rather well for more than half a century.

A much bigger contributory factor to the resounding No victory was the fragmentation of the Labour vote. While Miliband was strongly in favour – albeit not so strongly as to risk long-term discontent in his party – 130 Labour MPs came out vehemently against AV, and there was a strong Labour element in the 'No to AV' campaign, despite the fact that Labour had pledged to support AV in its 2010 manifesto. '[Clegg] felt a fair bit of despair,' says a close aide, 'not at Miliband's decision to refuse to share a platform with him, but at Miliband's inability to see the bigger picture, to see the importance of what was a historically unique moment for electoral reform, something Labour had in its manifesto, for the sake of short-term political gain and political headlines. That made him despair, as well as thinking Labour had shot itself in the foot.'

For those of the Ashdown–Blair persuasion who see the Conservative vote as largely static, and thus the chances of a non-Conservative government being forever dependent on a loose alliance of Labour, Lib Dems, Greens and other 'progressive' forces banding together, the decision by half the Labour MPs to back the old system might yet keep Labour out of office for longer than AV would have done. Part of the referendum deal was a concession to Conservative demands to redraw the parliamentary constituency boundaries, as it currently takes more votes to elect a Conservative MP than a Labour MP (and vastly more to elect a Lib Dem MP). When this happens, it is likely to make it harder for Labour to win a majority. How well Labour does remains to be seen, but the split in Labour ranks was a killer blow to the kind of alliance needed to deliver a change in the voting system. Clegg's unpopularity may have been a major factor, but Clegg believes the AV referendum was never going to be won without Miliband delivering Labour, and the Labour leader clearly failed to do this. It sheds a clearer light on Clegg's decision not to accept Gordon Brown's increasingly unrealistic offers on electoral reform made in the five days of post-election negotiations in May 2010.

Perhaps the biggest blow to the Lib Dems to emerge from the AV referendum was that most people appear simply not to care what voting system is used for parliamentary elections. It has been well known for many years that many people vote on national issues, whatever the elections, and therefore use local and European parliamentary elections as a chance to voice protests about what is happening nationally. With the No campaign tapping into a rich seam of anti-Clegg sentiment, it was able to mobilise all those people who were angry at what they saw as a betrayal by Clegg in the first year of the coalition government, so that the vote became a 'don't give Clegg what he wants' verdict, either as well as or more than a reasoned judgement on the relative merits of two voting systems.

There are two consolations for Clegg from the referendum and local election results. The first is that Labour used these elections to turn its fire on the Lib Dems, both to express its anger at the Lib Dems' decision to form a government with the Tories, and to try to establish itself as the sole progressive party. That job has been done for the short term, and Labour knows it cannot win a general election by fighting the Lib Dems – it has to target the Tories, so Cameron is unlikely to have such an easy ride for the remainder of the current parliament. Ed Miliband has also left various doors ajar to the possibility of Lib–Lab cooperation when the current coalition expires, so as long as he – or someone with his outlook – remains Labour leader, Labour fire on the Lib Dems is likely to be less intense in the immediate future.

The general view in the media after the referendum was that electoral reform is now dead for at least twenty years. Given how long it has taken to get electoral reform on the agenda, that may well be true, but not necessarily, and this is Clegg's second possible consolation. With elections to the Scottish and Welsh assemblies, the European Parliament and the London mayoralty all run on more sophisticated systems than first past the post, Westminster elections could come to be seen as increasingly out of sync with the developing British political consciousness, and if Labour fails to win an overall majority next time but can form a working coalition with the Lib Dems, there may be a parliamentary majority that would approve a change in the voting system without a referendum. Ironically, the 'No to AV' campaign has left a door open to those in favour of a proportional system – one of the arguments it listed on its anti-AV literature is that AV is not proportional, so those on the progressive wing of British politics might feel legitimised in using the argument that the resounding 'No to AV' vote is, at least in part, a vote in favour of a proportionally representative system. It would be a hard argument to sell, but could yet happen.

Yet such wishful thinking cannot dent the blow to Nick Clegg's political prestige caused by the defeat for AV. He had achieved more than any Liberal leader since the Second World War in getting the referendum, and had then seen his party's dream of electoral reform crushed because of his own unpopularity. There was only one thing to do: accept defeat with as much dignity as he could muster. 'This is a bitter blow for all those people like me who believe in the need for political reform, but the answer is clear,' he said.

The sense of resentment felt by the Lib Dems, and the sense of triumphalism felt by the Conservatives, changed the nature of the coalition in some respects. There were loud calls from within the Lib Dems for the party to assert its distinctiveness and not be seen as being a prop to an anti-state Conservative administration. There were equally loud calls from the Conservative Party, saying David Cameron should resist the temptation to make concessions to the Lib Dems, particularly over NHS and House of Lords reforms, as a consolation for the Lib Dems having had one of their biggest dreams obliterated.

One of Clegg's close aides says the nature of the referendum campaign underlined what would have happened anyway. In the early stages of the coalition it was important to show that the new government could work, and that once the two parties had convinced the world – especially the stock and money markets

– that it would last, then they would have to begin differentiat-
ing themselves more clearly. But even this aide says, 'The way the
campaign was conducted, and the fact that it was funded almost
entirely from Conservative sources, did leave a very nasty taste in
the mouth.'

Clegg says, 'David and I both assumed the referendum would
be much more non-partisan, and therefore we agreed to take a low-
profile role, but we were overtaken by events. The No campaign
decided to take a very different stance, so the idea that it would
be a non-partisan and non-personal campaign got overturned. Of
course there was a lot of anger on our side, but while we regret that
the AV vote was lost, the whole experience has made the coalition
more businesslike than it was before, and that's no bad thing. It's
very obvious at the beginning when you work very closely and have
to take big controversial decisions quickly with people you don't
really know – I hadn't met David Cameron more than a handful of
times and those were on official occasions – that the appearance of
government unity is a key priority in those early days. In many ways
it's a sign of how accepted coalition government now is that both
parties can afford to make it more businesslike.'

In some ways, the Conservatives probably did Clegg a favour.
'Until the Tories began their aggressive anti-Clegg personal
campaign in the AV referendum,' says Chris Rennard, 'Nick was
being pushed into a position that would make it hard to be equidis-
tant between Labour and Conservatives in any future negotiations.
Labour's aggressive campaigning in Sheffield and elsewhere was
jeopardising the chances of future deals with Labour, but once the
Conservatives' personal campaign had begun, it became clear that
the Conservatives were no better, and that emphasised the impera-
tive for him to carve out a distinctive platform for the Lib Dems
and not to be seen to be too close to Cameron.'

From the vantage point of May 2011, the launch of the coalition in the rose garden of 10 Downing Street was beginning to look
tactically dubious. The event had been designed to show the unity
of purpose between the two leaders, and it's easy with hindsight to

forget how important a show of unity was at that time, with the euro in crisis and sections of the British press having peddled the line that a coalition government would be a disaster. But Clegg's adherence to the 'owning everything' doctrine had left the public with an image of him joined to the prime minister but without much influence. Again, perceptions played a big part in this. Enough evidence can be assembled to suggest the Lib Dems were having a considerable influence on government policy, but the public perception was that they weren't, and that they were smoothing the way for a purely Conservative government. Peter Brookes's cartoon for *The Times* depicting Clegg as 'Cleggers', David Cameron's imaginary Etonian fag (to whom Cameron handed a pair of shoes and issued the instruction 'Polish these, Cleggers old son, then I'd like you to halve the deficit before prep'), only reinforced this image.

Despite the nastiness of the referendum campaign, relations between Cameron and Clegg – and between leading Conservatives and Lib Dems – remained remarkably good. They were not 'beer and sandwiches at No 10', as the Labour Prime Minister Harold Wilson had once initiated in negotiations with trade unions, but they were businesslike. As one insider put it a few weeks after the referendum, 'It's almost easier to start from a position where you disagree. The problem with the Labour Party in the Blair–Brown era was that all ministers came from a position where they were supposed to agree, so when they didn't, there was a sense that such disagreement wasn't meant to happen. At least with us, when Conservative and Lib Dem ministers sit down to thrash something out, there's a recognition at the start that we're not agreeing on things, so the discussion is then about how to make things work in the circumstances. In some ways it's cleaner. The relationships are certainly better than might have been imagined, and the relationship between Nick and David is still good and businesslike – they're both very effective at doing business, so that part of their relationship hasn't changed.'

This chimes with the comment of a former Labour Cabinet minister, who told a Lib Dem MP, 'Your coalition is characterised by a generosity of spirit, good nature, and give and take, unlike the last coalition – the one between the Blairites and the Brownites.' Admittedly that was said before the referendum campaign got nasty, but the fact was that both coalition parties still needed each other. The Lib Dems certainly wouldn't have relished a general election in the summer of 2011, and while the Conservatives would have done, there was no guarantee that abandoning the coalition would have brought about an election, as Ed Miliband would have fancied his chances of forming a Labour-led rainbow coalition. Generosity of spirit is easier to find when you have no alternative.

And Clegg always said the coalition was a five-year programme that would see some rough times on the way. Danny Alexander says, 'Nick told me during the spending review, "You've got to make sure you can look in the shaving mirror in the morning and can say we're doing the right thing," and I think we are. It doesn't mean some of the things aren't painful, some of them are very painful, but in two or three years people will look back and say we're stronger, fairer, freer and more prosperous, because these guys are in government and because they held firm. There are a lot of cheesed-off people about, but I don't think it's permanent. I think people will see that the country is in a better place as a result. When we went into this we knew we'd get a lot of criticism. I talked a lot to Jim Wallace [former Scottish Lib Dem leader] because they went through the same thing with a lot of abuse in the first Scottish Parliament coalition, so this didn't come as a massive shock to us.'

The biggest sustaining factor for both Clegg and the Lib Dems is a belief in their five-year project. The Lib Dems' chief executive, Chris Fox, says, 'What Nick and the party took on when we went into coalition wasn't just a glimmering five years in government, it was the opportunity to substantially and significantly change Britain – if you look at the scale of the agenda that the coalition has and the elements we put into that, this is a huge opportunity. Even if nothing else happens, at the end of this five-year period we will have changed Britain, and Nick will have done that.'

Political fortunes fluctuate considerably, occasionally wildly. It is easy to forget that, two years into her first term as Prime Minister,

Margaret Thatcher was massively unpopular. But a mixture of a recovering economy, a Labour Party in self-destruct mode, and a short victorious war delivered a 144-seat majority two years later. Clegg is clearly setting his chips on people gradually coming round to recognise that what he and his party did was the right thing to do rather than the popular thing, and even if such recognition is not forthcoming, he will be able to sleep at night knowing he did what he thought was right. But it's hard to escape the feeling that he could make life a little easier for himself if he could only accept a few more of the political tricks, notably the media techniques that allow him to play the game in interviews and then be himself when interacting with the public.

There is enough material for him to work with. In the weeks after the referendum and local/regional elections, the Lib Dems notched up some considerable successes, notably the concessions on Andrew Lansley's NHS reforms and Chris Huhne's achievement as energy and climate secretary in getting the UK to commit to a carbon reduction target of 60 per cent by 2030 (the target almost certainly won't be met, but the commitment means more reductions will happen than would otherwise have been the case, and the UK can wield more weight in international climate negotiations). The party's machinery has tried to publicise these Lib Dem contributions to government, but the media have been only moderately willing to take up the Lib Dem spin.

Indeed the media have not been keen to publicise Clegg much at all. It is possible to make the case that he has achieved the first stage of what he set out to achieve: providing the stability for the economy to weather the international economic and financial storms and start to recover gradually. Yet that may not be enough of a substantive achievement that makes people want to vote Lib Dem next time, especially when people are feeling the economic sacrifices in their everyday lives. As such, Clegg risks becoming the invisible man in the coalition government, as he is not associated with anything in particular. His PR team may need to shout a little louder about his successes, though one reason for a reluctance to do so may lie in his continuing enthusiasm for Britain joining the euro at some stage. He is with Tony Blair on this: both men believe the UK will have to join the euro somewhere down the track – with all the difficulties that will come with it – but both recognise that now is clearly not the right time. That's a hard argument to sell when the eurozone is in crisis and Britain is doing rather well by being outside it.

As a result, he may well need an initiative of his own to make his mark as a reforming Deputy Prime Minister, rather than risk being seen as merely an overblown administrator, but again there is ample scope. His belief that the extended family is very important has led him to initiate a Lib Dem working group on the 'third age', whose role is to discuss getting rid of compulsory retirement ages and establish grandparents' rights. Close colleagues says he gets very excited about the idea of grandparents' rights, so that might be an area in which he could make his mark with some pioneering family legislation that garners cross-party support.

Clegg's problem remains that, in a world where people don't see the alternative scenarios that could have resulted from the 2010 general election result, it is easy for the public to view him, and the Lib Dems, not as a moderating force working to tone down the excesses of Conservatism, but as complicit in cuts that are, in some ways, changing the fabric of British society. Clegg may be right by the terms by which he went into government with the Conservatives, but unless he gets his media and PR strategy right, he risks getting no gratitude for it in the long run.

Chapter 14

'WHAT IS THE MOST
LIBERAL THING TO DO?'

A **FEATURE** of the aftermath of the 2011 elections was the surprising lack of people – in particular leading Liberal Democrats – who called for Nick Clegg's resignation. A few councillors and the odd columnist said he should go, but there was no sense that he was irrevocably damaged. The elections and referendum results had been a serious setback, but they seemed to signal the start of a new chapter in the Clegg story rather than the end of it.

There were various reasons for that, not least of them that the history of the Liberal Democrats, and their forerunner parties, is littered with tales of predicted doom, only for the party to bounce back. If Clegg and Danny Alexander were right about the basic premise behind the immense potential for the Lib Dems – namely that most British people are liberal and thus there is ample scope for a liberal party that knows where it's going and has its engine well oiled – then there would be dents and gashes along the road but never a complete write-off. While electoral reform might be a holy grail for the Lib Dems, it was sufficiently marginal for many voters that they would happily use a referendum on the alternative vote to express displeasure at the third party, but would not necessarily vote against them in an election of greater perceived importance, especially if doing so would let in an undesired alternative. Or so the theory goes – it has never been tested with a liberal party in government.

When thinking of dumping a leader, the presence – or absence – of alternatives is also a factor. The obvious successor to Clegg was Chris Huhne, but while he was an impressive performer, he had never convinced his party that he was a natural team player, and in May 2011 his jilted wife Vicky Pryce hinted that he might have persuaded another person 'close to him' to accept three penalty points incurred for a speeding offence that he had allegedly committed. Huhne vigorously denied the suggestion, Pryce declined to go to the police, and Huhne remained in his job, pending a police investigation. But given that the offence, if proven, could land him in prison, the allegation hardly enhanced his political standing. Clegg even felt sufficiently strong to crack a joke at a journalists' lunch: 'Say what you like about Chris Huhne, but I know no-one better at getting his points across.'

After Huhne, Simon Hughes and Vince Cable were the next obvious potential leaders, but both were thought to be beyond the point at which they could become anything more than a caretaker. Hughes was playing a vital role as the membership's gateway to the Deputy Prime Minister, but had accepted after two leadership election defeats that he would never lead his party. Cable had come across as rather too misanthropic in the first year of coalition, which probably damaged his chances of becoming party leader more than either his age or his falling victim to a sting in December 2010 over his views on Rupert Murdoch's NewsCorp company taking full control of the television broadcaster BSkyB – Cable was recorded, by two undercover *Daily Telegraph* journalists pretending to be constituents, saying he had 'declared war' on NewsCorp and had the 'nuclear option' of resigning if necessary, an admission of prejudice that led to him being relieved of responsibility for making the decision. Clegg was clearly more desirable as party leader than any of these three alternatives.

Had Clegg fallen under the proverbial bus in early 2011, a possible successor would have been Tim Farron. Although little known to the public at large, Farron is a sparky Lancastrian whose down-to-earth straight talking laced with humour, all delivered in a broad Lancashire accent, evokes memories of David Penhaligon, the much-loved Cornish Liberal who many thought would lead the Liberals after David Steel, but who died in a car crash in 1985. Farron's speech to the Lib Dems' 2011 spring conference showed the party that you could be a traditional left-of-centre liberal and be OK with a Lib–Con coalition, and announced him as the brightest star of the up-and-coming generation. But at forty, he was far from ready to become Deputy Prime Minister, which also helped reinforce Clegg's position.

Perhaps the biggest reason for Clegg's security of tenure was confidence in the man himself. Those who survive the British syndrome of being put on a pedestal and then being shot down eventually find their appropriate level (in politics as much as sport, the arts or general entertainment), the good ones surviving as honest professionals, the bad ones quietly disappearing from the stage. Many Westminster journalists found themselves staggered at the dramatic incline of Clegg's rise and fall, but once they had got away from writing today's headline, which for sales purposes is always going to be more dramatic than a realistic assessment of the big picture, they began to admit in subtle ways that both Cleggmania and the demonising of Clegg were artificial, and that the man was likely to find a more realistic level of general appreciation. As Marcel Theroux says, 'The longer someone hangs around, the more they garner grudging respect.' The outlook was probably never as bleak for Clegg as it sometimes seemed in the dark days after the May 2011 results.

The Clegg story thus far has a few elements of the 1939 Hollywood film *Mr Smith goes to Washington*. That was a movie about a political novice thrust into the midst of American politics and buffeted around by the hard-bitten and seedy seasoned politicians who manipulated his inexperience. Jefferson Smith, played by James Stewart, eventually triumphs in a slightly corny but just-about-plausible tale of corruption shooting itself in the foot. It would be wrong to compare Clegg literally to Smith, if only because the decision to go into politics was his own. But there is an element about the Lib Dems' lack of street savvy in government that is a challenge to the British people – it's easy to dismiss it as naivety and inexperience, but in some ways it's an interesting response to the much-expressed concerns about the disrepute into which politics and politicians have fallen, which makes it fascinating to observe, whether as a partial or impartial observer.

Central to this is the Clegg personality. If the British populace do give him a chance, there's no question he has a collection of character attributes that people generally warm to. Such attributes have to be used wisely or he could become seen as a nice guy with poor judgement, but it is extremely difficult to find anyone who has personal experience of him willing to say a harsh word against his personality. Of course there are many who hate what he stands for, and translate that into a hate for him as a person, but those who have dealt with him personally universally speak of a decent character. That goes for the media as much as for politicians from other parties, campaign groups and trade unions.

There is no denying his affluent background, and Clegg himself never tries to. 'I was lucky, incredibly lucky and incredibly privileged to have gone to a great school and to have had a great education,' he says. 'I had luck and benefits that I'm acutely aware of and that are out of the range of many other people.' Some use that as a stick to beat him with, suggesting he cannot possibly understand the realities of people from less affluent backgrounds. A complete empathy, no, but to take that argument to its logical conclusion, you would ban anyone who had not worked down a mine from speaking up for the rights of miners, or anyone who had not suffered from persecution at the hands of their government from speaking out for refugees. The history of progressive politics around the world has been dominated by people from affluent backgrounds who use their position to fight for those less fortunate.

Marcel Theroux invokes a quote from John F. Kennedy, 'Of those to whom much has been given, much will be asked', to describe Clegg's approach to his politics. 'He's someone who's aware of how lucky he's been, he's never had to worry about material things, but the flip side of that awareness is that you have to do something with your life, you have to do something that's worth doing – he'll have got that from his mum and dad. Many of us are simply happy to get through, but he had this extra burden to do something worthwhile, however you define "worthwhile".'

One of the plaudits he has been given is that of taking his politics seriously. His wife talks of him as 'a vocational politician among professionals' (see page 81), and a former assistant to the liberal group in the European Parliament, Arne Richters, says he showed in his five years as an MEP a rare set of skills among politicians. 'I have great respect for the way Nick practises and commits to his politics. He sees it as a serious mission and vocation in life, and is consequently very professional about it. He's also somebody who would talk to anybody, he's not pretentious, he's not into hierarchy – which a lot of politicians are, they quickly become prima donnas or quite vain about their position, and that is certainly not him. He's very accessible, very approachable, he always made the effort – if he half-spoke the language, he would do so in that language. He's a good listener, which is quite a rare thing. And he's a real authority. He didn't always take an active part in meetings, but when he did say something, people listened, so when he intervened it was usually with a well-timed comment or a carefully thought-out objection – he wasn't someone who was there just to stage his presence, everything he did was carefully and purposefully done. People often laugh about politicians, they say "It's always the same", "It's hot air", "It's vanity", "They're all prima donnas" but Nick was one of those people who you could use as an example to say they're not all like that.'

The bit about him not being into hierarchy is a common theme among those who have worked with him. 'He always wants a really flat structure,' says one of his aides, who adds that Clegg's entourage are constantly struck by the hierarchy that surrounds David Cameron. 'He wants to be able to go to everyone who works for him and ask for stuff, ask for their opinion. It can be annoying if you feel he's just asking different people until he finds someone who agrees with him, but he is open to new ideas.' Another close associate says, 'You can always make a joke to lighten the atmosphere, if necessary at his expense, because he doesn't take himself too seriously, is friendly, quick with a joke, and nice to work with.' Another aide who has worked with him for several years adds, 'With him, what you see is really what there is. There aren't sides you discover once you've known him for six months. He's very bright, cares deeply about certain issues, and has no concern for establishment rules – protocol is pretty much a waste of time in his eyes. He finds it weird that he can't call someone by their first name in the House of Commons.'

Long-standing Liberal Democrats compare Clegg to Paddy Ashdown because of both men's immense capacity for hard work. Ashdown wins hands down on pure energy, but Clegg is well ahead on user-friendliness. Chris Huhne says of Clegg, 'He has a lot of charm, warmth, and an ability to listen to people very carefully.' And Norman Baker adds, 'I've always found him to be calm, in fact I've very seldom seen him other than calm. I've seen him looking frazzled on occasions when the press has been particularly unkind and unhelpful, and I've seen an occasional flash of temper, but very occasional. He's a well-grounded individual.'

It would be wrong to suggest that Clegg doesn't get angry. He does, and he admits that one of his reasons for abandoning Transcendental Meditation in his early twenties was that he felt it was stopping him experiencing emotions such as anger and sadness. But he has learned the politician's art of keeping the anger controlled or unseen. One long-time Lib Dem activist says, 'He's very personable and very charming, but he keeps the other side of himself very well covered, which is that he's very competitive, and sometimes gets very angry. I've seen it once or twice. I think he was furious with Chris Huhne for standing for the party leadership in 2006, and he was very angry with him at various points in the 2007 leadership campaign. He is able to rise above many of these petty political rivalries, but it does take some effort.'

Others say they have never seen him angry, only impatient and tetchy when tired. He apparently never shouts. The former Lib Dem leader Charles Kennedy says, 'For all that he gets uptight and can be short tempered or fractious or impatient – though he's not as impatient as Paddy was – he's a very balanced individual, commendably so. Like anyone in a high-performance job, he exudes great self-assurance whatever pressures or self-doubts he suffers from, but given the extraordinary rollercoaster period he's been through, he's remained extremely well balanced and good humoured about things.'

This is why the Lib Dems developed the concept, originally termed 'Clegg Direct', that became known as his 'Town Hall meetings'. He would go up and down the country, meeting a cross-section of people at their local town hall or other civic venue, and take their questions in an informal question-and-answer session. These meetings not only brought him together with people in the environment in which he shines best, but gave him direct contact with a range of voters. Since becoming Deputy Prime Minister, he has not abandoned these, but there are greater pressures on his time and they are organisational nightmares given the security detail that accompanies him, so he does a lot fewer of them than before the 2010 general election.

A quality all senior government ministers must have that is frequently underestimated is good health and a corresponding ability to get through masses of work. A colleague who knows him very well says, 'He has an immense ability to work long hours, to retain information and to survive on little sleep. He hardly ever refuses a request for more work. The only time he would refuse something is if he felt he hadn't spent enough time with his sons. He works like a horse.' This is why the idea that he stops work at 3 p.m. (see page 280) was so farcical.

And yet his primary survival mechanism is that he insists on getting away from politics and spending quality time with his children. 'The wonderful thing with little children', he says, 'is that they don't care what my job is. All Miguel wants to know is that I can put Waka-Waka on the iPad, Alberto wants to know that I can help him with his latest Mario Bros game on his DS, and Antonio wants me to take him to his football on Sundays. That has a wonderful liberating effect, because they're totally intolerant of these political preoccupations, and so I just relish every second of being a father.'

'He genuinely believes family is more important than politics,' says the former Sheffield MP Richard Allan, 'and yet he tries to do the big political job. They're in constant tension, but he rides that tension. It's one of the things that make him a bit different. Many politicians say their family is more important than politics, but most of them are lying.' Those who work with Clegg say the one thing that gets him down is not attacks from the press but failure to spend enough time with Antonio, Alberto and Miguel. 'He gets physical withdrawal symptoms if he doesn't see them enough,' says one aide.

A character trait that many people who have known Clegg over many years talk about is the fact that his basic sense of self never changes. Many talk about having seen him 'grow' in government, but no-one says his personality has changed. A member of the Westminster press pack, Isabel Oakeshott of the *Sunday Times*, says, 'I interviewed Nick for the first time since becoming Deputy Prime Minister a few months after the coalition had been formed. Because I've interviewed him a few times and we know each other professionally quite well, my antennae were absolutely out for any new behaviour since he'd become Deputy Prime Minister: was he going to be grand, would his attitude towards me have changed, was I going to pick up any "I'm very important now" signals? I was so totally gratified that he hadn't changed at all. He was as warm and as engaging as before – maybe there was a bit more self-editing going on, it was a bit more difficult an interview, but he was still happy talking about his kids, he told me how he'd spent several hours the previous day trying to fit batteries into annoying toys that needed to be charged up, that kind of banter which a lot of politicians are so scared about. They're so nervous about saying anything that's remotely off the subject, and I just thought "Oh good". It was a kind of relief that this was still the Nick Clegg I knew and enjoyed interviewing.'

Marcel Theroux says something similar. He saw Clegg on and off for about five years after the two left Cambridge University. 'I saw him most years, but had no idea of his daily life,' he says. 'You'd meet him, and however much his outward life had changed, you didn't get a sense that he'd had a personality makeover or conformed to a different value system. He has integrity.' And the former MP Mark Oaten describes a time when Clegg met up with his teenage niece while on a campaigning trip to Winchester: 'I watched the way he interacted with her, and he had the same easy-going manner he has with everyone. There was no difference between his public persona and him acting privately. He treats everyone the same way.'

If all this sounds a bit cheesy, it may be because it is genuinely difficult to find anyone with bad words about Clegg the person. There are plenty who don't like the Lib Dems, or who think he has too much faith in the private sector, or who believe his broader judgement is flawed, but on the personal front, he has masses of backers. That in itself may offer a part-explanation as to the extremes of his rise to and fall from the heights of Cleggmania: his likeable personality had a massive impact on an unsuspecting public desperate to believe in benevolent politicians, but the magnitude of that impact meant there was much greater disappointment and reaction against his personality when it transpired (inevitably) that he couldn't deliver as much as everyone had hoped. Whether Clegg was to blame for that disappointment is dealt with separately, but the British public hate being duped by a sweet-talking salesman, and when the nice guy from the TV debates was seen not to be sustaining his bright new world in government, the resentment was all the more vehement.

Even allowing for this, the vilification Clegg suffered over the first year of the coalition was starkly at odds with the personality of the man, and few who have known him take any personal pleasure (as opposed to political pleasure) in the demonisation of him. And it was interesting that, as the media started to move on from the carnage of the Lib Dems' electoral performance in May 2011, they began to be more willing to praise Clegg's personal qualities, even if they had taken great delight in his fall from the high of Cleggmania.

A political characteristic of Clegg is that he is no lover of the Westminster village. 'The party is best led by somebody who doesn't like Westminster very much,' says David Boyle, a member of the

Lib Dems' Federal Policy Committee and leading liberal and environmental thinker. 'Nick doesn't, like Ashdown didn't, while Kennedy and Campbell were Westminster people through and through, and I think Nick found it very frustrating when he was first elected. He wants to be at home, and he goes to great lengths to be at home, so he's not on the dinner party circuit like some of the Westminster insiders.'

'I am not a natural Westminster politician,' Clegg told Robinson College's magazine *Bin Brook*. 'The self-obsessed and introverted way that a lot of coverage of Westminster is done by a very small clique of people in the press who also spend all their time in Westminster is increasingly looking like a little bubble world that doesn't really have anything to do with the real world out there.'

Ah, but is that really true? Clegg is surely right that the Westminster media bubble is a law unto itself, but in a media-influenced world, it has immense ability to determine what picture large swathes of the country get of their politicians. To all people who see politics as a means to an end rather than an end in itself, Clegg's sniffy approach to Westminster is totally legitimate, but it is tactically risky. 'The key to leadership of any party is leading within the framework of the real world, not the reworked matrix that is somehow created in Westminster and Whitehall,' said the Lib Dems' chief executive, Chris Fox – but he said that six weeks before the Lib Dems suffered a drubbing at the polls, which suggests that playing the Westminster circuit is at least part of the game.

Where Clegg scores better is in his relations with his parliamentary party. 'He's more open than any previous leader of the party has been,' says Norman Baker, who has been an MP under all four Lib Dem leaders. 'He's more accessible and more open in the way he thinks. Even before we were in government, he had more of an open door than the others did, but without the downsides. I've found him easier to work with than any of the other three leaders.'

All this begs the question: is an attractive character enough on its own? In recent years, the British political culture has moved more towards an American-style presidential culture, where the personality of the leader determines to a large extent what the public thinks of the party. That bodes well for Clegg and the Liberal Democrats, as the personality of Clegg is a fundamentally attractive one, even if it needs some detoxifying after the coalition's first year. But in a party like the Lib Dems, which is based more on a mixture of free thinking and localism than loyalty to a class or brand, policies and political philosophies are very important.

'He's not a political geek,' says one of his colleagues. 'He works by instinct, but then if you can say "Gladstone said this" or "Beveridge said that", he'll say "Excellent, we'll use that". But he's not someone who'll bring up names from political history.' A member of the Lib Dems' Federal Policy Committee says of him, 'His gut feelings are very good, but because they're very good, he relies on them too much.'

No-one yet talks about 'Cleggism' as a political creed, but Clegg is clear what his own creed is, and even has a name from the Liberals' glorious past to throw in. 'I'm a liberal interventionist,' he says. 'It goes back to Gladstone – you can't be indifferent to people who are suffering, even if they may be in countries which seem a long way from us. You just have to do it for good moral reasons and legally, which in our world means multilaterally through the United Nations. I think we should never turn our back on the idea that we have duties to other people, and that where we can, we should help. You can't always, sometimes you're helpless, but where you can, where there are good humanitarian reasons, as a liberal you should intervene muscularly to promote good liberal values.

'I really just believe in the basic tenets of liberalism. I believe it's a basic view of the world. You can say we must keep the world as it is, which is a conservative viewpoint. You can think that everything should be done by getting the state to pull great big levers to get groups of people shifting around in society like pieces on a chessboard – that is a collectivist, socialist, Labour point of view. Or you have a liberal view, which starts from the premise that there's something wonderful about every person, there's something marvellous about their potential and talents, and you've got to do everything you possibly can in politics to emancipate individuals, to give them privacy, give them freedom, give them the ability to get ahead. I wouldn't depart from that very basic liberal viewpoint.'

That is his own interpretation of liberalism, and his view that everyone is born good is one that many liberals would share. But one of the growing pains of the Liberal Democrats has been that the party's growth has been based around targeted local successes. This means that putting a collection of elected Lib Dems together at national level inevitably means bringing together people whose electoral success is down to very different things, so deciding what everyone agrees on is not as easy as the yellow label and the distinctive 'bird of liberty' suggest.

The *Financial Times* journalist James Crabtree analysed this in an article for *Prospect* magazine in the summer of 2010. He said the inherent unfairness of the first-past-the-post voting system meant the Liberals – and later the Lib Dems – had no choice but to target a few seats and flood them with activists and local campaigning themes. The term given to this within Lib Dem circles is 'Rennardism' after Chris Rennard, whose greatest success was seeing the party grow from eighteen seats in 1992 to forty-six in 1997, fifty-two in 2001 and sixty-two in 2005. But targeting local issues meant making the Lib Dems seem the natural opponents to the Conservatives in the south (and thus they attempt to 'squeeze' the Labour vote to keep the Tories out), and making them the natural opponents to Labour in the north (which meant squeezing the Conservative vote to keep Labour out). It spawned the ubiquitous Lib Dem squeeze message bar chart that has become as much the party's logo as the bird of liberty. More importantly, it has led to a situation where a Lib Dem MP elected in a Lib–Lab fight can be a very different animal to one elected in a Lib–Con fight. It also leads to a patchwork of local policies, encapsulated when Vince Cable said at the party's south-east regional conference in Eastbourne in October 2010,

'I've always enjoyed my visits to Eastbourne, though I have to remember that we're in favour of bypasses here, and against them in Lewes.'

Crabtree says *The Orange Book* was the first attempt by the ambitious generation of Lib Dem MPs to mark out a coherent and consistent national policy framework that all the locally politicised representatives could feel comfortable with. He says Clegg never challenged his party to support his form of liberalism in the 2007 leadership election, and only as its new leader did he start calling for a less statist approach. This is a little overanalytical, and some-what unfair to Clegg, who set out his liberalism fairly clearly in the campaign. But it might well be fair to say Clegg's picture of liberalism was defined by the idea of 'Labour as the opposition, Conservatives as the competition' rather than the other way round. That, after all, was where he came from in his home and at the European Commission, and how a lot of European liberal parties see themselves. It also goes down very well in Sheffield, where the Lib Dems have very effectively swept up the potential Conservative vote so win in Hallam largely on an anti-Labour ticket. But it is a different philosophy to Lib Dems in, say, the West Country, where the party sweeps up the potential Labour vote to keep the Conservatives out.

Crabtree quotes a speech by Clegg in January 2008 in which he said 'the state must back off and allow the genius of grass roots innovation, diversity and experimentation' in schools and hospi-tals, and that he wanted to develop 'a new liberal model of schools that are non-selective, under local government strategic oversight but not run by the council'. It's easy to see from this where Clegg's willingness to support schools with 'academy' status comes from, as well as his readiness to go along with reforms he sees as 'improving democracy in the NHS'. But has he really put enough thought into whether the massed ranks of Lib Dem councillors, many of whom believe in a benign state making decisions to create a fairer society, are comfortable with his brand of liberalism, which invests a fair bit of trust in free market forces? His ability to take such people with him could be the key to his long-term effectiveness, to say nothing of his survival as leader.

All politicians are given more slack if they are doing well electorally, so part of Clegg's battle with the sceptics in his own party is to convince a lot of voters who would be minded to vote Lib Dem in the right circumstances that his liberalism really is for everyone and not just a form of conservatism with a social conscience. He himself is a convinced liberal – 'a liberal by temperament, by choice and by conviction' as he has described it – but his belief that the state should play a lesser role, and the private sector can have a bigger part to play in providing public services, has made some progressives sceptical about his credo. They find it easy to see his liberalism as a middle-class philosophy based on freedoms and liberties that are simply not relevant to those still trying to cope with the early steps in Maslow's hierarchy of needs. He needs to convince such people that his belief that universal happiness comes through opening people's minds at an early age is a genuine model for social progress rather than just a feelgood philosophy for the affluent classes.

It may not be fully appreciated that education is the driving force behind his political activity, edging ahead of the civil liberties and human rights that are often cited as his core values. Richard Allan, his friend and predecessor as MP for Sheffield Hallam, says, 'The importance of education for him cannot be overstated. This personal, individual liberation through education is a very strong theme, the one theme he believes in more than anything else. He sees the bigoted and illiberal person as one who starts closed, so when your mind is opened by education, you become a better person. That's the journey he went on at school. None of the other strands of political life get him in the way that the idea that "none should be enslaved by ignorance and poverty" does. It's what drives him on as a politician. He wants every child – and he loves children, they're really important to him – to have the experience of their mind being awakened so they have a whole range of opportunities in life. The idea of *enabling* is the common thread in everything he does with passion.'

As a result, Clegg believes that if you have a spare pound and you want to make a difference to social mobility, you have to spend it early in children's lives. He believes society is playing catch-up if too much depends on the structure of university fees, which is why he has always been more enthusiastic about pre-school and primary education than higher education. To what extent that is a product of having kids born in 2002, 2004 and 2009 remains to be seen; he may well be more into the structure of university fees ten years from now. But there is a logic about this belief in early-years education that chimes with the thinking of Friedrich Fröbel, the respected German educationalist who was convinced the key to happy and fulfilled adults came through meeting the needs of children between the ages of three and seven (Fröbel coined the term 'Kindergarten' as he believed the best way for children under seven to learn was to get them playing in the garden.)

Talking of spare pounds (not that there are many at present), Clegg believes that if we have a bit of extra money, it can be progressive to give it back to people rather than spend it on some service. This marks him out as an economic non-statist liberal in the mould of Jo Grimond, as opposed to the social liberals, who came largely from the SDP and who see a bigger role for the state than Clegg is comfortable with. One long-standing Lib Dem activist expresses complete non-comprehension of Clegg's approach: 'He at one stage floated the idea of using some savings for tax cuts rather than using them all for public services, which rang alarm bells among those of us on the left.'

He remains a committed internationalist, and while his enthusiasm for Britain joining the euro has taken a back seat while the euro goes through its own trials and tribulations, he remains convinced that Britain must play a significant and constructive role in the EU. The former assistant to liberal MEPs Arne Richters says, 'Europe is facing huge challenges, and the UK hasn't always been the most constructive EU partner, but if there's any politician in the UK that can breach those national barriers, it's Nick, not only because of the languages he speaks, but because he really is a European.' A close aide adds, 'He has an impatience with people who aren't liberal or internationalist. He can't fathom why anyone would not understand that we live in a world where Britain hasn't got an empire any more.'

Hand in hand with his internationalism goes a complete lack of prejudice. It may well come from his European family connections, but wherever it comes from, prejudice against people based on any aspect of their background or heritage simply has absolutely no currency for him. That may be an admirable trait, but when it comes to the battle for the hearts of voters, as well as their minds, failure to understand the roots of popular prejudice risks alienating a lot of people who might be willing to vote Lib Dem. It's interesting to note that one of the policies that gave the Lib Dems most grief in the 2010 general election campaign was their proposed 'amnesty' for illegal immigrants who have been in Britain for ten years without a criminal record – it was a perfectly reasonable policy, but it was very open to being hijacked and misrepresented by those sections of British society that fear Britain being overrun by immigrants.

And there is his wish to create a different governing ethos for Britain, a conviction that has been summarised in the shorthand 'a new politics'. This has been thought of synonymously with electoral reform, but it's wider than that. 'He talks about the evolution of Britain from a two-party system,' says a colleague. 'Charles Kennedy used to talk about the Lib Dems overtaking the Conservatives to become the second party. Nick doesn't want the Lib Dems to replace another party as the second party, he wants to blow up the two-party system as it currently operates, without gunpowder of course.'

The heavy defeat of the alternative vote in the May 2011 referendum is a serious setback to this aim, but it doesn't end the aim in itself, it just makes it a little harder to achieve. The eminent psephologist John Curtice of Strathclyde University says the chances of future hung parliaments are fairly high, as single-party majorities depend on a high number of Labour–Conservative marginal seats, and there are increasingly few of these as the number of Lib–Lab and Lib–Con marginals grows. There is a lot of comfort for Clegg in this argument, although the legitimacy of it depends on the Lib Dem vote holding up, which is not a given at present. In a way, Clegg is already breaking the two-party system by being in a coalition government, and he resents people suggesting he is part of a Conservative government. He memorably told the Lib Dems at one of its conferences, 'Will I ever join a Labour government? – no. Will I ever join a Conservative government? – no. Because any government that has us in it will be a coalition government.' He just has to make sure that it *looks* like a coalition government to the broad electorate.

According to one colleague, Clegg wonders how the party 'which talks the most about individual responsibility and freedom and general common sense' has ended up marginalised in the political debate. He believes the Lib Dems occupy the ground that most people occupy, and the party has a message that most sums up what most people think. That may be true, but arguments and philosophy alone don't win elections. Perhaps Clegg has been too dismissive of the role played by political tactics, too willing to trust the natural beneficence that he himself feels and radiates to do the work for him. He is, after all, still a relatively inexperienced politician, and while everyone can be wise with hindsight, a more experienced operator might have left more room in the Lib Dem general election campaign of 2010 for coalition compromises to be portrayed as such (especially in a country unused to coalitions). Instead, Lib Dem concessions were easy to depict as U-turns and betrayals, and created the bizarre spectacle in May 2011 of the Conservatives being able to escape largely unscathed from both their own concessions and a brutally unpopular round of cuts, while the Lib Dems took all the flak.

Clegg may also have been taken in by an excessive level of trust in David Cameron. Clegg's experience of continental politics has taught him that coalitions function if the people leading them get on, so there is a strong responsibility on him and Cameron to work well professionally. But he clearly trusted Cameron to stick to his word over the promise to keep a low profile in the campaign for the alternative vote, and Lib Dems at grass roots level are generally sceptical to the point of paranoia about trusting the Tories. That is not to say they don't recognise some good people in Conservative ranks, but too many Lib Dem fingers have been burned by what they see as the ruthless Conservative machine, such that even many Lib Dems who feel Clegg was right to go into coalition with the Conservatives feel he might have been a little naive in his relationship with the Prime Minister. Lib Dem activists want to know that Clegg really understands that Cameron leads a party which, however well-mannered it may be, bites back with venom when seriously threatened.

Clegg and Cameron are clearly two men who get on, but who disagree about the social fabric of British society. The fact that they are both from the affluent Home Counties classes means there isn't a gulf in day-to-day communication that can exist when people from wildly different backgrounds work together (the best example is the fictitious Labour Prime Minister Harry Perkins clashing with the upper-crust Cabinet Secretary Sir James Robertson in Chris Mullin's underestimated 1980s television play *A Very British Coup*). But if Clegg is doing his job well, he be should be making Cameron's job of balancing the interests of the Lib Dems and the Conservative right wing as hard as possible.

Somewhat reassuringly, for a man of great self-confidence, he is happy to admit to some doubts. 'I think it would be very unwise in politics, as in the rest of life, not to constantly ask yourself questions,' he says. 'I think people who are without doubts are very dangerous, or mad, or both. It's the most natural human thing in the world to ask yourself if you've got something right or not. And sometimes you have to accept that you have got some things wrong. So far, I'm absolutely happy to concede there might be certain words, or presentations or announcements, that we could have improved here or there. In terms of the really big judgements – putting the economy on a stable footing, trying to clean up politics, trying to restore civil liberties, and in the education field, making sure we've got a sustainable fair future for people going to university and that we're redirecting money to young kids so we have future generations of children who can even dream of going to university who presently can't – I'm totally unapologetic. I think it's exactly the right judgement, you won't get any repentance from me.'

If Clegg is to get his tactics right without selling his soul, he needs to perfect a very fine balancing act in his dealings with the media.

Despite the fact that he was elected Lib Dem leader because he was telegenic, and he did so well in the first TV debate, he is not a great media performer. He's fine when he has a speech to make, or some other scripted message, but in live interviews he seldom looks or sounds comfortable. This is largely because he hasn't yet made the transition from being good in an intellectual debate, where time is not really a limiting factor and where you stand or fall on the power of your arguments, to a media interview, where the most important thing is to get your point across. His close aides say he hates 'faking it', so his natural instinct when asked a question in an interview is to engage with it and offer a coherent answer. He is aware of the reality of the media interview – that it may be an interview when it's conducted, but it will be cut into sound bites for use on news bulletins in the subsequent hours – and therefore knows he cannot capitulate to the interviewer's agenda and has to get his point across in sound-bite-sized chunks, but it's not a natural process for him. As a result he comes across in some interviews as a little shifty.

This is a microcosm for all his media dealings: his natural gregariousness and love of human interaction mean he's happy to chat to journalists, often forgetting that they have their own agenda. 'He doesn't self-edit that much,' says Isabel Oakeshott. 'On the one hand, that's one of the most attractive things about him and why I've always enjoyed interviewing him, because you're unlucky if you don't come away with something fun to write, even if it's nothing to do with politics. On the other hand, that exposes him to the sort of stories that we all enjoy writing. He's got into a right old pickle on a couple of stories of no political importance, and it was the same with the Gina Ford opinion [Clegg was chatting with Oakeshott about methods of childbirth and volunteered a somewhat critical opinion of the controversial American baby guru Gina Ford]. He strays into left-field territory, which suits us but often doesn't do him much good.'

This presents a problem for Clegg. He has an irrepressible sense of humour, but when dealing with the media, it gets him into deep water. Richard Allan says, 'If you look at all the incidents when he's got into trouble, it's been his sense of humour. How many women has he slept with, Cameron forgetting to tell him he's in charge, etc. He has to fight it, but it's almost irresistible – if he's in a conversation, he wants to enjoy it and sometimes take it to the absurd, and you're just not allowed to do that in public life, because it looks bad on paper. It's a constant frustration for him that he can't enjoy a conversation because you've got to clamp down the whole time.' A related area in which he has to restrain himself is in getting into caricature while making a speech. 'People come up to me', he told the Lib Dem spring conference in 2011, 'and say...' and he looked as if he was about to lapse into some role play of a colourful character, but reined himself in, in case it would be misconstrued as mocking or offensive. The sad thing is that a part of him that makes him so popular to his mates becomes closed off to the public.

In her *New Statesman* interview with him, Jemima Khan suggested that being in a coalition government is 'a gag' on the gregarious Clegg. She describes asking him about the phone-hacking scandal that emerged in early 2011 and was traced back to the *News of the World*, one of the Murdoch newspapers, and observing him having to be so careful with his answer that he reminded her of Colin Firth in the opening scenes of *The King's Speech*. 'I know what he'd have said if he were in opposition,' she said, pointing out that some Lib Dem MPs were the victims of the *NOTW* hacking.

Clegg's wider problem is that if he plays the media game, he risks burying not just his sense of humour but the charm and engagement that are his biggest personal assets. He is consciously aware of this dilemma, as evidenced by what he said to Shelagh Fogarty in an interview in 2009 for *Total Politics* magazine. 'I've been very keen not to do what I think a lot of politicians do, which is retreat into a shell of repeated one-liners and try and evade. I try to be as frank as I can be. I think I've become tougher, but I hope I'm nonetheless candid in what I say.'

But the media are not into fairness or consistency. They will frequently lure a politician into saying something that can be taken out of context, have a field day with the story, and then label the politician 'gaffe prone'. Clegg admits he's fallen into a fair few media traps, but denies that he's deliberately setting out to say what he wants and be damned. 'I think it would be overegging it if I say it's a deliberate strategy, but I don't think I could do the job I do and feel comfortable with it if I felt I was constantly biting my tongue and suppressing views or humour. I try and minimise the hostages to fortune, but I don't think you can eliminate them and I'm not going to pretend I can.' It's an honest comment, but one that signals that there will be more Clegg 'gaffes' in the future.

He can also be indiscreet. One person who has known him since his MEP days says, 'You have to murder someone to get any publicity as an MEP, but he hasn't yet learned that you really have to watch for journalists round every corner.' And an MP says, 'Nick is an honest individual and tends to say what he thinks, and perhaps sometimes things are best left unsaid.'

A part of his relationship with the media concerns his three boys, and the decision he and Miriam took to keep them right out of the public eye. 'There's no subject I like more than talking about my sons,' he says, 'but either you cross the line and you start using your family for political purposes, or you don't – in fact you can be more precise: it's about whether you use them visually or not. I'm very happy talking about my family, but I don't want them to be the story. For me the winning argument was that I don't want my kids to go school on a Monday morning and have little Jack say to them "Oh, I saw you in a Sunday magazine"; I think if you're a six-year-old, that makes you feel rather different, and I don't want my kids to feel different, I want them to feel as "the same" as possible. Now they feel slightly different anyway because their friends say "Oh your dad does this and that", so they know I'm different for doing a particular job, but I don't want them to feel they are. I personally think you can place quite a strain on a little child if you make them feel different. They're lovely boys, I completely dote on them and am very proud of them. It's not their fault their dad's gone into politics. But Miriam and I won't take any risks with their happiness. We'll be knocked about a bit, but we want to insulate our children from that as much as possible.'

This is why the only protests that got to Clegg during the angry autumn of 2010 were ones that affected the family home. He could handle the burning effigy and demonstrations in central London, but while he conducted himself calmly in public and plays down the seriousness of the demonstrations outside his house, close colleagues say he was privately much more annoyed by those protesters who invaded his family's space than by any others.

There has been no shortage of suggestions that Clegg should invite in a film crew to meet his family, and he accepted one crew filming him and his mother in the parental home near Oxford. But while Miriam gets photographed with him at certain party functions, they remain resolute that the boys will remain off camera. This has largely been respected by the paparazzi. While the occasional photographer does turn up outside the family home when Clegg is taking Antonio and Alberto to school, it is always made very clear – by Clegg or an aide – that nothing must be published that features the boys. In this, the Cleggs are aided by rules laid down by the Press Complaints Commission to protect children, and they have worked very well so far.

And yet if Clegg's political fortunes don't start to rise before too long, he may come under pressure to show himself a little more as the family man. The image of Gordon Brown walking out of Downing Street with his wife and two sons, all holding hands, was such a charming one that many people wondered why he hadn't appeared with his boys earlier. It is perhaps to his and Clegg's credit that they refused to succumb to such a large temptation, but it does raise the question about whether there is a compromise situation that would allow Clegg to shine as a father and husband – perhaps a limited photo shoot with the family while on holiday. After all, the royal family engages in such photo shoots on holiday in return for being left in peace for the rest of the trip, and it wouldn't be painting a false picture of Clegg, merely allowing people to see him the way his friends do.

Perhaps because of the media blackout, little is known about Nick and Miriam's marriage. 'We have a very strong but private marriage,' he told Kirsty Young, and friends affirm it is very solid. 'He and Miriam are both strong characters,' says Neil Sherlock. 'They have an unbelievably strong marriage and a happy home, and Miriam is a very warm and fun person.' Some wonder to what extent she is the dominant personality in the relationship. She earns much more as a corporate lawyer than he does as Deputy Prime Minister, hence her occasional jokes about her husband 'having a hobby called politics'. The two clearly have a lot of love and mutual respect for each other, but occasionally a story seeps out that feeds the myth that Clegg is happy to be submissive at home. The latest came in February 2011, when the Cleggs went on a skiing holiday, only for Nick to have to fly back after just a day and a half because the Libyan civil war had blown up. At the end of the week, he was about to set off for the airport to meet Miriam and the boys, when a press adviser suggested it might be better if he wasn't seen at the airport welcoming back his family from holiday, as it might look bad if it coincided with British people returning home after fleeing the carnage in Libya. So Clegg phoned Miriam to say he'd been advised not to come to the airport and could she therefore take a taxi instead. What else happened in that conversation no-one knows, but Clegg was at the airport to meet Miriam and the boys as they came through customs.

Because of Miriam, the Clegg boys are being brought up as Roman Catholics. As a result, the Clegg family attends mass each Sunday, including Nick, even though he prefers to be considered an agnostic. 'I promised Miriam that if we had children, they would be brought up as Catholics, so I don't want to confuse my kids by not going to church,' is how he explains it. As for his own religious views, he told Simon Barrow in an interview for the Ekklesia website in March 2008, 'My moral frame of reference is clearly a Judaeo-Christian one. My ethics are not insulated at all from the world of faith and organised religion. I think that fundamental concepts of tolerance, of compassion, of love for your neighbour run very deep in our culture, but they are also intimately bound up with our Christian heritage. Many members of my family are very religious and I have a great deal of admiration for the strength of their faith. I take a great interest in people's religious faith, but I'm very non-judgemental about it. Maybe it helps a little bit that I personally don't share it.'

As for other aspects of his private life, he loves reading novels, and frequently has two on the go. He has a deep-rooted love of English literature and is comfortable with demanding works. The book he told Kirsty Young he would take to a desert island was *The Leopard* by Lampedusa, a fairly challenging Italian novel that charts the fall of the Sicilian aristocracy in the nineteenth century – it's only 200 pages, but every sentence is imbued with a hidden meaning, and is not the kind of book many would be found reading on the 7.20 into Waterloo. He loves dancing. 'I'm not going to pretend I'm a great dancer,' he said in 2008, 'but I love dancing with Miriam. The last thing I danced to was "Mamma Mia" with my kids.' He's big into music, largely classical but with a passion for Johnny Cash. If he could only take one piece of music to his desert island, it would be a piece for solo piano, Schubert's 'Impromptu No 3 in G flat'. As he has admitted in a couple of interviews, he cries at music quite a lot. 'Not buckets, but I can't understand people who can't weep at music. I think crying is a great thing. If what you're suggesting is "Do you as a politician have to emote to prove a point?", no, I think you just have to be yourself. But I'm perfectly happy to admit that I readily cry at something that I find moving – a lot of art, music, poetry. For some reason I find the combination of driving and moving music can switch on the tears like that. It can be a rip-roaring, romantic piece of Rachmaninov, through to soulful Johnny Cash.'

Despite representing part of a football-mad city, he says he doesn't have a favourite football team. He does admit to flip-flopping in the middle of the 2010 World Cup final, a match he had gone into heavily torn as the Netherlands, the country of his mother and her antecedents, were playing Spain, the country of his wife and in-laws – he began watching the final supporting the *Oranje*, but switched sides at half-time having been appalled by the physical display of the Dutch (he picked the winner, as Spain won 1-0). And he has his guilty nicotine habit. Very few people see him smoking, and he's very much a late-at-night-with-his-own-thoughts smoker rather than a serial puffer. Paddy Ashdown, a smoker himself who has been trying to cut down, is always prompted by his wife to get some cigarettes in whenever Clegg is invited round. 'Obama smokes too, or certainly did,' says Ashdown, adding quickly, 'Not that I'm saying there's any connection between us and Obama.'

Clegg's friend Ian Wright describes him as 'one of the funniest and most talented people I've ever met', while another friend, the extreme federalist MEP Andrew Duff says, 'He impresses me with his nervelessness, and his capacity to enjoy life.'

One of the things that easily gets forgotten about Nick Clegg as Deputy Prime Minister is that he had no apprenticeship for it. Ten years earlier he barely knew his own country other than the intellectual circles of London, Cambridge and the Home Counties. He first had the learning curve of the East Midlands, and then the city of Sheffield, described by David Blunkett as 'the biggest village in England'. In 2005 he became an MP, and in December 2007 became the first leader of the British liberals for more than a century to represent an urban constituency. It has been a phenomenal rise, and it would be utterly implausible if Clegg had not made a few errors of judgement along the way, whether through inexperience or a permanent state of near-exhaustion.

He's not entirely without advice from the grey-haired brigade. The former Labour Cabinet minister Shirley Williams is on the scene and played a crucial part in the campaign for reforming

Andrew Lansley's NHS reforms; Ming Campbell has played a low-key role since quitting as leader but offers occasional advice; and another septuagenarian, Paddy Ashdown, works closely behind the scenes when necessary, his undiminished personal energy fuelling a steady stream of offers of help. 'If he asks my advice I'll always give it,' says Ashdown. 'I said when I stood down as leader of the party that my motto would be what Mark Twain described as being written in the wheelhouse of a Mississippi steamboat: "Don't speak to the captain, don't spit on the floor." If the captain wants to speak to me, I'm happy to speak to him, but I don't go round spitting on the floor and making life difficult. He doesn't always take my advice, but he has always listened and then made his own decision, and that's right. My role is to make available vicarious experience to help him avoid the mistakes that I've made.' Clegg also has an occasional mentor from Conservative ranks, the former Home Secretary and European Commissioner Lord Brittan. 'I think he's doing very well,' Brittan says. 'Whether his party are happy with it is another matter, but objectively he's doing very well.'

It's not just a massive learning curve, it's a massive workload too. In the early months of the coalition, his office was severely understaffed, to the point where at the moment when the country was most looking to see how the Lib Dem leader would function as Deputy Prime Minister, he was desperately overstretched. 'I don't think the organisation around him was very good,' says David Blunkett. 'I don't think the government as a whole helped him, and I think that made a big difference. I think if he'd been able to say from the first three or four weeks "I'm sorry, this isn't good enough, I have to have key staff, and Gus [O'Donnell, the Cabinet secretary] has to allocate me some of the best people because I'm very isolated here and yet I have to keep the balance", he might have got off to a much better start. By the time he got the support, it was impossible to reach him on the phone, and near impossible to get him to answer letters.'

'It's the bit that worries me most,' says Ashdown. 'We have to find a way of giving him a bit of space and time with his family. He's a really good thinker but he isn't getting enough time to think. And we need some injection of challenging thinking – that isn't a criticism of Nick because when you're in government you're obsessed with government, but government parties need to be able to renew themselves, thinking new, having new projects. We're not hearing enough from that side, and at some stage fairly soon we need to make sure that being in government doesn't lead to sterility of thought. Mutualism is so important.'

Danny Alexander says Clegg gets energised the moment he leaves the capital. 'When he gets out of London, that's where his political energy comes from,' he says. 'I had him up to Boat of Garten [a small town near Aviemore] for a town hall meeting and a dinner for the Highlands parties with a couple of hundred supporters. Three of us – Nick, a local activist who had been a Liberal MP's agent in the 1960s and I – stayed up late, chatting over a glass of very good local malt whisky, and it ended up energising him.'

Traditionally, Clegg's thinking time has come when he's out in nature. He loves Stanedge Edge, a part of the Peak District National Park, not far from Sheffield, where he used to escape and allow the wind and new thoughts to ruffle his hair. 'It's a stunning view, a bowl-like valley, cliffs and a pine wood,' he raves. 'Amazing. Bleak but beautiful. When I'm there I literally start breathing more easily.' But such opportunities are very rare these days. 'I don't get out nearly enough. I grew up in the countryside, I was brought up in the tradition of scraped knees, camps, muddy fields, catapults, kicking rugby balls – if you asked my mum, she'd say that if ever I was cranky she'd just kick me out, come rain or shine, and I'd always come back calm and sweet as a lamb. I derive massive benefits from getting out into a wood, a valley, a mountain – it's an absolute tonic for me.'

A major problem for Clegg, shared with many other thinkers, is that the gulf between the politics that involves ideas about optimum systems of governance and the politics of what can be practically achieved is at times grotesquely vast. People join a party because of a conviction about what that party stands for, but then get sucked into the tactics and practical minutiae that pave the way for people to get elected. Clegg thinks deeply about the best way of running the country and enfranchising people, but then has to engage in media and electoral tactics if he's not to lose contact with the vast swathes of the population who don't really care about theoretical concepts of government and voting systems. It's a problem for all parties, but particularly for the Lib Dems, and it adds stress to Clegg's daily life, given that his motivation for being in politics is often far removed from much of his political activity.

The pressure of his immense workload and the steady stream of stick he's had to take from the press and other politicians worries some of those close to him. The MP Stephen Lloyd, who was elected for the first time in 2010, says, 'It's vital for a party leader to have the ability to make it look as if nothing is getting to you, even if you have to fake it. There's masses of sniping going on, most of which the public doesn't see, and it's very easy to let your guard slip and respond to some provocation. Nick is under so much pressure – not just the workload, but the fact that he is carrying so much of the responsibility for the party's future – that I do worry that one day when he's short of sleep he will react to something, and it could be damaging.'

So far, he has kept the lid on everything. Mark Oaten believes one of his greatest attributes under pressure is his ability to work efficiently. 'He's extremely quick thinking. He's a chess player in his approach. He will look at the chessboard, and instead of having to go through the six or seven moves that get him to check-mate, he gets to check-mate quite quickly, and he won't trouble you with all the bits and bobs about how he gets there. I've heard him say "What's the right thing to do, what's the liberal thing to do?" and I think that is inbuilt in him, so when we talk about getting quickly to check-mate, his starting point on the board is "Whatever move I make has to be motivated by what the most liberal thing to do is".'

This chimes with a comment made by Clegg's elder brother, Paul. 'He's pretty headstrong. That's really important, because he's bumped into some situations that are definitely a result of how headstrong he is and how convinced he is that he's doing the right thing. I don't think you could do what he does if you don't have strong convictions. He has understood that he has to work very hard to achieve what he wants to achieve, and he works his socks off – our younger brother Alexander is probably smarter than he is, but Nick has a much greater work rate, he's ambitious, and that's how he fights to get things done. Our grandfather used to say "All you need to do is to work 10 per cent harder than the next person, and then you'll succeed", and Nick takes that to an extreme.'

A senior Liberal Democrat staff member also talks about a very efficient work ethic. 'He's not an autocrat, he accepts that the leader of the Liberal Democrats is not a tsar, that you have to work things out. But he does have a clear idea of what he wants, and once a decision has been made, he's very much for getting on with it and can be quite impatient. He's very loyal to his closest staff, but he expects a lot of them, and once something has been agreed he's not interested in hearing why things can't be done. That's his approach to everything. He drives people around him pretty hard.'

The Conservative junior minister, Ed Vaizey, says Clegg is going down well with ministers and civil servants. 'I get the impression that the ministers he works with very much like him. There are no bad words said about him. If there were any rumours that he was a nightmare to deal with, they would soon start spreading, but there's been no such gossip.' He also inspires tremendous loyalty – at least he has so far – among those he works with, largely because he is very loyal to them. 'He's been incredibly loyal and supportive to me, kind, understanding and helpful,' says Oaten, whose political career is best known for his scandal over paying for the services of a male prostitute. 'There was absolutely no point in investing any capital in me, I was a dead hope, but he went out of his way to be nice, stop in corridors to ask how I was doing. Even since he's been Deputy Prime Minister he's chatted a couple of times on the phone, asking me how things are going and asking me what I think.'

Clegg showed no hard feelings towards the National Union

of Students' president, Aaron Porter, with whom he had crossed swords in the tuition fees controversy of autumn 2010. 'When I decided not to re-stand for president,' Porter relates, 'Nick was very gracious in what he said about me, which is a testament to him as an individual. The easy thing to do would have been to say "This bugger caused me a lot of trouble this year, I'm glad he's off and I lasted longer than he did", but actually he said, "We've had our disagreements but he's made the case for students very well, and I wish him all the very best for the future," which confirms that my personal dealings with him, although brief, have been remarkably impressive. I would agree with others in saying that he's been given a very hard time in the press – some of that is down to his own political naivety, some of that is down perhaps to a lack of preparation for government.'

A staff member at Lib Dem HQ says, 'Nick is very entertaining, good company, and he's also very loyal. He's a very decent chap apart from all else.' Loyalty is an admirable concept, but it can be a handicap in politics if used without sanguine judgement. Clegg's support for David Laws since the misuse of Laws's expenses first became public has been commendable from a human perspective, but given the fact that Clegg campaigned for a cleaner politics, it could be argued he should have been a little less supportive when the story broke, and a little keener to crush suggestions that he would like to see Laws back in the Cabinet. With Lib Dem nerves somewhat frayed at the thought that they are cuddling up too much to the Conservatives, it will do Clegg no good to have a man so closely associated with the party's right wing back too quickly, however much he may respect Laws's very thorough understanding of economics.

The staff team Clegg has brought into government from his work as Lib Dem party leader has largely remained intact, and he is immensely loyal to them, as they are to him, but eventually they will start to leave for pastures new. That will give him the chance to bring in new people who have not necessarily made the journey with him, which will be a test of his ability to pick people with the necessary skills, rather than just those who fit into the happy Clegg team. Loyalty can also work against Clegg's own position – Lib Dems are naturally loyal to their party leader (see how much leeway they gave Charles Kennedy), but the moment they sense Clegg is no longer an asset, he may find the party's affections are transferred to someone else.

So what of the future? Clegg is clearly walking a tightrope, being buffeted by several forces: the general state of the economy, the willingness of his own party to support the five-year project with the Conservatives, the ability of the Liberal Democrats to secure meaningful implementation of core liberal policies, and the corresponding willingness of the media to give publicity to such achievements.

There has been a general assumption that, if nothing else, the Lib Dems are acting as a brake on the worst excesses of the Conservatives, but that was not reflected in the election results of May 2011, when the Lib Dems took all the battering and the Tories emerged largely untouched. That is unlikely to continue, if only because Labour needs to focus its attacks on the Conservatives rather than Clegg or the Lib Dems. But the risk for the Lib Dems is that there could be a sizeable number of people who just don't accept the 'brake on the Tories' argument but feel they are a protective shield to let the Conservatives do more than they would be able to do on their own. Aaron Porter says, 'I don't think tuition fees would be as high as this if there had been a Conservative minority government. In fairness, I don't think the repayment mechanism would have been as progressive as it is, and I credit the Lib Dems with having had an impact on the raising of that threshold. But I just don't think a Tory government would have got away with £9,000 if they'd been on their own. The presence of the Lib Dems in government under the pretence of being progressive allowed for a worse deal.' Porter's comments need to be treated with caution given his Labour Party background, and research such as that from University College London (see page 268) makes its hard to make the case that the Lib Dems are soft gatekeepers allowing the Tory right to come and go as they please. But Clegg's political career will stand or fall not on what really happens, but on what the public perceives is happening, so such comments as Porter's are potentially very damaging. In this context, much will depend on the long-term outcome of the reformed NHS reforms, as any party that messes with the NHS without getting its PR right risks incurring the wrath of the massed ranks of deeply sceptical British voters.

If everything does go pear shaped for Clegg and he is bundled out of office after the 2015 election – or even before – he himself will be OK. He is eminently employable, both because of his own set of skills and personal attributes, and because of the experience he is gaining as Deputy Prime Minister. If he survives in politics, he is an obvious Foreign Secretary if the Lib Dems form part of a future government, and if he doesn't, one could see him as a British Commissioner in the EU, possibly even a future president of the EU, or working in a United Nations agency that fits his idealism, for example something to do with human rights or refugees. (It's also not far fetched to envisage him embarking on an acting career – his first film or stage role would certainly sell a few tickets in this country on the basis of his name.)

That suggests he can afford to be callous and slapdash about the fate of the Lib Dems, but such a conclusion would be very unfair. He cares deeply about 'being liberal' and has masses of his own self-esteem and purpose in life invested in using his period as leader of the Liberal Democrats to make Britain a fairer place. 'I would like to be remembered for being someone who, among many others, helped to usher in a very different way of govern-ing,' he says. 'I think this country has really suffered terribly from endless pendulum swings from one vested interest to the next, and I think we have the capacity to be quite a transforming government. I don't mean just the immediate stuff that's dominating all the headlines now, such as the difficult stuff with cuts, but the bigger stuff, such as cleaning up politics, showing a coalition government can work, restoring civil liberties, putting in place tax and educa-tion changes that can let children get ahead. I really hope that by the end of my time in politics, Britain will be a discernibly more liberal place.'

In a world where politicians are always seen to be propping themselves up first and looking to their idealism second, Clegg is something of an exception. He went into politics to make a difference, and when he reaches the point where he can't make that difference, he will get out rather than hang around going through the motions. Again, this could put fear into Lib Dem members who worry that he could be reckless in his political moves and walk away from a party in ruins. His friend and former MP Richard Allan says there's more to it than that. 'He's happy if he's done his best. "Doing the right thing" is vitally important for him, so it's important to him to feel he made the right calls on the big issues. It doesn't mean he doesn't care about the party, he does care deeply, but if the party was screwed and the election went up in flames, he would be able to live with himself if he felt he had made the right decisions. I think it comes from his mother.'

Clegg remains as much a challenge for the British people as they are for him. If there is any genuineness in the cries for a better form of politics – as opposed to people thinking they want honest politicians but in reality not being open to anything except what they want to hear – he should become popular again, as he does represent something different.

Of course people will replay the 'No more broken promises' broadcast from before the 2010 general election and say he's just like everyone else, but that's a hard argument to sustain. It was perhaps an unwise slogan, given that the Lib Dems were always going to have to compromise in a coalition government, and the risk of a compromise looking like a broken promise is immense. But he has already brought about something of a 'new politics' in British society. His role as Deputy Prime Minister in providing a filter for all legislation is new, and indeed a peace-time coalition government hadn't existed in this country for nearly eighty years. And he is not dogmatic in talking about the compromises needed in power; he is happy to admit that foreign policy often has to be 'pragmatic rather than pure', and gets 'messy and imperfect' when it proves to be in Britain's interests to prop up a disreputable government – this may well go down better than Robin Cook's attempt at an 'ethical foreign policy', something pretty much everyone approved of but which proved unrealistic and disappeared as rapidly as it had emerged.

The question then is: will the British people like what they appeared to be clamouring for? The election results of May 2011 suggest they might not, but it's possible to interpret the Lib Dems' hammering at those elections as being down to other factors, in particular the perceived amateurish way the party dealt with its compromise on tuition fees, the relative failure to project its successes in government, and the abject failure to enthuse the public about voting reform. But it's also possible that the people just don't want a new politics, that they are genuinely happy moaning and groaning about the old two-party system, believing that everything is rotten, and voting for the Lib Dems only as long as they are some cuddly protest vote. If that is the case, the Lib Dems will either have to seek refuge in permanent opposition or, to paraphrase Bertolt Brecht, seek to 'dissolve the people and elect another'.

In many ways, idealism in politics is at stake through the person of Nick Clegg. He believes in the intrinsic goodness of people, and has stuck his head above the parapet for certain things that are deeply unpopular with some, but which liberals believe are right – like human rights, the rehabilitation of offenders and international responsibility. Yet he is finding that many of the people who are facing genuine hardship because of the banking crisis and previous dubious management of the economy are taking out their anger on him. 'Seeing a friend go through this business in the public eye, you realise how much a three-dimensional person gets presented in two dimensions, and you see what kind of violence it does to that person,' says Marcel Theroux. 'But Nick's a good guy, and if you don't have good guys doing the job he's doing, then there'll just be arseholes doing it, so I want him to hang in there. He's gone from non-entity to saviour to this person being hounded, and that makes me hopeful that another huge change can happen. If he sticks around, I think people will realise that he's got a good heart and what he's doing is in good faith and with a hand he's been dealt that isn't the hand he wanted.'

Just as in sport, the arts and other walks of life, in politics being talented or personable isn't enough on its own. A wide-ranging package of attributes, including work ethic, ability to work in a team, health and judgement, and a large dollop of luck are essential for a politician to be successful. To that extent, it's not clear where Clegg's career will go from the mid-point of 2011. He may yet be headed for great things, as many have believed for some time. But he may also be headed for some form of premature demise. If that happened, it's likely that a lot more people than just Liberal Democrats would greet the news with considerable regret and dismay.

BIBLIOGRAPHY

MOST OF the quotes that appear in this book are taken from interviews conducted especially for it, but a few books and articles have provided background and foreground information:

Five Days to Power, Rob Wilson, Biteback 2010

My Autobiography, Menzies Campbell, Hodder & Stoughton 2008

Neither Left nor Right, Andrew Russell and Edward Fieldhouse, Manchester University Press 2005

The Third Man, Peter Mandelson, HarperPress 2010

Twenty-two Days in May, David Laws, Biteback 2010

'Balancing Act', Mick Brown, *The Telegraph* magazine, 10 April 2010

'Who Are the Liberal Democrats?', James Crabtree, *Prospect*, July 2010

'With Liberal Frankness', Shelagh Fogarty, *Total Politics*, December 2008

Journal of Liberal History, no. 30, 2001

Political Quarterly, vol. 78, 2007

University College London's School of Public Policy, http://www.ucl.ac.uk/constitution-unit/research/coalition-government/interim-report.pdf

INDEX

Adonis, Lord Andrew:
background of, 229; role
in attempted Coalition
negotiations (2010), 229–31
Afghanistan: British military
forces in, 193; Helmand
province, 193
Africa: 51
Alexander, Danny: 89–90, 186,
191, 207, 229, 247, 256, 303,
329; Chief Secretary to the
Treasury, 244; influence of,
106, 223; role in creation of
Liberal Democrat manifesto
(2010), 204–5; role in negotiating terms of Coalition
Government (2010), 223;
Secretary of State for
Scotland, 242
Allan, Richard: 124–5, 143,
322, 335; background of,
142; campaign manager for
Nick Clegg, 186; Director
of policy at London office
of Facebook, 147; MP for
Sheffield Hallam, 119, 141–2,
309–10, 316; opinion of

political ideology of Nick
Clegg, 119
Arnold House School: pupils
of, 45
Ashdown, Lord Paddy: 88–9,
91–2, 98, 130, 136, 159,
163, 166, 173, 187, 195, 222,
226, 232, 237, 241, 295;
background of, 153; chair
of FPC, 202–3; desire for
elected House of Lords, 155;
family of, 124, 235; influence
of, 105; Liberal Democrat
party leader, 65, 84–5,
154, 308; offer of position
in Brown administration
(2007), 174; resignation
of (1999), 122; support for
Nick Clegg, 215–16, 327;
support for UK residency
for British passport holders
in Hong Kong, 65
Associated Press: journalists
of, 43
Australia: Sydney, 80
Austria: 62; Hochfügen, 57–8

Bagehot, Walter: Bagehot
Club, 87
Bake, Herman Willem
Alexander van den Wall:
background of, 19; family
of, 19; president of ABN, 19
Bake, Hermance van den Wall:
De Aanspraak interview
(2010), 22–3, 35; back-
ground of, 28; family of, 21,
23, 26–7; ill–health of, 25;
influence of, 21, 34–5
Baker, Norman: 240–41, 257,
312; ideology of, 205; view
of Nick Clegg, 3, 183, 308
Balls, Ed: role in attempted
Coalition negotiations
(2010), 229
Bank of England: 26; influence
of, 228
Bassett, Kate: alumnus of
Cambridge University and
Westminster School, 70;
memories of Nick Clegg, 70
Batavian Oil Company: prop-
erty owned by, 24
BBC One: *Politics Show*, 184;
Question Time, 265, 269;
The One Show, 44
BBC News 24: 172
BBC Radio 3: *Private Passions*, 49
BBC Radio 4: *Desert Island
Discs*, 8, 16, 21, 35–6, 71,
265, 326; *The World at One*,
137; *Today*, 233, 292

BBC Radio 5 Live: *Breakfast*, 189
von Beckendorff, Count
Johann: background of, 13;
family of, 13
Beckett, Samuel: *Krapp's Last
Tape*, 70–71
Belgium: 31, 140, 266; Bagehot
Club, 87; Bruges, 72, 74;
Brussels, 61, 76, 84, 86–7, 89,
99, 102–4, 108, 121–3, 125–6,
164, 183; Collège d'Europe,
72–3, 82–3, 89; expatriate
communities of, 110
Benn, Tony: alumnus of
Westminster School, 43;
Labour MP, 109
Berkley, Michael: host of
Private Passions, 49
Blair, Ian: Metropolitan Police
commissioner, 171
Blair, Tony: 85, 91, 106, 138,
169, 210–11, 295; administration of, 134, 150, 170, 193,
279, 299; electoral victory
of (1997), 155; family of, 235;
languages spoken by, 254–5;
supporters of, 300; view of
UK joining Euro, 302
Blunkett, David: 215, 233, 328;
criticism of ending of financial loan to Forgemasters
(2010), 252–3; role in
introduction of tuition fees
(1997), 206; *The Guardian*
article (2010), 236

Blunt, Anthony: allegations of membership of Communist Party, 15–16; exposed as Soviet spy (1979), 16

Böningshausen, Baron Nikolai Budberg: family of, 15

Boulton, Adam: moderator of televised party leaders' debate on Sky News (2010), 213

Boyden, Malcolm: 38

Boyle, David: 204; member of Liberal Democrat FPC, 312; opinion of political ideology of Nick Clegg, 114–15

Brack, Duncan: role in compiling *Reinventing the State: Social Liberalism in the 21st Century*, 172; *Political Quarterly* essay (2007), 156

British Broadcasting Corporation (BBC): general election results coverage (2010), 219; request for televised party leaders' debate (2009), 211–12

British Medical Association (BMA): annual general meetings of, 18

British Sky Broadcasting (BSkyB): attempted purchase by NewsCorp, 304; request for televised party leaders' debate (2009), 211–12

British Telecom (BT): 101

Brittan, Sir Leon: 78, 82, 85–6, 92, 95, 113; British Home Secretary, 77, 328; Cabinet reshuffle (1996), 79; Conservative Party member, 77; support for Nick Clegg, 246, 250

van den Broek, Hans: European Commissioner for Foreign Affairs, 102

Brooks, Rebekah: former editor of *The Sun* and *NOTW*, 287; lunch with David Cameron, 287

Brown, David: choice of Nick Clegg as head of house at Liddell's, 46–7; housemaster of Liddell's, 46; memory of Nick Clegg's family, 27–8

Brown, Gordon: 106, 153, 175, 200, 213, 219, 226, 231–2, 235, 241, 324; administration of, 174, 177–8, 181, 199, 299; constituency of, 188; economic policies of, 202; family of, 139; Gillian Duffy incident (2010), 282; leader of Labour Party, 225, 229–30; performance in televised party leaders' debate (2010), 2, 56, 212, 215–16; presence at Cenotaph ceremony, 227–8; refrain from announcing general election (2007), 180; supporters of, 300

Brown, Mick: journalist for the Daily Telegraph, 141

Browne, Jeremy: 164

Browne, Lord John: Browne Report (2010), 208, 259–60, 263; former chief executive of BP, 259

Browne, Tom: 54–5

Budberg, Tania: *A Little of All These*, 16; death of (2004), 16; family of, 16

Buehler, Tom: alumnus of Westminster School, 57

Burgess, Guy: defection to USSR, 15

Burstow, Paul: 278; Minister of State for Care Services, 272; support for proposed NHS reforms (2011), 274

Bush, George W.: 138; administration of, 146, 210

Cable, Vince: 116, 151, 162, 169–70, 175, 195, 202–3, 242, 251, 253, 314; acting leader of Liberal Democrats, 194; *Daily Telegraph* sting (2010), 304; economic policies of, 194; essay contributed to *The Orange Book: Reclaiming Liberalism* (2004), 131–2; influence in creation of Liberal Democrat manifesto (2010), 204; media image of, 216, 248, 261; Secretary of State for Business, Innovation and Skills, 242, 260, 268; Treasury spokesman, 130; view of tuition fees, 206, 208–9

Caborn, Richard: criticism of ending of financial loan to Forgemasters (2010), 252

Caldicott School: 45; faculty members, 39; pupils at, 37–8

Callaghan, James: administration of, 239; Labour Party leader, 116

Cambridge University: 62, 113, 310; alumni of, 63, 65, 70; Clare College, 57; Conservative Association, 65; Magdalene College, 67; Robinson College, 41, 57, 63–5, 69, 312

Cameron, David: 41, 140, 183, 192, 200, 213, 219, 221, 226, 237, 241, 255–6, 277, 298, 307, 319; alumnus of Oxford University, 63; attempt to invite David Laws to defect to Tories (2006), 223; involvement in 'No to AV' campaign (2011), 290–91–2, 294–5; lunch with Rebekah Brooks, 287; performance in televised party leaders' debate (2010),

2, 56, 212, 215; presence at Cenotaph ceremony, 227–8; Prime Minister, 250; pupil at Eton College, 41; speech at Conservative Party conference (2005), 288; *Today* programme interview (2011), 292

Campbell, Alastair: 235

Campbell, Menzies 'Ming': 4, 136, 157, 162–3, 166, 182, 197, 234, 312; background in student politics, 63–4; chair of FPC, 202–3; family of, 179; Liberal Democrat party leader, 63, 139, 146, 154, 168, 173, 193, 202, 328; resignation from Liberal Democrat leadership (2007), 169, 175, 180; supporters of, 173, 187; view of British role in Iraqi War, 138, 149

Carmichael, Alastair: 234; sacking of (2010), 198

Carrington, Lord Peter: former Defence Secretary, 77; former Foreign Secretary, 77; recommendation of Nick Clegg to Sir Leon Brittan, 77

Carter, Helena Bonham: 43; alumnus of Westminster School, 56; memories of Nick Clegg, 56

Caviedes, José Antonio González: 111; death of

(1996), 81; influence of, 81; Mayor of Olmedo, 81; senator of Partido Popular party, 81

China: application to join WTO, 79; government of, 79

Chisholm, Scott: background of, 213; principle adviser to Nick Clegg for televised leadership debate (2010), 213

Clarke, Kenneth: 27; political ideology of, 115

Clegg, Alexander: 34, 38; languages spoken by, 32

Clegg, Elisabeth: family nicknames of, 31

Clegg, Hugh: 18–19; alumnus of Westminster School, 45; awarded CBE, 18; family of, 13, 16–17; editor of *British Medical Journal*, 17–18

Clegg, Nick: 5–6, 8, 11, 41, 55, 84, 92, 130, 158, 160, 162, 168, 172, 176, 227, 230, 234, 237, 250, 277, 289, 296, 303; alleged membership of Cambridge University Conservative Association, 65–6; alumnus of Cambridge University, 63, 65; alumnus of Westminster School, 42, 50, 52, 57, 60, 107; appearance on BBC News 24, 172; appearance on *Desert Island Discs*

(2010), 8, 16, 21, 35–6, 71, 265, 326; appearance on *Private Passions*, 49; article written for *The Guardian* (2002), 218; BBC Radio 5 Live interview (2007), 189–90; correspondence with Christopher Torchia, 47–8; Deputy Prime Minister, 3, 7, 221, 239, 246, 248, 255–6, 258, 280–81, 327; essay contributed to *The Orange Book: Reclaiming Liberalism* (2004), 130; experience as ski instructor at Hochfügen, 57–9; experience at Caldicott School, 37; experience working at European Commission (1994), 70, 79–80, 82, 246; experiencing working at GJW, 74–5; experimentation with Transcendental Meditation, 60–61, 68; family of, 7, 11–12, 14, 19–20, 24, 27, 31, 35, 37, 80, 82, 84, 110, 139–40, 144, 183, 192–3, 245–6, 248, 255, 287, 309–10, 324–6; family nicknames of, 31; former MEP, 2, 92–5, 97–100, 113, 120, 141, 145, 181, 246; *GQ* interview with Piers Morgan, 190–91; head of house at Liddell's,

46–7; Hugo Young lecture (2010), 245–6; interview with Jemima Khan, 287; languages spoken by, 11, 25, 32, 48, 254; Liberal Democrat party leader, 3, 5, 7, 26, 82, 128, 188, 267, 303, 308; MP for Sheffield Hallam, 119, 143–4, 149, 178, 226, 246; parliamentary expenses claimed by, 195–6; participant in Westminster Challenge (2007), 176–7; performance in televised party leaders' debate (2010), 1–3, 56, 197, 212, 286, 311; personality of, 305–6; presence at Cenotaph ceremony, 227–8; presence at François Bayrou convention (2007), 175; role in 'Unbundling the local loop' of telecommunications liberalisation measures (1999–2004), 101; support for UK residency for Gurkhas, 65, 199–200; tennis rating, 55; *The Guardian* interview (2005), 152; *The Guardian* interview (2010), 70–71; UN General Assembly speech (2010), 255, 258; use of image in 'No to AV' campaign literature, 291; view of UK joining Euro, 302

Clegg, Nicolas Peter: 36; background of, 25–6, 28; birth of (1936), 25; family of, 25; role in founding of Daiwa Anglo–Japanese Foundation, 26

Clegg, Paul: 12–13, 28, 34, 38; birth of (1960), 31; family of, 24, 74; languages spoken by, 32

Coalition government: 130, 240, 266; coalition agreement, 133, 238–9, 241, 262–4, 266, 271–2; formation of (2010), 2–3, 221, 237; Liberal Cabinet ministers, 3, 7, 192, 229, 268; political policy concessions within, 262–4, 269, 319–20; Tory Cabinet ministers, 229, 238, 241

Cogan, Jim: awarded OBE (2005), 51; role in establishing Students Partnership Worldwide, 51, 60; teacher at Westminster School, 51

Cold War: 15, 39

Conservative Party: 1, 43, 82–5, 107, 109, 113, 117–18, 136, 149–50, 209, 226, 232–4, 293, 297, 313; councillors of, 142; electoral performance of (2010), 219, 288; financial donors to, 292; ideology of, 114; involvement in 'No to AV campaign', 290; lack of support in Northern England, 290; members of, 77; MEPs, 119; partner in Coalition government, 5; party conference (2005), 288; politically dominant position of, 2; supporters of, 6, 27, 146

Cook, Robin: 64; foreign policy of, 336

Council of Europe: 89

Coward, Noël: *Blithe Spirit*, 56

Crabtree, James: article written for *Prospect* (2010), 314; view of *The Orange Book: Reclaiming Liberalism*, 315

Cresson, Édith: French Prime Minister, 103

Curtice, John: view of chances of future hung parliaments, 318–19

Cyprus: 25

Daily Mail: 56; article description of French farmhouse owned by Clegg family (2010), 28–9; 'Is there anything British about Nick Clegg?' article (2010), 217; report of Nick Clegg's activities at GJW, 75

Daily Telegraph: 197; 'Clegg Accused' article (2010), 217; David Laws expenses scandal (2010), 242–4; editorials of,

275; journalists of, 141, 162; magazine of, 33–4, 189, 201; Vince Cable sting (2010), 304

Daiwa Securities: Daiwa Anglo–Japanese Foundation, 26; Daiwa Europe Ltd, 26

Davey, Ed: 124, 157, 163, 186; chairman of Nick Clegg leadership election campaign, 197; Liberal Democrat foreign affairs spokesperson, 197

Davies, Chris: 105, 167; Liberal Democrat MEP, 101, 114, 147, 240; MP for Oldham East & Saddleworth, 127; opinion of political ideology of Nick Clegg, 114

Dean, Howard: Chair of Democratic National Committee, 210; Governor of Vermont, 210; relationship with Liberal Democrats, 210–11

Delors, Jacques: President of European Commission, 72

Dewar, Donald: 64

Dimbleby, David: moderator of televised party leaders' debate on BBC (2010), 213

van Dorp, Louise Hillegonde: family of, 19; tropical ulcer, 20

Duff, Andrew: 86–7; chair of English Liberal Democrats, 85; former MEP, 110, 115, 327; media image of, 121; opinion of political ideology of Nick Clegg, 115, 119

Dulwich College Prep School: pupils of, 45

Durántez, Miriam González: 74, 97, 248, 324; background of, 73; family of, 32, 37, 81–2, 84, 110, 112, 140, 325–6; interview with *El Norte de Castilla* (2007), 81; interview with *The Times* (2010), 281; Middle East desk officer in *cabinet* of Chris Patten, 80

Eagling, Russell: 99; regional organiser for Nick Clegg, 93

Economist, The: journalists of, 106

Egypt: Cairo, 25

El Norte de Castilla: Miriam González Durántez interview (2007), 81

Ellwood, Tobias: participant in Westminster Challenge (2007), 176

von Engelhardt, Baron Artur: background of, 12; family of, 12

von Engelhardt, Baroness Kira: birth of (1909), 12; family of, 12

Estonia: 12; Kalli Järv, 14

Eton College: 63; Conservative influence in, 42; pupils at, 41, 117

European Commission: 70, 74–7, 102, 246; *Concours*, 77; G24 Coordination Unit, 72

European Economic Community (EEC): 72

European Parliament: 77, 90, 96, 101, 112, 118, 120–21, 126, 141, 296, 307; elections (1999), 90–91, 92–5, 97, 99–100; European Liberal Democrat and Reform group (ELDR), 91, 104, 108; Liberal Democrat European Parliamentary Party (LDEPP), 104, 108; Members of (MEP), 2, 75, 83, 86–7, 91, 93–5, 99–103, 105, 121–3, 141, 163, 241; Volkspartij voor Vrijheld en Democraie (VVD), 104

European Policy Centre: 104

European Union (EU): 82, 102–3, 114, 334; Lisbon Treaty, 198; members of, 78, 100, 198; Treaty of Rome, 198

Falkner, Baroness Kishwer: 167; Liberal Democrat European and International Officer, 86

Farron, Tim: background of, 304; sacking of (2010), 198; speech to Liberal Democrats' spring conference (2011, 304–5

Field, John: 55

Fieldhoue, Edward: 'Neither Left nor Right: the Liberal Democrats and the Electorate' (2004), 136

Fields, Michael: background of, 52; memory of Nick Clegg, 52–3; teacher at Westminster School, 52

Financial Times: 76; journalists of, 314

Finland: 62, 69; Helsinki, 61

First World War (1914–18): 152; conscientious objectors in, 42; military units served in, 17; spies in, 15

Fogarty, Shelagh: interview with Nick Clegg, 190, 192, 322–3

Foord, Andrew: 47; alumnus of Westminster School, 57, 60

Fordham, Ed: 94, 187; candidacy for Hampstead & Kilburn constituency, 211; memories of Nick Clegg, 95

Fox, Chris: 109; Liberal Democrats' chief executive, 257, 288–9, 300, 312

Fox, Theodore: 18

France: 36, 254; Charente–Maritime, 28; government

of, 103, 172; Strasbourg, 89, 102–3, 108, 123, 126

Gellner, Ernst: influence of, 66; *Plough, Sword and Book*, 66
George, Andrew: criticisms of propose NHS reforms, 275
Germany: 15, 19, 24, 55, 254; Freie Demokratische Partei (FDP), 104, 268; Munich, 53–4; Nuremburg, 54; Oberammergau, 54
Gifford, Andrew: role in founding of GJW, 74
Gilligan, Andrew: article on Liberal Democrat's electoral campaign activity (2010), 197
GJW: established (1980), 74; staff at, 75
GMTV: *Sunday Programme*, 177
von Goethe, Johann Wolfgang: poetry of, 50
Gogol, Nikolai: *The Government Inspector*, 55
Gorky, Maxim: relationship with Moura Budberg, 15
GQ: Nick Clegg interview with Piers Morgan, 190–91
Grayson, Richard: former speechwriter for Charles Kennedy, 156; role in compiling *Reinventing the State: Social Liberalism in the 21st Century*, 172

Greece: economic crisis (2010–Present), 225, 228
Green Party: 129, 203; European Parliamentary election performances, 91, 154; influence of, 4
Grimond, Jo: 247, 317; background of, 117; influence of, 117, 133, 152; Liberal Party leader, 117; member of Unservile State Group, 118
Guardian, The: 198, 246, 249, 289; article on key people in general election (2010), 189; article written by David Blunkett (2010), 236; article written by Nick Clegg (2002), 218; journalists of, 106, 174; Nick Clegg interview (2010), 70–71
Guest–Albert, Corisande: family of, 74; relationship with Nick Clegg, 74
Gurkhas: challenge to right to residency in UK, 65, 199–200; ethnic identity of, 199; service in British military, 199

Hague, William: 154, 236, 255; British Foreign Secretary, 69, 254; ideology of, 119
Hall, Katie: political adviser to Nick Clegg, 110
Hall School, The: pupils of, 45

Hands, Greg: claim of Clegg's membership of Cambridge University Conservative Association, 65–6; Tory MP, 65

Hansen, Anders: 186

Harris, Evan: 277; criticisms of Nick Clegg, 185; criticisms of propose NHS reforms, 274

Harris, Peter: constituency chair for Nick Clegg, 95; family of, 105

Hart, Keith: background of, 66; influence of, 66

Harvey, Nick: call for resignation of Charles Kennedy (2005–6), 159–60; MP for North Devon, 122

Heath, David: sacking of (2010), 198

Heseltine, Michael: Westland Affair (1986), 69

Hilton, Steve: Director of Strategy for David Cameron, 279

Hitchens, Christopher: editor of *The Nation*, 71

Holmes, Paul: 93, 96, 109

Hong Kong: return to Chinese rule (1997), 65

Howarth, David: role in compiling *Reinventing the State: Social Liberalism in the 21st Century*, 172

Hughes, Simon: 122, 139, 225, 304; background of, 89; Bermondsey by–election candidacy (1983), 88–9

Huhne, Chris: 87, 107, 118, 130, 158, 162, 167, 169, 229, 308; alumnus of Westminster School, 43, 107; Brussels editor of *The Economist*, 106; criticism of George Osborne's role in 'No to AV' campaign, (2011), 292–3; environmental policies of, 5; driving license penalty points controversy (2011), 303–4; essay contributed to *The Orange Book: Reclaiming Liberalism* (2004), 131; former member of Labour Party, 106, 182–3; former MEP, 110, 141; influence of, 106; Liberal Democrat leadership candidacy (2007), 5, 43, 113, 124–5, 180; MP for Eastleigh, 141, 290; relationship with Carina Trimingham, 184; role in creation of Liberal Democrat manifesto (2005), 204; role in negotiating terms of Coalition Government (2010), 223; role in preparation for televised leadership debate

(2010), 213–14; Secretary
of State for Energy and
Climate Change, 242, 301
Humphreys, John: interview
with David Cameron
(2011), 292
Hungary: Budapest, 75
Hurst, Greg: biography of
Charles Kennedy, 138

Independent on Sunday: 291,
293; journalists of, 70
Independent, The: 289; article
written by Baroness Shirley
Williams (2011), 277
Independent Television News
(ITN): request for televised
party leaders debate (2009),
211–12; *News at Ten*, 2
India: 51; borders of, 60
Indonesia: 19; Bandung, 24;
Batavia, 24; Batujajar, 20;
independence movement of,
20; Java, 20; Palembang, 19
Iraq: Operation Iraqi Freedom
(2003), 135, 137–8, 150, 157,
166, 210, 255
Irvine, Derry: 64
Italy: 19, 36; Lucca, 37

Japan: 19, 22, 24–5; Hiroshima,
24; military of, 22
Jeger, Jenny: 75; role in founding of GJW, 74

Jones, Nigel: Liberal Democrat
MP for Cheltenham, 128

Kazakhstan: Almaty, 78
Kennedy, Charles: 4, 123,
136–7, 151, 193, 206, 312, 318,
333; alcoholism, 159; background of, 155; biography
of, 138; chair of FPC, 202–3;
contribution to *The Orange
Book: Reclaiming Liberalism*
(2004), 131; Liberal
Democrat party leader, 109,
122, 149, 155, 175; opposition
to formation of Coalition
Government, 238; opposi-
tion to tuition fees, 206;
resignation of (2006), 138,
163, 180; view of British role
in Iraqi War, 137–8; view of
Nick Clegg, 308–9; winner
of Politician of the Year
(2004), 156
Khan, Jemima: family of,
287; guest editor of *New
Statesman* 287; interview
with Nick Clegg, 287
Kirkwood, Archy: supporter of
Menzies Campbell, 173

Labour Party: 1, 27, 83–4, 109,
117–18, 129, 134, 142, 149,
153, 209, 233, 240, 249;
activists of, 283; electoral
performance of (2010),

219, 288; electoral victory
of (1997), 271; members of,
106; New Labour, 84; politically dominant position
of, 2; support for Iraq War
(2003), 210–11

Lamb, Norman: 160, 162–3,
176; appearance on *Question
Time*, 265; criticisms of
propose NHS reforms, 274;
ideology of, 134

Lansley, Andrew: 277; proposed
reform of NHS, 270–71,
279–80, 301; Secretary of
State for Health, 271

Laws, David: 87, 124, 162–3,
202, 209, 226, 234, 253,
332; *22 Days in May*, 222;
attempt by Tories to invite
defection of (2006), 223;
Chief Secretary to the
Treasury, 242; criticisms
of propose NHS reforms,
273–4; essay contributed to
*The Orange Book: Reclaiming
Liberalism* (2004), 130, 133,
136; expenses scandal (2010),
242–4; influence in crea-
tion of Liberal Democrat
manifesto (2010), 204;
role in negotiating terms
of Coalition Government
(2010), 223; role in preparation for televised leadership

debate (2010), 213–15; view
of tuition fees, 206

Lawson, Nigel: Chancellor of
the Exchequer, 43

Lee–Potter, Adam: observation
of conversation between
Nick Clegg and Danny
Alexander (2008), 191–2

Leech, John: opposition to
formation of Coalition
Government, 239

Lib Dem News: gazette page,
170–71

Liberal Democrats: 1, 6, 26,
33, 42, 64, 70, 84, 87–8,
96, 108–9, 222, 228, 337;
'Clegg Direct' concept, 309;
councillors of, 5; desire for
proportional representa-
tion electoral system, 224;
Eastbourne party confer-
ence (1997), 90; electoral
expansion of, 314; electoral
performance of (2005),
149; electoral perform-
ance of (2010), 219, 288;
established (1988), 64–5,
99, 118, 239, 282; Federal
Policy Committee (FPC),
202, 206–8, 312–13; ideology
of, 117, 188–9; impact of
local elections on (2011), 6,
275, 333, 336; *Liberator*, 129;
manifesto for general election (2005), 201; manifesto

for general election (2010), 196, 201; members of, 77, 182, 282; MEPs, 87, 103–4, 108; partner in Coalition government, 5; party conference (2010), 258; spring conference (2011), 274, 277, 304; supporters of, 266

Liberal Party: 152, 185; merger with SDP (1988), 64–5, 99, 118, 157, 239, 282; support of, 12; Unservile State Group, 118

Libya: Civil War (2011– Present), 325

Lloyd, Stephen: 330

Lockhart, Robert Bruce: affair with Moura Budberg, 14–15

Ludford, Sarah: MEP, 166

Lumley, Joanna: support for right to residency in UK for Gurkhas, 199–200

Luxembourg: 102

Mackenzie, Polly: background of, 161–2; policy officer for Nick Clegg, 178, 189

Malmström, Cecilia: European Commissioner for Home Affairs, 103

Mandelson, Lord Peter: 153, 231, 235, 237; offer of financial loan to Forgemasters (2010), 252–3; Secretary of State for Business, Innovation and Skills, 252–3; *The Third Man*, 222, 227

Marin, Manuel: 103

Marshall, Paul: background of, 130; role in compiling *The Orange Book: Reclaiming Liberalism* (2004), 130, 162

Martin, Chris: Head teacher at Bristol Cathedral School, 48–9

Mendes, Sam: *The Normal Heart*, 67

Metro, The: journalists of, 281

Mexico: 68

Miliband, David: media image of, 216

Miliband, Ed: 296, 300; leader of Labour Party, 183–4; position in AV referendum (2011), 290, 294; role in attempted Coalition negotiations (2010), 229

Moon, Christian: 90–91

Moore, Michael: 124; ambitions for Liberal democrat leadership (2005), 161; Liberal Democrat foreign affairs spokesperson, 197; Secretary of State for Scotland, 244

Moorhouse, James: defection to Liberal Democrats (2000), 119

Morgan, Piers: 56; interview with Nick Clegg for *GQ*, 190–91

Mulloy, Kevin: 97
Murdoch, Rupert: family of, 80;
    owner of NewsCorp, 304

Nation, The: journalists of, 71
National Health Service (NHS):
    131, 278, 280, 315; founded
    (1948), 18; funding of, 133;
    political issue of, 184, 270,
    273, 277, 297; proposed
    reform of, 270–71, 273,
    275–7, 279, 301, 328, 334
National Union of Students
    (NUS): pledge for candi-
    dates to not raise tuition
    fees, 208–9, 259, 261, 264,
    266, 270
Nepal: 51; borders of, 60
Netherlands: 25, 31, 80, 266;
    Amsterdam, 36; D66, 104,
    240, 266–7; Holland, 34, 80
New Statesman: editorial staff
    of, 287; Nick Clegg inter-
    view, 287
News of the World (NOTW):
    166; phone hacking scandal
    (2011), 322
NewsCorp: attempted purchase
    of BSkyB, 304; owner by
    Rupert Murdoch, 304
Newsnight: 147; John Reid
    interview (2010), 236
Newton–Dunn, Bill:
    Conservative Party MEP,
    119–20; defection to Liberal
    Democrats (2000), 119–20
Northern Rock plc: run on
    (2007), 193
Nottingham University: Senate
    adoption meeting (1999), 98
Nuttall, Simon: 86–7

Oakeshott, Isabel: 321–2; political
    editor of Sunday Times, 283,
    310; view of media image of
    Nick Clegg, 283–4, 310
Oaten, Mark: 124, 157, 171,
    175, 311, 330; ambitions for
    Liberal Democrat leader-
    ship, 165; background of,
    165; former chair of Liberal
    Democrat parliamentary
    party, 121
Oates, Jonny: adviser to Nick
    Clegg, 212
Obama, Barack: former smok-
    ing habit of, 327; presiden-
    tial campaign of (2008), 210
Observer, The: journalists of,
    178; video profile of Nick
    Clegg (2007), 147
Office for Standards In
    Education, Children's
    Services and Skills (Ofsted):
    inspections conducted by,
    50–51
Öpik, Lembit: 124, 166
Osborne, George: 256, 258,
    270, 279; attempt to

invite David Laws to defect to Tories (2006), 223; Chancellor of the Exchequer, 242; economic policies of, 180, 251, 262, 273, 291; role in 'No to AV' campaign (2011), 292–3

Owen, David: SDP leader, 88, 154

Oxford University: alumni of, 117; Brasenose College, 41, 63

Palestine: 80

Palmer, John: 126–7; European editor of *The Guardian*, 82, 104, 106–7; memories of Nick Clegg, 118

Patten, Chris: *cabinet* of, 80, 113; political ideology of, 115

Penhaligon, David: legacy of, 304

Pietsch, Lena: media spokeswoman for Nick Clegg, 189, 212, 216

Porter, Aaron: 333; appearance on *Question Time*, 265, 269; former President of NUS, 264, 268–70, 331–2

Press Complaints Commission: rules regarding protection of children, 324

Pugh, John: 277; criticisms of propose NHS reforms, 274

Rae, Dr John: Head teacher of Westminster School, 42, 48; member of Social Democrats, 43; opposition to Assisted Places Scheme, 42

Rawnsley, Andrew: journalist for *The Observer*, 178

Reid, John: 233; appearance on *Newsnight* (2010), 236

Reinventing the State: Social Liberalism in the 21st Century: contributors to, 172

Rendel, David: Federal Executive member, 238; opposition to formation of Coalition Government, 238

Rennard, Lord Chris: 123, 128, 257; chief election strategist for Paddy Ashdown, 154; Liberal Democrats' chief executive, 150, 233, 285, 314; view of 'No to AV' campaign (2011), 298

Rennie, Willie: MP for Dunfermline & West Fife, 188

Richters, Arne: Liberal MEP, 317; memories of Nick Clegg, 307

Robinson, Dr David: founder of Robinson College, Cambridge, 63

Robinson, Nick: 233; BBC political editor, 158, 222

Rogers, Tony: Chesterfield Borough councillor, 93, 109

Royal Bank of Scotland (RBS): 193

Royal Mail: discussions regarding privatisation of, 131, 134; industrial strikes, 188

Royal Marines: members of, 153

Rumsfeld, Donald: former US Secretary of Defense, 146

Russell, Andrew: 'Neither Left nor Right: the Liberal Democrats and the Electorate' (2004), 136

Russian Empire: family from, 12; Revolution (1917), 12–14; Smolensk, 12; St Petersburg, 13

Russian Orthodox Church: churches in London, 15

Salmond, Alexander: leader of SNP, 235

Scottish National Party (SNP): members of, 235

Scriven, Paul: former leader of Sheffield City Council, 283

Second World War (1939–45): 17, 22, 36, 152, 218–19, 237, 297; Atomic bombing of Hiroshima (1945), 24; Axis powers, 19–20; East Indies theatre, 22; Pearl Harbour attack (1941), 20

Secret Intelligence Service (MI6): 15; members of, 153

Security Service (MI5): 15–16

Sharkey, John: General election campaign manager for Nick Clegg (2010), 212

Sherlock, Neil: 88, 109, 187, 247, 325; co–founder of Lib Dems in Public Relations, 162; funding for Nick Clegg's parliamentary office, 217

Singh, Simon: 19

Sinn Fein: 117

Sky News: 177

Smith, John: 64

Smith, Peter: influence of, 38–9

Social Democrat Party (SDP): 106, 185; founding of (1981), 153, 182; members of, 43, 88, 317; merger with Liberal Party (1988), 64–5, 99, 118, 157, 239, 282

Sonei, Captain Kenichi: commander of Tjideng internment camp, 22

South Korea: Seoul, 32

Soviet Union (USSR): 39, 72; collapse of (1991), 78; defectors to, 15; Moscow, 15

Spain: 80; economy of, 225; Olmedo, 73, 81–2, 111; Madrid, 81, 111; Monuenga, 81; Santiago di Compostela, 255; Segovia, 110

Special Boat Service (SBS): members of, 153

Spectator, The: Politician of the Year award, 156

Steel, Lord David: 94; Liberal Party leader, 74, 93, 239, 304; media image of, 282

Stephenson, Richard: role in creation of Westminster Challenge (2007), 176

Stewart, Alastir: moderator of televised party leaders' debate on ITN (2010), 213

Stockley, Neil: chair of Liberal Democrats' environment policy review group, 205

Stokes, Richard: influence of, 50; memories of Nick Clegg, 49; teacher at Westminster School, 48, 53–4

Students Partnership Worldwide: established by Jim Cogan, 51, 60

Stunell, Andrew: role in negotiating terms of Coalition Government (2010), 223

Suárez, Adolfo: President of Spain, 81

Sukarno: President of Indonesia, 20

Sunday Mirror: journalists of, 191

Sunday Telegraph: 280

Sunday Times: journalists of, 283, 310

Suttie, Alison: 86–7; ELDR press officer, 110

Sweden: 266

Switzerland: 36

Tatchell, Peter: Bermondsey by–election candidacy (1983), 88–9

Teather, Sarah: 162–3, 206

Thatcher, Margaret: 70, 285, 290; administration of, 43, 64, 69, 101, 300–301; ideology of, 135; influence of, 249; Poll Tax (1989–90), 69; privatisation initiatives of, 101, 114, 135, 270; Royal Society speech (1988), 154; Westland Affair (1986), 69

The Orange Book: Reclaiming Liberalism (2004): 130, 132, 134, 136, 162, 172; contributors to, 130–31, 133, 136, 172–3, 202, 207; publication of (2004), 119; reaction to, 135–7

Theroux, Louis: appearance on *The One Show* (2010), 44; family of, 44, 57, 67

Theroux, Marcel: 44–5, 67, 72, 75, 102, 305–6, 336; memories of Nick Clegg, 45, 48, 57, 310–11

Thomas, Celia: Chief whip for Liberal Democrats in House of Lords, 179

Thomson, Paul: alumnus of Westminster School, 57

Thornberry, Emilly: participant in Westminster Challenge (2007), 176

Thorpe, Jeremy: 152

Times, The: Miriam González Durántez interview (2010), 281; political cartoons of, 299

Torchia, Christopher: Associated Press journalist, 43; correspondence with Nick Clegg, 47–8; memories of Nick Clegg, 47; memories of Westminster School, 43–4; tennis rating, 55

Total Politics: journalists of, 190, 192, 322

Trimingham, Carina: relationship with Chris Huhne, 184

Twitter: #nickcleggsfault, 218

Ukraine: 12

United Kingdom (UK): 31, 114, 234; Berkshire, 32; Broxtowe, 108; Buckinghamshire, 33; Chesterfield, 108–9; class system of, 21; Derby, 108; Derbyshire, 99; economy of, 225; Hampshire, 32, 290; House of Commons, 74, 105, 126, 158, 195, 203, 276; House of Lords, 155, 179, 276, 297; Houses of Parliament, 41, 63, 93, 125, 144, 266; Leicester, 108; Little Kingshill, 19; Lincolnshire, 97–8; London, 15, 35, 40–41, 46, 126; Northampton, 108; Nottinghamshire, 96; Oxfordshire, 33, 46, 77, 287–8; Royal Navy, 25; Skegness, 93–4; Waterloo station, 77; Westminster Abbey, 41

United Nations (UN): 111, 313, 334; General Assembly, 255, 258

United States of America (USA): 24; 9/11 attacks, 217; Democratic Party, 116–17; New York, 25, 71; University of Minnesota, 70–71

University College London (UCL): 333; School of Public Policy, 268

Vadher, Atul: 96; MEP candidacy, 92–3, 108

Vaizey, Ed: Conservative Minister for Culture, Communications and Creative Industries, 116; opinion of political ideology of Nick Clegg, 116, 119, 331; participant in Westminster Challenge (2007), 176–7

Van der Laan, Lousewies: 103; background of, 102; 'Everything You Need to Know About Coalition Politics You Already Know from Your Marriage', (2010), 267; MEP, 102;

former leader of D66,
266–7

Vietnam: Ho Chi Minh City
(Saigon), 32

Watson, Graham: Liberal
Democrat MEP, 87, 104,
108, 125

Watt, Peter: former Labour Party
general secretary, 179–80

Webb, Steve: 124, 191; essay
contributed to *The Orange
Book: Reclaiming Liberalism*
(2004), 130; Minister of
State for Pensions, 191

Weeks, Wilf: 75; role in founding of GJW, 74

West, Charles: criticisms of
propose NHS reforms, 274;

Westerwille, Guido: German
Vice–Chancellor, 254; FDP
leader, 254

Westminster School: 63, 90;
alumni of, 42–3, 45, 50, 52,
70; faculty members of, 42,
48, 51–4; tennis team, 55;
the Greaze, 44; Liddell's, 46

White, Michael: Political
correspondent for
The Guardian, 174

Wightwick, Chris: Head
teacher at King's College
School, 48

Williams, Baroness Shirley:
98, 327–8; article written

for *The Independent* (2011),
277; criticisms of propose
NHS reforms, 274; offer of
position in Brown administration (2007), 174

Williams, Stephen: 206

Willot, Jenny: participant in
Westminster Challenge
(2007), 176

Wilson, Harold: administration
of, 299; Labour Party
leader, 116

Wilson, Rob: 231; *Five Days
to Power*, 222, 229–30

Winyard, Graham: 278; background of, 274; criticisms of
propose NHS reforms, 274

Wolfowitz, Paul: Deputy US
Defense Secretary, 146

Woolas, Phil: Minister of
State for Borders and
Immigration, 199; MP
for Oldham East &
Saddleworth, 127

World Bank: 46

World Trade Organization
(WTO): 144; members of, 79

Wright, Ian: 109, 165, 186–7,
327; co–founder of Lib
Dems in Public Relations,
162; former speechwriter of
David Owen, 88; funding
for Nick Clegg's parliamentary office, 217

Wright, Peter: headmaster at
    Caldicott School, 39

Young, Kirsty: host of *Desert
    Island Discs*, 16
Young, Michael: background of,
    162; funding for Nick Clegg's
    parliamentary office, 217

Zakrevskaya, Alexandra
    Ignatievna: family of, 12
Zakrevskaya, Maria Ignatievna:
    affair with Robert Bruce
    Lockhart, 14–15; birth of
    (1892), 13; death of (1974),
    12–13; family of, 13–16; MI5
    file, 15; Moura Budberg,
    12–13; relationship with
    Maxim Gorky, 15
Zakrevsky, Ignaty: 14; back-
    ground of, 12; family of, 12